WESTMAR
VIA VERITAS VITA
COLLEGE

FUR TRADE AND EMPIRE

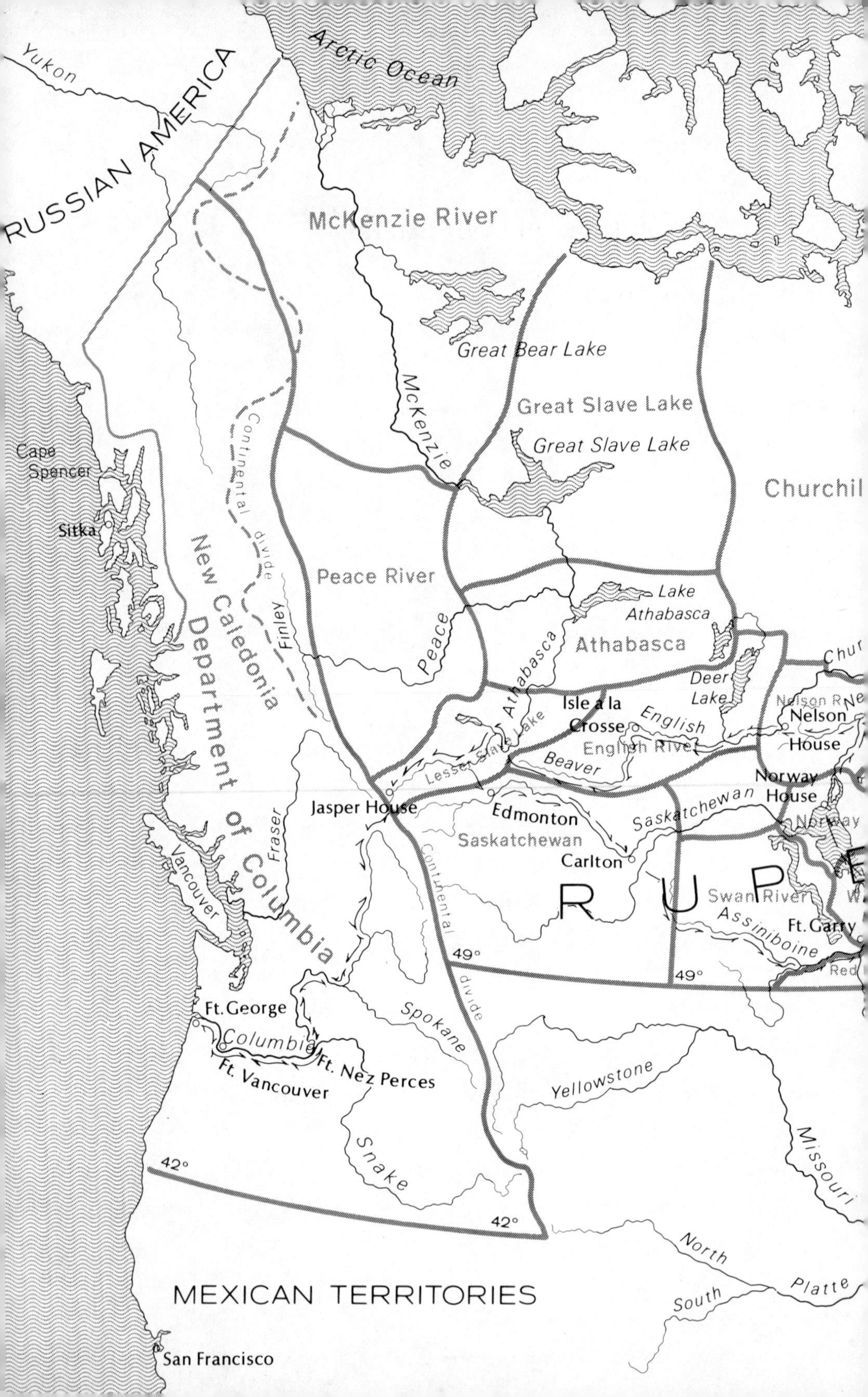

Arctic Ocean
Yukon
RUSSIAN AMERICA
McKenzie River
Great Bear Lake
Great Slave Lake
Great Slave Lake
McKenzie
Churchil
Cape Spencer
Sitka
Continental divide
New Caledonia
Department of Columbia
Peace River
Finley
Peace
Lake Athabasca
Athabasca
Athabasca
Deer Lake
Isle a la Crosse
English
English River
Beaver
Lesser Slave Lake
Nelson River
Nelson House
Norway House
Norway
Jasper House
Edmonton
Saskatchewan
Saskatchewan
Carlton
Fraser
Vancouver
Continental divide
R U P
Swan River
Assiniboine
Ft. Garry
Red
49°
49°
Ft. George
Columbia
Ft. Nez Perces
Ft. Vancouver
Spokane
Yellowstone
Missouri
Snake
42°
42°
North Platte
South
MEXICAN TERRITORIES
San Francisco

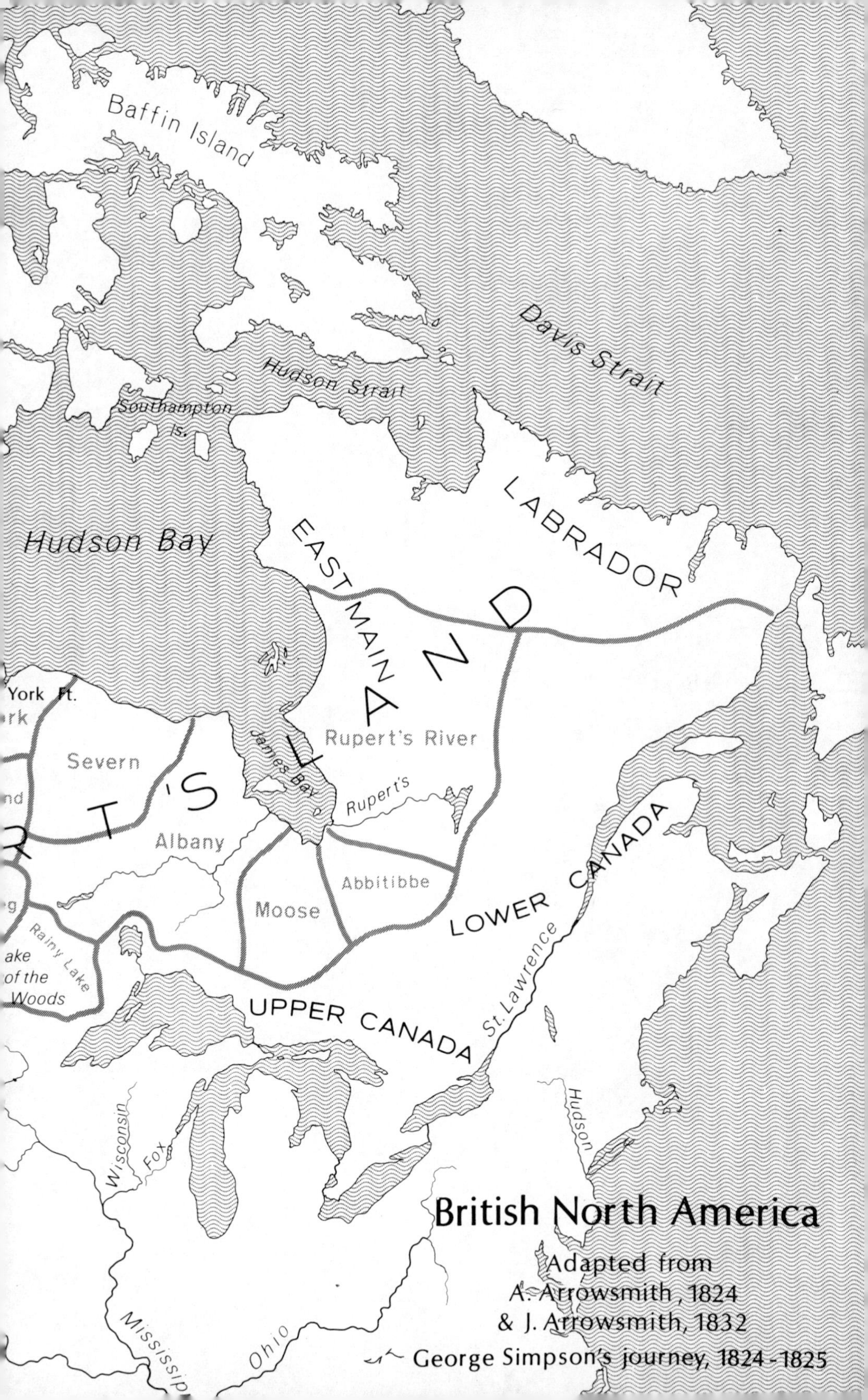

Baffin Island
Davis Strait
Hudson Strait
Southampton Is.
Hudson Bay
LABRADOR
EASTMAIN
R T 'S L A N D
York Ft.
rk
nd
g
Severn
Rupert's River
James Bay
Rupert's
Albany
Moose
Abbitibbe
Rainy Lake
ake of the Woods
LOWER CANADA
UPPER CANADA
St. Lawrence
Hudson
Wisconsin
Fox
Mississip
Ohio
British North America
Adapted from
A. Arrowsmith, 1824
& J. Arrowsmith, 1832
George Simpson's journey, 1824-1825

FUR TRADE AND EMPIRE

GEORGE SIMPSON'S JOURNAL

Entitled

Remarks Connected with the Fur Trade in the Course of a Voyage from York Factory to Fort George and Back to York Factory 1824–25

With Related Documents

Revised Edition

EDITED WITH A NEW INTRODUCTION

By FREDERICK MERK

THE BELKNAP PRESS OF
HARVARD UNIVERSITY PRESS
Cambridge, Massachusetts
1968

Distributed in Great Britain by Oxford University Press, London
Library of Congress catalog card number: 68–15646
Printed in the United States of America

The first edition, published in 1931 by Harvard University Press,
was volume XXXI in the Harvard Historical Studies, a series
under the direction of the Department of History, Harvard University

To the Memory of
FREDERICK JACKSON TURNER

CONTENTS

INTRODUCTION TO THE REVISED EDITION: THE STRATEGY OF MONOPOLY

BY FREDERICK MERK

June 1967

Two enormous North American territories were quietly brought by the British government into a union of a special sort in 1821. One territory was Rupert's Land, which lay east of the Rocky Mountains. The other was the Oregon Country, which lay to the west. Rupert's Land was an internationally recognized part of the British Empire. The Oregon Country was not; it was claimed by three powers—Great Britain, the United States, and Russia. The linking of these territories was, on its face, a reward given to the Hudson's Bay and North West companies for closing a stubborn trade war in Rupert's Land in which they had been engaged. It seemed to outsiders merely a phase of a domestic clash, and it was little noticed away from Great Britain. It was given only passing attention in the American press.

Rupert's Land was the drainage basin of Hudson Bay and Hudson Straits. It extended from Labrador to the Rocky Mountains and from the northern watershed of the St. Lawrence River to the southern watershed of the Arctic Ocean. It had been granted to the Hudson's Bay Company by Charles II in 1670 as a token of affection for a cousin and member of the Company—Prince Rupert. The charter conveying the grant gave soil, exclusive trade, and rights of government—even rights to make war and peace. But the grant had been contested by the French, then by traders inside the British empire who maintained that the charter was invalid. France as a challenger had been silenced after a succession of wars. But the domestic contestants, organized in 1784 as the North West Company, had taken up the fight, and for thirty-seven years Rupert's Land had been torn by a vicious fur traders' war. By 1821 the belligerents were on the verge of ruin and were ready for peace. On March 26 a merger of the two was effected. In the merger the charter and name of the older company were retained. The privileges of the charter were shared.

As a reward for the merger Parliament, on July 2, 1821, passed an act permitting the Crown to grant a license of trade in "parts" of North America. The "parts" were described in terms somewhat general. One was east of the Stony Mountains (the Rockies), embracing an area northwest of Rupert's Land draining into the Arctic. The other was west of the Stony Mountains—the Oregon Country. The license was to run for twenty-one years. Its recipient was not named, this being left for the Crown to fill in. The Hudson's Bay Company seemed, however, to be intended. A monopoly of all British trade rights would be part of the license, but west of the Stony Mountains it was not to prejudice the rights of American nationals, which were protected by the Treaty of Joint Occupation of 1818.

In the 1821 act a criminal and civil jurisdiction was set up. It was to apply to the "parts" east and west of the mountains, and perhaps also to Rupert's Land. It was to halt evils which the trade war had unleashed: breaches of the peace, injury to the Indians, and losses even to the belligerents themselves. It was to confer on the license holder the right to appoint justices of the peace who would have jurisdiction over minor causes in all that Indian country. The justices were to have the power to arrest and convey to Upper Canada for trial any persons resisting their authority. But no nationals other than British were to be subject to the justices west of the mountains. Even the British were not wholly at the mercy of the justices. They were to have rights of review in important cases in the courts of Upper Canada.

On December 6, 1821, the Crown designated the Hudson's Bay Company the beneficiary of the authorized license. The Crown gave the Company a monopoly of all rights of British trade with the Indians of the several "parts." It provided dutifully that its grant should not be deemed to authorize prejudice against, or exclusion of, any subjects of a foreign state in the region west of the Stony Mountains entitled to engage in the said trade under the force of an existing convention. The license merely concentrated British rights on a favored company. It could not be complained of as an infraction of treaty. If the monopoly should prove overwhelming to individual American competitors in the future, that would be due to the fragmented character of their competition. The judgment of the London press on the license and its antecedents was expressed in financial columns a few months after the Crown's action—in reports that the stock of the Hudson's Bay Company was trading on the market at an advance of 100 percent.

Legalized monopoly was an approved British principle in empire building, though it was forbidden within the realm of England by the Statute of Monopolies of 1623. It appeared in the navigation and trade systems adopted by Parliament for the colonies. It was part of the mercantile theory, and of most charters granted to colonizing companies. It was exemplified in the charter conferred by Queen Elizabeth on the East India Company in 1600, which granted sole British rights of trade throughout the East Indies—in other words between the Cape of Good Hope and the Straits of Magellan. It appeared also in the exclusive trade privileges which the charter of 1670 conferred on the Hudson's Bay Company. Centuries of imperial precedent were reflected thus in the monopoly principle of the license west of the mountains. Even though no more than British trade rights were within the scope of that monopoly, still the license was expected to produce economic control and to bear fruit ultimately in imperial control.

In the United States free competition in trade seemed essential to life. It certainly seemed essential to republican freedom. Legalized monopoly was detested. It was a manifestation of monarchical favoritism. At best it was a gift to the favored few at the expense of the many, at worst an instrument of oppression. Americans associated it with Parliament's attempt, just prior to the American Revolution, to confer a monopoly in the sale of tea in the colonies on the East India Company as a means of breaking down colonial resistance to an oppressive principle of taxation without representation. The attempt of the East India Company to implement the act had led to the Boston Tea Party—a preliminary of the American Revolution. American repugnance to legalized monopoly became intensified after independence. It appeared in diplomatic clashes over the closed trade of the British West Indies and, in 1823, it was an element in Monroe's famous announcement of objection to any extension of European colonization to the Americas.

Especially irksome to Americans was the choice of the Oregon Country as a field for experimentation in monopoly. That country had been opened to free enterprise by Americans. An American mariner had discovered its great river—the Columbia. American explorers and scientists had made known its interior. An energetic American merchant, John Jacob Astor, had established its first settlement, and this had been conceived of as the germ of a new independent Pacific republic.

American plans had miscarried, however. They had suffered from a succession of accidents and had finally been shattered by war. Astoria had been sold to the North West Company virtually under the guns of the British navy. It had later become, by reason of the merger and license, a prospective entrant into the British empire.

A decline in the trade of the Oregon Country followed the close of the War of 1812. The trade of both the coast and the interior was affected by it. The decline resulted from overdone competition on the coast. The coastal trade before the war had kept fourteen American vessels busy. After the war the number had fallen by two-thirds, the effect of depletion of the furs. The survivors eked out a livelihood by transporting supplies to Sitka for the Russian American Company. But in moving northward they had sold rum and firearms to the Indians and this had created peril for the Russians, even for those behind stockaded forts. This, in turn, had brought down on them the Russian Czar's ukase of 1821, which closed the coast and the adjoining waters of the Pacific, as far down as parallel 51°, to non-Russian vessels. The Hudson's Bay

Company hoped by diplomacy to effect a cancellation of the ukase and then, by a tight contract with the Russians, to eliminate the American suppliers.

As for the inland trade, the British dominated it after the war. Americans made little effort to recover it. Those operating out of St. Louis were discouraged by the remoteness of the Oregon Country. They had earlier tried the Missouri River route to it which Lewis and Clark had opened. But they had found this roundabout. Also, the towering masses of the Rockies lay between the Missouri's upper waters and those of the Columbia. And on the upper Missouri were the implacable Blackfeet.

Overland routes to the mountains and through them were as yet little known. Overland traffic would, in any case, be beset by logistic obstacles, especially obstacles in supplying traders and trappers, and in bringing home the fur harvest. More attractive opportunities lay nearer American centers of strength —the Great Lakes region, the middle Missouri, and the Far Southwest.

A psychological impediment troubled American traders also. It was the uncooperative spirit of the American government. The American government not only did nothing to encourage traders; it actually impeded them. It enacted laws setting up government trading posts, known as "factories," in the Indian Country. It had begun to do this in 1796. The rationale of the laws was protection of Indians against excesses of private enterprise, against distributing spirits and shoddy goods in payment of furs, against frauds and violence of the debased which drew reprisals from Indians upon farming frontiers and induced them to lend ear to foreign intriguers. In government factories Indians were given goods of honest quality and at reasonable rates in exchange for furs. Rum was withheld and fair dealing was required. This was felt by many private traders to be unfair competition.

Likewise considered unfair by traders—and restrictive of access to the Oregon Country—was legislation forbidding whites to hunt or trap on Indian lands. Legislation "to regulate trade and intercourse with the Indian tribes and to preserve peace on the frontiers" was on the federal statute books as early as 1802. The pertinent language of the 1802 law was: "if any citizen of, or other person residing in the United States (or in the territories), shall cross over or go within (Indian Country) to hunt, or in any wise destroy the game; or shall drive, or otherwise convey any stock of horses or cattle to range on any lands allotted or secured by treaty . . . to any Indian tribes, he shall forfeit a sum not exceeding one hundred dollars and be imprisoned not exceeding six months." This act was basic Indian law until 1834, and had it been at all enforced would have prevented, on lands leading to the Oregon Country, all trapping and hunting.

Of the two restrictions, that of the factory system was the more unpopular among traders and trappers, since it was actually operative. It was disliked even by the Indians since it forbade extension of credit to them and, worse yet, trade in liquor, for which most of them had a strong taste. The law was especially unpopular among entrepreneurs of the fur trade and was under persistent attack from them and from politicians representing them. Senator Thomas Hart Benton, the spokesman of St. Louis traders, was successful in persuading Congress in 1822 to abolish it. This was a triumph for laissez faire, and gave the St. Louis traders a lift of spirits. The lift was well timed. It came just after the British monopoly system had been extended into the Oregon Country.

In August 1822 the *St. Louis Enquirer*, a faithful defender of the city's traders, observed:

> Since the abolition of the United States factories a great activity has prevailed in the operation of this [Indian] trade. Those formerly engaged in it have increased their capital and extended their enterprize; many new firms have engaged in it, and others are preparing to do so. It is computed that a thousand men, chiefly from this place [St. Louis] are now employed in this trade on the waters of the Missouri, and half that number on the Upper Mississippi. The Missouri Fur Company, which alone employs upwards of 300 men, have reached the mountains, and will soon be on the Columbia river.

Others have the same destination, so that the rich furs of that region will soon cease to be the exclusive property of the Hudson's Bay Company.

In Congress the problem of the Columbia and its trade gave concern as early as the opening of the decade. Agitation among enthusiasts to induce the government to move to a political occupation of the mouth of the river began on December 19, 1820, when Congressman John Floyd, an imaginative Virginian in close touch with Senator Benton and with the fur magnates of St. Louis and New York, brought a motion into the House of Representatives to appoint a committee "to inquire into the situation of the settlements upon the Pacific Ocean, and the expediency of occupying the Columbia River." The motion was routinely approved and Floyd was named chairman of the committee. Under his leadership the committee submitted a hastily prepared report and bill on January 25, 1821. The bill authorized the President to occupy the portion of the territory of "the United States on the waters of the Columbia river," to extinguish Indian title there in an undefined district, and to give land there to American settlers. It recommended providing a government for said district as soon as expedient, also a customs house and Indian agents for the natives of the river. It proposed the abolition of the superintendency of Indian affairs in Washington and repeal of so much of every Indian act as had established government factories among the Indians. It initiated a persistent congressional debate on the Oregon question which was destined to become more extreme and inflammatory until it generated the crisis of 1845–46.

In the meantime, on the day following the bill's appearance in Congress, the British minister in Washington, Stratford Canning, dropped in at the office of the Secretary of State, John Q. Adams, to inquire about the intentions of the American government regarding it. He announced portentously by way of introduction that he was making the inquiry in his official capacity. He seemed to feel that the executive department was responsible in some way for what happened in Congress. This annoyed Adams, who was short-tempered. He took strong exception to the inquiry because of its impropriety and because of its inference that the British possessed any rights at all in the Oregon Country. The argument became so heated that it had to be adjourned to the next day. Instead of cooling off then, it became hotter. Adams wished to know how the British Foreign Secretary (Lord Castlereagh) would respond if some member of Parliament should propose in a speech to send a regiment of British troops to the Shetland Islands or to New South Wales and the American minister in London should at once go to the Foreign Secretary and talk to him in an injured and tragical tone about a violation of treaties. The Briton replied that the cases were not parallel. "Have you," said he, "any *claim* to the Shetland Islands or New South Wales?"

"Have you any *claim*," replied Adams, "to the mouth of the Columbia River?"

"Why, do you not *know*," replied Canning, "that we have a claim?"

"I do not *know*," said Adams, "what you claim nor what you do not claim. You claim India; you claim Africa; you claim . . . ."

"Perhaps," interjected Canning, "a piece of the moon."

"No," said Adams; "I have not heard that you claim exclusively any part of the moon; but there is not a spot on *this* habitable globe that I could affirm you do not claim; and there is none which you may not claim with as much color of right as you can have to [the] Columbia River or its mouth." (C. F. Adams, ed., *Memoirs of John Quincy Adams*, V, 251-252.)

This episode was indignantly reported home by the British minister. He complained that it represented an about-face in Adams' attitude, for in personal relations he had hitherto been agreeable. The correspondence got into the hands of George Canning, distinguished cousin of Stratford, momentarily out of the cabinet. He wrote back chiding his relative gently for having laid himself open to attack on such insecure ground. He observed:

> You will perceive when you consider the article in our last convention that we have no reason to complain of the Americans sending an expedition to the Columbia River: the only thing we could complain of would be . . . if they hostilely dispossessed us from any settlement we might have on it. This is *all* that can be said against the step you took; and then it must always be confessed on the other side that Adams behaved in a most boisterous and shameful manner to you. I cannot help thinking that he must have in some degree deceived you into a belief by his former conduct that he meant always to treat you with the greatest confidence, and that then the animal turned round & bit you when he thought he could do it with effect. (George Canning to Stratford Canning, April 14, 1821. Public Record Office, F.O., 116:6.)

The bite apparently was good for the minister's soul, for he did not again expose himself so carelessly to the animal. Indeed, when he returned home for a new assignment in 1823, his parting from Adams was actually amiable.

Americans in Congress and in the press nursed the belief in these years that the Oregon Country was full of furs and that these were immensely enriching British subjects. Congressman Floyd, the Missouri senators, and portions of the New York and Missouri press incessantly spread this view. It was a delusion. The furs in the well-worked areas of the lower Columbia were far from numerous, and the trade was so unprofitable in the years 1818 to 1821 that some of the leading persons in the North West Company were strongly recommending abandoning it and moving northward to fresher areas. Disappointment over meagerness of profit and prospect persisted even after the merger of 1821, and so did proposals to leave the river and move northward to New Caledonia.

The reason for scantiness of profit was in part the scarcity of beaver in the more accessible streams. Beaver had been trapped there unremittingly for a dozen or more years. But defective management in the Columbia Department was probably more at fault—at least the field governor of the Hudson's

Bay Company's territories, George Simpson, so believed. He had retained North West Company personnel in the management of the Department following the merger. He had been receiving disquieting reports, however, of slackness there on the part of these men, and of waste and dissension which they had imported from the scene of the trade war in Rupert's Land. He had been unable to verify the reports personally, his time and energy being engrossed for three and a half years after the merger in the vast task of restoring the economy of Rupert's Land. Reform, where needed, was essential, however, if profit was to be realized in the Department and if the grant of the royal license to the Company was to be justified. In the autumn of 1824 his arrangements for the east having been completed, he set out from York Fort (York Factory) on Hudson Bay on the dramatic canoe drive to the Pacific coast with which his *Journal* opens.

By the time he was half way down the Columbia he was aware that the reports of mismanagement in the Columbia Department had been true. On being reassured, as he arrived at the mouth of the Spokane River, that the Department was in a state of peace and quiet, with the affairs of the Company going on as usual, he wrote impatiently that this was not saying a great deal, as, "if my information is correct the Columbia Dep^{tmt} from the Day of its Origin to the present hour has been neglected, shamefully mismanaged and a scene of the most wasteful extravagance and the most unfortunate dissention. It is high time the system should be changed and I think there is ample Field for reform and amendment." (*Post*, 43.)

Reform and amendment began as soon as Simpson was at his journey's end at Fort George. It was pressed with an energy and a relentlessness that was already a byword in Rupert's Land. The neglect, shameful mismanagement, wasteful extravagance, and unfortunate dissension were removed by surgery. So also was the management which had tolerated them. He had brought with him to the Department a new administrator, Dr. John McLoughlin, to see that the reforms he outlined were implemented and extended. Indeed they were. The

Department under McLoughlin was rejuvenated, though its returns did not reach anywhere near the 100 percent improvement predicted by Simpson and others.

Improvement was contingent from the outset on government support in diplomacy. Such support was implicit in the license of 1821, creating as it did a partnership of government and corporation. The partnership was based on the assumption that the Oregon Country would be divided in the future between the states having claims there. This had been taken for granted in the Anglo-American negotiations of 1818 and of 1823–24. The British government had indicated a willingness to draw a partition line along the 49th parallel from the Rocky Mountains to its intersection with the Columbia River and thence along the river to the sea. The American government had offered a line along the 49th parallel straight to the sea. The area between the offers seemed especially valuable to both governments for its water appendages. At the south the appendage was the Columbia River; at the north it was the body of harbor waters inside the Strait of Juan de Fuca.

In the light of this history the Foreign Office had already suggested to the Hudson's Bay Company that the Company transfer its base of operations in Oregon from the south bank to the north bank of the Columbia River. Canning had proposed this as Foreign Secretary in 1824. The proposal was approved by the Company, and, in the winter of 1824–25, Simpson arranged for the erection of Fort Vancouver on the north bank of the Columbia opposite the point at which the Willamette enters the river. The shift would in no wise reduce the Company's opportunities to exploit the south side of the Columbia and it would increase the prospects of holding the north side in any future negotiation for a partition.

Simpson brought reorganization of the Columbia Department to completion during the winter of 1824–25, and in the spring he was on his way back to Hudson Bay by a different route from the one taken going out, which permitted inspection of added areas. By December 1825 he was in England consulting with the directorate of the Company concerning the years ahead. Prominent in the consultations was a proposed government negotiation with the United States for continuing or replacing the Joint Occupation agreement of 1818 when it expired in 1828. If the agreement could be renewed or if the government could effect a partition which would secure to the Company continued use of the Columbia, a trade expansion over the license area might be undertaken with assurance.

On December 9, 1825, J. H. Pelly, the London governor of the Company, opened the subject with George Canning. He asked in a letter whether the Company might be permitted to expect a continued use of the Columbia in any new agreement with the United States. He suggested that if a partition of the Oregon Country were made, an equitable line would be the continental divide from the 49th parallel to the source of the Snake, the Snake to the Columbia, and the Columbia to the sea. He wrote that the field governor of the Company was in town and would be pleased to furnish the Foreign Office first-hand information. The letter led to a conference and a correspondence which gave Simpson an opportunity to make clear that unless the Hudson's Bay Company could retain the right to use the Columbia River it would probably be constrained to abandon the whole Columbia Department and, indeed, all the country west of the mountains.

The outcome of the conference and correspondence was a negotiation in 1826–27 in London for a partition of the Oregon Country. It was the third such negotiation with the United States in a period of eight years. It proved not successful as to partition. But it did produce a renewal of the joint occupation for another ten-year period and an extension of the agreement thereafter until one side or the other served notice of a wish to terminate it. This was quite satisfactory to the Hudson's Bay Company. It gave ample time to implement the program Simpson had in mind.

In the Oregon Country the region south of the Columbia contained areas relatively unexplored and believed to be rich in furs. These Simpson proposed to harvest as promptly as possible, both for quick profit and for removing temptation from the eyes of the Americans. Absence of beaver there would increase distances to profitable trapping country for those setting out from St. Louis. A fur desert south of the Columbia would intervene as a *cordon sanitaire* for the area north of the river.

A forthright formulation of this policy was sent by Simpson to McLoughlin on July 10, 1826:

It is intended that a strong Trapping Expedition be kept up to hunt in the country to the southward of the Columbia, as while we have access thereto it is our interest to reap all the advantage we can for ourselves, and leave it in as bad a state as possible for our successors; this party may be called the Snake, Umpqua, or any other Expedition you please, but our wish is that it should scour the country wherever Beaver can be found (but on no consideration cross the Mountains) take its returns to Fort Vancouver annually in sufficient time to be sent home by the Ship of the Season and return to its hunting grounds immediately. (R. Harvey Fleming, ed., *Minutes of Council Northern Department of Rupert Land, 1821–31,* 154 n.)

The program of "scouring," of creating a *cordon sanitaire,* was local. It was not applied in areas secure from Americans. There the rule was conservation, especially of beaver. Indians were encouraged to take only winter beaver, not summer, or cub-beaver. A quota system was imposed on district heads to protect beaver. The Governor took a long-range view where it was possible. But it was not possible south of the Columbia.

Complementing the scouring policy in trapping was a rigorous price competition in trade wherever Americans might appear, whether inland or on the coast. That policy was likely to be especially feasible in areas tributary to the Company's trading posts. In such areas Indians were ordinarily paid for furs at predetermined rates. As soon as some wandering American party was learned to be in the neighborhood, the rate would become whatever was necessary to fetch the furs. The Company could afford to outbid competitors—indeed to bid regardless of sales value. It could take a momentary loss; the competitors could not. The same tactics were employed along the coast where the Company ultimately employed a small steamer, which was quicker in its movements than sailing competitors. The combination of thorough trapping south of the Columbia and cutthroat price competition elsewhere was the essence of Simpson's program.

The renewed American advance into the Oregon Country began early in the 1820's. The Missouri River was the route relied on—the route of Lewis and Clark. The upper waters of the river proved to be still stocked with beaver, but these were, as before, jealously guarded by the Blackfeet. Two St. Louis companies—Ashley & Henry and the Missouri Fur Company, in which Joshua Pilcher was a partner—took the lead in the new advance, using as road, the river. They sent parties forward in 1822, as already noted. In the spring of 1823 they sent reinforcements of men and supplies. The reinforcements of Ashley & Henry were roughly handled on the way, especially by the Arikara Indians, who first sold horses to the party and then made a venomous attack on it even though no hunting had been done on their lands. They had a taste for pillaging which was ingrained in the character of some Indians. In the upper Missouri the trappers suffered heavily at the hands of the Blackfeet. But a contingent of the Ashley-Henry men did return alive to St. Louis in the autumn of 1824 with a valuable cargo of furs, and with a valuable report. The report was that a new route to the Oregon Country had turned up during the operations of the preceding year. The new route was feasible because of the discovery—perhaps "rediscovery" would be the better word—of South Pass.

The route through South Pass, taken thereafter, was in all respects superior to the old. It was more direct, and its ascent to the mountains was more gradual. As a gateway through the mountains it was lower than any at the north. The Indians encountered on it were not a great problem. Pack horses were necessary all the way, but they were necessary anyway in the mountains. The first pack-train via South Pass went out with the Ashley-Henry men in 1825.

The trapping system thereafter used by the St. Louis entrepreneurs was a model of efficiency. It was based on the principle of year-round maintenance of trappers in trapping country—no time lost going back to base. An expedition initially sent out would be divided in the mountains into brigades of thirty or forty men. Each would be assigned an area believed to be promising. Each would be strong enough to hold off any ordinary Indian attack. Each had its own string of ponies for moving from stream to stream—transporting supplies and whatever beaver was taken. Each had auxiliary hunters to seek game to supplement the flesh of beaver as food. At the end of a season's hunt, normally in July or August, when furs were not in the best condition, the brigades would meet at some prearranged rendezvous.

Each trapper would deposit his season's catch of furs and settle his accounts with the company. If he was operating on his own—as a so-called "free trapper"—he would turn in his furs at a prearranged rate. If he was working for wages he would collect his pay. The normal pay for this rough and hazardous work was $130 a year.

To the rendezvous would come new supplies from St. Louis—also fresh men. Any trapper wishing further enjoyment of the freedom of the mountains took a new outfit of traps and equipment. Any wishing to leave the mountains and return to civilization went out with the caravan transporting the catch to St. Louis.

Trappers usually stayed in the mountains a number of years. Often they had to, for at the rendezvous they commonly drank and gambled away the earnings of a year and enough more to create a debt to the company. The rendezvous usually attracted friendly Indians who joined in the festivities. The Indians brought their daughters too, who easily found favor with the trappers.

In consequence of these developments two divergent frontiers were brought face to face in the 1820's in the mountains south and east of the Columbia. One was British. Its home base was London—Fort Vancouver was its outpost. Its traditions were those of monopoly, of receiving government support and supporting government in turn. Its mode was long-range planning, synchronized with that of the Foreign Office, and corporation finance, with capital limited only by ability to pay dividends on it. The opposing frontier was American. It was based on St. Louis. Its traditions were those of individualism and laissez faire. All it asked of government was to be let alone. Its makers of tactics were petty entrepreneurs, rival and secretive. Unthought of was long-range policy coordinated with that of government. Financing was of the individual mortgage variety, and the labor relied upon was youths bent on adventure.

The Simpson plans were well carried out. Experienced trapping parties systematically traversed the area south of the Columbia, relieving well-canvassed streams of remnants of their beaver, and seeking out new grounds. An excellently appointed party, led by Peter Skene Ogden, for six years trapped the south side of the Columbia and both sides of the Snake. Another party wrought the upper waters of the Willamette, Umpqua, Klamath, and Sacramento. None of the parties balked at trespassing on Mexican territory. Trespassing was unavoidable in a region as confused in its topography as the Enclosed Basin. But the trespassers discovered the unpleasant fact that the Enclosed Basin was for the most part an area of aridity to be avoided by trappers, a fact Americans also learned. In coastal areas and on the lower Columbia, McLoughlin pressed the tactic of relentless competition in price as a corollary to interior scouring policies.

The Simpson plan in all the area south of the Columbia was highly successful. American trappers and traders, broken by repeated failures, dwindled in numbers, and then quietly withdrew in the 1830's. The Missouri Fur Company wound up business in 1830. The Rocky Mountain Fur Company (successor to Ashley & Henry) did the same in 1834. Captain B. L. E. Bonneville, an adventurous West Pointer, threw in the sponge a year later. The New Englander Nathaniel Wyeth, who had erected Fort Hall on the upper waters of the Snake, sold out to the British company in 1836.

The coastal waters were freed of American competitors by 1837. Simpson made sure that these waters would stay free of them by a ten-year contract signed with the Russian American Company early in 1839, whereby he leased their coastal strip south of Cape Spencer for a rent paid in furs of a specified type, agreed to sell other furs at a stipulated price, and agreed to provide at favorable rates whatever trade supplies and farm produce the Russian American Company would need. The Hudson's Bay Company became overlord of Oregon. McLoughlin became "King" of the combined departments of Columbia and New Caledonia—the license area of 1821. Fort Vancouver served as the *de facto* capital of all the Oregon Country.

And yet this triumph did not translate itself into empire. It was reversed in the Treaty of 1846. In the reversal the American mountain men had their final word. Numbers of them had settled as broken-down trappers in the valley of the Willamette. They formed there the nucleus of a steadily growing pioneer force. None of the force had any love for the colossus of the Oregon Country. When they became numerous enough to be feared they did create fear in the mind of Simpson for the safety of the great Company stores housed at Fort Vancouver. They added urgency in 1845 to other forces inducing the Company to shift its headquarters from the exposed location at Fort Vancouver to the security of Fort Victoria on the southern tip of Vancouver Island. That shift in turn revealed to the British government the truth that the Columbia was not as indispensable a highway to the British interior as it had once seemed and could safely be given up.

In the meantime an incendiary article on the issue of the Oregon Country appeared in December 1845 in a leading American journal—the *Democratic Review.* It was by Caleb Cushing, a prominent American statesman and diplomat. He had long served as a member of Congress and in 1844 had won national acclaim by obtaining in China the Cushing Treaty opening five new treaty ports to American trade. His article was entitled, "English Politico-Commercial Companies," and it was a well-documented account of the British system of enlarging empire. The system was "politico-commercial companies." Cushing began with a vivid description of the system as exemplified in the East India Company's operations in India. That company had won for the British, he said, in the course of centuries, the greatest empire on earth except that of the Manchus. It had done this by pitting rival Indian princes against each other, by levying brutal wars on them, by wholesale bribery, and by every other imaginable variety of black deeds. The British government had kept its hands clean throughout. To the protests of moralists in Parliament it had been able to say that not the government but the East India Company was responsible for what was happening. It merely retained the gains of empire. Also Parliamentary orators were able to take a high moral stand (anti-slavery) on a proposal of the independent state of Texas to join the American Union. All this seemed to Cushing hypocritical.

In the Oregon Country, Cushing pointed out, another of the "English Politico-Commercial Companies," the Hudson's Bay Company, was at work. It, too, had an ancient charter conferring semi-governmental powers. It also had immense resources, and in addition, a license which was a grant of monopoly. It had succeeded in driving all American traders by cutthroat competition from the Oregon Country, and the British government had not needed to lift a finger. Moreover, the license had subjected Americans in the Oregon Country, Cushing wrote, to British judicial process.

Cushing was an intense Anglophobe. He inherited this feeling from his father, who had been driven from the Northwest coast as a trader by the Hudson's Bay Company. The son had already denounced the Company in 1839 in two reports, while a member of the House Committee on Foreign Affairs. He had given there a preview of the article in the *Democratic Review*. In the *Review* he was able to present his case more dramatically and stridently than in congressional reports. This was because the periodical was a journal for literary productions and especially for those favoring Manifest Destiny. He was also able to give full expression to a view that the British had no legitimate claim to any part of the Oregon Country. He had a reputation in the nation for legal learning and his writing carried conviction with believers in the doctrine of Manifest Destiny.

Cushing had once been a Whig but had followed President Tyler into the Democratic Party. He had fought for the annexation of Texas. He had come to believe that Texas extended all the way to the Rio Grande. In the Mexican War he became a general and he wished all Mexico to be absorbed by the peace treaty. He also wished Cuba to be acquired. In the Pierce administration, in which he held the post of Attorney General, he enthusiastically supported the "Ostend Manifesto." He was more favorable to it than even Marcy, the Secretary of State. He was a "Northern man with Southern principles," in short a "doughface" to his Massachusetts anti-slavery critics. His article in the *Democratic Review* was typical of the propaganda of expansionists of the era. It thrummed every chord of antipathy to the British that could be played in Democratic circles. It was more effective than such propaganda would have been from the pen or lips of ordinary demagogues, since Cushing was an intellectual and a great legal scholar. He later was actually nominated to fill a vacancy in the United States Supreme Court as chief justice, though this did not succeed. He could reason well in terms of legal precedent, law, and history, and could skillfully conceal exaggerations.

His article gave to Oregon extremists in the United States a lawyer's brief on imperialist precedents and methods of British monopolies. It exhibited the process by which one of the monopolies had migrated from its original home to an area to which the United States had valid claims. It described a contest thereafter in which Americans, striving to uphold democratic principles, had been bested by imperial agents resorting to unfair means. It warned that a wilderness intended for a republic was being taken over by a monarchy that already encircled the globe. In the article two theses especially useful to extremists were stressed—one, that the British had no genuine claim to any part of the Oregon Country, the other, that American nationals were being subjected in Oregon to the jurisdiction of British courts. The effect of the article was to inflame the Oregon issue in its critical last months and to render an adjustment of it by compromise more difficult. For the reader it ties the events of the early stages of the Oregon contest to the later ones, and reveals the ideologies, British and American, in conflict in the crisis years 1845 and 1846.

A growing body of literature on the history of the fur trade of the Pacific Northwest, and the diplomacy growing out of it, has appeared in print since the first edition of *Fur Trade and Empire: George Simpson's Journal* was published in 1931. This literature includes source materials and secondary accounts.

Of the source materials, the most relevant to this journal and to the correspondence accompanying it are those made available by the Governor and Committee of the Hudson's Bay Company. Especially useful is a volume appearing in the Publications of the Champlain Society (Toronto), *Minutes of Council Northern Department of Rupert Land, 1821–31* (R. Harvey Fleming, ed., 1940), which contains valuable Simpson letters in an appendix. Three other volumes in the same series are Edwin E. Rich, ed., *Letters of John McLoughlin to the Governor and Committee, 1825–38* (1941); 1839–44 (1943); and 1844–46 (1944). The Hudson's Bay Record Society has published two volumes of *Peter Skene Ogden's Snake Country Journals,* one for the years 1824–26 (London, 1950), and the other for the year 1826–27 (1961).

Of secondary accounts two are useful for the period under review: Edwin E. Rich, *History of the Hudson's Bay Company, 1670–1870* (London, 1959), II, Chs. 1-25; and John S. Galbraith, *The Hudson's Bay Company as an Imperial Factor, 1821–1869* (Toronto, 1957), chs. 1-12. These studies are more convincing for the fur trade than for the diplomacy of the Oregon question. For an admirable account of the American mountain men of the Rockies the reader is referred to

Dale L. Morgan *Jedediah Smith and the Opening of the West* (Indianapolis, 1953), and Morgan, ed., *The West of William H. Ashley, 1822–1838* (Denver, 1964). A recent bibliography of the North American fur trade is found in Paul C. Phillips, *The Fur Trade* (Norman, Okla., 1961), II, 577–656. The diplomacy of the Oregon question is dealt with in my *The Oregon Question: Essays in Anglo-American Diplomacy and Politics* (Cambridge, Mass., 1967). Essay Four in that volume—"The Snake Country Expedition, 1824–25," and accompanying correspondence—has special relevance to the present volume.

A detailed map of the Hudson's Bay Company territories divided into districts, including the area covered by the license of 1821, will be found in the map pocket of the first edition of this volume. The map is a reproduction of A. Arrowsmith, *Map Exhibiting All the New Discoveries in the Interior Parts of North America* (London, 1795, Additions to 1824). A simplified version of the map is reproduced as a frontispiece in this edition.

I wish to acknowledge the courtesy of my colleagues in the Harvard History Department who permitted the volume to be reproduced outside its original niche in the Harvard Historical Studies.

INTRODUCTION TO THE FIRST EDITION

October 1929

THE accompanying journal of George Simpson is a memoir of trade and of empire. The author was Governor of the Hudson's Bay Company Territories in America, and as such, director of the economic life of the greater part of what is now the Dominion of Canada and the Pacific Northwest of the United States. At the time of writing this journal he was primarily interested in the task of rehabilitating the fur trade of one section of this vast empire, the Oregon Country, stretching westward from the Rocky Mountains to the sea and from California to Alaska. His account opens with his embarkation in a North canoe on Hudson Bay bound for the Pacific and for the work of reorganizing this trade. He gives a lively narrative of his swift journey across the continent, with comments interspersed on the state of trade along his route. In Oregon the record becomes a memoir of Indian life, of trade problems, of the slashing reforms by which he revived a demoralized and profitless industry, and of his plans for holding possession of the country against any future competition of Americans. By the spring of 1825 he was on his way back to the east to report the results of his tour to his Council, a journey which proved to be a perilous one, and which is correspondingly exciting in the narrative.

The account is one of varied interest. In the field of economic history it offers a summary of the industry of half a continent, a survey as swift and keen and hard as the pace which the Governor set the crew of his North canoe; it presents in sharp contrast the technique of monopoly and of free competition in the fur trade; and at every point it reveals the method and the outlook of a great business executive. The journal contains material for business history; nor is it choked with the dry dust of the ledger, for through these pages runs the breath of swift movement and of perilous adventure in the Indian Country. There is material here also for the student of statecraft. The

Oregon Country, which is the central theme of the document, was in 1824-25 a region in dispute. Not only was it contended for by Great Britain and the United States, but it was claimed also by the Russian Czar, though he was preparing in 1824-25 to give up such rights as he had there for recognition of his sovereignty north of the parallel of 54° 40′. Governor Simpson was ambitious to win the Oregon Country, or as much of it as possible, for Great Britain and for the Hudson's Bay Company. His methods, as richly illustrated in this document, are suggestive of the processes of early nineteenth-century diplomacy.

The journal opens with a reference to the "Honble. Committee," a reminder that there is a charter and a corporation's history in the background. The charter dates back to the period of the Stuart Restoration. It was conferred by Charles II on his "dear and entirely beloved Cousin, Prince Rupert," and a group of associates incorporated as "The Governor and Company of Adventurers of England trading into Hudson's Bay." With the charter the King gave a province named in honor of the cherished kinsman "Rupert's Land." The bounds of the province no man knew. The grant was described in the deed as embracing the lands and waters draining into Hudson Bay and Hudson Straits. That meant extension on the east nearly to the shores of Labrador; on the south to the northern watershed of the St. Lawrence, the Great Lakes and the upper Missouri; on the west to the Rocky Mountain sources of the Saskatchewan River and the eastern sources of the Athabasca River, Great Slave Lake and Back's River; and on the north to the line of the watershed of Hudson Straits. This immense territory was granted free from seignorial reservations; it was given to the Governor and Company to hold as "absolute lords and proprietors" in "free and common soccage." The charter gave all mines of gold, silver, gems and other precious stones in Rupert's Land, and exclusive rights of trade and of fishing. Subjects of the King other than those authorized by the Governor and Company were straitly forbidden to intrude on the Company's exclusive privileges or to "directly or indirectly visit, haunt, frequent, or trade, traffic or adventure by way of merchandizing into or from any of the said territories" under penalty of forfeiture of all goods brought from thence to England and such other punishment as should seem meet to the King for so high a contempt. For this grant of principality and privilege the price exacted in the charter was two elks and two black beavers, to be paid each year to the King and his successors "whenever they should happen to enter into the said territories."

Governmental rights over Rupert's Land, as well as proprietorship, passed with this charter to the Governor and Company, the power to legislate for the territory and for the servants of the Company, the right to impose pains and penalties provided they be reasonable and not repugnant to the laws of England, and the authority to administer justice in all causes, whether civil or criminal, according to the laws of the Kingdom. These were imperial powers, ample for the erection of regular governments as the later history of Red River Colony showed. The Company was entrusted with military authority, the right to enter into peace or war "with any prince or people whatsoever that are not Christian," to send ships, men and munitions into Rupert's Land, to build there castles and fortifications and to garrison them, and to choose and commission commanders and officers. Rupert's Land under this charter was the proprietary colony of the Hudson's Bay Company and as such for two centuries it was held.

But it was not held in peace. The gifts of the charter were challenged in England and abroad. France had claims to the territory as part of the province of New France; she had bestowed the region on one of her colonizing companies much before 1670 and she was not disposed to give up her rights there without a struggle. This was one of the questions that was fought over in the long Anglo-French duel for mastery in the New World; and Rupert's Land, or parts of it, changed hands repeatedly with the fortunes of war before its fate was finally determined in 1763 by the expulsion of France from the continent of North America.

But the removal of this foreign threat served only to stimulate domestic challenge to the charter. Almost from the beginning there had been question as to the charter's validity on the ground that it emanated from royal authority without legislative ratification, and that it granted monopoly rights which, after the Statute of Monopolies of 1623, the crown could not legally bestow. It was argued also in later years that in 1670 Rupert's Land was not Charles II's to give, being then the soil of France, that England gained it first in 1763, when it came by conquest and unencumbered by Stuart gifts of monopoly. Supported by such arguments, free traders from England and Canada defied the exclusive privileges of the Hudson's Bay Company and after 1763 did so with increasing determination and success.

Among the free traders who intruded on Rupert's Land was a group which in 1784 united to form the North West Company of Montreal. This was a redoubtable organization, characterized on the one hand by the dash and aggressiveness of adventurers, and on the other by the stability and the foresight of men of money. Two classes of shareholders were in it: eastern partners, merchants of substance in Montreal and Quebec, who supplied the capital, and the so-called "wintering partners" who contributed the skill and experience which went into leadership in the field. Zeal on the part of employees was stimulated by holding out to promising young men brought into the service the prospect of promotion to the wintering-partner status. There were in the employ of the Company at one time not far from two thousand men—clerks, voyageurs, laborers, interpreters, guides and various other functionaries of the trade. The Company had a route to the interior, less direct, to be sure, than the Hudson Bay passage but advantageous in other respects. This was the southern highway consisting of the broad St. Lawrence and the Ottawa to the Great Lakes, and the Rainy Lake passage thence to the waters of the Saskatchewan. At Montreal and at Fort William on the western shore of Lake Superior the Company had great warehouses assuring to interior posts regularity of supply. This was no mean antagonist for the great British chartered monopoly.

For fifteen years the North West Company and the Hudson's Bay Company clashed in the forests of Rupert's Land. It was a bitter war in which each party wielded weapons of trade and of violence mercilessly in turn. Rival posts fought each other at close range; there was undercutting and overbidding; Indians were competitively plied with liquor; there was covert bargaining by each side with faithless employees of the other, and seizure and confiscation of each other's supplies and furs. Such was the musketry of trade. From the arsenal of war were drawn raids, the levelling of each other's trading posts, incitation of Indians and of half-breeds to violence, open fighting and secret stabbing and shooting in the shadows of the forest. Red River Colony, established in 1811 under the aegis of the Hudson's Bay Company, was in 1816 the scene of a pitched battle in which Governor Semple of the Hudson's Bay Company Territories and twenty men fell before the fire of a party of half-breed retainers of the North West Company. Violence was succeeded after this "Battle of Seven Oaks" by a renewal of cut-throat competition and by litigation in the courts of Upper and Lower Canada.

The result of this war was complete disorganization of the northern fur trade. Prices paid to Indians for furs rose to levels which rendered profit out of the question. Ruin faced even the Indians who in competitive traffic were paid for furs in the currency of rum. Game was recklessly wasted. Furs reach prime condition only in the winter, but competition led to the trapping and hunting of pelts in all seasons, which meant not merely defective furs but extermination of the young with the full grown in the breeding season. Discipline among employees became lax; extravagance and waste crept into the conduct of the trade, a disease that spread even to the Oregon Country which lay outside the boundaries of Rupert's Land and therefore beyond the immediate war zone. By 1820 the struggle had brought the two belligerents to the verge of bankruptcy and to the will to peace.

Peace came by way of a coalition agreement entered into in London in 1821. In the merger the Hudson's Bay Company retained its identity; it took over the assets of the North West Company, evaluated like its own at £200,000, and to finance the consolidation doubled its outstanding stock. The charter and the ancient privileges of the Hudson's Bay Company remained undisturbed. To the privileges a princely addition was made. The British government as a reward for the peace and as a means of preventing any future outbreak of war conferred upon the reorganized Company, under an act of Parliament of 1821, exclusive trading rights for twenty-one years in all that part of British North America lying between Rupert's Land and the Rocky Mountains, and, in addition, the sole British trading rights in the whole of the Oregon Country. Thus the entire area which is now the Dominion of Canada excepting only the valley of the St. Lawrence and the maritime provinces was, after 1821, under the control of the Hudson's Bay Company, either as proprietor or as possessor of exclusive trading rights, and besides the Company held sole British rights of trade in all of what is now the Pacific Northwest of the United States.

The Company divided this empire, for purposes of trade, into four great Departments. Of these the Northern Department of Rupert's Land was the largest and most important, embracing the area lying between the Arctic Ocean on the north, the United States on the south, Hudson Bay on the east and the Rocky Mountains on the west, together with New Caledonia west of the mountains. The Southern Department extended from James Bay southward to the provinces of Upper and Lower Canada, and also East Main, the eastern slope of Hudson Bay. The Montreal Department comprised whatever business was done in the Canadas, and included the Kings Posts, and at a later date part of Labrador. The Columbia Department embraced the valley of the Columbia and after 1825 the province lying to the north of it—New Caledonia. Departments such as these were principalities!

This territorial expansion and the exigencies of the coalition made necessary a revision of the administrative structure of the Hudson's Bay Company. The machinery of central control alone remained in the form prescribed by the charter. It consisted of a governor of the Company, who in Simpson's time was John H. Pelly; a deputy governor, who was Nicholas Garry; and a committee of seven directors. Together these constituted the "Honourable Committee" referred to in the journal. Their choice was determined, or at least confirmed, by the stockholders or proprietors of the Company at their annual General Court in London. The Governor and Committee constituted the ultimate executive authority; they had charge of the voyages, the shipping, the sale of the merchandise brought to England, "and the managing and handling of all other business, affairs and things belonging to the said Company."

It was in the field structure of the Company that the most radical reorganization took place, the whole of the well-designed field machinery of the North West Company being incorporated into it under the cover of old charter forms. This change had for its principal purpose the centralization of field responsibility. Prior to the war the Hudson's Bay Company organization had been defective in this respect, its fort and factory commanders being without nearer supervision than the Governor and Committee in England. The weakness had been exposed in the struggle with the well-knit and locally controlled North West Company, and in 1815 the General Court had taken the step of appointing to America a governor-in-chief and a council, who should have administrative supervision over all Rupert's Land. That innovation the Company wisely retained at the coalition. In 1822, for special reasons, it appointed to its territories two governors instead of one, Williams, the older encumbent, being named to the Southern and Montreal Departments and our author, George Simpson, taking over the great Northern Department and the territories to the west of the Rocky Mountains. In 1826 Williams was recalled to England, and George Simpson became the Governor-in-Chief of all the Territories of the Hudson's Bay Company in America.

The most distinctive feature of North West Company field structure taken over by the reorganized Company was partnership for field officers. This institution was built into the charter by means of a covenant called the Deed Poll of 1821. By this agreement the field officers and wintering partners of the two old companies were erected into a partnership body called the "fur trade" and the relations of this group to the body of proprietors or stockholders in London were put upon a contractual basis.

Two grades of field partners—otherwise referred to as "commissioned gentlemen"—were established: chief factors, of whom the number was fixed at twenty-five, and chief traders, of whom the number was twenty-eight. The chief factors and chief traders were chosen in the first instance under the coalition agreement from among the field officers of the Hudson's Bay Company and the wintering partners of the North West Company. Chief factors were the senior in position and function. They had the more responsible duties as, for instance, the supervision of entire fur-trade districts. Chief traders were of lesser grade; they were assigned to the supervision of single posts or other duties of like weight.

The Deed Poll provided that the profits of the Hudson's Bay Company should be divided annually in the proportion of sixty per cent to the proprietors and forty per cent to the field partners. The forty per cent was to be divided into eighty-five equal shares, two of which were to go to each chief factor and one to each chief trader. Seven of the eighty-five shares were available for a retiring fund. This made it possible for a chief factor or chief trader under certain restrictions to receive on retirement his full interest in the profits of his partnership for one year, and a half interest thereafter for a further period of four years.

With field partnership was associated another North West Company institution, the annual partners' council. In North West Company days this had consisted of a yearly meeting at Fort William of the winterers and the Eastern proprietors, and had been made the occasion for bringing out the season's harvest of furs, distributing new outfits of trading goods and supplies, balancing accounts, deliberating as to the arrangements and projects of the ensuing year, and in the intervals of labor holding those picturesque baronial wassails so dear to the heart of Washington Irving. It had proved a valuable means of unifying and coördinating the far flung activities of a continental fur trade, and when, in 1815, the Hudson's Bay Company appointed a field governor to its territories, it associated with him a general field council. At the coalition, as the result of the extension of partnership to field officers, this was developed into the Council for the

Northern Department of Rupert's Land, a body that, by 1826, had become the supreme consultative organ of all the territories and business of the Hudson's Bay Company in America. Within Rupert's Land it occupied a position analogous to the earlier governor's councils in the proprietary colonies of the American seaboard, except that in the inhospitable climate of the north it could not develop important legislative functions. To establish rules and regulations for the conduct of the fur trade, to examine the results of the trade of the previous year, to determine the outfits and general arrangements for the trade of the ensuing year conformably to the provisions of the Deed Poll of 1821, these were its chief duties. It had the right to review decisions of subsidiary councils in Rupert's Land; its own decisions on the other hand were reviewable by the Governor and Committee in England.

The membership of the Council comprised the entire body of the chief factors of the Company. Chief traders, if they were in charge of fur-trade districts, were expected to come to its annual sessions, and such other chief traders as were at the Council seat when it was in session were invited to attend. Chief traders in attendance exercised the same rights of discussion and ballot as chief factors, except that they could not vote on questions of promotion to their own class or to that of chief factors. The Council was presided over by the Governor, in our day George Simpson. In his first years, before he had thoroughly established himself and while he was still seeking to assuage the sensibilities of men who had been active partners in the North West Company, he presided over the body in the manner of the chairman of a legislative assembly. Later he tended to dominate the meetings.

The Council met in the summer while the fur trade was slack and the routes of travel from the otherwise frozen north were open. Though the place for meeting varied, it was always a depôt accessible to the east, since to it the supplies of the trade must be brought and from it the annual harvest of furs exported. Norway House, near the northeastern outlet of Lake Winnipeg, Red River Settlement and York Factory were the favorite places of assembly. In the appendix to this volume are presented the Minutes of the Council for the year 1824. Those for 1825 are published in the *Canadian Historical Review*, VII, 302-320, and those for the years 1830 to 1843 may be found in E. H. Oliver, *The Canadian North-West*, I, 641-688; II, 689-869.

Beneath the rank of field officers of the Company were employees known as clerks and apprenticed clerks. These were young men, Scotch by birth oftener than otherwise, of fair education and promise, who went through a rigorous training and were expected, after a given period, to recruit the ranks of the field partners. To the apprenticed clerks fell the task of keeping accounts and attending to necessary writing at the posts. They were paid a salary of £20 the first year, from which they rose by stages of £5 and £10 to £50 in the fifth year. They were eligible after five years of service to become clerks. Clerks had duties of greater responsibility. They were in charge of small posts or of expeditions and they received a salary of from £40 to £150 a year. They were eligible, after a period of about fourteen years, if they showed promise to promotion to chief traderships.

Beneath the rank of clerks and apprentices were the ordinary employees, the so-called engagés. These were men of the lower orders for whom there was no hope of high preferment. They had, however, among them grades and classes ranging from the highest, that of post master, down through interpreters, mechanics, guides, steersmen, bowmen, voyageurs and laborers, to the lowly order of apprenticed laborers. Post masters were men who, though barred by lack of education from further promotion, had the confidence of their superiors, and were entrusted with such duties as the keeping of accounts at minor posts or even temporary management of posts in the absence of their principals. Their salaries went as high as £40 a year, and they were nearly in the ranks of gentlemen. Next stood the interpreters, who had a smattering of the Indian dialects of their neighborhood, and whose services might bring them as high as £25 a year. Mechanics followed, then the guides, steersmen and bowmen, the aristocracy of the voyageurs. Common voyageurs or middlemen were the most numerous order, commanding wages of £17 a year, followed at the bottom of the list by laborers and apprenticed laborers. The Company recruited its voyageurs and laborers largely from French Canadians and half-breeds. Orkneymen were also employed, together with some Indians and Hawaiians. The Canadians were the favorites of the officers, a docile, happy, lovable, shiftless, irresponsible class, capable of great exertion while on the voyage, of rowing, paddling and portaging sixteen hours a day for months, and then living over extended periods in thriftless idleness. These elements were to be found, with their Indian or half-breed women and children, around every considerable trading post, but the chief center for them was Red River Colony, where they eked out a precarious existence in the intervals of employment by the Hudson's Bay Company, and in old age, by a little irregular farming and by hunts in the spring and autumn upon the buffalo herds of the Great Plains.

George Simpson who stood at the head of this great field organization was in 1821 a man with a future rather than a past. He was the illegitimate son of George Simpson, born at Loch Broom in Ross-shire, Scotland, in 1792. Of his early life little is known except that he was given a fair education, was brought to London in 1809, and as a clerk entered the employ of a firm engaged in the West India trade. His native heath in the early nineteenth century was a nursery ground for North American fur-trade leaders, but his own entrance into the industry was the result of his having attracted the favorable notice of Andrew Colvile, an influential member and later governor of the Hudson's Bay Company. In the spring of 1820 he was sent by the Hudson's Bay Company to the Athabasca Country to acquire experience in the Indian trade, and there he spent the winter of 1820-21. At that time the war with the North West Company was in the litigation stage, and Governor Williams was under indictment in the courts of Lower Canada. In order to be prepared for the contingency of his removal to Quebec, the Hudson's Bay Company, in November, 1820, appointed Simpson governor *locum tenens*. At the coalition, at the age of twenty-nine, he was promoted to joint governorship, with Williams, of the Company Territories, with special charge of the Northern Department of

Rupert's Land including the Department of the Columbia. By 1826 he was governor-in-chief of all the Hudson's Bay Company Territories in America.

To be governor of the Northern Department of Rupert's Land in 1821 was to be brought face to face with harassing problems of post-war reconstruction. Rupert's Land was strewn with the wreckage of battle. There was material wreckage in the form of exhaustion of fur preserves, the duplication of trading posts and the multiplication of equipment and men. More difficult to cope with was the psychological wreckage, mutual bitterness and hate of subordinates of the old companies now brought together in the coalition, habits of drunkenness which competition had fostered among the Indians, relaxed habits of discipline among servants, and the propensity to waste and extravagance formed by the whole fur-trading community. These were the rehabilitation problems of the new governor and they were a test of his quality.

He came to his task with an intellectual equipment that promised much for his success. He had, to be sure, only scant experience in Rupert's Land, but that was an element of strength rather than of weakness in 1821 since it had as its corollary freedom from the rancors of the war. Indeed, it was one of the chief reasons for appointing him rather than his senior colleague to the great Northern Department. He combined with a sure judgment an exterior of affability that enabled him to heal old wounds and to reconcile men to a new order. As an administrator his talents were exceptional. He had the imaginative vision of a Clive; he drew his plans on a scale that was continental. With vision he combined a grasp of detail that was extraordinary. There was no element of the fur trade from the Athabasca Country to the Sandwich Islands, from Hudson Bay to the steppes of Siberia, that he did not acquaint himself with by personal visit. He was a dynamo of energy, tireless at his work, whether at his desk or on the march. His journeys were famous for their speed; on the present voyage, though he took a route that was unfavorable in passing from Hudson Bay to the Columbia and lost many days by halts for business, he cut the record for the distance from 104 days to 84. On his return, to save time in an emergency, he made a perilous and exhausting overland march from Carlton to the Red River Settlement. His party, when it met relief within a half-day's march of the Settlement, was half famished and utterly spent, but not the Governor. Without pausing for food or rest he threw himself upon a horse brought by the relief party and galloped off to his duties at Fort Garry. He put the spurs as remorselessly to his subordinates, high and low, as to himself. There is an unsubstantiated legend, which used to circulate in the Red River Colony, that on one occasion his goading drove one of his favorite voyageurs to the point of seizing him by the collar, lifting him into the water, and holding him there until he promised to relent his pace.

With drive he combined a penchant for orderliness, a product of his counting-house experience and a source of frequent discomfiture to unsystematic clerks and post officials whose accounts he examined on his unannounced tours of inspection through the country. He was the never wearying apostle of economy. To be wasteful or to indulge in what he called "luxuries," which were ordinary European supplies, were offences that grated like a rasp on his Scotch soul. "One would think," is his indignant reply to a requisition sent in by a post officer for mustard, "from the quantity you order, that it is intended to be used in the Indian trade."

A typical nineteenth-century captain of industry is the Governor as we meet him in these pages, a self-made man with all the traits of the type emphasized by his being still in the making—imperious, aggressive, self-assured, severe in his judgments, painfully eager for success. If the reader finds some portions of the journal on this account grating, let him remember that Rupert's Land in 1821 was no place for the gentler arts of leadership. It was a raw, fierce wilderness calling for an administrator as hard and as indomitable as itself, a leader who had edge, a scythe of steel to clear away the weeds and tares of war.

Under Simpson's direction Rupert's Land passed through a swift process of rehabilitation. Posts that were no longer useful were abandoned, those that were not well located were shifted.

A sweeping reduction was made in the number of employees of the Company—from 1983 to 827 between the years 1821 and 1825. The discharged men as a matter of economy were gradually transferred with their native families to the Red River Colony, which took on as a result a new character and a new permanence. Wages were cut to half what they had been and an end was made to perquisites and gratuities of every sort. Fur prices were standardized; only along the international frontiers and along the Pacific Coast were the flexible standards of competition retained. The liquor traffic was put under restraint, though by uneven stages owing to Indian resistance in the interior and trade competition along international frontiers. In 1822 and 1823 the Company reduced to a half the quantity of liquor distributed and never again returned to the old scale. Along international frontiers agreements were made, with the American Fur Company in 1830 and with the Russian American Company in 1842, mutually renouncing trade in spirits. The transport service of the Company was overhauled, new routes were opened and old ones improved. Wherever stream conditions permitted York boats were substituted for North canoes as freighters at a saving of a third in wages. The Governor himself took a brigade of York boats to the Athabasca Country in 1822-23 to demonstrate that they could be advantageously used in the transport of the Far North.

Discipline in every rank of the service was toned up. The Council became the whip of the Governor for this purpose, formulating as occasion required new rules and regulations and enforcing them even on its own membership by stiff fines. The old semifeudal freedom and individualism of the fur trade became a thing of the past; "wintering partners" were no longer, as in the days of the North West Company, "lords of the lakes and forests." They had become cogs in an efficient machine, the levers of which were in the firm grasp of the Governor of the Northern Department of Rupert's Land. Ferdinand Wentzel was right when he wrote at the end of a page of lament from Athabasca in 1824, "the North-West is now beginning to be ruled with an iron rod."

One region there remained in 1824 to rehabilitate, the great area west of the Rocky Mountains, known, in the northern half, as New Caledonia and, in the southern, as the Department of the Columbia. This was a region less capable of subjection to the rod than Rupert's Land. No solid foundation for authority existed there since its sovereignty was still undetermined. Russia, Great Britain and the United States, as we have seen, all had claims to it, though Russia in 1824 was on the eve of withdrawing to the parallel of 54° 40′. Great Britain and the United States, after failure to agree to its partition, had concluded in 1818 a ten-year treaty of joint occupation which gave to the nationals of each the right to engage in its trade. To reduce to order a traffic kept open to competition by international treaty was a task calling for capacity and flexibility even beyond that of Rupert's Land.

The trade was of two types, coastal and interior, each with its own background and problems. That of the coast in 1824 was in the control chiefly of Americans. They had entered upon it after Captain Cook's notable voyage of discovery in 1776-79 revealed its richness to the English-speaking world, and they had come to dominate it in the period of the Napoleonic struggle when European rivals were drawn off to more compelling fields of contest. New England and New York were the particular contenders for it. From their ports in the late summer or early autumn of the year went forth adventurous craft, laden with goods adapted to Indian taste—blankets, iron works, firearms, cutlery, beads, trinkets, finery of various sorts and plentiful quantities of rum. Rounding the Horn in December, in the Antarctic summer, and touching on their way northward at the Sandwich Islands for fresh food and water, they arrived off the Northwest Coast ready for barter in the spring. They devoted the summer to the gathering of furs, visiting Sitka on occasion to dispose of supplies to the Russian American Company. Late in the summer they were ready to depart for the Orient, stopping again on the way at the Sandwich Islands for food and for sandalwood to fill up cargo. Toward the end of the year they were at Canton where furs and sandalwood and, perhaps, ginseng from New England were exchanged for teas and silks and nankeens destined for the markets of Boston and New York. It was a romantic trade, somewhat speculative but alluring in its prospects of exceptional profits. Many a New England fortune was founded on it, and no doubt also some failures. At its height in the early years of the nineteenth century there were as many as fourteen American vessels engaged in it. But by 1821 its great days were over, and by 1824 only a few New England trading firms or adventurers still pursued it. Governor Simpson's task was to salvage what could be saved of it and, by careful management along the coast, to protect more important interests in the inland trade.

The inland trade similarly had its background in national rivalry. That of the Columbia may be said to have been opened by Robert Gray, a Boston ship captain, who in 1792 turned the prow of his vessel, the "Columbia," into a white line of breakers between Capes Disappointment and Adams, found a channel through them, and on the other side disclosed the mouth of the great stream which bears his ship's name. A dozen years later Lewis and Clark supplemented this momentous achievement by exploring from the eastward the southern half of the interior valley. To the north New Caledonia was left for the adventurous partners of the North West Company to open up—to Alexander Mackenzie, who in 1793 crossed the continental divide from Fort Chippewyan and came out upon the sea at Bentinck Inlet; to Fraser and Stuart, who in 1808 descended the turbulent Fraser to the Gulf of Georgia; and to David Thompson, who made his way in the years 1807-11 down the northern arm of the Columbia to the Pacific.

Priority in the erection of trading posts was distributed along the same national and geographic lines. In 1806 Simon Fraser of the North West Company built in New Caledonia the first British trading post established west of the Rocky Mountains. In 1811 John Jacob Astor made at Astoria the American bid for fortune and for empire. But the American venture proved unsuccessful. Misfortune dogged it at every step and the War of 1812 sealed its fate. In October, 1813, after a series of adventures by sea and land that rival the imaginings of fiction and that still give thrill to the pages of Washington Irving's *Astoria*, the partners of Astor accepted from the North West Company terms of surrender. The entire inland trade of the Columbia passed with this capitulation to the North West Company, and there for eight years uncontested it remained.

But despite this exclusive enjoyment of it the North West Company was never able to bring the Columbia trade to a profit. This was partly due to the difficulty of marketing the fur catch. Though China was the natural outlet for the furs of the Pacific Northwest, under the laws of Parliament the rights of British subjects to trade there were vested solely in the East India Company. The East India Company was willing to permit British traders to dispose of their furs within its precincts under license, but under no circumstances to take away the proceeds in the form of tea or other China produce. That rendered almost impossible competition with American coastal traders who were able to take profitable cargo not only to Canton but from it. The North West Company, indeed, experimented with restrictive licenses of the East India Company for the first three of its Columbia shipments (1813 to 1815). Then in 1815 it sought refuge from them in an arrangement with the American firm of Perkins & Company. That concern, it was agreed, should take charge at Boston of supplies for the Columbia sent over from England, ship these to Fort George at the mouth of the Columbia, take on there the furs of the North West Company, transmit them to Canton, convert the furs, under the protection of the American flag, into teas and other China produce, bring the latter to Boston to be disposed of for cash, and receive in compensation an agreed percentage of the net returns. That arrangement proved better than dependence on the East India Company licenses, and it continued for the remainder of the existence of the North West Company. But it was far from a satisfactory solution of the Columbia River marketing problem, and accounts in part for the failure of the North West Company to turn this trade to a profit.

There were other reasons for failure, the competition, already noted of American coastal traders, the distance of the Columbia Valley from the seat of North West Company control, the absence of such compelling leadership as Simpson was later to give, jealousy and bickering between the wintering partners in the region, the lax and wasteful methods which had crept into the trade when the country was virgin and its opportunities rich, and, not least, the war psychology finding its way in from Rupert's Land which destroyed interest in mere efficiency and created indifference to those humble economies which in a large-scale business often spell the difference between success and failure. When the North West Company turned over this trade at the coalition to the Hudson's Bay Company, there seemed so little prospect of its ever becoming again a source of profit that the Governor and Committee of the Hudson's Bay Company were prepared, despite the gift from Parliament of exclusive British rights to it, to give it up.

"We understand," they observe in a despatch to Governor Simpson in February, 1822, "that hitherto the trade of the Columbia has not been profitable, and from all that we have learnt on the subject we are not sanguine in our expectations of being able to make it so in future. But if by any improved arrangement the loss can be reduced to a small sum, it is worth a serious consideration, whether it may not be good policy to hold possession of that country, with the view of protecting the more valuable districts to the North of it; and we wish you to direct the attention of the Council to this subject and collect all the information which you can obtain from individuals acquainted with the country . . . . Should the result of all your enquiries be unfavorable to the plan of continuing the trade of Columbia it will be proper to consider" at what time and by what mode the withdrawal to New Caledonia may best be effected.

It must have been profound discouragement that induced the directors of the Hudson's Bay Company to consider a step so grave as withdrawal from the valley of the lower Columbia. For here lay the core of the Oregon boundary dispute. Nominally the British and American governments claimed each the whole of the Oregon Country from California to Alaska. Actually both were prepared for some sort of partition. In the negotiations of 1818 the American government had proposed as the line of division the 49th parallel drawn to the sea; the British government had intimated the line of the 49th parallel to the great northern branch of the Columbia River and thence down the channel of the river to the sea. Between the Columbia River and the 49th parallel lay the bone of contention, that triangle of territory which comprises the central and western thirds of the present state of Washington, and embraces on one side the channel of the Columbia River and on the other the valuable cluster of harbors in and about the Gulf of Georgia. Throughout the period of Anglo-American negotiation from 1818 to 1846 this region constituted the stakes of Oregon diplomacy and in the play for it economic control was an ace card. Yet this was the region from which the London directors of the Hudson's Bay Company and most of the chief factors in America, in discouragement over its unprofitableness, were thinking in 1822 of withdrawing.

Discouragement was no part, however, of the thinking of the Governor of the Northern Department of Rupert's Land. At the opening of this journal we find him at York Factory on Hudson Bay chafing over the delay which the nonarrival of the annual ship from England was making in his departure for the Columbia and for the work of reorganizing its trade. On August 15, 1824, he determined to wait no longer and, though it was then the Sabbath and a gale of wind was whipping the waters on which his North canoe was to be launched, he set off. That was the beginning of a merciless drive of the kind for which he was already famous and which brought him by November 8 to the scene of his labors. There, as usual, he found much to reform and little to commend. Everything in the Columbia seemed to him to be on too extended a scale "*except the Trade* and when I say that that is confined to Four permanent Establishments the returns of which do not amount to 20,000 Beaver and Otters altho the country has been occupied upwards of Fourteen Years, I feel that a very Severe reflection is cast on those who have had the management of the Business, as on looking at the prodigious expences that have been incurred and the means at their com-

altruistic, the founding of missions among the Columbia River Indians was recommended to the London office with important later results.

An outstanding need of the Department was vigorous new local leadership. This the Governor provided by appointing to its superintendence one of the ablest of his eastern chief factors, a man destined to achieve in the Columbia a standing hardly second to the Governor's own, Dr. John McLoughlin. We are given in this journal an interesting glimpse of the future "King of Oregon" as he appeared when overtaken by Governor Simpson in Riviere la Biche on his way to his new charge. "He was such a figure as I should not like to meet in a dark Night in one of the bye lanes in the neighbourhood of London, dressed in Clothes that had once been fashionable, but now covered with a thousand patches of different Colors, his beard would do honor to the chin of a Grizzly Bear, his face and hands evidently Shewing that he had not lost much time at his Toilette, loaded with Arms and his own herculean dimensions forming a tout ensemble that would convey a good idea of the high way men of former Days."

Under a leader of such stature the Columbia Department ceased to be a liability, though on the other hand it did not achieve the riches predicted for it by the sanguine Simpson. The precise degree of its improvement is difficult to determine, for the account books of the Company are not accessible and information found elsewhere is not conclusive. We have a report from Governor Simpson to the London office ten years after his voyage to the Columbia in which he describes the Departmental returns, including those of the coast and New Caledonia, as more cheering and satisfactory than any hitherto received from that quarter, amounting to £47,500 with a profit balance of £23,000, an increase over the preceding season of 38 per cent. These figures, however, are but a preliminary estimate, the actual gains of any season being determinable only after the furs had been sold in London and the costs of transport and distribution ascertained. We have a letter from Dr. McLoughlin to the Honorable Committee in 1843 replying to an assertion made in Congress by Senator Linn that the Columbia Department had been immensely profitable, an assertion which, he says, "as you know is not the case." Governor Pelly comes to the same conclusion in a survey prepared for the Lords Committee of the Privy Council For Trade in 1838 when the Company was an applicant for the renewal of its exclusive license of British rights in the Indian Territories. He does not, however, in this statement make a clear distinction between the profits of the coastal trade, which were low, and those gained by the Department as a whole.

"The principal benefit the Company derive," he declared, "from the exclusive License of trade is the peaceable occupation of their own proper territory [Rupert's Land], from which they draw nearly the whole of the profits of their trade, and for the protection of which they have a right to look to the Government in common with the rest of Her Majesty's subjects, as the trade of the country embraced in the Royal License is as yet of very little benefit to them, and affords greater advantages to the mother country in the employment of shipping, and in the revenue arising from imports and exports, than the Company derive from it.

"The country denominated 'Indian Territories,' comprehended in the Royal License, is principally situated on the west side of the Rocky Mountains, the most valuable part thereof being the north-west Coast, bordering on the shores of the Pacific.

"For many years previous to the grant of exclusive trade to the Hudson's Bay Company, the trade of that coast was engrossed by the subjects of the United States of America and Russia, the only establishment occupied by British traders being 'Astoria' afterwards named 'Fort George' at the mouth of the Columbia River, while no attempt was made, through the means of shipping, to obtain any part of the trade of the coast; and so unprofitable was it in the years 1818, 1819, 1820, 1821 and 1822, and so difficult of management, that several of the leading and most intelligent persons in the country strongly recommended that the Company should abandon it altogether. The Company, however, felt that the honour of the concern would, in a certain degree, be compromised were they to adopt that recommendation, holding as they did under Government the License in question, and with a degree of energy and enterprise, which I feel assured your Lordships will admit, reflects much credit on themselves and on their officers and servants in the Country, they directed their efforts so vigorously to that branch of the business, that they compelled the American adventurers, one by one, to withdraw from the contest, and are now pressing the Russian Fur Company so closely, that although that association is supported by its government to the extent of affording them the assistance of a strong military guard at each of their establishments, which, with their shipping, are officered by naval and military officers of the Imperial army and navy, we are gaining ground upon them, and hope at no very distant period to confine them to the trade of their own proper territory.

"The outlay and expense attending this competition in trade are so heavy, that the profits are yet but in perspective, none worthy of notice having been realized, the result showing some years a trifling loss, and in others a small gain, fluctuating according to the degree of activity with which the contest is maintained; but by energy and perseverance, we hope, in due time, to bring it to a more favourable issue, if the facilities of protection now required of Her Majesty's Government be afforded.

"This trade, nevertheless, affords employment to about 1000 men, occupying 21 permanent trading establishments, two migratory trading and trapping expeditions, a steam vessel, and five sailing vessels from 100 to 300 tons burthen, all armed, and so dangerous is the trade, that I lament to say that it has not been unattended with loss of life....

"That the Hudson's Bay Company have the strongest possible claims upon Her Majesty's Government for a renewal of the exclusive License of trade, without any rent or pecuniary consideration whatsoever, cannot, I should hope, admit of a question after the explanation I have given; but when it is considered that the greater part of the country to which the License applies is Indian Country, opened by treaty to citizens of the United States of America, as well as to British subjects, and, consequently, the License of exclusive trade does not protect the Company from the competition of citizens of the United States, it must appear evident that no substantial benefit is likely to arise from the boon we are soliciting, beyond the probable means of affording peace to our own territories, in the tranquillity of which Her Majesty's Government ought to feel as deep an interest as the stockholders of the Hudson's Bay Company."

Whether the revenues of the Hudson's Bay Company in the Columbia Department were large or small is after all not a matter of much historical importance. What is significant is that by reason of Simpson's elimination of major losses the Company had found it possible to remain in the valley of the lower Columbia, that by the vigor and energy of the new administration it had succeeded in reversing American domination of the coast, that it had compelled American competitors one by one to withdraw from the field, and that in the interior, no less than on the coast, it had completely carried the day. What George Simpson had achieved by his reforms was to reduce Oregon to economic vassalage to a British corporation. He had converted the Columbia Department into a new principality of the Hudson's Bay Company, ruled over from Fort Vancouver as by the viceroy of a king.

For a decade this dominion of trade conditioned Oregon diplomacy. For a decade this was the great obstacle to a settlement of the boundary dispute. British negotiators found in it motive and support for an unwavering refusal to retreat from the lower Columbia River. American negotiators found in it, and particularly in British possession of the Columbia River, an insurmountable barrier to their reaching the coveted harbors in and about the Gulf of Georgia.

What the consequences of this deadlock would have been if it had continued during the critical years of Oregon diplomacy we need not conjecture, for it did not continue. By the early forties new forces had come into play: the advent particularly of American pioneers in the valley of the Columbia, and the growth of their settlement opposite Fort Vancouver, the great western base of the Company. Under the threat of pillage of the rich

the striking differences in spirit and method between the fur trade of the Hudson's Bay Company and the American trade to the south. For the most part the American trade was under the direction of men who were in the midst of its harsh realities, men who were traders themselves or had been, who had braved the Indian menace of pillage and murder, who knew the sordidness and cruelty of savage life, and who had little compunction in profiting by its weaknesses and vices. St. Louis, which was the center of this trade, was a frontier community which accepted the frontier philosophy that the only good Indian is a dead Indian. Native Canadians took much the same attitude in trafficking with the Indians as, for instance, the partners of the North West Company who were notorious for their realism. George Simpson in his earlier years was not free from this contagion as is attested by some of his intimate letters to his London patron, Andrew Colvile, a number of which are here presented from the Selkirk Papers. On May 20, 1822, for example, he expresses strong objection to establishing schools for Indian children in Rupert's Land; they will serve merely to fill the pockets and bellies of hungry missionaries, they will rear the natives in habits of indolence, and "an enlightened Indian is good for nothing." A proposal to have a chaplain at York Factory is objected to as a nuisance. The heavy restriction placed by the London Committee on the export of rum to Rupert's Land is lamented; such restriction, if too severe, will discourage the Indians, and "the people will not have an opportunity of disgorging their heavy wages." Here is a philosophy as harsh as the wilderness from which it sprang and George Simpson, left without outside supervision, would have been as realistic and as hard-bitted as any American or Nor'Wester.

But in London there was kindlier soil. In its sheltered security humanitarianism was able to take root and escape the chill blasts rising from barbarism. The London Committee contained men some of whom were philanthropists, sincerely concerned for the welfare of natives who, under the terms of the charter and the exclusive license of trade, were the Company's wards. Monopoly in itself was a support to humane councils, providing a permanent stake in the Indian country as compared with the transitory interest of American trappers, and justifying as a matter of enlightened self-interest a policy of conserving and strengthening Indian life. Monopoly served also as a spur. There was strong and increasing opposition in England to the perpetuation of any exclusive trading privilege, and the London Committee was keenly alive to the fact that at any moment it might be called upon to defend its stewardship of the charter and the license at the bar of public opinion and of Parliament. London thus nurtured a policy of humane moderation in the fur trade as naturally as the American environment stimulated exploitation.

Governor Simpson took his cue from the London Committee, and the views which in 1824-25 he expressed in this journal are in striking contrast with those of his letters to Andrew Colvile three years earlier. He is now a friend of the school for native children at Red River, to which, on his return from the Columbia, he took two Indian boys to be educated; he is vigorous in his denunciation of the liquor traffic in the Columbia Department; and he is almost evangelistic in his earnestness for the establishment of missions among the Columbia River Indians. Dr. McLoughlin's patriarchal sway over the natives of Oregon need find no other explanation than his own kindly spirit, but it was in entire accord with the policy of Governor Simpson and of the Honorable Committee.

London paternalism and St. Louis individualism gathered each its own fruits. The territory of the Hudson's Bay Company, inhabited by a numerous and diverse Indian population, was an area of peace and order. Throughout its length and breadth the Company's transportation service was maintained, without interruption, by boat crews barely large enough for the requirements of the portage; the murder of a white trader was an event that was infrequent and that was visited when it occurred with prompt punishment; and even intertribal wars yielded at times to the intervention of the Company's officers. On the American side of the line, violence and murder were the order of the day. Senator Benton in 1829 placed at five hundred the number of

American trappers and traders who had already lost their lives to the Indians of the Rocky Mountains; the hostility of the natives was so inveterate that the Senator felt it necessary to find some explanation for it, which he did by the atrocious charge that it was instigated by the officers of the Hudson's Bay Company. How great the distance was between London and St. Louis is illustrated in the episode of the famous American trapper, Jedediah Smith, which appears in our correspondence. Smith's party was overwhelmed and, with the exception of its leader and three others, destroyed by Indians on the Umpqua in 1828. When the news reached Fort Vancouver Dr. McLoughlin sent out a party of Hudson's Bay Company trappers which was able without force to recover and restore the bulk of the pillaged property.

This striking contrast between British and American Indian relations was no mere temporary phenomenon disappearing with the passing of the fur trade. It persisted as long as the red man and the white faced each other in the coveted land of the Far West. Trapper and trader gave way on both sides of the international boundary to miner and cattleman and they in turn to the pioneer farmer. These harbingers of a new day on the American side entered a region of already established strife and perpetuated there traditions two centuries old of Indian massacre and border retaliation. On the Canadian side civilization entered a region reduced by the Hudson's Bay Company to a tradition of law and order and the history of this frontier was one of almost unbroken peace.

In preparing these documents for publication I have had to reconcile two conflicting purposes. One was to emphasize the natural unity which geography, business organization and the Convention of Joint Occupation gave to the Columbia Department. The other was to preserve as far as possible the ties which related this Department to the wider empire of the Hudson's Bay Company. As a practical matter I have made concessions to each of these ideals and, though the center of interest of the volume lies in the Columbia Department, I have felt free to depart from a unity which, overemphasized, would have been misleading.

The reader will find in Appendix A frequent evidence of selection and excision. Selection was necessary even within documents, more particularly within the longer despatches of Governor Simpson and the Honorable Committee which dealt with the whole range of Hudson's Bay Company interests. Some omissions were the result of censorship. Still others were due to a desire to avoid redundancy, produced in the original documents by the requirements of business, the factor of distance, the uncertainties of communication, and the distribution of authority between England and America. It was the practice of Dr. McLoughlin to report to Governor Simpson by the Columbia Express; and by the annual Columbia ship to the Honorable Committee. Governor Simpson made his report on the basis of the despatches received from the Columbia and elsewhere to the Honorable Committee, often without significant variation of idea or even of phraseology. The Honorable Committee on its part sent its general instructions by the Columbia ship to Dr. McLoughlin and by the Bay ship to Governor Simpson; and the latter completed the circuit of communication by the Columbia Express. Where the omitted portions of despatches consisted of paragraphs which were serially numbered, I have not burdened the printed page with the conventional symbols of omission, but all other excisions have been properly indicated. I have undertaken in editing these documents to reproduce them as nearly as possible in their original form. In some cases, however, in the interests of economy of space or clarity I have paraphrased letters in part or in whole, plainly indicating this fact.

I am under obligations to Sir William Schooling, K. B. E., and to the officers of the Hudson's Bay Company for the greater part of the documents presented in this volume. I did not have access to the Company's archives themselves, the documents being selected by me from a manuscript catalogue and brought for transcription to an outside office. Some records which I applied for could not be located, and others containing the accounts of the Columbia Department I did not have access to. My transcripts were censored as I have indicated. I consider it permissible to say that the record of the Hudson's Bay Company in the Oregon County, so far as I saw it, contains nothing that cannot bear the light of day. The standards imposed by the Honorable Committee on its servants were high in themselves and much superior to those of the American adventurers who competed for the trade. I believe the Company could but enhance its reputation by throwing open its archives without restriction to historians.

For the minutes of the Council of the Northern Department of Rupert's Land I am under obligations to Dr. Max Farrand and to the Huntington Library. For the Simpson-Colvile correspondence I am indebted to Sir Charles Hope-Dunbar of Scotland, who owns the originals, and to the Public Archives of Canada which has the transcripts. I am, in addition, indebted to Sir Charles Hope-Dunbar for courtesies in collating my copies with his originals. I am under obligations to Messrs. F. C. C. Lynch and J. B. Tyrrell of Canada for kindly assistance in my editorial labors, and to Miss Elizabeth F. Hoxie for valuable help in seeing the volume through the press.

FREDERICK MERK

Cambridge, October, 1929.

GEORGE SIMPSON'S JOURNAL

ENTITLED

Remarks Connected with the Fur Trade in the Course of a Voyage from York Factory to Fort George and Back to York Factory 1824–25

GEORGE SIMPSON'S JOURNAL

Sunday, Aug. 15, 1824. The Honble Committee having signified a wish that I should visit the Columbia Deptm^{t} I used every diligence to get through the business of the season at York[1] sufficiently early to ensure a passage to the Rocky Mountain before the Navigation closed, and with much perseverence and labour my correspondence was finished and the principal transactions of the Year completed by the 15th of this Month when after conveying my sentiments fully to M^{r} McTavish[2] on all matters connected with the business and leaving to his managment the final arrangements of the season, I took my departure from York accompanied by Chief Trader McMillan[3] in a North Canoe[4] with a complement of Eight Men besides my own Servant and an Indian Guide.

D^{r} McLoughlin who was appointed to succeed Mr Kennedy in the superintendence of the Columbia Deptm^{t} left York on the 27th of the preceding month with two Light Canoes and Fourteen

[1] York is Simpson's abbreviation for York Factory—the chief depôt of the Northern Department of Rupert's Land. This establishment was located on the west shore of Hudson Bay at the mouth of Hayes River, and at the outlet of a vast interior transport system. Thither were brought the furs of nearly all the region between Hudson Bay and the Rocky Mountains, and between the American boundary and the Arctic. From it likewise went out the supplies of this area, imported in the annual ship from England. Near the depôt site were the ruins of an earlier fort of the same name built in 1682, which had been a bone of contention between England and France throughout their long struggle for dominion in the New World, and had been destroyed in 1782, at the close of the War of the American Revolution, by the La Pérouse Expedition. For a contemporary description of York Factory see the "Diary of Nicholas Garry" in Royal Society of Canada, *Proceedings and Transactions*, 2nd series, VI, sect. ii, 167, 195; see also R. M. Ballantyne, *Hudson's Bay* (London, 1848), chap. i.

[2] J. G. McTavish, the chief factor in charge of York Factory. He is best known for his earlier North West Company connection and particularly for his part in the taking over of Astoria from the Pacific Fur Company in the winter of 1813-14. He became a chief factor of the Hudson's Bay Company in 1821 at the time of the coalition.

[3] See for him *post*, 68 n.

[4] See Appendix B, *post*, 345.

Men having the start of us by Twenty Days; he took the route by Norway House[5] and the Object of sending so many hands across the Mountain this Season was to replace others expected to retire next Year and to reinforce the Snake Country Expedition[6] which had sustained considerable loss in the recent Conflict with the Slave Tribes[7] of the East side the Mountain.

I was most anxious that the Ship from England should have arrived at York, previous to my departure, in order that I might be in possession of the Coy[s] instructions as they did not anticipate my undertaking the present Voyage in the course of this Season when the Spring Despatches were forwarded, but for important reasons which I have already explained to the Hon[ble] Committee and which it is here unnecessary to repeat, it appeared highly desirable for the interests of the concern that my visit to the Columbia should not be deferred 'till an other Season and the opinions of Gentlemen conversant with the Navigation and climate in the Mountain agreed that there was no probability of accomplishing the Voyage by Water if my departure was delayed beyond the 10th of this Month; and by Snow, the Journey would be so tedious as to occupy nearly the whole Winter and extremely dangerous and uncertain without much precautionary arrangement on account of the hostility of the Blackfeet and other plain Tribes; I therefore spun the time of departure out as long as it could be done with safety say until the 15th Inst. in hopes that

[5] The route by Norway House was that which ran from York Factory via Hayes River and Norway House to Lake Winnipeg. Thence for craft bound to the Pacific Ocean it ran up the Saskatchewan to Cumberland Lake, north via the Frog Portage to the waters of English River, up the English River and the Beaver River to Beaver Lake, north to the waters of the Athabasca via Portage La Biche, up the Athabasca to Athabasca Pass, and down the Columbia to the sea.

[6] Refers to the annual trapping expedition which the Hudson's Bay Company maintained in the country tributary to the Snake. See Alexander Ross, *Fur Hunters of the Far West* (London, 1855), II, chaps. x-xiii; also *post*, 46.

[7] The Indians here referred to were the Siksika or Blackfeet Confederacy, an Algonquian group comprising the Blackfeet, the Bloods and the Piegans. Why they should have been known among fur traders as "Slave" tribes is not clear. The Indians to whom that name properly applied were the northern Athapascans. The conflict with the Slave Indians to which Simpson refers was one in which the Snake Expedition of 1823 lost eight men. See Ross, *Fur Hunters*, II, 5. The Blackfeet were the terror of the fur traders in this period.

the Ship would have arrived and was exceedingly mortified and disappointed at her non appearance up to that Date beyond which I could not venture to wait.[8] I am thus particular in order that if any misfortune or inconvenience to the general interests should have arisen in consequence of my absence it may be known that the subject was duly weighed in all its bearings and that every precaution was taken to guard against difficulties of which the Honble Committee are no doubt already informed by my Despatches and general Correspondence Book.

In order to acquire a more perfect knowledge of the Navigation of Nelsons River and the route from Split Lake to the Frog Portage likewise conceiving it to be the shortest track I determined on proceeding by that communication but in the very outset of the Voyage we had the misfortune to encounter a strong Gale of Wind which prevented our Doubling Point au Marsh so that at the Mouth of the Factory River[9] we were obliged to put ashore the surf running so high that in order to save the Canoe it became necessary to get into the Water up to our Necks and there hold our weak bark until the Lading was taken up to the Beetch when she was carried ashore. Time was now too precious to admit of our waiting until the Storm blew over; we therefore shouldered our Craft and Baggage for Fifteen long Miles which was a tedious Service on account of the badness of the road and strength of the Wind rendering it necessary to employ Six Men in the transport of the Canoe alone two being the usual number in short and Four in long Portages; by great exertion however and some danger having re-embarked before the Storm abated by Wading through the Surf in like manner as on landing we had the satisfaction of finding ourselves at liberty to prosecute the Voyage in defiance of the Weather having got within the shelter of the banks of Nelson River the second night from York and encamped near Seal Island as high as the influence of the Tide is felt in the River. From hence we may be said to have only

[8] In the Geological Survey of Canada, *Reports, 1879-1880*, 84C, appears the date of the arrival of every Hudson's Bay Company ship at York Factory from 1789 to 1860. The ship for which Simpson was waiting arrived five days after his departure.

[9] Refers to the Hayes-Hill River at the mouth of which York Factory stood.

commenced our Voyage as we were still in sight of the Factory Smoke across the Point. At 2 O'Clock A. M. of the 17th we left our Encampment and in the Even^{g} of the 20th got to the Establishment of Split Lake having fallen in with no occurrence worthy of remark.

Split Lake, Friday, Aug. 20. Here I received a letter from Mr Keith[10] Dated at this place the 8th Inst. en route to Athabasca containing some suggestions relative to the Outfit of that District for next Year, which I transmitted to M^{r} McTavish at York; also Duplicate of papers received from England connected with the Arctic Expedition.[11] To that Gentleman I wrote fully on several points which had escaped my attention before parting with him. John Scott the person in charge of this place during M^{r} McKenzie's absence is a plain stupid æconomical Man but competent to the management of a small post in this part of the Country, he is at the height of his ambition on a Sal^{y} of £40 p Annum and it is to be regretted we have so few of his description in the Service instead of Young Gentlemen of higher expectations who can never be provided for by shares in the concern and to whom the business cannot afford such Sal^{ys} as their qualifications and respectability might appear to entitle them and who consequently become dissatisfied and disaffected. I do not concieve that the business of the North^{n} Deptm^{t} requires at any time exceeding Twenty Clerks whose Education & abilities should lead them to expect preferment in the Service, while there are Thirty Four commissioned Gentlemen attached thereto; if those

[10] Chief Factor James Keith in charge of the Athabasca district. See for him Captain John Franklin, *Narrative of a Second Expedition to the Shores of the Polar Sea* (London, 1828), 6.

[11] Refers to the preparations under way for Captain John Franklin's second expedition to the Arctic. Franklin's party came from England to York Factory aboard the annual ship of the Hudson's Bay Company (the one for which Simpson had been waiting). From York Factory it was taken by Hudson's Bay Company craft to Cumberland House on the Saskatchewan, where it wintered, and thence, in the following spring, to the North Country. See *ibid.*, ix-xxiv, 1-6; also H. A. Innis, "Minutes of Council 1825," *Canadian Historical Review*, VII, 315. The Hudson's Bay Company was interested in Arctic exploration partly as an obligation of its charter and partly as a means of opening up knowledge of its own northern territories.

Gentlemen would condescend to lay aside the "great men" and attend to their own business which I am concerned to say is not generally the case as many of them concieve that they ought only to look on while Clerks act for them. The young Gentlemen of expectation should be sent to New Country where they can find opportunities of distinguishing themselves but if they are kept in the exhausted Districts of the Comp[ys] Territories their abilities if they possess any remain latent and they and the Chief Factors and Chief Traders with whom they are placed become a useless burthen on the concern as at very few Establishments within the height of Land dividing the Waters that run into the Bay from those falling to the Westward and Northward is there employment for more than one commissioned Gentleman or Clerk and at the small outposts such men as Scott before alluded to who have risen through good conduct from the rank of common Labourers answer the purpose better than more dignified people as they are not above putting their hands even to menial offices when necessary, require no establishment of Domestic Servants, do not load the Craft with Luxuries and Families and who consider themselves well paid at £40 p Annum which in my opinion ought to be the ultimatum of their prospects and emoluments.

At this place I likewise found a M[r] Brown a Clerk of three Years standing and apparently about 25 to 28 years of Age; this Young Man is an apprentice but altho' he has had the advantages of a good Education (being the Son of Professor Brown of Aberdeen) he possesses neither mental nor corporal abilities for the line of life in which he has been placed; his memory is so defective or he is so extremely inattentive that no duty can be entrusted to him; the very sight of an Indian he detests, he cannot live on the ordinary provisions of the Country, he cannot even keep the common accounts or Memoranda of a Trading Post, he cannot command the people, he can neither venture on Snow Shoes nor in a small canoe, cannot provide a Meal for himself with his Gun and it would be certain Death to trust him out of Doors in the severity of the Winter; I therefore in justice to the Young Man as also to the concern recommended his giving in his resignation as he is in no way adapted for the Country, unfrequented and dismal place which our Canadians very appriately named *Chemin le Diable.* At 1 O'Clock A. M. the 26th we got to Nelson House which is pleasantly situated on an Island in White Fish Lake[16] and which will this Winter be the residence of Chief Factor Charles.[17] Here I found one Mowat in charge a confidential labouring man with an other Orkneyman and a little Boy (Raymond) Son to Mowat's Woman. This Boy did not know his own age but from appearance I should take him to be about 12 or 13 years and has been on the Books at Wages for these last *Six Years.* I knew it to be a practise in former Days in the Compys Service to place the children of Gentlemen and favorites on the Books in order that they might be entitled to Wages (a species of Robbery which certain examinations in the British house of Parliament brought to light some years ago and which the Honble Committee are not perhaps aware had got the length of Hudsons Bay) but this is the first instance of the kind that I have discovered now to exist and it is with much concern I trace it to Mr Charles's Deptmt [District], which, up to the time I looked upon as one of the best regulated in the Country and himself one of the most upright and correct men in the Service. On landing at Nelson House Mowat informed me with an air of some importance that he was the Summer Master and at same time begged to know my Name and business (it being impossible for him to recognise a *great man* in a long beard Check Shirt and Blanket Coat which had once been Green but had assumed a different Colour in the Muddy Portage of the preceding Day,) but the poor mans terror & amasement when informed that he was in the presence of the Govr was quite laughable, I however relieved him by a hearty shake of the hand and immediately proceeded with him to the object of my unexpected visit; in this however I met with a serious disappointment as there was not a person at the Fort who had ever been Fifty Miles in the direction I wished to go except Mrs Mowat and she had only passed across land on Snow Shoes; Mowat however very civilly offered the

[16] White Fish Lake is probably the southeastern portion of what is now Nelson Lake.

[17] John Charles was the chief factor in charge of the Nelson River district.

Services of his Lady as far as her knowledge of the route went, but on conversing her I found we should not benefit thereby and therefore declined them. Nothing remained for us now except to go in search of Indians or retrace our steps to the Cepewisk[18] River and take our route by Lake Winnepeg Cumberland and the Saskatchawann[19] which would be a loss of much time and terminate the hope of effecting the Voyage by Water. I was thus embarrassed with a choice of difficulties but after a little consideration determined on giving a fair trial to the present route before abandoning it, took leave of Nelson House and pushed on to the further end of the Lake which we reached about 11 O'Clock P. M. After passing Four Sleepless hours at an Encamp^t my present situation exciting much uneasiness & distress of mind as I fully anticipated the failure of the Voyage which would be attended with most serious inconvenience to the general business, I pushed across a point of Woods at 3 O'Clock A. M. the 27th which formed a Portage to an other Lake while the people were preparing to pass the carrying Place and to my inexpressable delight in searching the opposite side of the Lake with an anxious Eye, I discovered an Indian Canoe as it was disappearing behind an Island and which one moment later would have been lost to my view. Not waiting to embark the Baggage I dispatched our Canoe in the direction the Indian had taken and in about an hour our people brought us a Guide which afforded me greater satisfaction than the sight of an Indian ever did before; in a few minutes we were once more on our route and about Mid Day of the 30th got to the Frog Portage[20] where I touched in order to see if we could pick up any tidings of the Craft that had gone by the Norway House track. Here I was surprised to find Mr Clark[21]

[18] Sipiwesk River.

[19] Lake Winnipeg, Cumberland, and the Saskatchewan was the ordinary Hudson's Bay Company route from Hudson Bay to the Pacific. See C. O. Ermatinger, "York Factory Express Journal," in Roy. Soc. Can., *Proceeds. and Trans.* 3rd series, VI, sect. ii, 132.

[20] Frog Portage was the famous carrying place between the waters of the Saskatchewan and the English rivers near Wood Lake north of Cumberland House.

[21] Chief Factor John Clarke in charge of the Lesser Slave Lake district. He was an American of unsteady judgment and character whose record in the various companies he served—the Pacific Fur Company, the North West Company, and

with the Lesser Slave Lake Brigade of Four Canoes making the Portage, as from his having left York so early as the 28th of July I did not expect to have overtaken him on this side the Athabasca River. He did not explain the cause of this detention satisfactorily and I consider his conduct to be highly reprehensible. This Gentleman left York as before stated on the 28th of July in compy with his Brigade but on losing sight of the Factory he started ahead taking the precaution of being lighter and better manned than the other Canoes, pushed on to Norway House with his own Canoe leaving his Brigade to make the best of their way after him which is in direct opposition to the established regulations as p Resolution of Council 1823 and as might be expected when Craft and property are thus left to the charge of careless Servants, due diligence was not observed and one of the Canoes was upset in Jack River where several of the pieces[22] were lost and others much damaged. I shall not say what induced all this haste on the part of Mr Clarke and the neglect of his duty yet will hazard an opinion that this accident and delay would not have taken place had he bestowed more attention to the charge with which he was entrusted and less to *Domestic* affairs. This breach of one of our most important regulations I mean to bring

the Hudson's Bay Company—is marked by a succession of unpleasant incidents. See for him H. H. Bancroft, *History of the Pacific States* (San Francisco, 1882), XXII, XXIII, index; Elliott Coues, *Henry and Thompson Journals* (London, 1897), II, 766-767; and E. H. Oliver, *Canadian North-West* (Canadian Archives, *Publications*, no. 9, Ottawa, 1914), I, 236-248. For a portion of a journal kept by him at Isle à la Crosse in 1819-20, see J. J. Hargrave, *Red River* (Montreal, 1871), 491.

[22] "Pieces" were packages of merchandise wrapped and encased so as to be safe for transport in the fur trade. Their weight was about ninety pounds, a limit fixed by the requirements of packing into canoes or boats or carrying on the portage. Other units of transport in the fur trade, the pack of furs, the bag of pemmican, the bale of dried meat, the keg of grease, were also of this approximate weight. Two pieces constituted a normal portaging load, which the voyageur carried on his back with the aid of a "tump line." The tump line was a leather strap, broad at the center and tapering at the ends, of which the broad part passed across the forehead and the ends were tied around the piece so as to hold it on the small of the back as in a harness or sling. A second piece rested on the first, and sometimes a third on the second. Such a load was carried by the voyageur at a kind of dog trot, by "poses" or "lifts" of 500 to 800 yards if the portage was a long one.

under the consideration of the Council[23] and to move that the loss and expence occasioned thereby shall be placed to his private account;[24] 'tis probable the Council may not be inclined to go this length as they are nearly all *Family Men* and have a fellow feeling in such cases but if Mr Clarke is allowed to escape in the present instance the evil may be repeated. From Mr Clarke I was rejoiced to learn that all the other Craft and Brigades had passed Norway House in safety and that some Boats had arrived from Red River previous to his departure bringing favorable reports of the Crops and state of things generally at the Colony. By a Note found on the Portage I learnt that the Dr[25] had passed Ten Days ago so that in the distance between York and this place we have gained Ten Days on him.

It may here be proper to say a few words regarding this Communication which is little known and much spoken against. The worst and most dangerous part of the Navigation I conceive to be almost within sight of the Factory in doubling Point au Marsh. Boats[26] half Laden have nothing to fear unless blowing unusually hard if the Point is doubled at the proper time of Tide say about half flood as the Shoals and bar at the Mouth of the River prevent any considerable Sea rising and the Tide sets in so strong that in the course of an hour or two they are within

[23] Refers to the Council for the Northern Department of Rupert's Land. See *ante,* xl ff.

[24] Simpson carried out this threat and the Council at its next meeting in 1825 voted to charge Clarke's private account with "all expenses attending loss of property ingoing."

[25] Refers to Dr. John McLoughlin.

[26] Refers to the so-called "inland" or "York" boats which the Hudson's Bay Company used as cargo carriers wherever stream conditions permitted. They were craft shaped like ordinary whaleboats, with a cargo capacity of fifty to sixty pieces and a crew of six or seven men. They were propelled by oars or, in difficult waters, by the tracking line; also by sail in crossing lakes when the wind was favorable. For sailing purposes they were provided with masts, which could be unstepped at will. They were steered by an ordinary rudder lever, also by a long sweep operated by the steersman who sat on a platform or deck at the stern, and who also served from that vantage point as captain. York boats were safer than North canoes and cheaper to operate. Simpson, who brought them into general use as cargo carriers in the Hudson's Bay Company Territories, maintained that they effected a saving of thirty-three and a third per cent.

shelter of the Banks of Nelson River; the other half of their ladings may easily be taken by the small Leighter as high as Seal Island. In like manner the Cargoes of Canoes may be taken by the Vessel the same distance and the people can carry their Canoes light from the lower to the Upper Beakon where a light Canoe may venture out in almost any Weather; but at the Season the Northern Brigades arrive at and leave York it rarely blows so hard as to prevent Craft doubling the Point with their ordinary Ladings. From Seal Island there is a strong steady current, the Water too deep and the bottom too Muddy to use setting Poles so that it is necessary to go up with the Tracking Line.[27] The tracking ground is generally good. The Rapids are very strong but plenty of Water and the Current runs with great force at the points but there is no danger of breaking and little of being upset if the Bow & Steersmen[28] are careful not to allow the head of the Craft sheer too far out into the Current. The Portages six to Eight in number according to the state of the Water are good and none exceeding ¾ths of a Mile; in short after having passed up and down I consider the Navigation from York to Split Lake perfectly safe if anything like common prudence is observed indeed far preferable to Hill River in every point of view. Early in the Season however there is some danger at the Steep Banks which to a great height are faced with Drift Snow & Ice and it is necessary to pass nearly under those Banks as the rapid is too strong and Shoal to be run outside, so that Craft and people must incur the risk of accidents from the Fragments of Snow & Ice falling, but if they take the precaution of passing down there late in the Even^g or early in the Morning there is less danger than in the heat of the Day. In going up latter end of July or beginning of August there is no danger as little Snow or Ice remains so late in the Season. From Split Lake

[27] Line by which boats or canoes were hauled up stream from the shore where water conditions rendered other means of propulsion impossible. For an illustration of the manner of use see Sir William Schooling, *The Hudson's Bay Company* (London, 1920), 14.

[28] Bowmen and steersmen were crew leaders in North canoes and in inland boats. Bowmen had chief command in North canoes, steersmen in inland boats.

to the Frog Portage there cannot be a finer navigation[29] as far as regards safety as people cannot drown unless they are really so disposed; they cannot run risks as the falls are so heavy that they will never be attempted; the access to the carrying places is good & no danger of being swept into the current; the portages are frequent but tolerably good and none exceeding half to ¾ths of a Mile in length. But the great objection of the people to this track is the want of Lakeway & Establishments not affording them any rest by head Winds or by Gentlemen indulging themselves in taking a few holydays at the Establishments of Norway House[30] & Cumberland[31] en passant, and this very objection on their part is to me the strongest recommendation it can have as the time to be occupied by the Voyage may be calculated to a Day whereas by the other route much delay is occasioned by bad Weather in the Lakes and by amusements at the Establishments and these amusements are attended with a certain heavy expence as extra provisions are consumed Balls are given and the business frequently neglected. The Establishment of Norway House alone has occasioned more expence in this way since the Coalition than the profits of its Trade would defray.

The Country between York and the Frog Portage is much exhausted, indeed we did not see a single animal on the whole route exceeding the size of a Musk Rat and not so much as the vestige of a Beaver, the Indians however say that the latter are not entirely extirpated and that if the District was allowed to recruit for a few Years it would still be productive in Furs. I

[29] Simpson presents too favorable a view of the Nelson-Burntwood-English river route as a highway from York Factory to the North Country. More advantageous though it was in some ways than the old route via Norway House, Cumberland House and Frog Portage, and better for canoe transport, it was not good for cargo carriage, and no attempt was ever made to put it to such use. For a discriminating contemporary evaluation of it see the "Diary of Nicholas Garry" in Roy. Soc. Can., *Proceeds. and Trans.* 2nd series, VI, sect. ii, 153-156, 190-191.

[30] Norway House, at the northern end of Lake Winnipeg on Norway Point, was one of the chief interior outfitting posts of the Hudson's Bay Company, and a council seat of the Northern Department of Rupert's Land.

[31] Cumberland House on Cumberland Lake was the point of departure from the Saskatchewan River to the North Country. It was the oldest Hudson's Bay Company post in the prairie region, having been built by Hearne in 1774.

shall not here dwell on the state of the Trade of Nelson River District as my time at the Establishments was too limited to look narrowly into its affairs; in reperusing however my report thereon of this Season forwarded to the Honble Committee I find the information it contains to be correct and corresponding with such parts of it as came under my own observation in passing through the Country and I do not see that any change of System from that laid down this Season at York[32] would be likely to ameliorate its condition except one which the Senr and retiring members of our Council would not willingly adopt altho in my opinion it should not be delayed an other Season in justice to the permanent interest the company holds in the Country, and that is to interdict the killing of Beaver for Four or Five Years throughout the District; if that was done it would still become rich and valuable and it is high time to give it a few Years rest as it has been constantly wrought for ages. The Indians would of course suffer inconvenience from this change as we could not afford to indulge them with Cloth and Blankets, but if their time is merely occupied in search of a living they can dispense with such articles of Luxury while Rein Deer are so plentyful. In Trapping Martens and hunting Rats they are not much exposed to the severity of the Climate and their industry in that way will enable us to supply them with Ammunition Iron Works and absolute necessaries.

After passing an hour with Mr Clarke at the Frog Portage, where I wrote to Mr Charles by the return of our Indian Guide whose Services we could now dispense with I continued my Voyage, passed Cunningham the Athabasca Guide[33] in charge of Four Boats at their Encampment on Beaver Lake at 3 O'Clock

[32] For the proceedings of the Council at York in the summer of 1824 see Appendix A, *post*, 210 ff.

[33] "Guides" of the type here referred to were not mere wilderness pathfinders like the Indian guide mentioned earlier in the sentence, but a special class of company employees charged with the care of brigades of boats or canoes en route. They were trusted men, the aristocracy of the voyageur class, distinguished for exceptional expertness in the arts of the stream, for intelligence and for a high sense of responsibility. They had the function of directing the movements of a brigade, supporting the authority of those in charge of individual craft, and at exchange points, in the absence of officers of the Company, transacting brigade business.

A. M. of the 2nd; he had made a tolerable voyage of it by the Nelson River track[34] from York and spoke favorably of the Navigation; he had the misfortune of losing one poor fellow the preceding Day who was taken ill early in the passage. In Lake Primeau we lost nearly a whole Day by a strong head Wind and in making a Traverse[35] had much difficulty in keeping the Canoe afloat altho' Two Men were constantly baling. Passed several bands of Chipwyans who all recognised me, but I had nothing but a little Tobacco to present them with, and they were nearly starving being destitute of ammunition. This says little for the management of affairs in English River and will render it necessary for me to give Chief Factor Keith[36] a rub, which I would not willingly do having generally found his Deptmt well regulated.

Isle a la Crosse, Sunday, Sept. 5. We arrived at Isle a la Crosse on the 5th Inst. having performed the Voyage from York in 22 Days or 18 Working Days (4 Days being lost by unforseen detensions) the quickest passage ever made. Here I found Mr James Heron in charge and was by no means satisfied with the state of things in the Deptmt. The Indians instead of being furnished with Ammunition for the purpose of laying up a stock of Provisions for next Year were employed in hunting Furs which is permanent destruction to the Country and attended with no immediate benefit as the unseasoned Skins[37] are not worth the prices paid for them and this is solely done from a mistaken ambition to shew large returns. The excuse of a Scarcity of Ammunition is inadmissible as such scarcity is the clearest proof

[34] Nelson River was usable as a communication between York Factory and Lake Winnipeg instead of Hayes River. From Lake Winnipeg brigades bound for the north proceeded via Cumberland House, Frog Portage, English River and the Methye Portage.

[35] "Traverse" is a technical term as used here for crossing a lake. Making a canoe traverse of a large lake, especially a lake subject to sudden storms, was a dangerous operation, and voyageurs preferred to do it at night when it was quiet or early in the morning.

[36] George Keith, in charge of the English River district. Not to be confused with James Keith, mentioned a little later, a brother, who was in charge of the Athabasca district.

[37] Refers to skins taken out of season, as in the summer.

of extreme mismanagement and want of foresight. Here there is a large Stock of costly articles on Inventory such as Cloth Blankets and useless fineries burthening the Trade with a large interest Account and of which there ought to be barely sufficient to meet the demands of the Winter while the most essential article is wanting and one which costs us next to nothing, enables the Indians to live in comfort and lay up a stock of Provisions & Leather without which they cannot exert themselves in the inclement Season. This Mismanagement likewise exposes us to a most Serious loss and inconvenience in an other point of View as thereby we run the risk of having our Northern Brigades Stopped on the route by Starvation; they depend on Pemican at Isle a la Crosse[38] to take them to Split Lake on the Voyage down & to Portage La Loche[39] on the homeward Voyage but if the provision trade is there neglected it becomes necessary to haul supplies across from the Saskatchawann in Winter which cannot be done without much expence labour and great Waste and in the event of a failure of the Buffaloe Hunts at Carlton which is not unusual the Brigades are stopped for want of Provisions or the people exposed to the miseries of Famine. There are at present attached to the District a Chief Factor Chief Trader three Clerks and Twenty Four Men. I think however we shall be able next Season to reduce the Clerks and Servants to two thirds of their present number a saving of about £350 p Annum as two commissioned Gentlemen two Clerks and Sixteen men should be quite sufficient for Isle a la Crosse and its dependencies in the present state of the Trade.

Here I was favored with letters from Chief Factors McLoughlin, Smith[40] & Ja^{s} Keith, likewise from Chief Traders Connelly[41]

[38] The importance of Isle à la Crosse as a provision point is evidenced by the order of the Council for the Northern Department of Rupert's Land in 1824 that 220 bags of pemmican of 85 pounds net weight each be provided there the ensuing season for the outcoming and ingoing Athabasca and New Caledonia brigades.

[39] Portage La Loche is the name sometimes given to Methye Portage, the key to the transportation system of the north, an eleven-mile carry between the waters of the English River and the Athabasca River.

[40] Edward Smith, in charge of the Mackenzie River district.

[41] William Connolly, in charge of New Caledonia. There is a good account of him in A. G. Morice, *History of the Northern Interior of British Columbia* (Toronto, 1904), index.

& Laroque.[42] The D^r is still Eight Days a head of me and does not expect I can overtake him before he reaches Nez Perces on the Columbia, but in this he is mistaken as we shall assuredly be up with him if no accident happens before he can reach the Athabasca River. Wrote Messrs Smith George & Ja^s Keith and Mr Connelly from this place. Our Canoe was altered here by Cadotte and Pierre Muce being too crank and learning that the Beaver River was unusually low I got a half sized Canoe from Mr Heron and two Men, with whom I put in two of our own Crew and part of the Baggage to lighten us. There being no certainty of getting provisions on this side the Mountain I took in six bags Pemican at Isle a la Crosse which is sorry fare as the Materials are bad of their kind, and for the carelessness of the maker the being compelled to Eat it would be a sufficient punishment; on such provender however must M^r McMillan and I now content ourselves as we could not get a Load of Shot here which is the more vexatious as in the Beaver River we could nearly feed ourselves & people with Game had we ammunition indeed since leaving York we have lived almost entirely on the produce of our Guns.

Left Isle a la Crosse on the 6th at Sun Set, made very slow progress up the Beaver River on account of its lowness, the people almost constantly in the Water dragging the Canoe; the Weather cold raw and disagreeable thick fogs and raining at intervals Daily. I had a serious quarrel with Cadotte our Guide one morning for tapping the Liquor Keg and getting Drunk; this fellow was a crack Man at Isle a la Crosse in the Days of opposition and got spoiled by over indulgence, indeed he has never been thoroughly curbed until this Voyage but I have succeeded in humbling his pride and on the present occasion put him in the terrors; he is however one of the most adroit men I ever saw in the Bow of a Canoe and not only does his duty well himself but keeps the others at it; on the whole I believe the Indian Country cannot produce a better crew. Saw several

[42] Joseph Larocque was in charge of the Rocky Mountain House in the Athabasca Pass. There is a sketch of him in Joseph Tassé, *Les Canadiens de L'Ouest* (Montreal, 1878), II, 321-338.

bands of Indians but they were all starving being quite destitute of Ammunition which reflects much discredit on the Chief Factor in charge of the District. No Scarcity of Animals indeed we see Moose & Buffalo Tracks Daily but altho we have a few Ball and are getting nearly tired of Pemican I am so eager to get on that no time is lost in hunting. M[r] McMillan and I are obliged to cool our toes occasionally by a walk in the river to lighten the Canoe in the Shoal places. On the 16th near Sun Set we found M[r] Laroque encamped about three Leagues above the Moose Portage, he had accompanied the Doctor from York this length where finding the Water so low he determined on Waiting the arrival of the Lesser Slave Lake Brigade with his outfit; the D[r] had passed this place on the 10th so that we have gained two Days on him from Isle a la Crosse.

M[r] Laroque accompanied us a few Miles higher up to our Encampment and passed the Night with us, he gave me some useful information respecting the Indians and Trade of Thompsons River where he had Wintered two Years. Raised Camp[t] at Day break the 17th but found the little Beaver River nearly dry in consequence of a Severe Frost during the Night so that we were obliged to carry the Baggage along Shore while two Men took the Canoe up light with great difficulty; abandoned the small Canoe at the Jolie Bute and sent the two men I had from Isle a la Crosse back; wrote M[r] Keith by them. On the 18th I found it would be impossible to get along the Beaver River, many parts of it not even having an appearance of moisture; we had now got to where an Indian Winter Track strikes off to the Northward and falls on Lake la Biche after passing several lakes and Portages; the D[r] had taken this Track with an Indian Guide and I now determined on following him altho we had no person who knew the route. M[r] Laroque however offered to go ahead with a small Canoe and Search out and mark the track for us and if possible to find a Guide. The 18th likewise the 19th and until the Even[g] of the 20th was occupied in passing through the track in which we had a Portage of 7 Miles, then a Lake of about 8 Miles where we had much difficulty in embarking and Landing on account of a great depth of soft Mud at the edges in which it was scarcely possible to drag the Canoe and through which the people had the utmost difficulty in Wading, indeed one poor fellow was nearly drowned having sunk up to the chin but saved by the timely assistance of one who had got ashore; we then made a portage of a Mile to an other Lake of about 6 Miles where we had fully as much trouble in getting through the Mud as in the former and where we encountered the heaviest Gale of Wind I have experienced in North America. At a small Narrows of this Lake we Encamped being unable to make a Traverse; throughout the Night the Trees were continually falling by the Violence of the Wind so that our situation was rather uncomfortable being obliged to put up for the night on the Wet Mud at the Waters Edge exposed to Wind & Weather as it was unsafe to get within reach of the falling Timber, the crashing of which together with the dismal houling of the storm and the fear of having our Canoe blown away interfered seriously with our repose; from hence we made a portage of 1½ Miles then crossed a Swamp of 100 Yds then another Portage of 1½ miles then a Lake of one Mile then a portage of 2 Miles then a Lake of ½ Mile then a portage of 200 Yds where we met Mr Laroque on his return with two Boys to conduct us; proceeded accompanied by that Gent^n^ through Island Lake 6 miles in length at the end of which we encamped and found Cardinal[43] the Freeman[44] who hearing of our distress came from Lake la Biche to assist us.

[43] Jacques Cardinel, well-known half-breed horsekeep, who frequented the region between Lake La Biche and Jasper House.

[44] Freemen in the language of the fur trade were ex-servants of the fur companies free in the sense of being no longer under indenture. They were usually worn-out voyageurs, differing from ordinary discharged engagés in that they did not retire to Red River Colony or to Canada, but chose to remain in the Indian country living among the natives. Shiftless and irresponsible, they found in the Indian country refuge both from necessity of regular labor and the restraints of civilized life. They were usually tied to the wilderness also by Indian wives and half-breed childern. They are described rather harshly by Alexander Ross, who had no love for them, as a kind of civilized savage having all the faults of both races and none of the virtues of either, despised alike by whites and Indians. "They live in tents or in huts, like the natives, and wander from place to place in search of game, roots, and herbs. Sometimes they live in the utmost abundance; but as they are not always expert hunters, nor industrious, they have at times to undergo the extremities of want." The region between Lake La Biche and Jasper House

At Day break the 21st Mr Laroque took his leave of us and returned to his Encampt near the Moose Portage, there to await the arrival of his outfit and we proceeded on our route making a Portage of about two Miles where one of the Canoe carriers fell and broke the Canoe which occasioned a delay of three hours in repairs; we then passed through Beaver Lake Ten Miles long to Portage La Biche[45] where we found Ottawa, Cardinals Son and an Indian waiting to assist us across the Portage which is about Four Miles in length and by Dusk had every thing across and encamped on the Banks of Lake la Biche where we found old Dejoilais[46] the Freeman and his Family likewise Cardinals Family and a posse of Freemen and their followers. These people with a few Cutonais[47] and Soteaux[48] were preparing to go on a War Expedition against a poor helpless inoffensive tribe of Indians "Shewhoppes"[49] natives of the North branch of Thompsons River knowing them to be weak and unprovided with the means of defense and solely with a view to plunder and gain themselves renown as Warriors by taking a few Scalps without incurring

was one of their favorite haunts. A number were to be found also in the valley of the Columbia. Most of them were French Canadians or half-breeds, but some were Iroquois Indians from Caughnawaga, brought originally to the Far West by the fur companies on account of their expertness as canoemen.

[45] Portage La Biche is the carry between the waters of the Beaver and Athabasca rivers.

[46] Antoine Déjarlais was a trapper formerly in the employ of the North West Company. He had long been a resident of Lake La Biche. See Gabriel Franchère, *Narrative of a Voyage* (R. G. Thwaites, *Early Western Travels*, Cleveland, 1904-07, VI), 366.

[47] Kutenai Indians. They occupied the region between the two forks of the Columbia. See F. W. Hodge, *Handbook of American Indians* (*House Docs.*, 59 Cong. 1 sess., no 926), under caption "Kitunahan."

[48] Soteaux or Saulteaux were members of the great Chippewa family inhabiting the region around Lake Superior and Lake Huron. These people were often employed by the North West Company in an earlier day as servants, and probably the presence of the individuals here referred to so far from the tribal home is thus accounted for.

[49] Shuswaps were the great Salish tribe of British Columbia, the main body of which lay along the North Branch of Thompson River. The band here referred to was an isolated one, the Shuswaps of the Rocky Mountains, occupying the country "in the neighborhood of Jasper House and as far as Tête Jaune Cache on the western slope." See for them Viscount Milton and W. B. Cheadle, *The North-West Passage by Land* (London, 1866), 240-242.

danger. On these poor wretches they made War a few Years ago and treacherously massacred a whole camp in the Mountain on their way to the Fort.[50] I have been anxious to encourage those Indians to frequent the Establishment in the Mountain[51] in order to draw them from Thompsons River as in the event of their being prevailed on to go to the former place for their supplies and with their returns we should be enabled to abandon that heavy and unprofitable Establishment[52] for a Year or two, but this unprovoked warfare was likely to defeat my plans; on the score of humanity as well as of interest I therefore spoke my Mind very plainly to those freemen, told them we meant to protect the Shewhoppes and if they did not instantly abandon their cruel intentions they should not this Winter have even a particle of ammunition at any of our Establishments and that next Season they should be bundled down to Canada where starvation & misery would follow them. This lecture had the desired effect and they promised that they would no longer entertain hostile feelings towards those people. Those freemen are fully in our power and if they break their promise I shall keep my word in regard to them. With Cardinal the Freeman I made an agreement that he should in the course of this ensuing Winter and Spring get a Horse track or road cut from Fort Assiniboine to Edmonton House Saskatchewaine which I shall have occasion to speak upon hereafter. Left our Encampm[t] on Portage La Biche before Day break the 22nd crossed the Lake of that Name about 20 Miles and fell on River La Biche which we descended and a more disagreeable navigation or piece of Road I never travelled; the River itself was nearly dry so that it became necessary to carry the Baggage at least four fifths of the way, two men took down the Canoe light with great difficulty and M[r] McMillan and I walked the whole way and most abominably dirty Walking it was, the banks of the River having been recently overrun by Fire and while still smoking a light rain had fallen so

[50] The fort here referred to is Thompson or Kamloops at the confluence of the north and south branches of Thompson River.

[51] Refers to Rocky Mountain House in the Athabasca Pass.

[52] Fort Thompson.

that we were up to the knee every step in Charcoal and ashes, and by the termination of each Days March as black as Sweeps. On the 24th we killed a fine large fat Buck Moose and as ourselves and people were a good deal harrassed by continual marching since we left York and but indifferently fed I thought the present a good opportunity of indulging both them and us with a half holyday it being now about 3 O'Clock P. M. Preparations were forthwith on foot, the Moose was soon relieved of his Skin a rousing Fire made and all hands employed to the utmost of their skill in the art of Cookery; a haunch the Nose and Tongue Mr McMillan laid aside for ourselves and the rest of the Animal made over to the people, who were occupied from the time of putting ashore until the sound of leve—leve—leve the following morning in a continued succession of Eating roasting and boiling. On the 26th at 7 O'Clock A. M. came up with the Dr before his people had left their Encampment altho we had by that early hour come from his Breakfasting place of the preceding Day; himself and people were heartily tired of the Voyage and his Surprise and vexation at being overtaken in Riviere la Biche notwithstanding his having a 20 Days start of us from York is not to be described; he was such a figure as I should not like to meet in a dark Night in one of the bye lanes in the neighbourhood of London, dressed in Clothes that had once been fashionable, but now covered with a thousand patches of different Colors, his beard would do honor to the chin of a Grizzly Bear, his face and hands evidently Shewing that he had not lost much time at his Toilette, loaded with Arms and his own herculean dimensions forming a tout ensemble that would convey a good idea of the high way men of former Days. About 2 O'Clock A. M. we got to the Athabasca River and put up for the Day in order to repair our canoes which had got much shattered in the shoal Waters of Riviere la Biche. Continued our route the following Morning but Slackened our speed in order to give the Dr an opportunity of keeping up with us. Got to the entrance of Slave River on the 29th at 2 O'Clock P. M. where we found two men waiting for us with a supply of Provisions Bark & Gum. By them wrote to Mr

Pambrun[53] directing him to proceed to New Caledonia[54] in the course of the Winter as after rec[t] of his instructions to join M[r] Connelly at Dunvegan that Gentleman would have been past and neither the Establishment of Lesser Slave Lake nor Dunvegan could spare men to take him on to the Rocky Mountain Portage[55] after the New Caledonia Brigade. Proceeded up the Athabasca River and recognised my Winter Encampm[ts] of two Years ago; we had during that Journey most unfavorable Weather yet I find we made longer Days Marches altho' the Snow was about 3 feet Deep than we now do with the Canoes.

On the Morning of the 1st about 2 hours before Day break soon after the people were called our Guide and Shorkie had a Boxing Match but after 4 or 5 good rounds it was a drawn battle in consequence of my interference being afraid they might hurt each other which would necessarily retard my progress. Passed the 5 Islands at 10 O'Clock A. M. the same day and got to F[t] Assiniboine[56] on the following morning at 9 O'Clock A. M. say Saturday the 2nd October.

Here I found Letters from Mess[rs] John Stewart[57] and Rowand,[58] these Gentlemen had left York Factory with the Saskatchawaine Brigade on the . . . July; the former addressed me from Carlton and the latter from this place where he arrived Four

[53] P. C. Pambrun, a clerk, who had been assigned to service in New Caledonia. He was to be associated with Chief Trader Connolly at Stuart Lake. There is a sketch of him in Tassé, *Les Canadiens de L'Ouest*, II, 299-320.

[54] New Caledonia was the district comprising what is now the northern interior of British Columbia. Within it in 1824 lay the posts of Stuart Lake, Fraser Lake, McLeod Lake, Fort Alexandria, Fort George on Fraser River, and Babine.

[55] Rocky Mountain Portage is the portage around the heavy rapids of the upper Peace River at about longitude 122.

[56] Fort Assiniboine was located on the Athabasca River northwest of Edmonton at the junction of the Athabasca and Freemen rivers.

[57] John Stuart was the chief factor in charge of Carlton House on the Saskatchewan. He had recently been transferred there from New Caledonia. He is the John Stuart who accompanied Fraser on the famous journey down the Fraser River in 1808. See Morice, *Northern Interior of British Columbia*, index; also Coues, *Henry and Thompson Journals*, II, 783, 784.

[58] John Rowand was the chief trader in charge of Edmonton House on the Saskatchewan. See Ross, *Fur Hunters*, II, 209-213; also Coues, *Henry and Thompson Journals*, II, 602, 603.

Days ago in hopes of seeing me and returned to Edmonton Yesterday; the circumstance of Mr Rowands having got to this place from Edmonton after accompanying his loaded Brigade from York thereby performing the Voyage in . . . Days shews how much shorter the route is by the Saskatchawaine than by the Beaver River and accounts for some arrangements I am about to suggest and have taken steps for carrying into effect without further delay which I have no doubt the Honble Committee & Council will approve. From several remarks in the course of this narrative will be seen the tediousness and uncertainty of the Beaver River Navigation even to half laden North Canoes rendering the Voyage extremely harrassing to the people requiring much expensive and precautionary arrangement in regard to provisions assistance from Freemen &c &c and in dry Seasons incurring the risk of not getting to the Wintering Grounds before the Ice sets in, but above all, the heavy expence occasioned by this route in Men's Wages it being impossible to substitute Boats for Canoes.

According to the present mode of conducting the transport business of Cumberland, Saskatchawaine, Lesser Slave Lake Districts and Columbia Express,[59] there are required for Cumberland Eleven men, for the Saskatchawaine Forty Three Men for Lesser Slave Lake Seventeen men and the Columbia Express Canoe Eight Men say Seventy Nine Men for Transport alone, but by the change of System I am about to suggest (besides other important benefits and facilities which shall be hereafter noticed in connexion with the business of New Caledonia and Columbia) a saving of thirty Two Men will be effected in these Districts and a vast deal of trouble and expense in hauling provisions from the Saskatchewaine to the Beaver River and employing Hunters on that communication will likewise be saved. For this purpose I would recommend that the route by the Beaver River be aban-

[59] The Columbia Express was the mail canoe of the Hudson's Bay Company which carried despatches back and forth annually between the Columbia River and York Factory. It also transacted incidental business of various sorts on the way. See for the Express journal for the years 1827-28, C. O. Ermatinger, "York Factory Express Journal," in Roy. Soc. Can., *Proceed. and Trans.*, 3rd series, VI, sect. ii, 67.

doned altogether and by forming one Brigade of Seven Boats to start from York at the usual time say about the 20th July Forty Five Men instead of Seventy Nine will do the transport business of those Districts as follows vizt:—2 Men in addition to the Summer Establishment are quite sufficient for the Winter business of Cumberland House, those Men with the outfit of that District to be left en passent. 28 Men in addition to the Summer Establishment are quite sufficient for the Winter business of the Saskatchewaine, even should it be considered necessary to establish the Rocky Mountain House[60] for the accommodation of the Piegans. 9 Men in addition to the Summer Establishment are quite sufficient for the Winter business of Lesser Slave Lake District say the Posts of Lesser Slave Lake, Fort Assineboine and Cranberry Lake; these Men can take the outfit of Lesser Slave Lake District across Land about 50 Miles by Horses to Fort Assineboine on the Athabasca River, from whence the outfit of the Post in Lesser Slave Lake and Cranberry Lake can be taken by Boats or Small Batteaux as there is sufficient Water in the Athabasca River at all times. The 8 Men usually employed in taking the Columbia Express will thus be occupied as far as Edmonton in assisting to Work up the Brigade of Boats, from thence they can proceed across to Fort Assiniboine and have abundance of time to cross the Mountain and reach their destination before the Winter sets in. A strong Brigade of Seven Boats and Forty Five Men is thus formed to pass the Saskatchewaine which the Natives[61] must respect and the outfits got to their destinations.

For the outgoing:—The principal part of the returns of Lesser Slave Lake Posts can be hauled across to Edmonton in the course of the Winter & Spring and the few packs that cannot be hauled on Ice can be taken by Horses so as to reach Edmonton on or before the 20th of May. The Columbia Express can be there at

[60] The Rocky Mountain House here referred to is probably the old North West Company post on the North Saskatchewan opposite the mouth of the Clearwater River which the Hudson's Bay Company took over in 1821.

[61] Refers to the Blackfeet Indians, the dread of the fur traders of the northern Great Plains.

the same time and thus a Brigade will be formed sufficiently strong to take out the returns should the Saskatchawaine be even more productive than at any time for these last Ten Years; the Cumberland returns will be embarked en passant. By this arrangement no risk or inconvenience can be sustained and an Expence of about £1,000 p Annum saved. Towards carrying it into effect I have as before mentioned given directions that a good Horse road be cut in the course of this Winter; in order to shew that it is practicable, the returns of Fort Assiniboine will be taken out by that route this ensuing Spring and I shall cross over to Edmonton instead of going by the Beaver River and employ my Crew in working out the general Brigade.[62]

Mr Deschambeaut Clerk and McKay the Blackfoot Interpreter arrived from Edmonton at Fort Assiniboine about an hour after we landed, the former to Winter with Mr McIntosh[63] at this place and the latter to accompany us across the Mountain on his way to join the Snake Country Expedition. Being extremely unwell for some time past I was recommended by Dr McLoughlin to lay

[62] Simpson's proposal, not very clearly set forth here, was to bring together two transport routes that had hitherto forked at the Cumberland House on the lower Saskatchewan. One of these routes was that used by the Lesser Slave Lake brigade and the Columbia Express, which ran from the Cumberland House to the Athabasca River via Frog Portage, English and Beaver rivers and Portage La Biche. The other was the route used by the Cumberland and Saskatchewan brigades—the north branch of the Saskatchewan River. The difficulty with the first was the Beaver River, a trying piece of navigation which made necessary the use of the uneconomical North canoe not only on this link, but all the rest of the way. The handicap to the Saskatchewan route was the danger of attack from the hostile tribes of the Plains, which necessitated the employment of more men in the brigades than would have been required for the work of transport alone. Simpson's proposal was to unite the Lesser Slave Lake and the Columbia Express transport with the Cumberland and Saskatchewan transport as far as Edmonton House on the North Saskatchewan which would provide safety in the zone of danger without extra cost. From Edmonton House the Lesser Slave Lake brigade and the Columbia Express could reach the Athabasca River by means of a horseroad which Cardinal, the freeman, was to cut. That would obviate the need of using the difficult Beaver River route and would permit the use of boats instead of North canoes. This was so clearly a good plan that, as indicated in the journal, Simpson ordered it into effect at once. Subsequently it was ratified by the Council of the Northern Department of Rupert's Land, and in the season of 1825 only forty-four men instead of seventy-nine were assigned to the work of transport here under consideration.

[63] Chief Factor William McIntosh in charge at Fort Assiniboine.

by the remainder of the Day in order to benefit by his professional skill which I accordingly did and experienced much benefit therefrom and I availed myself of this opportunity of addressing Govr Pelly,[64] Chief Factors McTavish, Geo. Keith, John Stewart, McKenzie[65] & McIntosh, likewise Chief Traders Rowand and Laroque & Mr A. Robertson Clerk. Fort Assiniboine is beautifully situated on the North Bank of the Athabasca River; Mr Fraser Clerk in charge at present but M^{r} McIntosh expected Daily from Peace River to take the Winter management. On account of the contemplated change in the mode of Transport for Lesser Slave Lake District I am of opinion that this Post should be attached to the Saskatchawaine Deptm^{t} in order to prevent the chance of misunderstandings between the Gent^{n} of these Neighbouring Districts as such an evil would be productive of serious consequences to both and this arrangement would greatly facilitate the Transport of the Outfits from Edmonton and the returns thither. The Horses would of course be kept at Fort Assineboine where they can be safe from Thieves and where Hay may be had in abundance and with little trouble.

Left Fort Assiniboine at Day break on the 3^{d} and in the course of the Forenoon met old Burleigh the Freeman coming down the River alone on a raft; he had made a tolerable Hunt in the Neighbourhood of McLeod's branch where he represents Beaver to be pretty numerous indeed this part of the Country seems generally well stocked. Poor Burleigh was some Twenty Years ago one of the most active enterprising Canadians of his standing in the Country, a first rate Hunter and possessing a strength and acuteness of mind rarely to be met with in his Walk of Life; he had amassed a fortune of about £7,000 & returned to Canada but so enchanted was he with the roving Life of a Freeman and the charms of some half Doz Wives (natives of the Soil) that he could not sit down quietly at Home to enjoy his good

[64] R. H. Pelly, Governor of Assiniboia, is the person probably referred to here. See for him *post*, 152, and note. J. H. Pelly, his cousin, was the Governor in London of the Hudson's Bay Company.

[65] Chief Factor Donald McKenzie, in charge of Fort Garry and of the Red River district. See for him *post*, 358.

fortune but must revisit the Indian Country since which time he has met with nothing but reverses; his Money disappeared, his talent as a hunter forsook him and as he advanced in Years Wife after Wife deserted him, the last having given him the slip this morning taking with her his favorite Child and the greater part of his little property. This fresh misfortune quite distracted the poor man who was in the utmost agony when we met him and the only consolatory advice I could give after upbraiding him with his folly and lamenting his infatuation was to retire to Canada with the Wreck of his fortune & that I would provide him and . . . with a passage free of expence. We met a few Indians who gave us some fresh meat and without falling in with any adventure worthy of remark we got to the Rocky Mountain House commonly called Jaspers House,[66] where Mich^l^ Clyne was in charge on the Even^g^ of the 10th.

The Athabasca River is one of the finest streams I have seen in the Country, the current strong and steady with few rapids except at the Upper parts and navigable by Boats of the largest size. The Country seems rich in large and small Animals as we saw numerous tracks Daily, the banks finely Wooded and as we approach the Mountain high and prominent and the face in many places exhibiting strata of Iron & Coal; the Soil rich which with the Climate in the lower parts would be favorable to cultivation.

At Jaspers House we found Mr Thos McKay Clerk[67] who had arrived some Days previous from the Columbia and brought Letters from Messrs Kennedy & Ogden[68] conveying satisfactory accounts of the Companys affairs in that quarter.

[66] This post was located where the Athabasca opens into Second or Burnt Lake. It was built by the North West Company, and was named for one of its employees, Jasper Hawes, who was long stationed there. See for it Ross Cox, *Adventures on the Columbia River* (London, 1831), 254; also Ross, *Fur Hunters*, II, 203, 204. The name Rocky Mountain House is used by Simpson also to refer to two other Hudson's Bay Company posts in the Rocky Mountains. See *ante*, 22, 26.

[67] Thomas McKay is a well-known figure in the fur-trade annals of the Columbia Department, a son of Alexander McKay, the famous Astorian, and son-in-law of Dr. McLoughlin.

[68] Chief Trader P. S. Ogden of Spokane House, a notable trapper and explorer, after whom the city of Ogden, in Utah, is named. He was a member of the Board

The 11th was occupied in preparations for attacking this formidable Portage[69] which is in between Latitude 52 & 53 North and longitude 118 West according to Mr D. Thompson's observations.

The situation of Jaspers House is beautifully Wild & romantic, on the borders of the Athabasca River which here spreads itself out into a small Lake surrounded by Lofty Mountains. From hence I wrote to several Gentlemen on the East side of the Mountain. This is merely a temporary Summer post for the convenience of the Columbians in crossing; the Winter Establishment was last Year on the borders of the Smoky River about 80 to 100 Miles to the Northward, but it was this Season determined that it should be removed to Moose or Cranberry Lake situated more in the heart of the Mountain near the height of Land and where we suppose Frazers River takes its source; the object of this change is to draw the Freemen further into the Mountain than they have been in the habit of going, where they are expected to make good Hunts as it has been rarely Wrought and thereby the lower parts of Smoky River and the Country they used to occupy towards Lesser Slave Lake will be allowed to recruit, we have it likewise in view to draw the Shewhoppes or natives of the North branch of Thompsons River to the Mountain from the Establishment of Kamloops or Thompsons River which they have hitherto frequented as that Post on account of the heavy Establishment of people required for the purpose of defence yields little or no profit so that it is desirable we should abandon it; by this change a few Packs Furs may be lost (the hunts of the Natives occupying the South branch of Thompsons River) but that deficiency in the returns will ultimately indeed immediately prove a gain as the people can be employed to greater advantage in other parts of the Columbia, and the absence of a

of Management that in 1845 succeeded Dr. McLoughlin at Fort Vancouver. See for him the excellent sketch by T. C. Elliott in *Oregon Historical Quarterly*, XI, 229.

69 Refers to the famous Athabasca Pass over the Rocky Mountains, the road that was used by the Hudson's Bay Company across the continental divide until the forties. Here the portage was made between the waters of the Athabasca and those of the Columbia. David Thompson, the geographer, discovered the pass in the winter of 1810-11 and was the first white man to traverse it.

Post will in the course of a year or two humble the Natives and ensure its safety when re-established at one half the present expence.

Sent Thos McKay and six men ahead of us this morning across the Portage in order to build a Canoe as the two Craft laying there are not sufficient to take the whole of our party down the heavy rapids of the Columbia. Jacco Findlay[70] and a band of followers (Freemen) were here watching the Shewhoppes in order that they might trade their Furs before they got to the Establishment[71] and thereby make a profit on the hunts of these poor Indians, but I gave them notice that that practise must be discontinued as we should not allow Freemen interfere with and impose on the Natives & I addressed a circular Letter to Messrs Clarke McIntosh Rowand and Laroque begging they would narrowly watch the conduct of Findlays band and if they did continue this nefarious Traffick[72] (as from timidity and the late unprovoked hostilities against these Natives they are become an easy prey) that no supplies of any description be given to them. These freemen are a pest in this country, having much influence over the Natives which they exert to our disadvantage by inciting them against us, but if such measures as I have recommended to those Gentlemen are followed up they will soon be quite at our disposal as their very existence depends on us and were more firm and decided conduct observed to freemen generally throughout the Country it would be much to our interest as their present independence and high toned importance is very injurious and in my opinion frought with danger to the concern.

On the Morning of the 12th we sent the Horses ahead under the charge of M^r McMillan and the D^r and I followed in the Canoes to William Henrys old House[73] as far as the River is Navigable

[70] Jacques Finlay, a half-breed trapper and trader, who was at one time an interpreter of the North West Company.

[71] Refers probably to Fort Thompson.

[72] Nefarious because in contravention of the monopoly rights in the fur trade of this region granted to the Hudson's Bay Company by Parliament in 1821. The Hudson's Bay Company held by virtue of the same grant a monopoly of the British fur trade west of the Rocky Mountains.

[73] Henry's House was an old North West Company post used by the Hudson's Bay Company as a winter establishment. It was located where the Miette River

about 50 Miles higher up where they were laid carefully past in order to be ready for use next Spring and on the Morning of the 14th we started in a body with a cavalcade of Twenty-one Horses.

Our route is about due West through defiles in the Mountains; the track for Cranberry Lake[74] takes a Northerly direction by Cow Dung River which falls into the Main Stream at Henrys House. Our Road was rugged and bad frequently covered with fallen Timber the country having been over run by Fire; it appears well stocked with Animals as we found many tracks of Buffalo & Deer; the Mountain Goat and Sheep are likewise numerous, our Hunter killed two of each kind say of the Goats & Sheep; they were in good condition but tough and not well flavoured tasting strongly of Musk and so much alike that my palate could not distinguish the one from the other. The Goat frequents the highest pinnacles of the Mountains where there is scarcely a particle of herbage or vegetation of any kind to be seen; they are not so numerous as the Sheep and the utmost skill of the Hunter is required in approaching them as their retreat & means of defence render them inaccessible even to the Wolves; Hunting them is a duty of some danger as no sooner do they discover an Enemy than they roll down showers of Stones when it is high time to give up the chace and look for safety under the cover of some projecting rock.

The Goat is larger than any I have been accustomed to see covered with fine Wool of a dingy white colour instead of Hair; the horns smaller than those of the English Goat but of the same form. The Sheep are not so shy, keep together in bands and do not frequent such inacçessible places; on the least alarm however they clamber up the Mountains and are equally expert in rolling down Stones on their pursuers they are larger than any breed we have in England and are covered with White hair instead of Wool, the horns large & circular indeed so cumbrous that they

enters the Athabasca. See Ross, *Fur Hunters*, II, 202, 203; also Cox, *Columbia River*, 252.

[74] The track here referred to is the Yellowhead Pass, which turns off from Athabasca Pass toward the northwest at the Miette River (Simpson's Cowdung River). The Canadian National Railway crosses the Rockies by this route at the present time.

appear out of all proportion to the size of the Animal. I am not sufficiently conversent with the articles of Hair & Wool to say any thing as to their qualities or the uses to which they could be applied but I have directed a few Skins to be taken care of for the purpose of being sent home next Season and if the Manufacturers could afford a tolerable price say 10/ @ 15/ p Skin nett they might become an object of Trade worthy our attention. I have likewise directed that a specimen of each of these Animals be provided next Season for the purpose of being sent to Mr Sabine[75] as I believe they are not much known to Naturalists. The Mountains now encrease to a stupendous Size; the Summits of many obscured from our sight by Clouds and of others covered by eternal Snows. We crossed the River once to Day the ford bad and the current strong and Encamped at the Grand Traverse. 15th Left our Encampment after Breakfast; the road hilly craggy & rugged and in many places dangerous but the Horses are accustomed to it and rarely make a false step; one of them however, my wardrobe forming part of his Load Slipped from the bank of the River and was swept down by the current some Hundred Yards but saved by the activity of his Driver; forded the River twice to Day and put up at Campement D'Orignal. After a thorough drenching of Sleet & Rain we renewed our March on the Morning of the 16th the Weather continuing exceedingly bad throughout the Day; as we proceed the Road gets worse and the Mountains rise perpendicular to a prodigious height; the scenery Wild & Majestic beyond description; the track is in many places nearly impassable and it appears extraordinary how any human being should have stumbled on a pass through such a formidable barrier as we are now scaling and which nature seems to have placed here for the purpose of interditing all communication between the East and West sides of the Continent. We forded the River about a Doz times to Day and put up at Campement Fusel near the height of Land.

[75] Refers probably to Joseph Sabine the eminent British zoologist and horticulturist. Might refer also to his distinguished younger brother Edward Sabine, astronomer and naturalist to the Polar expeditions of John Ross and Edward Parry.

Sunday, October 17th. We had a regular fall of Snow of about 8 inches last night with severe frost; started from our encampment early; towards the height of Land the Road is as bad and dangerous as it can well be and Glaciers are seen which have bidden defiance to the rays of the Sun since the beginning of time wherever the Snow & Ice has room to collect in the face of the mountains and the valleys or passes underneath exhibiting the ravages of the avalanges which sweep down every tree and shrub also loose rocks that happen to be in their way.

At the very top of the pass or height of Land is a small circular Lake or Basin of Water which empties itself in opposite directions and may be said to be the source of the Columbia & Athabasca Rivers as it bestows its favors on both these prodigious Streams, the former falling into the Pacific at Lat. 46½ north and the latter after passing through Athabasca & Great Slave Lakes falling into the Frozen Ocean at about 69 North Lat. That this basin should send its Waters to each side of the Continent and give birth to two of the principal Rivers in North America is no less strange than true both the Dr. & myself having examined the currents flowing from it east & West and the circumstance appearing remarkable I thought it should be honored by a distinguishing title and it was forthwith named the "Committee's Punch Bowl."[76] From hence the descent is extremely rapid down the West side, in many places nearly perpendicular and the changes of climate and consequent difference in the character of the country and its productions which takes place in the course of a few minutes walk would to a person who had not experienced it appear almost incredible. About the height of land and on the East side thereof for several Days Journey the Timber is small and stunted but no sooner do we begin to descend the West side than we fall on the most noble trees I ever beheld, principally Cedar, Hemlock White & Red Pine and Ash all of prodigious

[76] Committee's Punch Bowl, still so known, is in reality a pair of tarns or mountain pools, one of which empties into Whirlpool River, the headstream of the Athabasca, the other into Wood River, a tributary of the Canoe River, which flows into the Columbia at the great bend. *Cf.* Franchère, *Narrative* (Thwaites, *Early Western Travels*, VI), 353; and Cox, *Columbia River*, 248.

size. From the Committee's Punch Bowl to the Base of the Mountain on the West side we occupied 4½ hours in walking, 2 hours of which were consumed in what is called the Grande Côte where our descent could not be less than 40 feet p minute; the other part is not so steep but the descent may be safely reckoned at 15 to 20 feet p minute so that after making a fair allowance for time lost in falls breathing &c. I think without exaggeration I may estimate the height of this single mountain at not less than 4500 feet; this is the lowest pass in the mountain behind which and on each side thereof are immence masses of mountain piled upon and overlooking each other, the principal of which is a huge mountain known by the name of McGillivray's Rock in honor of the Honble W^m^ McGillivray the top of which was enveloped in fog but as far as we could judge by the eye double the height of that described which would make it exceeding 13,000 feet.[77] At and before reaching the height of Land the Cold was intense but immediately after we began to descend the difference of climate was as great as between Summer & Winter and in vegetation the contrast was fully as much.

This was a most harrassing Day to our poor horses and many a cruel blow they got from their unfeeling Drivers, it was evident that the Honble member for Galway's Bill against cruelty to Animals was not in force in the Rocky Mountain.

Monday, Oct. 18th. Heavy Rain without intermission since we put up yesterday afternoon which continued until 12 O'Clock to Day. Started at the usual hour passed about 3 miles of

[77] McGillivray's Rock, mentioned by Franchère and Cox, is probably the present-day McGillivray Ridge. It is not over 8779 feet in height. There was something about Athabasca Pass which led early travellers greatly to exaggerate the height of its mountain peaks. David Thompson thought them 18,000 feet high, Alexander Ross estimated a thousand feet less, and David Douglas who named Mt. Brown and Mt. Hooker thought them 16,000 and 17,000 feet high respectively. For three quarters of a century these peaks enjoyed the reputation of being among the loftiest in America. As a matter of fact Mt. Brown is only 9156 feet high and Mt. Hooker not more than 10,505. The person after whom McGillivray Ridge was named was a partner of the North West Company who took a leading part in 1821 in arranging the coalition between the North West Company and the Hudson's Bay Company.

Bottoms through which the River has formed a number of small channels, then crossed two points of Woods the first about one mile the second about six miles in length, the road one continued mire frequently waist deep and large fallen timber laying across the track every 10 or 20 yds.; then crossed Bottoms of about 7 miles in length in which are many quicksands; the River winding through these Bottoms compelling us to ford it more frequently than agreeable; in high water it must be dangerous. Put up at Campement Point des Bois.

Tuesday, Oct. 19th. The Weather fine, left our Encampment after Breakfast, passed a Bottom of two miles then a point of Woods six miles fully as bad as those of yesterday, afterwards a Swamp of about two miles crossing the River repeatedly and got to the Boat Encampment;[78] having disposed of the celebrated Athabasca Portage which altho not exceeding from Jaspers House 120 miles and from Henry's House 80 to 90 occupied us six Days in crossing.

This portage as connected with the Columbia Trade I shall have occasion to touch upon hereafter and shall now make some remarks on the mountain and its environs in relation to the trade of New Caledonia District.

At our Encampment fell in with a band of free Iroquois who have for several years hunted in the neighbourhood of Canoe River Cranberry & Moose Lake New Caledonia and the North branch of Thompson's River; they had a good many Skins and were on their way to Mr Laroque's Establishment[79] for the purpose of trade; they had numerous families & their women of the Carrier tribe[80] natives of New Caledonia.

[78] Boat Encampment was the point at which parties moving eastward across the Athabasca Pass stored their boats, and where those coming from the Pass embarked for the lower Columbia. It was situated near the junction of the Canoe River and the Columbia.

[79] Refers to Henry's House. See *ante*, 31 n.

[80] This tribe received its name from a strange funeral rite imposed upon widows. When a warrior died his body was committed to a funeral pyre upon which his widow remained prostrate until the flames had consumed her hair and touched her body. Then she gathered the dead man's ashes and carried them about in a basket for two or three years. During this time she was in a state of servitude to the

These Iroquois informed me that the Canoe River which falls into the Columbia about a mile below this Encampment is navigable by half sized or Soteoux Canoes to its Sources in the Mountain from whence two small portages can be made to Cranberry Lake which is the head Water of Frazer's River and by that route Fort George,[81] New Caledonia is not exceeding Ten Days march from hence; this information does not answer any good end as regards the trade of that Dep^{tmt} but shews that the distance between New Caledonia and the Athabasca River is very inconsiderable and led to further enquiries the information derived from which induces me to think that great advantages would arise from changing the route now pursued by the New Caledonia Brigade, which is the most tedious harrassing and expensive transport in the Indian Country[82] the business of that Dept^{mt} which does not yield 100 Packs of Furs requiring this year no less than 80 officers & men whereas according to my present view of the subject Forty of all descriptions would answer the purpose. My plan would therefore be to forward the New Caledonia outfit in two Boats & thirteen men in company with the Saskatchawann Brigade; from Edmonton cross over to Fort Assiniboine in three or Four Days then proceed in two Boats to Henry's House in the mountain in Ten Days; thence by Horses to Buffalo Dung Lake[83] (1 pipe across) in Two Days; thence by Land or Water to the head of Frazer's River in Three Days and thence by a fine bold stream to the different Posts. The returns to be taken out in like manner. The only objection appears to be the risk of damaging the Furs in the transport by Horses, I shall however be better able to give an opinion on that head after crossing the mountain & from Fort Assiniboine to Edmonton on

family of the deceased husband. At the end of the period at a feast given for the occasion her thralldom was lifted, and she was free to marry again if she wished. For a good account of this tribe see D. W. Harmon, *A Journal of Voyages and Travels* (Andover, 1820), *passim*; also Hodge, *Handbook of American Indians*, under caption Takulli.

[81] Fort George on the upper Fraser, not to be confused with the better known Fort George at the mouth of the Columbia.

[82] See Appendix B, *post*, 349.

[83] Buffalo Dung Lake is the present Yellowhead Lake. Simpson's measurement of it is in voyageur terms.

my way out in Spring. Wrote Messrs Connelly and Laroque fully on the subject requesting them to get the route properly examined in the course of the Winter and Spring. From this place wrote to Messrs Keith Clarke McKenzie & McTavish, Here we were occupied in making repairing & Gumming Craft until the morning of the 21st and our provisions running short we were under the necessity of killing three Horses; the loss to the Comp^{y} was not serious as they were so old & worn out that they could not have recrossed the portage. I omitted to mention that from Jasper's House I wrote Mr Rowand to provide 20 good young cut Horses and a few breeding mares and entire Horses for the mountain transport. These Establishments of Horses for the Athabasca Portage and Fort Assiniboine Portage to Edmonton are attended with little Expence, at the former place a regular Horse keeper is required who can take care of a large as well as a small number, at the latter place a Horsekeeper is likewise required whether this transport business is undertaken or not and by watching the proper opportunities Horses may be traded from the Indians at from 8 to 10/ each and after the first stock is provided they may rear as many as can be required.

The Craft used on the Columbia are of a different construction to those on the east side of the mountain; they are called Boats but are more properly speaking Batteaux & wrought by Paddles instead of Oars, intended to carry 50 pieces Trading Goods besides Provisions for the Crew of Eight Men but they have of late reduced the size altho' they have not reduced the number of the Crew so that Eight Men are employed in the transport of about 35 pieces; I do not know whether this innovation is meant as an indulgence to the Masters or the Men, but suspect it is aggreeable to both altho' injurious to the Comp^{y} as thereby one third more people are employed in transport than necessary. I shall however take care that this evil is remedied before my departure and endeavour to improve on the originial plan Seven Men being in my opinion quite sufficient to Navigate a Boat containing Fifty pieces Cargo and the Crews of two Boats equal to the transport of One across the Portages.

Left the Portage after Breakfast in Two Boats and a Cedar

Canoe; passed the Mouth of the Canoe River which is a considerable Stream; found the Columbia River in a fine state; the Water Deep the current bold and strong and the Rapids perfectly safe altho' the Waves or broken Water rise to a considerable height, yet by watching the proper lead craft can pass tolerably dry. The current is so strong that at first sight one would scarcely suppose it possible to stem it even with the Towline but on more attentive observation it is found that in every reach there is a strong back current or Eddy which renders it easy of ascent and this appears to be occasioned by the Serpentine course of the River the current running with great strength against the Points which force the Water up in shore. Encamped about a League below the Grand Rapid. In the course of to Day I imparted to Mr McMillan my views in regard to extending the trade to the Northward of Fort George[84] and pointed out to him the importance of having an Establishment at the mouth of Frazer's River; this was done with a view that he should volunteer his services to explore the Coast that length in the course of the Winter but he did not see my drift or would not take the hint; in the Evening however I again opened the subject and intimated that rather than allow an other Season pass without obtaining a knowledge of the Coast natives & resources of that part of the Country (our ignorance of which after being established on the Coast upwards of Fourteen years being a disgrace to the whole concern) I should undertake it myself; this had the desired effect and Mr McMillan immediately offered his services on this dangerous and unpleasant mission; the Dr likewise declared his readiness to undertake it so that we are likely to get some business done this Winter. When the plan is sufficiently matured I shall give my views fully on this subject in connexion with a project I mean to submit for the consideration of the Honble Committee in regard to the extension and future management of the Columbia Trade generally.

Continued our march at Daybreak the 22nd the current so strong that we must be making upwards of 100 miles p Diem. The River now runs about S. S. W. and the mountains gradually

[84] Fort George at the mouth of the Columbia River.

diminishing as we descend, they are still however formidable the tops covered with Fog & Snow: the Weather cold raw and disagreeable with occasional Showers of Sleet & Rain. Passed a Lodge of Indians part of the Kettle Fall Tribe[85] they appeared more wretched than any I had seen on the East side of the Mountains not having a single article of British Manufacture in their possession but a Gun & Beaver Trap; they were not sufficiently numerous to enable us to form any correct opinion of their disposition or habits. Encamped within a League of the first Lake.[86]

Saturday, Oct. 23rd. Raining in torrents throughout the Night. Left our Encamp^t^ about 2 hours before Day break met several Indian Canoes and passed through a Lake of about 60 to 70 miles in length and from 1 to 3 miles in breadth;[87] the Country still mountanous but altho' late in the Season no appearance of Winter.

Sunday, Oct. 24th. Started before Day, from the Lake fell on a wide smooth Stream of about 8 to 10 miles leading to an other Lake similar to that passed yesterday but about ⅓^d^ longer;[88] the shores thereof covered with rotten salmon which the natives were collecting for their Winter stores. Those Fish ascend the Stream from the Sea in immense shoals in the month of July for the purpose of Spawning and find their way to the foot of the Mountain penetrating every little Creek; they however never get back to their native element as towards the Fall they become lean exhausted and diseased and are cast ashore in large quantities or found in nearly an inanimate state on the surface of the Water; they are even in this putrid condition acceptable to the Natives who dry them for Winter stock[89] indeed they are the only

[85] Known commonly as the Colville tribe. They occupied the region between Kettle Falls and Spokane River.

[86] Refers to Upper Arrow Lake.

[87] Refers to Upper Arrow Lake.

[88] This is Lower Arrow Lake.

[89] The Indian method of preserving salmon was to split the fish into four strips and hang the quarters to dry on scaffolds erected along the river bank. Sometimes

support of those in this part of the Country with the exception of a few roots they collect in the Fall. Encamped about an hour after Dark having passed about ⅔^{ds} of the Lake.

Monday, Oct. 25th. Heavy Rain during the Night but it did not damp the mettle of the D$^{r's}$ men two of whom amused themselves with a regular set too as we were embarking about an hour before Day break this morning and served each other out as gallantly as if they were exhibiting before a Moulsey hurst Ring; they certainly did not want for training as I do not know any thing more likely to put a man's bellows in order than a voyage from York Factory to the Columbia. Got to the end of the Lake about mid Day. Three Leagues lower down the Coutonais[90] or McGillivray's River joins the main Stream from the South; it is a considerable body of Water navigable for Canoes but strong and rappidy; it takes its source in the mountain a little to the Northward of the Portage of the same Name; a few miles lower down an other River falls in from the South name unknown and not navigable. The banks of the River to Day are covered with Red or Norway Pine. Encamped soon after Dusk.

Tuesday, Oct. 26th. At Day break passed the mouth of the Flat Head or Ponderais River[91] from the South, it appeared a large Stream but I understand is full of dangerous rapids; it has never been explored which appears somewhat extraordinary considering the short distance between it and Spokane House and the length of time that place has been established; I shall take care that it be examined next Season as it would be highly important for us that the Flat Head Post could be supplied by Water instead of Land Carriage. About a League below the mouth of Flat Head

the process was carried further, the dried salmon being pounded between two stones to a flaky pulp after the manner of pemmican. In this readily preservable form it was packed into large baskets (2 ft. x 1 ft.) made of grass matting, lined with cured salmon skins and closed with a covering of the same material. Twelve such baskets made a stack, seven at the bottom and five on top, over which was thrown matting made fast with cords. Salmon cured in this way could be kept sound and sweet for several years.

[90] Kootenay River.

[91] Pend d'Oreille River.

River a stream of some size falls in from the North called Rivière de Mouton blanc.[92] The Country from hence to the Kettle Falls is beautiful with all the varieties of Hill Dale Wood & Water but the Soil poor a mixture of Clay & sand. Got to the Kettle Fall about 1 o'clock P. M. where we made a portage of about ¾ths of a mile occasioned by a heavy cascade. The Portage would be a good situation for a fort as the soil is tolerably good and extensive Gardens might be made and Fish collected in any quantity at little Expence: it has been suggested to me that Spokane Establishment should be removed to this place but I shall be better able to form an opinion on that head after visiting the latter place.

At a little distance below the Kettle Falls we came upon the Grand Rapid an ugly looking Fall but run in high Water we however made a portage of about 100 yards. Passed a great number of Indian Lodges and Encamped about an hour after Dark. Were visited by some of the Natives at our Encampment who informed us that Mr. Ogden was waiting our arrival at the Forks of Spokane River.[93]

Wednesday, Oct. 27th. Embarked at the usual hour, the country still continues very beautiful and the Banks of the River studed with Indian Lodges. All the natives we have hitherto seen are called Kettle Fall Indians as they assemble there from the surrounding country during the Summer for the purpose of fishing. They appear to be a mild inoffensive race of people very good looking and generally stouter than the natives of the East side the Mountain. Throughout the Summer they remain about the Banks of the River collecting Fish for immediate use and Winter stores and at the close of the Fall they go inland in search of Roots and in order to pick up a few Skins to enable them to purchase the triffling articles of British Manufacture they require but those are very few indeed; as they are perfectly independent of us for any necessary; arms they merely require for show or defence as they rarely hunt; tobacco however is becoming

[92] Sheep Creek.

[93] Refers to the junction of the Columbia and Spokane rivers.

almost a necessary of life with them. Got to the Forks of Spokane River where we found Chief Trader Ogden and Mr Work[94] with about 30 men who had come up from Fort George with the outfits for the interior after the arrival of the Vigilant.[95] Mr. Ogden had arrived from the Coast about a Week ago. He represents the Country to be in a state of Peace and quietness and the Comp^{y}'s affairs going on as usual which is not saying a great deal as if my information is correct the Columbia Dep^{tmt}. from the Day of its Origin to the present hour has been neglected, shamefully mismanaged and a scene of the most wasteful extravagance and the most unfortunate dissention. It is high time the system should be changed and I think there is an ample Field for reform and amendment. Spokane House is about 60 miles to the Southward of this place on the Banks of a River of the same name, it is not navigable at this season I mean therefore to leave my craft and people here and proceed thither on Horseback tomorrow.

Thursday, Oct. 28th. Messrs McLoughlin McMillan & Ogden with Thos. McKay and two men accompanied me to Spokane House leaving our Craft and people at the Forks; the distance is about 60 miles and being well mounted we got to the Establishment in the same Eveng. the road tolerably good and the Country interesting being a succession of Hills plains and points of Wood the winding course of the River bringing it frequently to our view and adding much to the beauty of the scenery. The Soil a mixture of Clay & Sand producing short Grass stunted underwood and Red Pine every thing having a parched & withered appearance on account of the continued Droughts as for about 8 months in the year there is little or no rain in this part of the Country. Spokane House[96] is delightfully situated near the

[94] John Work was a clerk stationed at this time at Spokane House. There is a sketch of him in W. S. Lewis and P. C. Phillips, *Journal of John Work* (Cleveland, 1923), 55-69.

[95] The "Vigilant" was the Hudson's Bay Company vessel which brought the supplies of the Columbia Department from England to Fort George.

[96] For an account of Spokane House by T. C. Elliott see *Washington Hist. Quart.* XXI, 3.

banks of the Spokane & Skichew[97] Rivers in a fine plain or valley and surrounded at the distance of two or three miles by Hills clothed with Grass and fine Timber to their summits. Here we found Messrs Finnan McDonald & Kittson[98] Clerks and a large concourse of Indians of the Spokane & Nez Percés Tribes encamped about the Fort. The remainder of this day and the 29th was occupied in making the following arrangements connected with the trade. The Spokane District comprises the Posts of Spokane House Coutenais & Flat Head Rivers the former about 8 Days and the latter 7 Days march from Spokane House with Loaded Horses. The Snake Country Expedition is likewise attached to this District.

The aggregate returns were last year equal to about 9000 Beaver of all sizes of which about one half was the produce of the Snake Country Expedition. The appropriation of Officers & men as follows Spokane House Messrs. Ogden & Work with 7 men; Coutenais M[r] Kittson with 5 men; Flat Head M[r] McDonald with 7 men; Snake Country Expedition M[r] Ross[99] with 9 men in all 5 officers & 28 men the superintendence devolving on M[r] Ogden.

It has hitherto been usual for the Snake Country Expedition to start from the Flat Head Post in the month of February, and return in the month of November laying idle at that place all Winter; but several objections presented themselves in my mind to this arrangement:—viz., By laying idle at the Flat Head Post from the month of Nov. till Feby. the best hunting season when Fur bearing animals are in their prime is lost their hunts are

[97] Skichew River is the Skeetshoo of David Thompson and the Little Spokane of the present day. See David Thompson's map in J. B. Tyrrell, *David Thompson's Narrative of his Explorations, 1784-1812* (Champlain Society, *Publications*, XII), map pocket.

[98] Finan McDonald and William Kittson were on temporary duty at Spokane House. McDonald's regular charge was Flathead Post; Kittson's was Kootenay House. McDonald was a well-known character in the Columbia Valley, a clerk for many years in the service of the North West Company, associated particularly with David Thompson. There is a good account of him in Cox, *Columbia River*, 164 ff. See also Ross, *Fur Hunters*, *passim*, and Tyrrell, *Thompson's Narrative*, 378, 379. For William Kittson see Ross, *Fur Hunters*, *passim*.

[99] For Alexander Ross see *post*, 351.

consequently of little value the Furs being out of Season; a great deal of time is also lost in going to and returning from their hunting Grounds, say half the year unprofitably consumed and the very season when they could be most usefully and industriously occupied as then there is little danger comparatively speaking to be apprehended from roving War parties it being well known that Summer is the favorite time for those excursions and that the plain Tribes of the East side the Mountain are following the Buffalo about the North and South branches of the Saskatchawann all Winter. In the next place by laying at the Flat Head Post such a length of time the Freemen consume in the course of the Winter their ammunition and other supplies which they receive in the Fall and will not start in the Spring until they have a second outfit which they cannot afford to pay for. Moreover if there is a scarcity of Provisions at the Flat Head Post in the Winter their Horses are consumed and the company must supply them anew which is at times a difficult matter each hunter requiring three Horses to do his duty well; and lastly when such a worthless and motley crew are collected together laying idle for Four Months on end they are forming plots and plans quarrelling with the natives and exposing themselves and us to much trouble and danger. This band of Freemen the very scum of the country and generally outcasts from the Service for misconduct are the most unruly and troublesome gang to deal with in this or perhaps any other part of the World, are under no control & feel their own independence they therefore require very superior management to make any thing of them but I regret to find that Mr Ross has not that talent and that his presence among them has been attended with little good. Their Hunts however are more respectable this year than last amounting to upwards of 4000 Beaver. The Snake Country Expedition has hitherto been considered a forlorn hope the management of it the most hazardous and disagreeable office in the Indian Country therefore no Volunteer could be found for it among the Commissioned Gentlemen since Chief Facter McKenzie[100] crossed

[100] For Donald McKenzie's experiences in the management of the Snake Country Expedition see Ross, *Fur Hunters*, I, 182-283. See also *post*, 358.

the Mountain. This important duty should not in my opinion be left to a self sufficient empty headed man like Ross who feels no further interest therein than in as far as it secures to him a Sal[y] of £120 p Annum and whose reports are so full of bombast and marvellous nonsense that it is impossible to get at any information that can be depended on from him.[101] If properly managed no question exists that it would yield handsome profits as we have convincing proof that the country is a rich preserve of Beaver and which for political reasons we should endeavour to destroy as fast as possible. A charge of such consequence I therefore conceived should be in the hands of a Commissioned Gentleman and knowing no one in the country better qualified to do it justice than M[r] Ogden I proposed that he should undertake it and it affords me much pleasure to say that he did so with the utmost readiness.[102] It was therefore settled that he should proceed to the Flat Head Post without delay to meet the Expedition which by a Letter received this Day from M[r] Ross would be there about the 1st November; that he should outfit it immediately re-inforce it by Fifteen of the Comp[y's] regular servants furnish it with 30 to 40 additional Horses and proceed direct for the heart of the Snake country towards the Banks of the Spanish River or Rio Colorado pass the Winter & Spring there and hunt their way out by the Umpqua and Wilhamet Rivers[103] to Fort George next summer sufficiently early to send the returns home

[101] See Appendix B, *post*, 351.

[102] This is the inception of Ogden's four historic Snake Country Expeditions which opened up the unexplored wilderness of the northern Great Basin in the years 1824-29. Ogden kept a record of these expeditions in a series of day-to-day journals, the last three of which are published in the *Oregon Hist. Quart.*, X, 331; XI, 201, 229, 355, 381. A journal by him of the first and most notable expedition—the one proposed here—was unavailable for years to historians in the archives of the Hudson's Bay Company. A progress report, however, written near the close of the expedition and containing a graphic account of its adventures, was located there by the present editor and was published with an introduction and accompanying documents in the *Mississippi Valley Historical Review*, XXI (1934-35), 49-75.

[103] The country through which Ogden was here directed to hunt his way home was the unexplored wilderness of the northern Great Basin. He would have found it a difficult country to cross. But he had to change his plans and come out by the familiar road of the Snake, and the mysteries of the northern Great Basin were not revealed until his later expeditions.

by the Ship; and in future instead of incurring the heavy Expence of sending the Equipment round by the Spokane & Flat Head Posts and dragging the Expedition such a distance from the hunting Grounds outfit it direct from the Depot on the Coast. The Expedition will this season consist of Mr Ogden, Dears[104] a Clerk, McKay a Blackfoot Interpreter, 25 men (Coy's servants) and about 35 Freemen say about 60 in all. Mr McDonald and Four men will transact the business of Spokane House Mr Kittson and Five men that of the Coutonais Post and Mr Ross and Eight men that of the Flat Head Post. Mr Work I mean to take down to Fort George for the purpose of accompanying Mr McMillan to Pugets Sound & Frazer's River. Had the Chiefs of the different Bands encamped here into the Hall and made them a speach with the usual formalities.

The good people of Spokane District and I believe of the interior of the Columbia generally have since its first establishment shewn an extraordinary predilection for European Provisions without once looking at or considering the enormous price it costs; if they had taken that trouble they would have had little difficulty in discovering that all this time they may be said to have been eating Gold; such fare we cannot afford in the present times, it must therefore be discontinued and I do not see why one oz. of European Stores or Provisions should be allowed on one side of the Mountain more than the other; its great distance from the Seat of Government has of late been the only cause—no other can be assigned. From 80 to 100 pieces Trading Goods, Skins, Luxuries, &c or the Cargoes of Two Boats navigated by 16 men is as much as can be required or as the trade of Spokane District can afford if it is meant that any thing like respectable profits should be realised; but for these three years past Five and sometimes Six Boats have been annually sent and these principally loaded with Eatables Drinkables and other *Domestic Comforts*. Thompson's River and Nez Percés Districts in the same proportions as it has been considered that what was good for the one must be so for the others and to accommodate Gentle-

[104] Thomas Dears, a clerk without definite assignment at this time. His appointment to the Snake Country Expedition was later cancelled.

men in this manner about 35 to 40 men (commonly called extra men) have been kept merely to transport this Superfluous property. These extra men alone (valuing the Eatables Drinkables & Luxuries they brought up at nothing) were sufficient to run away with a large share of the Columbia profits. The articles of Provisions and Luxuries are in themselves at Prime cost of little value but when the Expence of conveying them to their destination is taken into the account that acquired value is a matter of very serious consideration.

I do not know any part of the Country on the East side of the Mountain that affords such resources in the way of living as Spokane District; they have abundance of the finest Salmon in the World besides a variety of other Fish within 100 yds. of their Door, plenty of Potatoes, Game if they like it, in short every thing that is good or necessary for an Indian trader; why therefore squander thousands uselessly in this manner? The old Hackneyed plausable answer of Mr Haldane[105] is always at hand, that the Brigade must come up formidable on account of the hostility of the Natives; that a Ship must come out annually and that therefore the provisions cost nothing beyond Invoice prices which is cheaper fare than Dog or Horseflesh but I contend that thirty men in all is sufficient force to pass with safety from one end of the Columbia River to the other if any thing like firmness and discretion is observed as shall be exemplified by my own ingress and egress; that, that number is adequate to bring up all the outfits and sufficient to establish all the Country about Fort George a few Summer men excepted; and further that as they consider Dog & Horseflesh expensive articles they need not indulge in them as the Waters at little cost and trouble will supply all their Wants. I have therefore given intimation that they had better Hoard the European provisions and Luxuries they have got now in Store as their future supplies will be very scanty barely the allowance determined on by the Honble Committee.

Everything being settled at Spokane House to the satisfaction

[105] Chief Factor John Haldane in 1822 shared with J. D. Cameron the command of the Columbia Department. His headquarters were at Spokane House.

of all parties we started to rejoin our Craft on the Morning of the 30th and after a hard ride got to the Forks the same Evening, the Dr quite knocked up being unaccustomed to such violent exercise.

The Climate of this part of the Country is delightful scarcely a Cloud to be seen for Months together, little Frost or Snow Some Winters not exceeding a few Days but the Rains Spring and Fall are constant when they set in for about a Fortnight or three Weeks at a time; there are occasional refreshing Showers in the course of the Summer. I mean to send some Garden and Field seed across next Season to be tried at Spokane House and I feel confident that they will thrive, *Indian Corn cannot fail.* Rattle Snakes are very numerous in this part of the Country but rarely do mischief; they are always on the defensive and give notice by shaking their Rattle when approached so that accidents seldom happen indeed none of our people have ever been bitten altho instances are known of Indians having lost their Lives.

Sunday, Oct. 31st. Took leave of Mr Ogden at the Forks of Spokane River early this morning and pursued our route. The San Poil River falls in from the North about three Leagues below the Forks. The Country now becomes dreary and wretchedly sterile scarcely a shrub to be seen and merely here and there a solitary Red Pine. Saw a few Indians collecting the exhausted fish that float down on the surface of the Water half dead and alive, they are quite putrid and have scarcely strength to move out of the way of the Fisherman.

Monday, Nov. 1st. Left our Encampment before Day break, had a good deal of Strong current and some heavy Rapids particularly the Dalles[106]—got to Okanagan at 10 A. M. Mr Birnie[107] Clerk in charge with two men. Here we found Mr Annance[108] with

[106] Refers to the Great Nespilem Rapids, consisting of Kalichen Falls and Whirlpool Rapids which were commonly known at this time as the Dalles. See Ermatinger, "York Factory Express Journal," in Roy. Soc. Can., *Proceeds. and Trans.*, 3rd series, VI, sect. ii, 74. There is a graphic description of the running of these rapids in T. W. Symons, *Upper Columbia River* (*Sen. Docs.*, 47 Cong. 1 sess., no. 186), 33-34.

[107] James Birnie. See for him Bancroft, *Pacific States*, XXIII, 276.

[108] F. N. Annance, a clerk in the Thompson River district.

some of the Thompson River people who had been sent by M^r McLeod[109] for supplies brought up by Mr Ogden after the arrival of the Vigilant which could not be got at Fort George when they went for their outfits in the Summer on account of the non-arrival of the Vessel from England.

This Post is agreeably situated in a fine plain near the Forks of the Okanagan and main River; the Soil is much the same as at Spokane and produces the finest potatoes I have seen in the Country. Grain in any quantity might be raised here, but cultivation to any extent has never been attempted, indeed throughout the Columbia no pains have been taken to meet the demands of the trade in that way which was a great oversight or neglect as corn in abundance might have been procured at little or no Expence at the Door of every Establishment but those in charge have preferred the less troublesome and more costly mode of Importing them from England Boston or California and employing extra men to deliver it into their Stores. It has been said that Farming is no branch of the Fur Trade but I consider that every pursuit tending to leighten the Expence of the Trade is a branch thereof and that some of our Factors and Traders on the other side are better adapted for and would be more usefully employed on this side in the peaceable safe and easy occupation of Farming than in Councilling Dealing with Indians or exploring new countries for which many of them are totally unfit but it unfortunately happens that in these savage regions Gentlemen sometimes imbibe the exalted notions of Indian Chiefs who consider that to Slaves or inferiors alone belong the less important yet useful and necessary duties of providing for their Daily wants by their own personal exertions; in short they have no notion of acting but think that their business only is to legislate and direct and are not satisfied unless they have a posse of Clerks Guides Interpreters & supernumeraries at their disposal while they look on with a pair of Gloves on their hands.

In order to acquire a thorough knowledge of the communication and country from hence to Fort George round by Thomp-

[109] John McLeod, a chief trader, in charge of the Thompson River district from 1822 to 1825.

son's & Frazer's Rivers and from the mouth of the latter by Puget's Sound to the entrance of the Columbia River, I was desirous to have dispatched an Expedition from this place under the charge of M^r McMillan as there would be more of the Season before him than by starting from Fort George and a better opportunity afforded of examining the navigation of Frazer's River as there is a probability that by the latter route he may not be able to ascend that Stream on account of the drift Ice at a more advanced period of the Season but I found that many essential requisites for such a hazardous and formidable undertaking could not be obtained here it was therefore determined on outfitting the Expedition from Fort George after our arrival there. This Establishment (Okenagan) is an outpost from Thompson's River District under the direction of Chief Trader McLeod the principal establishment Kamloops (the Indian name) on Thompson's River being situated on the banks of that Stream about Eight Days March from hence due North with loaded Horses.

The District I am concerned to say has not improved under the management of M^r McLeod; for these last two years there has been a continual outcry for more officers men goods & Provisions which the state of the trade does not authorise and if a very great amendment does not this year take place it ought in my opinion to be abandoned.

The Indians of Thompson's River I understand have been more daring and independent since that Gentleman has had the charge than they ever were before which does not say much for his management as if any thing like proper treatment is observed towards the Natives they must necessarily become more attached to us in measure as our residence among and intercourse with them advances and I concieve that an Indian trader who cannot obtain personal influence and secure to himself the respect and esteem of the Indians he has been in the constant practise of dealing with for three years successively is unworthy the title he bears and unfit for the situation he holds.

The Post of Okenagan I think ought to be maintained it requires an Establishment only of a Clerk and two men and produces about 600 Beaver but if the Post of Thompson's River cannot be kept up with a Gentleman and Eight or Nine Men say Ten in all and yield about 1500 Beaver it should be abandoned as we can turn the Services of our officers & men to better account in many other parts of the Country even by outfitting them as trappers. There were no less than Seventeen people attached to that post last year and Eighteen this, the expense of whose Wages and Equipments besides the outfit, its returns cannot defray and the fears of Mr McLeod have magnified the dangers to be apprehended from the Indians to such an alarming pitch that it was with great difficulty he could be prevailed on to undertake the charge even with the formidable Establishment now at his disposal. In regard to Provisions and Luxuries not one oz. is required for this place beyond the established allowance as excellent fish can be got in abundance with little cost or trouble, and at merely the expense of a little ammunition the table of the Gentleman in charge can be occasionally supplied with Game.

The distance from Okenagan to Spokane House across land does not exceed 5 or 6 Days march with loaded Horses. Spokane House is situated from hence in the direction of about S. S. E. and the junction of Thompson's River with Frazer's River about N. W.

Tuesday, Nov. 2nd. Took our departure from Okenagan at Day break; about Four leagues lower down a small River falls in from the West and about Five leagues farther a larger Stream called Piscahouse River[110] deriving its name from a Tribe who inhabit the banks in the interior, and from the sources of these Rivers there is a communication formed by small lakes narrows and Portages to Puget's Sound the distance not exceeding Six or Eight Days March with small canoes. Saw no Indians on the communication to Day and the character of the Country much the same as that passed yesterday. Encamped about an hour after Sun Set.

[110] Pisquows or Wenatchee River. For the Indian tribe of that name see Hodge, *Handbook of American Indians.*

Wednesday, Nov. 3rd. Started at the usual hour passed several strong Rapids, that of Isle de Pierre and du Pretre[111] require skilful management and by a blunder of my foreman who in the latter took the wrong lead we narrowly escaped being upset; it was such a close shave that I began to peel for a swimming match. In the course of to Day passed some Hundreds of Indians all busily employed in laying up Salmon for the Winter. Since leaving Okanagan there is scarcely a Tree or Shrub to be seen and Fire Wood is so scarce that the Brigades passing frequently burn the pallisades that surround the Graves of the Natives; this is a most unwarrantable liberty and would on the other side of the mountain be considered the grossest insult that could be offered and accordingly resented by the Natives; but the Indians here are so passive and well disposed that they take little notice thereof, we should not however impose on their good nature as it cannot fail of giving offence and I mean to issue instructions that it be discontinued in future as it might some Day lead to serious quarrels. Put ashore about two hours after Sun Set and were visited at our Encampment by 60 odd Nez Percés who smoked and were very friendly with us but as they mustered strong and might be inclined to pilfer we embarked after Supper and paddled 'till Sun rise the 4th when we arrived at Fort Nez Percés, Chief Trader John Dease[112] in charge.

The South branch of the Columbia commonly called the Nez Percés or Lewis's River is a fine large Stream navigable by small craft falling into the North branch or Main Stream about 3 to 4 Leagues above this place. In the year 1805 Captns Lewis & Clarke of the United States Army in command of a discovery Expedition fitted out by the American Government after ascending the Missouri Crossing the Rocky Mountains and descending this Stream to its junction with the Columbia at Lat. 46.15 North by their observation proceeded down to the Coast where they passed the following Winter and we are given to understand

[111] Refers to the Rock Island Rapids and Priest Rapids. There is a good description of them in Symons, *Upper Columbia River*, 43-48.

[112] John W. Dease, brother of P. W. Dease, the Arctic explorer. He was in charge of Spokane House until it was abandoned for Fort Colvile, and remained at Fort Colvile until his death in 1830.

that the American Government claims the Sovereignty of the tract of Country laying on the South side of the River Columbia from where Capt^{ns} Lewis & Clarke fell upon it (say at the Forks of Nez Percés or Lewis's River) to the coast on the ground of discovery altho it is perfectly ascertained that Lieu^{t} Broughton of Vancouvers Expedition had taken possession of the whole River and country adjoining it on behalf of G^{t} Britain as far back as October, 1792 determining Vancouver's Point in Latitude 45.27 North & Longitude 237.50 situated about 100 miles up the River.

The Walla Walla River a smaller Stream likewise falls in from the South and it is at the Forks of this River say about 3 to 4 Leagues below Nez Percés River that Fort Nez Percés is situated. This post has been progressively improving for these last three years but the profit it yields is still very moderate. There is an Establishment of Eleven in all attached to it which will admit of reduction and by lopping off superfluities in the outfit I am in hopes that next year it will shew a very material amendment. Its returns this season are estimated at 2000 Beaver got principally from a branch of the Nez Percés tribe called the Caiuses[113] and it does not appear to me that there is a prospect of any considerable increase unless trappers are introduced as the Indians cannot be prevailed on to exert themselves in hunting; they are very independent of us requiring but few of our supplies and it is not until absolutely in need of an essential article or an article of finery such as Guns & Beads that they will take the trouble of hunting. There is a Lake in the Blue Mountain about 4 Days march from hence in a S. Easterly direction into which a number of small rivulets fall where it is supposed there are a good many Beaver but we have no accurate information on the subject a few men will however be sent to explore it next Season.

It has been suggested to me that the Snake Country Expedition could be outfitted with greater facility and more advantage from the Nez Percés Fort than from Spokan House as by the former

[113] The Cayuses are not a branch of the Nez Percés, as Simpson and other early travellers supposed, but an independent linguistic stock. This is the tribe that later gained notoriety by its massacre of the Marcus Whitman missionaries.

route the transport of the outfit to Spokan and the Flat head Post would be saved and the Freemen would not be taken from their hunting grounds exceeding half the distance that they now come for their supplies thereby saving much time and considerable expence and further that by getting their outfits at the Nez Percés they could be supplied with any number of Horses at a less expence than is now incurred as those they are annually furnished with are traded from the Nez Percés tribe and forwarded to Spokan from that Establishment [Nez Percés]. My objections to that plan however I think ought to set the question at rest for ever. The Nez Percés tribe is by far the most powerful and Warlike in the Columbia and may be said to hold the Key of the River as they possess and are Masters of the country from Okenagan down to the Chutes a distance little short of 300 miles by the course of the River. Their lands to the South border on the Snake Country and with the Snakes they are almost continually at War. If a reconciliation is effected between those tribes it is by our interference and presents are made by us to both parties indeed their only object in coming to this temporary arrangement is to secure those presents;[114] they then smoke a Pipe of Peace and part with professions of Friendship but their treaties are no sooner ratified than broken as the moment the conference is over and we turn our backs they are ready to pillage each others Women and Horses and cut each others throats. The Nez Percés might by mere weight of property be induced to allow us pass through their lands to the Snake Country for a year or two while such a temporary peace existed but we have no security or guarantee for its continuance and in the event of a rupture they would identify us with their enemies the Snakes on account of our furnishing them with the Sinews of War Arms and Ammunition and if we were in self defence to kill any of the Nez Percés not only would we have thereafter to pass through an Enemy's Country on our way back with the returns & for fresh supplies but all communication be-

[114] For an account of such peace negotiations see Ross, *Fur Hunters*, I, chaps. vi-ix.

tween the interior and the Coast might be cut off which would be certain ruin and destruction to the whole Department. I therefore consider it an object of the first importance to keep on terms of friendship with the Nez Percés and not even venture the chance of a rupture with them which would involve such serious consequences. There is an other objection of nearly equal Weight. The Snake Expedition with all its followers am^{ts} to exceeding One Hundred Souls men women and children; in coming to the Nez Percés Fort for their supplies, they would require provisions for a Twenty Days March which they are not sufficiently provident to lay up; they would remain at the Nez Percés Fort about Twenty Days where it would be difficult and at times impossible to maintain such a body of people and they would require Twenty Days Provisions to take them back to the Snake Country which we could not furnish unless a Brigade of extra men were kept specially to take European Provisions from Fort George for their use which would eat up all the profits of the Expedition. Furthermore our Freemen are composed of Europeans, Canadians, Americans, Iroquois, half breeds of all the different Nations on the East side the Mountain and the Women are Natives of every tribe on both sides; such a motley congregation it is quite impossible to keep under any controul or restraint; they would be constantly gambling buying chopping & changing of Women Slaves Horses & Dogs with the Natives, quarrels would follow as a matter of course and the consequences might be fatal both to the Establishment and Expedition. I therefore conceive that the less intercourse we have with the Nez Percés beyond what is absolutely necessary the better; and I am decidedly of opinion that the only way in which we are likely to turn the Snake Expedition to advantage is that which I have already settled on with Mr Ogden, viz.:—to outfit them this season at the Flat Head Post take them at once to their hunting Grounds in the heart of the Snake Country pass the Winter & Spring there come round hunting their way either by land or Water to the Umpqua River, across the Mountains that divide it from the Walhamot River, down the last and thence direct to

Fort George with their returns,[115] there enjoy themselves for a Fortnight or 20 Days re-equip them from thence and send them back to pass the Winter in the Hunting Grounds from whence they came but on no consideration to visit any Establishment throughout the year except Fort George. Thus will their time be fully and usefully occupied; we shall be relieved of the expence and trouble of inland transport we shall avoid the risk of quarrels with the Natives and the people will have an opportunity of Spending their money to their satisfaction.

The Nez Percés Tribe when Chief Facter McKenzie first visited them were much more bold saucy and independent than they are now and hostily inclined towards the Whites but he by extraordinary good management obtained much influence over them he however kept a Watchful Eye upon them and never allowed them enter the Gates of his Fort except for the purposes of Trade and then not exceeding two or three at a time and occasionally a few of the Chiefs or principal men; Mr Ross (Clerk) who succeeded him followed up M^r McKenzie's plan as far as precaution went but Mr Dease has altered it, allows them more indulgence does not keep the same strict Watch and is not so much on his guard; his system has done well so far as the Natives appear well disposed but they are a capricious and treacherous race and I have recommended that while they are kindly treated the utmost caution and vigilence should be observed in regard to them. This Gentleman (Chief Trader John Dease) I understand is very *sober* steady and attentive to his business, but his extreme *sobriety* rarely tasting and never exceeding one Glass of Wine in *public* when contrasted with certain reports of ancient Date, his appearance in the morning, want of appetite, the Oceans of Tea he Swallows and the deranged state of his Nerves, I must confess looks a little suspicious; people are however wonderfully delicate in regard to each others character on this side the mountain and altho I have fished for information I can merely learn that he is a

[115] Ogden was compelled by disasters in the Snake Country to abandon the program here outlined and to make his homeward march by a familiar route to Fort Nez Percés. It was at Fort Nez Percés, therefore, the very post Simpson considered so objectionable for the purpose, that the expedition of 1825-26 was reëquipped.

great Tea Drinker. Were he to drink a pint of Wine with his Friends on extraordinary occasions, get up earlier in the morning eat a hearty breakfast and drink less Tea I should have a much better opinion of him. At Fort Nez Percés as at Thompson's River & Spokan House large quantities of Luxuries and European provisions are annually consumed at a prodigious cost and for no other good reason than that they are preferred to the produce of the Country which is cheap and abundant; while this ruinous system continues it is not surprising that the Columbia Department is unprofitable but from what I can see and learn no question exists in my mind that by introducing economy and regularity with the necessary spirit of enterprize and a disregard to little domestic comforts it may be made a most productive branch of the Company's Trade and the result of this and perhaps an other visit from me will shew that I do not take a visionary or speculative view of the business: it must however be understood that to effect this change we have no petty coat politicians, that is, that Chief Facters and Chief Traders do not allow themselves be influenced by the Sapient councils of their *Squaws* or neglect their business merely to administer to their comforts and guard against certain innocent indiscretions which these frail brown ones are so apt to indulge in. The extent of evil arising from this source strangers can have no conception of and the Honble Committee would scarcely believe that their business is frequently a matter of secondary consideration compared to little family affairs and domestic arrangements, that their people and Craft are employed in transporting Women & Children with their Baggage Pols Pans Kettles & Bags of Moss and that if these Women and Families were not appendages to the Brigades there would not be so many extra men employed in the Columbia and the Services of Commissioned Gentlemen would be turned to better account.

The Pacific Fur Co^y^. had an Establishment situated some distance up the Nez Percés River which was cut off by the Natives in the Winter of 1813/14 when Mr Reed the Clerk in charge and 8 or 10 men were massacred. This melancholy occurrence was in revenge for a cruel Wanton and ill advised murder

(I may call it) on the part of Chief Facter Clarke who was then a Clerk in that concern having hung one of the principal Indians without any kind of trial or formal examination merely on suspicion of his having Stolen some triffling article of Table Furniture;[116] the only remark I shall offer on this affair is that it is to be lamented the innocent should have suffered instead of the guilty.

In the event of the Americans establishing their claim to the Country laying on the South side of the Columbia below Nez Percés or Louis's River it would be necessary to remove this post to the North side of the Main Stream which could be easily done and instead of being at the expence of sending a body of extra men from Fort George to erect the new Fort the people of the different Brigades might be detained here for about a month on their way to the interior where there is plenty of Fish for their maintenance and in that time they could pull down the present establishment raft it across the River and rebuild it on the other side.

There are Eleven people including the Gentleman in charge at this place which complement is kept up Summer & Winter but I think that Nine in all are sufficient for the duties of the Post, i. e.

[116] The facts of this case are told by Ross Cox, an eye witness: "In the tent in which Mr. Clarke slept he kept a large *garde-vin*, which he had locked on retiring to rest, but the key of which he had omitted to take out; the tent was closely fastened, and while he was asleep, the strings were untied, the *garde-vin* opened, and a valuable silver goblet stolen thereout! Several loose articles were also taken, and bundles belonging to many of the men were carried away. Mr. Clarke immediately assembled the principal Indians; told them of the robbery; declared if the stolen property were returned he would pardon the offender; but added, if it were not, and that he should find the thief, he would hang him. The chief, with several others, promised they would use their best exertions to discover the delinquent and bring back the property; but the day passed over without tidings of either. On the second night, . . . two sentinels were placed at each end of the camp with orders to conceal themselves, and keep a sharp look out. Shortly after midnight they observed the figure of a man creeping slowly out of one of the tents, and carrying with him a bundle of clothes, a powder-horn etc. They silently watched his progress, until they saw him in the act of jumping into a small canoe which he had in the creek, upon which they sprung forward, stopped the canoe, and seized him . . . . We had not the slightest suspicion of this man, who had been remarkably well treated by us; in consequence of which, and the aggravated nature of the robbery, Mr. Clarke determined to put his threat into execution . . . ." Cox, *Columbia River*, 106, 107.

Four to be employed in the Summer in the Transport business to and from Fort George and the other Four with the Gentleman in charge to remain inland as it is quite unnecessary for him to visit the Depot occupying room in the Craft with his Family and incurring many Expences which attach as a matter of course to the movements of a commissioned Gentleman while his services may be more usefully employed inland; indeed for the whole interior business I do not see the necessity of more than one commissioned gentleman going to the Depot and that one should be a Chief Facter appointed to superintend the affairs of the interior generally accompanied by any Clerks that can be spared from the different posts in order.to assist in the management of the Brigades and as a support in case of trouble or difficulty with Indians.

Changed some Iroquois with Mr Dease for Canadians to accompany M^r^ McMillan on the coasting discovery Expedition. Wrote Mr Ogden on the subject of the Snake Expedition and directed Mr Dease to forward my letter also thirty Horses for the Freemen to Spokan House in the course of a Day or two. Killed two Horses for the people, they were in good condition and bought from an Indian for a few triffles value about 3/ prime cost.

From hence to the Coast is considered the most dangerous part of the communication as regards the Indians who are very numerous and disposed to be troublesome we therefore provided ourselves with three Arm Chests containing Twenty Four Muskets and 200 round of Ball Cartridge and having nothing more to do at this place we took leave of Mr Dease and continued our route on the morning of the 5th after Breakfast against a strong head Wind which raised such a broken Swell the River being here wide that we were continually wet throughout the Day; that however was not so disagreeable as the Clouds of sand and dust flying across the River the banks of which and the Country behind being nothing but a sandy desert. About 12 O'Clock passed the mouth of the Utella River[117] falling in from the South and in the course of the Day several large camps of Indians; at Sun Set came in sight of Mounts Hood and St Helens

[117] Umtella River.

the former on the South and the latter on the North side of the River at a considerable distance; they appear high are covered with Snow and are the principal land marks seen from Sea on making the Coast. Put up about an hour after dark.

Saturday, Nov. 6th. Left our Encampment soon after midnight and in the course of the morning passed Hundreds of Indian Lodges; at Day break many of the Natives came off to us in canoes begging a little tobacco which was given them some even attempted to come on board while we were at full paddle but we endeavoured to keep them off without quarrelling, one of their Canoes however shot across our Bow and was run down before our people could stop the way of the Canoe; the passengers thought nothing of it as they rose from under the water round the canoe like so many Seals; this accident entitled them to a little more Tobacco than their neighbours; they appear quite at home in the Water and altho their Canoe was rendered useless by the Blow they took it all in good part and laughed heartily at their misfortune. About 7 we passed John Day's River a small rapid stream falling in from the South: at 8 put ashore to Breakfast and examined our arms as we were now approaching the Chûtes Portage[118] which has been repeatedly a scene of Warfare between the Natives & Whites. At 10 got to the Portage and were followed by numbers of Indians in Canoes and on Horseback who were hurrying down to see us. They mustered about 250 men, very few of them had Guns but nearly all were armed with Bows and Arrows and each had a small Stilletto or

[118] Chutes Portage is the portage around Celilio Falls, the first of a series of obstructions in the Columbia River, fourteen-miles long, known as "The Dalles." This includes, beside Celilio Falls, the Little Dalles and the Great Dalles. Here several portages had to be made and here the Indians undertook to collect toll or to pillage as opportunity offered. Washington Irving has named one of these portages by reason of its evil history, "the pirate pass." Accounts of conflicts between the Indians and the whites occurring here are to be found in Cox, *Columbia River*, 67, 79, 160; Ross, *Fur Hunters*, I, 18, 129-135; and Washington Irving, *Astoria* (London, 1836), I, 108-111; II, 70-73, 94-104, 203-205. When Simpson traversed the Chutes portage again in 1829, from 400 to 500 of the neighboring Indians undertook to pillage him and his crew, and he held them off only by a narrow and exciting margin. See Sir George Simpson, *Narrative of a Journey Round the World* (London, 1847), I, 164-167.

Knife hung by a thong to the Wrist. They were very orderly and good humoured drawn thither principally by curiosity and with the hope of getting a little Tobacco. The Portage is about a mile in length, the path through heavy sand and across several Rocks; it is crossed in two poses or lifts; at each end of the pose a guard is stationed for the security of the property while the people transport the Canoes and Baggage; at the lower end of the Portage where the Canoes were Loaded and ready for starting, Mr McMillan and Thomas McKay (who are well known to every Indian in the Columbia having sent a few of their Friends to the other World for their misdeeds) ranged the Natives on the bank gave to each a pipe of tobacco and on embarking & pushing off threw some crumbled leaves and tobacco dust into the River where there was a general scramble all hands young and old male and female plunging in to secure a share of the Spoil thereby affording themselves and us a good deal of amusement and so we parted very good Friends. About two miles below this portage there is a very strong deep rapid[119] forming a heavy broken swell and considerable whirlpools which we ran but in high water a portage of about half a mile is made on the South side; here we saw great numbers of Seals playing about, I fired at them, but they are so quick that on seeing the Flash they are under Water before the Ball can reach them. Proceeded about 30 miles further down the River passing some large Encampments of Indians and put up about Two hours after Dark nearly opposite Mount Hood; the country now begins to get more pleasant the banks of the River being clothed with fine Timber and occasionally exhibiting a pretty spot. The Indians are frequently obliged to change their Encampments on account of the miriads of Vermin that collect about them and in passing the sites of some of these deserted habitations on the Portage to Day, it appears that we did not keep at a sufficiently respectable distance as no sooner had we landed this Evening then all hands were actively employed in dislodging those filthy and loathsome visitants a duty requiring a considerable stock of patience, good Eyesight and active Fingers.

[119] This is the Great Dalles of the Columbia. Compare *ibid.*, I, 168-169.

Sunday, Nov. 7th. Left our Encampment at 2 A. M. and got to the cascade portage[120] about 7; it is about half a mile in length; the Road is bad over Crags and uneven ground. This portage is occasioned by a heavy Fall or Rapid which cannot be run at any Season. Here we found about 80 to 100 Indians who were more peaceable and quiet than I ever saw an equal number on the other side of the mountain; it was not so some years ago as on this very spot they attempted to pillage a Brigade under the charge of Messrs A. Stewart and Jas Keith when the former was severely wounded and two of the Natives killed;[121] but since that time they have given little trouble and this favorable change in their disposition I think may be ascribed in the first place to the prompt and decisive conduct of the Whites in never allowing an insult or outrage pass without retaliation & punishment, and in the second to the judicious firm and conciliatory measures pursued by Chief Factor McKenzie who has had more intercourse with them than any other Gentleman in the Country; he even passed the greater part of a Winter among the Natives of this portage (having been taken by Ice on his way to the interior) placed a great part of his property under the charge and in possession of some of the Chiefs and took his departure without the loss of an individual article,[122] and this very circumstance has in my opinion done more towards restoring tranquility and establishing confidence and a Friendly intercourse with them than either our numerous forces or presents. Having made the portage without any trouble or accident, we distributed a little tobacco among the Natives and took our leave of them. The River now assumes the appearance of a Lake as it widens in some places to the extent of 2 & 3 miles is studed with Islands and the current slack; towards the afternoon we had the benefit of an aft wind, passed a branch of the Wilhamot River and several fine points named after Vancouver Broughton and others and at dusk

[120] This is a portage around the Cascades of the Columbia, a series of obstructions where the river breaks through the Cascade Mountains.

[121] For this incident see Alexander Ross, *Adventures on the Columbia* (Thwaites, *Early Western Travels*, VII), 254-261.

[122] See Ross, *Fur Hunters*, I, 109-114, 120-128.

put ashore at the Jolie Prairie. The country here is very pleasant well wooded & Hills plains and beautiful openings coming to the view at every reach. Several Indians came off from their Villages in Canoes bringing us a variety of excellent Fish, they appeared glad to see us and we received a hearty Welcome from two of their principal Men "Slyboots" & the "Little Chief" to each of whom we gave about 6 inches of Tobacco and to the others about a pipe each. After Supper all hands were busily occupied in shaving scrubbing and changing[123] as by continuing our march during the night we expected to reach Fort George the following morning we accordingly embarked about 10 P. M., kept our people at their Paddles until Day break the 8th when we put ashore to Breakfast; wrought hard all day against a strong head Wind and got to Tongue Point about 5 P. M. where we found Chief Facter Kennedy & Mr McDonald amusing themselves Boat Sailing; they embarked with us and we landed at Fort George about Sun Set having performed the Voyage from Hudson's Bay across the continent of America to the Northern Pacific Ocean in 84 Days thereby gaining Twenty Days on any Craft that ever preceded us. By taking the Saskatchewann route however instead of the circuitous and tedious course we pursued I shall undertake next Season if necessary with Eight men to perform the Voyage in not exceeding Two months so that if any object is to be gained by waiting the arrival of the Ship from England no danger or inconvenience can arise from remaining at York Factory until the 1st Septemb as thereafter there is sufficient Season to get to Carlton by open Water from thence to

[123] It was a custom among voyageurs to end any extended journey with a flourish. Simpson encouraged the practice, as it cost nothing, gratified the men and impressed the Indians. Preparations consisted of scrubbing and packing away the soiled clothing worn on the journey and donning in its place show garments, including a flashy sash tied about the waist, ribbons braided into the hair, and moccasins embroidered with gay beadwork. Generally a stop was made for the purpose of "changing" shortly before reaching the point of destination, but on this occasion Simpson had his men perform the function on the preceding evening as a matter of saving time. On coming in sight of the place of destination it was customary to set up a chorus of boat song, double the beat of the paddles or oars, and drive the craft with a dash to her landing place. See Malcolm McLeod, *Journal of Archibald McDonald, 1828*, (Ottawa, 1872), 4, 24-25.

the head Waters of the Columbia by Land and by making no delays en route to be at Fort George by the 1st Novem^{b}, by which means the Compan$^{y's}$ Dispatches may in less than Four Months from the Date thereof be at the most distant Establishment on the borders of the Pacific and through their medium the E. I. Comp^{y} may communicate with China by North America in less than Six Months which I have no doubt will be found the shortest most direct and least expensive route that has yet been discovered; to this subject I shall take the liberty of drawing the attention of the Honble Committee, it may become an object of much importance to both the H. B. & E. I. Co^{ys} nay even of National importance and if so the credit of being the first who discovered or suggested it will be a source of gratification to me through Life.

Having finished the Voyage and touched on every point connected therewith which appeared to me worthy of remark I shall now without reference to Dates continue my remarks on the Trade and observations generally as they occur to me.

The Establishment of Fort George is a large pile of buildings covering about an acre of ground well stockaded and protected by Bastions or Blockhouses, having two Eighteen Pounders mounted in front and altogether an air or appearance of Grandeur & consequence which does not become and is not at all suitable to an. Indian Trading Post. Everything appears to me on the Columbia on too extended a scale *except the Trade* and when I say that that is confined to Four permanent Establishments the returns of which do not amount to 20,000 Beaver & Otters altho the country has been occupied upwards of Fourteen Years I feel that a very Severe reflection is cast on those who have had the management of the Business, as on looking at the prodigious expences that have been incurred and the means at their command, I cannot help thinking that no economy has been observed, that little exertion has been used, and that sound judgment has not been exercised but that mismanagement and extravagance has been the order of the day. It is now however necessary that a radical change should take place and we have no time to lose in bringing it about.

In the Columbia Department comprehending the Posts of Spokan House, Thompson's River, Walla Walla and Fort George with their temporary Outposts, viz. the Coutonais and Flat Heads outfitted from Spokan, and Okanagan outfitted from Thompson's River; likewise the Snake Country Expedition outfitted from Spokan there are employed at present Two Chief Factors Three Chief Traders Ten Clerks and One Hundred and Thirty Six Men in all One Hundred and Fifty One officers and men appropriated as follows, viz.:

Fort George	2 Chief Facters	—Chief Trader	3 Clks	65 Men
Nez Percés	—	1 Do	— Do	10 Do
Thompson's River	—	1 Do	2 Do	20 Do
Spokan	—	—	4 Do	18 Do
Snake Country	—	1 Do	1 Do	23 Do
	2 Chief Facters;	3 Chief Traders;	10 Clerks;	136 Men

Whereas the following complement would answer every useful purpose, viz.:

Fort George	1 Chief Factor	— Chief Trader	2 Clks	20 Men
Nez Percés	— Do	1 Do	— Do	8 Do
Thompson's River	— Do	1 Do	1 Do	12 Do
Spokan	1 Do	— Do	2 Do	12 Do
Snake Country	— Do	1 Do	1 Do	20 Do
	2 Chief Factors;	3 Chief Traders;	6 Clerks;	72 Men

in all Eighty Three officers & men which is a reduction of Sixty Eight officers and men or a saving of Two Thousand Forty Pounds p Annum averaging the Wages and allowances of officers & men all round at £30 p Annum.

The Goods Provisions &c transported from Fort George for the Interior have, taking the average of the last three years, amounted to 645 North West pieces of which 183 pieces were trading goods private orders and Equipments and the remaining 462 pieces Provisions Luxuries &c &c. A very large proportion of the last item is quite superfluous and unnecessary as I am of opinion that 200 pieces should cover the whole outfit or supplies for the interior including Trading Goods, private orders & luxuries & these 200 pieces ought to be taken up in Four Boats the Crews of which with the officers accompanying the Brigade being as far as I am able to see or learn a sufficient force to pass from one end of the Columbia River to the other.

In the event of the Americans establishing their claim to the Trade of the South side of the Columbia as far up as Nez Percés or Lewis's River and that the Honble Committee did not consider it expedient to enter the Lists of opposition on the Coast I think that a great proportion of the Trade of the interior might still be secured by conducting the business from York Factory.

The Posts I should in that case recommend being kept up would be Spokan with its dependencies the Coutonais & Flat Head Rivers, Thompson's River and a post either near the Nez Percés on the North side of the River or on the Lands of the Tacamos & Pescahouse Tribes[124] who occupy the Country opposite Nez Percés between that & Puget's Sound and stretching North West towards Thompson's & Frazer's Rivers which is supposed to be well stocked with Beaver; the communication thereto from the Main River would be by the Pescahouse River which falls into the Columbia about Ten Leagues below Okenagan.

I shall not include the Snake Country as 'tis probable that the British Government in relinquishing the South side of the Columbia River as high as Fort Nez Percés would in like manner wave all claim to the Snake Country as it forms part of the Discovery of Lewis & Clarke's Expedition on which I suppose the present claims of the American Government to be founded. The probable returns of these Posts above mentioned might be estimated at 8000 Beaver or with small Furs at 150 North West Packs of about 90 lbs. each.

The most direct communication with York would be by the Coutonais Portage[125] and the Saskatchawann River but it is doubtful that the plain Tribes of the East side the mountain would allow supplies to be taken through their Lands into an Enemy's Country as they are almost constantly at War with the

[124] The Tacamos or Yakimas are an important Shahaptian tribe related to the Nez Percés. For the Pescahouse see *ante*, 52 n.

[125] Coutonais Portage is the pass which Simpson describes earlier in this journal, *ante*, 41, as situated a little to the south of the source of Kootenay River. Probably it is the present White Man's Pass with its western extension Sinclair Pass. See Geological Survey of Canada, *Reports*, 1885, B 9, 10; 112-118.

Natives of the West side; they would not however it is supposed object to our bringing out the returns by that route which would be a matter of great importance to us as by the Coutonais Portage we should be enabled to cross the mountain at least a Month earlier than by the Athabasca Portage. [*Pencilled marginal note*] It is to C. T. McMillan[126] I am indebted for this suggestion & indeed for the principal information I possess in respect to this part of the country & no one is so well qualified to give a correct opinion thereon, as he has had more experience therein than any other Gent^{n} in the Service.

If the Athabasca Portage was followed, out and in, it would not be possible to send the returns to Market the same year they are taken across the Mountain as the Road is impassable before the Month of August. It would likewise be necessary that the outfit should remain in Depot en route from York a year in advance as the Brigade would not be able to go the length of York Factory at that late Season so that a year's interest would be lost on the returns and the outfit would in like manner be burthened with a years Interest which would be a heavy draw-back on the Trade.

The plan I should therefore beg leave to propose would be to have the Furs taken across the Coutonais Portage by about 70

[126] Refers to Chief Trader James McMillan, mentioned earlier by Simpson in this journal as his travelling companion to Fort George. He was a veteran of the fur trade of the Columbia River, having been active there as early as 1808 in the capacity of clerk of the North West Company associated with the geographer-explorer, David Thompson. He became a chief trader of the Hudson's Bay Company at the coalition in 1821, and by the time of this writing was already high in the favor of Governor Simpson. We shall see him carrying out, to the Governor's satisfaction, the exploration of the lower Fraser, and in the spring of 1825 accompanying Simpson across the mountains to Norway House to attend the Council of Rupert's Land where he was appointed to the charge of Fort Assiniboine. He reappears on the Pacific in 1827 as builder of Fort Langley at the mouth of the Fraser and as a chief factor. He left Fort Langley in the winter of 1828-29 to accompany Simpson again across the mountains, and in the spring of 1830 he was assigned to the charge of the Experimental Farm at the Red River Settlement where he seems to have been unsuccessful. He was a man of more than ordinary capacity, possessing intelligence and education in addition to the outstanding qualities of character that went into the making of a successful fur trader. It was upon him and upon Chief Factor Donald McKenzie that Simpson seems chiefly to have relied in his preliminary reorganization of the Columbia Department.

Horses accompanied by 35 Officers & Men; by the ~~1st of July~~ 1 June+ they would reach the head of the Saskatchawann or Rocky Mountain House;[127] from thence the Horses should cross over to the Athabasca Portage in charge of 2 Horsekeepers and an Indian Hunter, there to remain until the Fall. Six canoes to be provided at the Rocky Mountain House Saskatchawann, the Water being high at that Season they would be at Cumberland by the ~~12th~~ 14 June+ at Norway House by the ~~17th~~ 20 June+ and at York Factory by the ~~25th of July~~ 28 June. Leave York with 150 pieces goods on the ~~1st August~~ 5 July be at Norway House by the ~~12th~~ 21 July, at Cumberland by the ~~20th~~ 30 July at Carlton by the ~~30th~~ 10 Augt. at Edmonton by the ~~10th September~~ 22 Augt., cross from thence to the Athabasca River by Horses, be at Fort Assiniboine by the ~~15th~~ 27 Augt. there find two Boats or Batteaux, be at Henry's old House on the Athabasca Portage by the ~~25th~~ 6 Sept. there find the Horses that were sent across in July from the Rocky Mountain House Saskatchawaine; cross the Mountain from Henry's House and be on the banks of the Columbia by the ~~1st October~~ Sept. 13. In the whole course of this route provisions may be had with due precaution as large animals are numerous.

At the West end of the Mountain 5 Days may be lost in building Two Boats or Batteaux to descend the Columbia but by the ~~13th October~~ 25 Sept. the Spokan outfit may be at the Forks of Spokan River, the Thompson's River Outfit at Okenogan by the ~~15th~~ 27, and the Nez Percés or Tacamos outfit at the Pescahouse River by the ~~16th October~~ 28 Sept., so that the outfits will get to their destinations sufficiently early for all the purposes of Trade. The same band of Horses will transport in both Portages outgoing and incoming as after taking the supplies across the Athabasca Portage they would be left in charge of the two Horsekeepers and Hunters and pitch leizurly in the course of the Fall and Winter back towards the Coutonais Portage so as to be ready for the Spring transport. All these plans and arrange-

[127] Refers probably to the old North West Company post on the North Saskatchewan opposite the mouth of the Clearwater River which the Hudson's Bay Company took over in 1821.

ments look very well, very easy and very regular on paper but it would require the assistance of our practical Chief Traders to carry them into execution. Our Chief Factors generally speaking are so much care worn with state affairs and have the happy talent of foreseeing so many dangers and insurmountable difficulties when their own Services are likely to be called into action and hardship anticipated that I would not recommend any member of Counsel (or at least very few individuals among them) being required to trust his precious frame across the Rocky Mountain under the arrangement in question. A Summer Establishment would be required at some of these posts in order to provide the means of living for the Winter say at Spokan House 1 Clerk and 4 Men, at Thompson's River 1 Clerk and 4 Men and at the Tacamos Post 1 Clerk and 4 Men. The complement of officers and men would therefore be as follows, viz.:—

Spokan House	1 Chief Trader	2 Clerks	4 Summer Men	14 Voyageurs
Thompson's River	1 Do	1 Do	4 Do	8 Do
Nez Percés	1 Do	1 Do	4 Do	8 Do
	3 Chief Traders	4 Clerks	12 Summer Men	30 Voyageurs

The result of the Trade on this plan might be estimated as follows, viz.:—

8000 Beaver & small Furs in 150 packs @ £60 p pack		£9000
Wages of 4 Clerks and 44 men at £30 p Annum each	£1440	
Outfit......150 pieces goods at £8 each	1200	
Contingencies	1000	
		3640
Probable amount of Gain		£5360

So that with proper management I have no question that the Columbia District even on the limited scale proposed would yield a profit of about £5000 p Annum.

If it was not contemplated to extend the Trade of this side the mountain beyond its present limits no loss would in my opinion be sustained by abandoning Fort George altogether even if the Americans did not settle the Columbia as the Expence of chartering a Ship from England annually, the large retinue of people at the Depot together with the infinity of et ceteras in the way of Expence which necessarily attach to an Establishment of such magnitude amount to fully as much as we should lose by having no Post on the Coast and if there was none lower down than the Nez Percés I think we might still secure a considerable proportion of the Fort George returns as the Coast Indians are such keen traders that many of them would even bring their Skins as high as the Cascades at appointed times in order to obtain our supplies indeed I think the greater part of the Fort George returns would find their way to our Establishment near the Nez Percés Country. This is however merely a passing remark as whether we are assailed by opposition or not I think there is a Field for commerce on this side the mountain which has been shamefully neglected and which if properly cultivated would become an object of the first importance to the Honble Hudson's Bay Company.

The enterprising spirit of the British Merchant shews itself conspicuous in all parts of the World except on the North West coast of America altho' our discoveries in that quarter have been pushed at a heavy Expence and in a manner that reflects highly to the honor of our nation and the individuals employed therein; but it is mortifying to feel that up to the present hour two rival nations should alone benefit thereby and that a profitable and extended Source of Trade is lost to G^t^ Britain who alone has any just right thereto. I shall not here examine into the claims set forth by the Russian and American Governments to this line of Coast as it is with peculiar satisfaction I understand the Government is at length roused and beginning to assert its rights which have been so long usurped by Foreigners.

The Trade of this Coast and its interior Country is unquestionably worth contending for and if the British Government do take that interest in the Welfare of the Fur Trade which it is wonted to do in every other branch of its widely extended Commerce the Americans will not talk so vauntingly of their discoveries and the sweeping and absurd Ukase of the Russian

Government[128] will prove of little avail to its Rus. American Comp-y.

The trade of this side the mountain if sufficiently extended and properly managed I make bold to say can not only be made to rival, but to yield double the profit that any other part of North America does for the Amount of Capital employed therein but in order to turn it to the best advantage New Caledonia must be included and the Coasting trade must be carried on in conjunction with the inland business. The support and assistance of the East India Company would however be essential to its prosperity; that powerful body has already evinced a Friendly disposition towards the Hudson's Bay Compy in the late Contract entered into for the supply of the China Market[129] and from their well known liberality and patriotism it is not to be doubted that they would go great lengths to secure to Gt Britain and their fellow citizens a profitable branch of Commerce which has hitherto been enjoyed by their Country's most powerful and dangerous Neighbours. This assistance cannot be considered a sacrifice on the part of the East India Company as we should only wish them to grant a priviledge to the British Fur Trade which the American Fur Cy enjoy without their consent or approbation. The priviledge alluded to would be that after delivering our Furs at Canton direct from hence instead of sending them by England we should be permitted to invest the proceeds in China produce to be disposed of on the South American Coast on the return Voyage.[130] The advantage to be derived from this indulgence is

[128] Refers to the Russian ukase of Sept. $\frac{4}{16}$ 1821, which forbade commercial vessels of other than Russian subjects to approach within 100 Italian miles of the northeast coast of Asia and the northwest coast of America down to latitude 51°. To the extravagant pretensions of this edict the United States and Great Britain quickly gave challenge, and eventually the Russian Government agreed by the conventions of 1824 and 1825 to withdraw its claims to the whole of the Northwest Coast as high as latitude 54°40′. See *post*, 241 n.

[129] Refers to a contract made by the East India Company to purchase 20,000 beaver skins and 7000 land otter skins from the Hudson's Bay Company in each of the years 1824 and 1825 for resale in the China market. See *post*, 207.

[130] Simpson has reference to the fact that British trade to China was vested by law exclusively in the East India Company. His proposal was to obtain from this Company a double relaxation of its rights—permission to dispose at Canton of the

that the heavy Expense of chartering a Ship annually from England to bring our supplies and take home our returns would be avoided as from ~~thirty~~ 40 to ~~forty~~ 50 tons of every description of British produce or Manufactures is all that can be required for the Trade and which could be got at an easy Freight say about £10 p ton to Lima or some of the Ports on the Spanish Coast from whence we could transport it to our Sea Side Settlements at no additional charge by our own Shipping; that our Furs would be at Market and in Cash from 18 Months to 2 Years earlier than they are at present thereby saving a considerable amount of Interest and that we should have the advantage of a Freight on the return Voyage of our Ship from China and the probability of realizing something by the sale of our China investment on the Spanish Coast on our way back for the returns of the following year.

Having now given the outline of the plan on which I should beg leave to recommend the Trade of this side the Mountain to be conducted I shall endeavour to shew the advantages thereof and to point out the practical mode of carrying it into effect.

Whether the Americans come to the Columbia or not I am of opinion that the principal Depot should be situated North of this place about Two to Three Degrees at the Mouth of Frazer's or as it is sometimes called New Caledonia River as it is more central both for the Coast and interior Trade and as from thence we could with greater facility and at less expence extend our discoveries and Establishments to the Northward and supply all the Interior Posts now occupied. Frazer's River we as yet know little about except from Indian report as neither Cook, Vancouver, nor any of the Traders on this Coast take any notice thereof; in the year 1808 Mess[rs] Frazer & Stewart descended it

furs taken by the Hudson's Bay Company on the west side of the Rocky Mountains, and the right to carry away from Canton in exchange a cargo of China produce to be sold on the west coast of South America. In view of the fight which the East India Company was making, and had been making, in Parliament to preserve its China monopoly against such encroachments these proposals appear rather naive, and the officers of the Hudson's Bay Company in London declined to act on them. The monopoly came to an end by the terms of its grant in 1834. See *ante,* xlix.

to the Sea[131] but were so much alarmed on account of the numbers of Indians they saw that they did not take time to enquire into the resources of the Country, to ascertain the disposition of the Indians, to thoroughly examine the state of the Navigation or even to determine its situation.

In respect to the resources of the Country as to the means of living we know them to be abundant as the population is very numerous and the natives excessively indolent and where a large population of Indians would barely exist a trading Establishment properly managed ought to live in the midst of plenty; it is however ascertained that the soil is fertile, the Climate Salubrious, that the Rivers are periodically visited by immense shoals of Salmon Sturgeon and other Fish and that Wood Animals are numerous.

In respect to Fur Bearing Animals, we know that the Natives are Wretched Hunters yet nearly all the returns of Fort George come from that quarter and that the Americans found the Coasting Trade alone so profitable that in the year 1801 they had no less than Fourteen Vessels employed thereon, of the Riches of the Country however there cannot be the slightest doubt. In respect to the natives they will as a matter of course take advantage of Strangers when in their power until Friendship and confidence is established but it would be paying a very poor compliment to ourselves if a doubt was entertained of our being able to secure a safe footing among the most treacherous and ill disposed savages that North America produces; no stronger proof of their good disposition however is necessary than Mess[rs] Frazer & Stewart having passed up and down between the mountain and Coast without being molested altho' their party did not exceed Ten men and the latter Gentleman has assured me that on one point of the River he shook hands with no less than Fifteen Hundred Indians at one short interview. In regard

[131] Fraser's journal of this expedition is published in L. R. Masson, *Les Bourgeois de La Compagnie du Nord-Ouest* (Quebec, 1889), I, 155-221. John Stuart, Fraser's companion, was in 1824 a chief factor of the Hudson's Bay Company who had just been transferred from the command of New Caledonia to Carlton House on the Saskatchewan.

to the navigation it is sufficient to say that those Gentlemen went down and returned safe altho total strangers to the River in the months of June and July when the waves are at their full height and when the Columbia River is impassable and from the Natives of Thompson's River we know that when the Water subsides it is a fine large deep navigable River indeed from the character and extent of the Country through which it passes and the number of tributary streams that fall in from the North and South it cannot be otherwise.[132] And in regard to its situation we know from Indian report that it falls into the Strait or Sound that divides Vancouver's Island from the mainland near about Burrards Canal or 49 to 50 North Latitude. In order however to remove all doubts I despatched Chief Trader McMillan with a party of about Forty (who would otherways have been laying idle here all winter) a few Days after my arrival at this place altho the Season was extremely unfavorable for such an Enterprize and I entertain sanguine hopes that he will accomplish the object of his mission with credit to himself and to the satisfaction of all concerned by bringing a favorable report on the various points on which we require information and which is so essential to carrying the present plan into effect. Taking such for granted I would establish the principal Depot at the Mouth of Frazers River from whence a Vessel for China would sail annually with the returns, where the Coasting Craft would receive their outfits and deliver their returns and from whence all the posts of New Caledonia would be outfitted likewise those of Thompson's River Spokan Nez Percés Flat Head and Coutonais also Fort George if we are allowed to occupy a Post on the Columbia and in that case the Snake Country Expedition from the last Establishment if we are at liberty to continue it; but if any serious objection exists to outfitting that Expedition from Fort George it can be supplied by Thompson's River across Land to the Flat Head Post. The Country between Frazers and Babine River as also

[132] This is much too sanguine a view of the character of Fraser River. More correct is the letter Simpson wrote to the British Foreign Office in January, 1826, in which he represented the river as unnavigable. See Appendix A, *post*, 264, 265. See also McLeod, *Journal of A. McDonald, 1828*, 21-39.

to the North of the latter we know little about but we are given to understand that its inhabitants are numerous and that they have either directly or through the medium of the Tribes on the Coast intercourse with the Russians as many articles of Russian Manufacture find their way to our Establishments in New Caledonia & McKenzies River which is to a certain degree proof that there are Furs on their Lands as the Rus. American Co^y^ are not proverbial for their liberality and not likely to expose themselves to the accusation of giving their property away to their Savage Neighbours without recompence. No time should therefore be lost in exploring that country and if its Trade induced us to establish Posts therein, it could be done with greater facility, from Frazers River than either Fort George or the other side of the Mountain. In short Frazers River appears to be formed by nature as the grand communication with all our Establishments on this side the mountain.

The great advantage of outfitting New Caledonia from this side instead of from York Factory is that the business can be done with greater facility and less expense.[133] According to the

[133] Simpson indicates in this passage that he has come to a new solution of the transport problem of New Caledonia. His earlier proposal (see *ante*, 37) of a route via York Factory, the Saskatchewan River and Yellowhead Pass is given up, and he has arrived at the thought of a Pacific outlet via Fraser River. That the middle Fraser had been found by Fraser and Stuart in 1808 to be unnavigable for all practical purposes does not seem to have been fully realized by him, and James McMillan who was sent to examine the river during the winter did not succeed in bringing back a report on anything but its lower reaches. Simpson, therefore, left the Columbia in the spring of 1825, apparently still believing that the Fraser could be made a highway for New Caledonia to the sea. But he was disillusioned, perhaps by Chief Factor Stuart, before the meeting of the Council of Rupert's Land in 1825, and the route which the Council adopted—one that Stuart had experimented with in 1813—was one that made use of the Fraser only as far as Fort Alexandria, from which it ran by a pack-horse trail via Fort Thompson to the Okanagan River, and thence down the Columbia by batteaux to Fort Vancouver.

This was the route which the Hudson's Bay Company used from 1826 to 1846. Then a change had to be made on account of the fact that the Oregon Treaty ceded the lower Columbia to the United States, rendering British goods transported on it liable to American tariffs. The new route chosen—a very difficult one—ran up the Fraser from Fort Langley to the junction of the Fraser and the Coquihalla, thence by pack-horse trail up the valley of the Coquihalla to Fort Thompson on Thompson River and thence northward by the old route. See "Minutes of Council 1825" in *Can. Hist. Rev.*, VII, 306; Harmon, *Journal*, 228, 236.

present mode of conducting the affairs of that District there are upwards of Sixty officers & men employed therein whereas little more than half that number would answer every purpose if Frazers River was its Depot on account of the labour in Land and Water transport that would be saved and by substituting Boats for Canoes. A Sum amounting to 25 p Cent on the value of the returns would likewise be saved as the damage sustained in transport as the business is now conducted reduces their value in that proportion at the very lowest calculation. On the communication down to the Forks of Thompsons River there is no danger to be apprehended from the Natives but from thence to the mouth of Frazers River it is necessary that the Brigade should be formidable on account of the numerous population on its banks as is now the case below Nez Percés on the Columbia; the Craft of Nez Percés Spokane and Thompsons River alone would not present such a respectable force as to ensure safety but with the New Caledonia people they would be sufficiently strong and without them it would be necessary to have about Twenty Extra Men merely for the sake of protection which would be a heavy drawback on the Trade; it is therefore evident that important benefits would result from making but one Dep^{tmt} of all the Establishments on this side the mountain and that the mouth of Frazers River should be its Depot.

The outfit from England required for the Trade is so inconsiderable that it would not be an object to charter a Ship: from ~~thirty~~ 40 to ~~forty~~ 50 Tons will one year with an other be the outside of our demands and as the late political changes in the affairs of South America will occasion a regular and extended intercourse between G^{t} Britain and that country[134] there will in all probability be little difficulty in getting Freight for that quantity to Lima or some other port on that Coast and I would beg to recommend that the outfit be divided among as many Vessels as

[134] British trade to South America, which had been illegal in the Spanish period, grew to considerable proportions during the South American struggle for independence, and by 1824 was an important factor in British policy. Canning was influenced by it when he gave British recognition to the South American Republics in 1825. See F. L. Paxson, *The Independence of the South American Republics* (Philadelphia, 1903), chaps. i and iii.

possible to guard against the risk of loss in that long and dangerous Voyage.

Provisions for which there has been such a hue and cry from Fort George since its first Establishment is not only not required but by attention I am of opinion that we might actually make it an article of Trade from this Coast say Beef Pork Fish Corn Butter &c &c.

If the East India Comp^{y} would contract for all our Furs it would give them the entire command of the China Market as if we manage our business properly we must put down all competition on the Coast at least from the Americans; the Russians do not interfere so much with us as their Furs are principally Sea Otters and Fur Seals which find their way to the Northern parts of China through Siberia but the prodigious Expences incurred in transport render it impossible that they can affect us by competition. The East India Company therefore by contracting for the whole of our Furs would insure to themselves the entire monopoly of the Trade. Another important advantage that would result therefrom is the reduction of the Export of Bullion from England to China for the home investments as the present export of British Manufactures I believe is inconsiderable compared with the Imports of China produce and the difference being made up in specie or Bullion turns the balance of Trade greatly against England.

Such a contract would likewise be advantageous to us by saving commission to an Agent in China[135] and protecting us from the

[135] British merchants trading to China made a practice of evading the East India Company's monopoly by engaging the services of non-British agents at Canton. Such agents were generally British-born persons parading under the naturalization papers or the consular diplomas of some Continental state, or they were Americans. Among the latter Perkins & Co. and James P. Sturgis & Co. of Boston, with branches at Canton, did an extensive British agency business in addition to their own trade. Perkins & Co., for instance, from 1816 to 1821 did the marketing in China of all the North West Company's Columbia Department furs, and they continued for a few years to serve the Hudson's Bay Company after the coalition of 1821. The business was carried on as follows. The North West Company sent a consignment of British trading goods from London to the Boston house of Perkins & Co. This was taken by Perkins & Co. to the Columbia River to be exchanged at Fort George for the season's catch of furs. The furs were taken to Canton to be ex-

shameful impositions practised on Strangers at the Port of Canton. By delivering our Furs to their Agents at Canton direct instead of sending them via England nearly Two years interest on the amount would be saved of which we should of course derive the benefit and by employing our own ship in the transport they would naturally allow the Freight and Port dues they thus save from England or an increased price to cover those charges and they could not reasonably object to our taking a cargo of China goods back to the Spanish Coast in order to secure us a Freight as it could not interfere with that Market in England...

The Shipping required for the business as proposed to be conducted would be a Vessel of about 150 Tons Register commanded by a man of character and ability with two respectable officers and a Crew of Fifteen Men and Boys; to Sail from hence for Canton annually on or before the 1st November by which means she would be in time to receive the Company's latest dispatches from England up to the departure of the Bay Ships and take advantage of the proper season for crossing the China Seas. An average passage from hence to Canton occupies two months so that by sailing on the 1st November she may be supposed to leave Canton by the 1st of February allowing her a month there to discharge & reload, deliver her return Cargo at Lima or rather some port more to the Northward if it presents a Market equally good, receive the 30 to 40 Tons goods brought from England and be at Frazers River Depot by the 1st of June which is allowing her 7 months for the Voyage to and from Canton and 'tis probable it may be done in less time and by allowing her a month at the Depot on arrival and an other before her departure for Canton the following November for the purpose of refitting &c she would have three months to perform a trading Voyage on the Coast.

A small Vessel of about 50 to 60 Tons would likewise be required for the Coasting Trade; this Vessel could however be built here at little or no expence by having a good steady hard

changed for teas and other China produce, and this cargo in turn was sent to Boston for sale. Perkins & Co. retained as their compensation for these services an agreed percentage of the net proceeds.

working carpenter or Shipbuilder attached to the Depot and the only complement of people required for her would be a Commander Mate and Four good Seamen, the rest of the Crew could be made up of Landsmen in the Service. This Vessel would find constant employment on the coast and in case of any accident happening to the larger Vessel could make a Voyage to Canton with the Furs and on her return bring supplies from Lima or such other Port on the Coast as might be fixed upon as an entrepôt. Provisions for these Vessels we could undertake to furnish.

The Vessel intended for the China Trade would of course be sent from England and her cargo could be filled up with such heavy & bulky articles of little cost as would be required for the Trade one or two years in advance so as to save Freight afterwards and it would be necessary to send by her Stores for the Small Vessel and spare stores for two Vessels one of about 150 & the other of about 50 to 60 Tons as by having a Ship builder at the Establishment we could from time to time prepare such craft as might be required for the Trade arising either from loss damage or a wish to extend our commerce.

The East India Company have frequently occasion to forward Dispatches to India at a very heavy Expence and as formerly hinted it might be an object of much importance for them to have a regular Annual communication with China, that could be had through the medium of our Ships as within Six Months from the Date of the Dispatches we could undertake to deliver them at Canton, such a facility might be an additional inducement for them to fall in with the H. B. Coy's views or perhaps they would allow a certain Sum annually for the benefit thereof which would go towards meeting our Expences. Two respectable men would be required to command these Vessels so that our business might not be at a stand in case of any accident happening to either and great care should be taken in the Selection of them as more evil from roguery mismanagement or misconduct is to be apprehended from that Source than any other; it is not necessary that these Gentlemen should be general men of business, on the contrary I think the less they know of any business beyond their own the better; the commanders of Merchant Men brought up in the Merch^{t} Service are too frequently inclined to look to their own interest in the first place and make that of their Owners a secondary consideration at least I have found it so and from what has come to my knowledge in this country I do not believe that either the Honble Hudsons Bay Co^{y} or North West Comp^{y} have yet had a correct man in their employ in that capacity, it is not therefore to be wondered at if we should look on the whole craft or fraternity with suspicion and distrust; there are however hundreds of Naval Officers now out of Employ about England, men of respectable Connexions of Conduct of Honor and of talent whose half pay being barely sufficient to keep them in existence are looking out for employment in the Merchant Service and to whom the Lords of the Admiralty will on application give leave of absence of 3 to 5 years as may be required at least they were in the habit of doing so before I left England. Two of these Gentlemen (Lieu^{ts} in the Navy) I would take the liberty of recommending for this Service at respectable Sal^{ys} say about £300 p Annum to cover all perquisites privi-ledges and allowances with the prospect of advancement in the Service if they afterwards chose to throw up their half pay as we have a greater number of Facters and Traders than necessary for the Indian trade alone, indeed our List of Commissioned Gentlemen without increasing their number should in my opinion comprehend Legislators real Indian Traders Agents both in the Country and wherever the business required such and com-manders for our Vessels. The Mates I think ought to be intro-duced on the footing of Clerks expecting promotion and by that means every person coming under the denomination of Gentleman in the service will feel themselves amenable for their conduct to the Govr & Councils in this country as well as to the Honble Committee at home which is highly essential to the well being of the whole concern. In regard to Seamen after the first comple-ment is provided from England we shall be enabled to fill up any vacancies that take place by Death or otherwise by landsmen from the Service and apprentices Natives of the Country who I think would soon become excellent Seamen. . . .

I shall now endeavour to come at a rough estimate of the Expence or capital required for carrying this extended scheme into effect, viz.:—

Wages of 110 Canadians and Europeans @ £25 p Annum[136] . .	2750
Wages of 42 Sandwich Islanders @ £12 p Annum . . .	504
Salys of 2 Comnders for Ships at £300 p Annum each[137]	600
Salys of 16 Clerks & Mates for Vessels @ £60 each	960
Amt of Annual requisition for the Trade	~~2600~~ 3000
Frt of 40 Tons Goods from England to Spanish Coast @ £10 p ton	400
Vessel for the China Trade of about 150 tons supposed to cost about £3000 will cost annually about . . .	~~500~~ 1000
Insurance and Sundry Contingent Expences	~~1~~786
	£10,000

The Data on which the Salys & Wages of Officers & Men is calculated is as follows, viz.:—

Depot Frazers River		
Chief Factor in charge	2 Clerks	2 Blacksmiths
		1 Shipbuilder
		1 Assistant
		1 Carpenter
		1 Taylor
		1 Tin Smith
		1 Cooper
		2 Sawyers
		10 Labourers
Fort George		
Chief Trader in charge	1 Clerk	1 Blacksmith
		1 Carpenter
		1 Butcher or
		1 Cooper
		7 Labourers

[136] The wages paid by the Hudson's Bay Company to its various classes of voyageurs in the period of this journal are given at *post*, 211 ff.

[137] This item chargeable only until the Comns are provided for by commissions. [Marginal comment by Governor Simpson].

Post	Officers	Clerks	Men
Spokane including Coutonais & Flat Head Posts			
	Chief Factor in charge	2 Clerks	16 ~~12~~ Labourers
Thompsons River			
	Chief Trader in charge	1 Clerk	10 Labourers
Nez Percés			
	Chief Trader in charge	1 Clerk	8 Labourers
New Caledonia			
	Chief Factor in charge	4 Clerks	36 Labourers
Shipping	2 Commanders	3 Clerks or Mates	25 Men
New Countries to be explored & settled			
	Two Chief Traders	2 Clerks	30 Men
	2 Commanders for Vessels;	16 Clerks & Mates;	156 ~~152~~ Men.

It is impossible to form any correct estimate of the returns that may be collected by conducting the business according to the Scheme now projected; they are at present equal to 20,000 Beaver and Otters but by attaching New Caledonia to the Department and extending the trade along the Coast I think that at a moderate calculation it may be doubled or even trebled[138] and this extension of the trade will not be attended with any material additional Expence to that incurred on the System and Scale now pursued as will be seen by the following Estimate of the Expences of the current outfit 1824/25, viz.:—

Wages of 147 Officers & Men now employed in the Columbia.......................................£ 4600
Am^t Invoice Insurance & Charges on outfit 1824/25........2800
Freight as p Charter Lively...............................1575
Sundry Contingent Expences...........................1025

£10,000

[138] Simpson is oversanguine as to the possibilities of expansion of the trade in the Columbia Department, but a material increase did take place as a result of the reforms he introduced. See *ante,* liii ff.

Many of our Commissioned Gentlemen are so little acquainted with general business that they will not readily fall in with the view I have taken of the affairs of this side the mountain and others who are getting beyond the prime of life and attached to their Families would in order to be exempt from the laborious duties to which they would be exposed in settling a new country have no objections to relinquish all interest in its affairs and confine themselves to the business of the East side. The Services of those may be dispensed with and a sufficient number of enterprising men can still be found among our Chief Facters and Chief Traders who would readily enter into it and I am myself so Sanguine and confident of its success if properly managed that in order to give it a certain tone in this country I should not hesitate to exchange my fixed Sal^{y} for an interest in the trade thereof.

In order to see the whole machine put in motion I should wish to pass one or two Winters on this side indeed if the Honble Committee thought that my Services on the other side could be dispensed with for a whole year say 1826/27 I have the vanity to think that much benefit would be derived by my presence and I shall here take the liberty of pointing out how I conceive my time could be turned to the best advantage. The Vessel intended for the China trade would leave England in November or December 1825 so as to reach Fort George in June or July 1826 deliver the Outfit take in the Furs for China and be in readiness to take her departure from and after the 20th October. I should propose starting from York Factory after the arrival of the Bay Ship from the 20th of August to the 1st September and be at Fort George by the 1st November, accompanying the Ship to Canton, dispose of the Cargo either by delivery to the E. I. Co$^{y's}$ Agent, bringing it immediately to Sale or putting it into the hands of a respectable mercantile House to be disposed of afterwards as the state of the market or other circumstances might render expedient; take in a cargo of China Goods, proceed to Lima Acapulco or some port on that Coast most likely to present an advantageous market which the Honble Committee would be able to ascertain from some of the London Mercantile Houses in that line and of which I should have information by the Bay Ships; dispose of the Cargo and remit the proceeds or leave it (the Cargo) in the hands of a respectable House of business to be disposed of afterwards as the state of the market would authorize; take in the goods required for the outfit of the following year and reach the Columbia in June or July 1827 by which time the interior Brigades would have delivered their returns and gone inland with their outfits. Embark the Furs people & property and proceed to the mouth of Frazers River; remain there until the 1st November by which time our Establishment would be completed and the York Factory Express arrived; dispatch the large Vesel for China and then proceed in the small Vessel along the Coast on a Trading Expedition, touch at the Russian Settlement in Norfolk Sound and see if any business could be done there, return to Frazers River in March proceed from thence to the mountain meet the different Brigades from the interior going with their returns and for their outfits to the Depot and be at Norway House by the opening of the Navigation about the middle of June 1828 thereby being absent from the Councilling business at York only one Season.[139]

In order that the important arrangements connected with the business may be in simultaneous operation (as no doubt exists in my mind that the Honble Committee will see the propriety of extending the business on this coast) I shall forward a Carpenter who understands something about Shipbuilding from York next Fall (1825) for the purpose of cutting down & preparing Timber for the Small Vessel so as to be seasoned by the time the regular

[139] Simpson did not carry out this program partly because of decisions by the London Committee, partly because of changes in his own views. The London Committee decided not to attempt to bring the Columbia Department furs to market at Canton. This disposed of the need of a China vessel. The only ship sent out to the Northwest Coast was therefore a small coasting vessel, the "Cadboro," which put in her appearance at Fort George in the spring of 1827. Simpson was constrained on learning of the true character of the Fraser River to give up the project of locating the Columbia Department depôt at its mouth, and though Fort Langley was built there in 1827-28, it was built as a secondary trading post. Simpson did not return to the Pacific until 1828-29. He came then by way of the Peace and Fraser rivers, and saw for himself the hopelessness of the Fraser as a highway of commerce. See McLeod, *Journal of A. McDonald, 1828*; Bancroft, *Pacific States*, XXIII, 477 ff.

builder arrives from England in the months of June or July 1826 who would immediately commence laying down the Small Vessel and under the Superintendence of one of the two Naval Gentlemen who would come out in the capacity of Commanders she could be launched Rigged and ready for Sea by the time the large Vessel arrived from Canton and proceed together as before stated with the Establishment of people goods and Stores &c &c to Frazers River.

The Russian Settlements have hitherto been principally supplied with goods for their trade by the American adventurers on this coast payable by Bills on St Petersburg or in Furs; but if we conduct our business with good management according to the present plan that channel will be shut up as we ought to be able to put down all competition on the Coast in which case 'tis probable we should be enabled to do business with the Russians on advantageous terms; it would be with a view to see what could be done in that way I should purpose visiting the Director Von Baranoff at their principal establishment of New Archangel in Norfolk Sound.[140]

In abandoning the Establishment[141] and removing so high up the River as the Jolie Prairie or Belle vue Point I do not think that any loss will be sustained by the Trade; nearly the whole of the Furs got now at this place pass through the hands of three Chiefs or principal Indians viz. Concomely King or Chief of the Chinooks at Point George, Casseno Chief of a Tribe or band settled nearly opposite to Belle vue Point and Schannaway the Cowlitch Chief[142] whose track from the borders of Pugets Sound strikes on the Columbia near to Belle vue Point; the first is much attached to us and will follow wherever we go; his favorite

[140] New Archangel is the present Sitka. Norfolk Sound is Sitka Sound. Simpson was unaware of the fact that Baranof had died in 1819 and that Governor Mouravief presided at New Archangel in his place.

[141] Refers to the abandoning of Fort George and the building in its stead of a new post, Fort Vancouver, on the north bank of the Columbia River opposite the mouth of the Willamette.

[142] For these chiefs see *post*, 104. Schannaway is the Schachanaway mentioned by David Douglas in his *Journal kept by David Douglas*, 1823-27 (London, 1914), 62.

Daughter is kept by Mr McKenzie one of our Clerks[143] and he offers to place his Grandson (eldest Son of the Prince of Wales)[144] under my care in order to be Educated at the Missionary Society School Red River so that his trade and that of his band may be considered as secured to us.

Casseno who is the most intelligent Indian I have seen and who endeavours to imitate the Whites in every thing is likewise much attached to us declares he is not an American but a Relative and subject of King George and residing nearly opposite our Door is not likely to desert us and go a distance of 70 miles with his Furs to our opponents. . . . Between the mouth of the River and Belle vue Point there is not a spot of Ground fit for the site of Establishment on the north side as the Banks are either high perpendicular Rocks or low points which are overflown by the River in the Season of high Water. The place we have selected is beautiful as may be inferred from its Name and the Country so open that from the Establishment there is good travelling on Horseback to any part of the interior; a Farm to any extent may be made there, the pasture is good and innumerable herds of Swine can fatten so as to be fit for the Knife merely on nutricious Roots that are found here in any quantity and the Climate so fine that Indian Corn and other Grain cannot fail of thriving; it is much better than that of the Coast say at Point George being less exposed to the Sea Air. The distance from the Harbour is the only inconvenience but that is of little importance being now a secondary Establishment;[145] the small Vessel however

[143] Fur traders were quite ready to make such alliances with the daughters of tribal chiefs, with the view, partly at least, to winning the good will of the tribes, while the chiefs on their part were eager for the prestige and profit that flowed from such connections. Concomely, for example, boasted two white sons-in-law, Duncan McDougal, senior partner of the Pacific Fur Company, whose nuptial ceremonies in 1813 are picturesquely described by Washington Irving in *Astoria*, I, chap. xxvi, and A. McKenzie, the Hudson's Bay Company clerk here referred to. Servants of the fur-trading companies almost without exception kept Indian women and had children by them.

[144] Cassicus, eldest son of Concomely, was known to the fur traders as the Prince of Wales. Concomely's daughter, the consort of A. McKenzie, was known as the Princess of Wales.

[145] This refers to Fort Vancouver which was intended at first to be a secondary establishment. Simpson had in mind at the time to locate the main depôt of the

can run up a considerable way and a Leighter or large Batteaux can work or drift down in a couple of tides.

The Establishment of officers and men at this place is very large no less than Seventy in all about thirty five of whom may be considered extra men for the purpose of assisting in the transport of the outfits & Provisions inland as the people attached to the interior posts could not take up the whole; these extra men are not therefore chargeable to the Post of Fort George alone but to the Deptm^t generally. According to the System now laid down however the Services of these Men would be dispensed with altogether if there was no prospect of extending the Trade and in that case I should have taken them across the mountain this Spring but as there is a probability that the Honble Committee will see the propriety of conducting their business on a more enlarged scale I have thought it advisable to keep such of them as are useful on hand in the meantime but not to be employed as heretofore. The outfits of the interior will therefore be taken by the people immediately belonging to those Establishments only, forming a Brigade of about Thirty Two officers & men, and the Supernumeraries or extra men in question will be equipped for a whole year and sent off from Fort George on a Trapping Expedition in the month of May accompanied by all the Freemen in this neighbourhood so as to form a party of between Fifty & Sixty under the command of Messrs Finnan McDonald & Thos McKay[146] their route will be up the Wilhamot River across a Mountainous Country which we know little about to the Umpqua River and from thence Hunt their way to the Banks of the Rio Colorado keeping either inland or towards the Coast as the state of the Country in regard to Fur bearing Animals and the means of living may direct; they will remain out all Winter and Spring and return to Fort George in the month of

Columbia Department at the mouth of Fraser River. Fort Vancouver did not become the main depôt until after the Fraser had been determined to be unnavigable in its middle reaches.

[146] Simpson inserted the names of McDonald and McKay into the manuscript at some time subsequent to his first writing.

June following (1826)[147] about the time the Ship will arrive from England by which conveyance the Hon[ble] Committee will be pleased to intimate to the Gentlemen in charge of this place their future intentions and the party will be re-equiped and sent back to their Hunting Grounds from whence they came or sent on another Expedition to the Northward to pass Winter 1826/27 as the Committee may direct or the state of the Country render expedient and return to Fort George in the Spring or Summer of 1827 for the purpose of going to Establish Frazers River Depot or returning to the East side of the mountain if the Co[y] should unfortunately determine on not extending the Trade. If my Despatches from hence which shall be forwarded from Norway House in June reach the Committee sufficiently early to make the arrangements proposed (in regard to the purchase of a Vessel, preparing the Indent or requisition and engaging Commanders for the Vessels &c) before the month of Novem[r] 1825 (say the usual time of Sailing) instead of November 1826 the plan of establishing Frazers River Depot can be carried into effect after the arrival of the Vessel from England in Summer 1826 but on the contrary which is more than probable it must be postponed until 1827.

There are several old favorite Canadian Servants and useless Iroquois about this Establishment who we must get rid of altogether as they are merely a burthen on our hands, I shall therefore take them out with me this Spring for the purpose of being sent either to Red River Colony or to Canada and it is highly necessary

[147] This is the Umpqua Expedition subsequently mentioned in the journal. It did not carry out the program here sketched for it. It started late because of Indian troubles in the Columbia, and consequently could not take the route to the Umpqua Country which Simpson had ordered. It took instead a southeasterly course, crossing the Cascades, probably by the near-lying Santiam Pass, and proceeding thence up the Des Chutes River toward the unexplored Klamath Country. It had been ordered to penetrate that country and to proceed as far southward toward California as possible. but it did little more than cross the outer edge of its objective. Somewhere on Williamson River it turned back, making for the Des Chutes River, where it effected a junction with the crippled Snake expedition, and accompanied it thence eastward on a long hunt to the upper waters of the Snake River. See *post*, 281; also *Oregon Hist. Quart.*, X, 336-365; XI, 210, 211, 218.

to reduce the number of Families at this place as altho' the Company do not feed them their consumption of Provisions added to the regular demands of the Fort creates a competition in the Market which the Indians avail themselves of and raise the price of their Fish and other supplies accordingly; the population now exceeds one hundred and fifty Souls but I am in hopes it will this Season be reduced to less than a hundred.

The Inland Brigades arrive here generally about the latter end of April or beginning of May and remain idle until the arrival of the Ship in the month of June or July thereby exposing us to the Expence of their maintenance, and both men and officers losing the three most valuable months in the year whereas if any thing like activity or Enterprize had been observed these people might have been usefully employed in exploring the Coast to the Northward & Southward of which to our shame be it said we are still nearly totally ignorant:—such indolence and indifference is unpardonable must be broke through this year and I am satisfied my Friend the D^r^ will not allow it be repeated during his administration; we have therefore determined that the Gentlemen who come from the interior this Season shall immediately after their arrival proceed in charge of the people of their Brigades from hence by the Willamot River so as to fall on the Coast about 100 miles to the Southward and push forward as far as their time will admit on a trading excursion and in order to acquire a knowledge of the Coast Natives and Country.[148] We have every reason to suppose that the Country is rich in Furs and that Sea Otters are numerous on the Coast and if the report of this party is favorable we shall endeavour to open a regular communication with the Natives or fit out a small trapping & trading Expedition the following Season. Indeed the Southern shores as far as California we know to be very productive in Sea Otters and I have no doubt that considerable advantage may be derived from paying that line of Coast an Annual visit with one or other of the Vessels; the Natives are not Hunters but if the different Spanish Missions encouraged it and rendered their protection we

[148] No such expedition appears to have been sent in 1825, but one went out the following year under A. R. McLeod. See *post*, 290.

should in all likelyhood be enabled to prevail on some of the Pugets Sound Indians or the Natives of the Coast more to the Northward who are very expert at hunting the Sea Otter to go thither for that purpose annually to be taken to the Hunting Grounds and back to their Homes at the proper Seasons by our Vessels on the Coast.[149]

A few Sandwich Islanders mixed among the Canadians and Europeans can be usefully employed here as Guards and for common drudgery about the Establishments but they are not generally disposible men being unfit for the laborious duties of the Voyage; they are however valuable in establishing new Countries as they can be depended on in cases of danger from the natives; when they first came here and until last year their terms were merely food and cloathing which is sufficient recompence for all the Services they render, Mr Cameron[150] however by way of following up the strict Letter of the Minutes of Council regulating the Wages of Servants (which did not provide for Sandwich Islanders) advanced theirs to £17 p Annum thereby putting them on an equality with the Canadian & European Servants which occasioned much dissatisfaction and very naturally so as they are by no means such serviceable people, we have therefore reduced them to £10 p Annum which satisfies all parties; there are about 35 of them now on this side the mountain but we can employ 15 more to advantage if the trade is extended and in that case I would beg to recommend their being taken on board as the Vessel intended for the China trade passes Owyhee on her passage hither from England.

Having now worn the subject of the trade of the North West Coast nearly threadbare I shall conclude my remarks thereon by giving it as my humble opinion that if the Honble Committee enter into it on the scale proposed it will turn out highly advantageous to the concern and at no very distant period become an

[149] It was a common practice for the Russian American Company to transport parties of native northern hunters with their sea canoes to the California shores in search of sea otters. Some American adventurers did likewise. But the California sea otter was not as valuable a fur as that found further north.

[150] Chief Factor J. D. Cameron was one of the officers in charge of the Columbia Department for several years prior to the advent of John McLoughlin.

important branch of Commerce in a national point of view and so anxious am I to see it set agoing on a regular and well organised footing that if I find my Services can be dispensed with at York by the 1st of next July and that the Committee have not chalked out any particular duty to occupy my attention during the following Winter I purpose starting for England via Canada so as to be there in the course of the month of September which might enable them to make the necessary arrangements for commencing the business in the Summer of 1826 instead of waiting until 1827 and the object of my presence at Home would be to give information on many points that might be essential to its future interests which do not at present occur to me and cannot be anticipated & sufficiently explained or understood by correspondance.

In regard to the navigation of the River Columbia there is not an officer or Servant belonging to the concern who is qualified to Pilot a Vessel even of Twenty tons Burthen from outside the bar to the Establishment of Fort George which shews how very little trouble has been taken to acquire useful information and so badly arranged are we for extending our trade along the Coast or assisting our Shipping if such was required that there is not a Boat at the Establishment fit to cross the River in bad Weather nor a person competent to Sail one; promotion in the service had nearly resulted from this wretched state of our Marine Deptmt as a few Days after my arrival here being desirous of visiting Bakers Bay and Cape Disappointment in order to ascertain if there was a spot thereabout fit for the site of a new Establishment Chief Factors Kennedy & McLoughlin with Thos McKay Clerk accompanied me in an open Craft called the Gun Boat; previous to starting I made no enquiry in respect to the state of the Craft or rigging, abilities of the Crew or dangers of the Voyage conceiving that all was right as a matter of course but we had not got a mile from the Wharf when owing to the crazy condition of our Vessel it became necessary to Bail with Buckets Hats &c, she was so unmanageable that we could not regain the Shore our rigging so rotten that the Sails came down by the run and so ignorant were we of the River that we touched on a sand bank but fortunately drifted off otherwise we must have perished among the breakers; we exhausted our strength at the Oars in order to get ashore but to no avail as we were drifting rapidly past Point Adams towards the Breakers on the Bar of the River,[151] when the Tide providentially turned and brought us up under the Lee of Chinook Point where we landed and returned on Foot to the Fort; during this perilous excursion the melancholy accident that occurred to Messrs McTavish & Henry and their Crew[152] frequently came across our minds and we momentarily expected a similar fate. The mention of this circumstance is merely to give one instance of the gross mismanagement and wretchedly bad system on which the Coy's affairs have been conducted in this quarter and which is inexcusable and unpardonable as with very little trouble and no expence we might have good Sea Worthy Boats expert Boatsmen and a thorough knowledge of the navigation of the River; the last we cannot attempt to improve but we ought to know its dangers and be prepared to meet them instead of which we are as ignorant of it below Fort George as our Friends on the East side of the mountains and know little more of the Coast having never been Twenty Miles either North or South along Shore from its entrance until I fitted out the Expedition under Mr McMillans charge this Season. Mounts Hood & St Helens and Cape Disappointment are the most remarkable objects in making the Coast and cannot be mistaken but getting into the mouth of the River is a dangerous Service on account of the Sand banks that stretch across its entrance outside Cape Disappointment & Point Adams; if blowing hard from Sea no Vessel should attempt the Channel as it is then filled up with sand but when the Wind moderates the current opens to itself a passage, narrow but of sufficient depth Soundings being from 3 to 7 fathom and when

[151] There is a good chart of the outlet of the Columbia River in Lynn's report, *Sen. Docs.*, 25 Cong. 2 sess., no. 470, opposite page 9.

[152] Donald McTavish and Alexander Henry were partners in the North West Company who, with five other persons, were drowned in 1814 while proceeding from Fort George to a vessel at the mouth of the Columbia. See Coues, *Henry and Thompson Journals*, II, 916.

once across the Bar there is good anchorage and safe harbours. In the event of our being permitted to retain possession of the Columbia I think some expence should be incurred in placing Buoys & Beacons on the bar and a person should be attached to the Establishment qualified to Pilot a Vessel in and out as in the whole Navigation of the outward and Homeward Voyage I do not believe there is so much danger to be apprehended as in making & leaving the River.

The population on the banks of the Columbia River is much greater than in any other part of North America that I have visited as from the upper Lake to the Coast it may be said that the shores are actually lined with Indian Lodges; this I account for by the River affording an abundant provision at little trouble for a great part of the year and as they do not turn their attention to Hunting the whole of the Interior population flock to its banks at the Fishing Season. Those above the Cascade portage go into the Interior or back country about the latter end of October for the purpose of gathering Roots, leaving their Winter Stock of Fish in Security and return with what they may have collected early in December. Towards Spring such as have not been sufficiently provident are reduced to the greatest distress by Starvation and many perish annually from this cause; but those who are careful may live in the midst of plenty the whole year round as Fish and Roots may be secured at the proper Season sufficient for the maintenance of any population merely at the expence of a little industry; but unfortunately they are indolent and lazy to an extreme and cannot be roused into habits of activity.

There are a few large Animals on their Lands but they are unaccustomed to the Chase and I believe there are many among them who have never tasted any other meat than Horse or Dog Flesh. The few Skins they barter with us are taken in the Fall when they go in search of Roots but they have not much occasion for our supplies and therefore take little pains in that way. Cloth Blankets and Iron Works they rarely purchase and they merely take the trouble of looking after a few Beaver (which is considered a wonderful exertion) in order to supply themselves with Tobacco Beads Guns and Ammunition.

There are few or no Beaver on the Banks of the Columbia owing to the rapidity of the Current and great rise and fall of the Water sweeping away their Young and not enabling them to form Lodges or Dams; they are however numerous on some of the small Lakes and Creeks in the back country and if the Natives would but apply themselves to Hunting during the Winter Months the Trade would be greatly increased.

The population is divided into a great variety of tribes or bands speaking different Languages and are generally on Friendly terms with each other as it rarely happens that they have Serious differences or form themselves into War parties. The Spokans, Nez Percés and Flat Heads however do sometimes make incursions on their Territory and carry away Scalps, Women Slaves and Horses. The Spokan Language is understood from the Lakes down to Nez Percés or Louis's River and that of the Nez Percés Tribe down to the Cascades or lowest Portage but every thirty or Forty Miles a different Language is spoken, having little affinity with each other as will be seen by a specimen of the different Languages[153] (which might be interesting to philologists) spoken by the various bands or tribes that inhabit the Banks of the River from the Mountain down to the Coast.

All the Natives of the River appear well disposed indeed I never saw such good humoured inoffencive Indians in any part of the Country; those of the Cascade and Chûte Portages have on three or four occasions attempted to pillage the Brigades when the Country was first established but the example made of them at the time and subsequent conciliatory yet firm and judicious conduct of the traders has deterred them from offering any insult or violence for several years past.

From the Cascade Portage to the Coast they are collected into Villages of Ten to fifteen Houses and three or Four Families inhabiting the same House. They live in great comfort throughout the year, as Fish are taken at all Seasons, Roots abundant

[153] This was not found in the journal.

close to their Houses and Wood Animals are numerous so that they may have a variety of choice fare.

The Chinook tribe is the most powerful and having been resident among them for a considerable time I am enabled to give a sketch of their customs mode of life &c which will serve to give an idea of all the Natives below the Cascade Portage as they may be considered one and the same Nation altho speaking different Languages.

Their looks on the whole are pleasing being more fair and their features more resembling those of the Whites than any other tribe I have seen. They have however a strange practise of flattening the upper part of the Head which at an early age disfigures them very much but as they advance in Life it is not offencive to the Eye at least was not so to me at first sight and as none but the wretched Slaves have round heads I begin to fall into the Chinook way of thinking that they do not look so well (particularly the Ladies) with round as with Flat Heads. The Child is almost constantly kept laced down on its back on a Cradle or Wooden frame the back part of the head leaning against the board, on the forehead a pad is laid and tied lightly to the board which keeps the head in the same position and by constant pressure in this manner until the child is about 18 months old it becomes flattened or assumes the shape of a Wedge and the flatter it is the more dignified and fashionable the Wearer; this operation does not seem to give pain as the children rarely cry and it certainly does not affect the brain or understanding as they are without exception the most intelligent Indians and most acute and finished bargain Makers I have fallen in with. A couple of those Heads will be sent to the Honble Committee next Season as a curiosity. They frequently tattoo the Legs arms and breast but not the Face; the Ears are perforated all round and Beads or Hyaques[154] suspended there-

[154] *Hyaque* or *haiqua* is the Indian term for a species of shells (*ioquas*) found along the shores of Nootka Sound and to the northward, white in color, tubular and tapering in shape like a game cock's spur, and a quarter of an inch to three inches in size. They were used by the Indians for ornamentation and for shell money. Their value increased with size.

from in quantity according to the rank or taste of the party; Mr Corney states in his Journal[155] lately published in the Literary Gazette that the rite of circumcision is observed among them but this and many other circumstances he has introduced probably with the intention of giving interest to his Narrative I find to be incorrect.

The Dress of the Men consists of a Wood Rat Skin Robe, or Blanket fastened over the shoulder by a Gun Worm or Wooden Pin, the opening down the side leaves the right arm at liberty but they can use both by casting the blanket or robe round at pleasure; breech Cloths they never use and their sense of delicacy or decency is moderate; the only other article of Dress they Wear is a straw or Chip Hat or Cap of a conical form which the Women make very neatly; on their War excursions however they Wear a double Shirt or kind of guernsey frock of thick Deer Skin two fold which is arrow proof. The Women wear a Kilt or Short petty Coat made of rushes fastened round the loins and hanging in fringes down to the knees and occasionally a small pin-a-fore of Rat Skin hanging over the breast or a piece of Cloth or Blanket but are more frequently without any other article of apparel than their Kilts or Petty Coats.

Concomelly is the principal man[156] of the Chinook tribe from the circumstance of his being the most wealthy having a number of Slaves and a large stock of Hyaques Beads and other property but he has little controul over them, indeed every Flat Head Indian who is possessed of a Slave considers himself a Chief.

In cases of quarrels or misunderstandings with other Natives they either compromise matters by an exchange of presents or determine on fighting it out. Their mode of Warfare is much

[155] Peter Corney, "Journal," in (London) *Literary Gazette*, 1821. The author was the chief officer of an English trading vessel plying the Northwest Coast, who in 1816 had the opportunity to observe the Chinooks for five months in their village at the mouth of the Columbia River, while his vessel lay there refitting. His account is a good one on the whole. It was reprinted in 1896 at Honolulu under the title *Early Northern Pacific Voyages*.

[156] There is a good account of this picturesque chief in Alexander Henry's journal see Coues, *Henry and Thompson Journals*, index. See also Irving's *Astoria*, and the three "synoptical writers" of the Columbia: Franchère, Cox and Ross.

more honorable and manly than that practised on the East side of the Mountain; they appoint a time for Meeting and the Belligerents go to the scene of action in their War Canoes, the neighbouring tribes or Nations observing a strict neutrality; they never come to close quarters and sometimes fight from Sun rise till sun Set, that is, fly their Arrows at each other, from a safe distance without drawing blood; in the course of their battle they occasionally exhibit a flag of truce when a cessation of hostilities immediately takes place and a parley is held on the subject of their differences but if a reconciliation cannot be effected they resume the combat which may be spun out for several Days until two or three fall when the losing party makes the necessary concessions and then they settle matters amicably and sometimes enter into offensive and defencive alliances.[157]

In their marriages they follow the example of many great Folks in the old World, as love is entirely out of the question, these alliances being formed solely on political considerations when presents are exchanged according to the means of the parties.

The Chinooks never take the trouble of hunting and rarely employ their Slaves in that way, they are however keėn traders and through their hands nearly the whole of our Furs pass, indeed so tenacious are they of this Monopoly that their jealousy would carry them the length of pillaging or even murdering strangers who come to the Establishment if we did not protect them. To the other tribes on the Coast they represent us as Cannibals and every thing that is bad in order to deter them from visiting the Fort; and in order to strengthen their commercial relations men of consequence or extensive traders have sometimes as many as half a Doz Wives selected from among the best Families of the Neighbouring tribes and each of those is entrusted with a small Outfit and sent on trading excursions to Her Friends & relatives and this is her constant employment.

When any serious offence is committed one against an other such as Robbery seduction or Slander the party agrieved some-

[157] There is a good description of such a contest in Coues, *Henry and Thompson Journals*, II, 855, 879-880.

times takes revenge by Murder but it is generally settled by presents or through the intervention of Friends.

The Young Women previous to Marriage are allowed to indulge the full scope of their inclinations and chastity is not looked upon as a virtue except in regard to the Ladies of the very first rank when the parents are desirous that they should be allied to White great men in which cases they are closely watched indeed are never allowed to cross the Door except after Dark and then attended by Slaves it however strangely happens that these precautions are of little avail as the Young Ladies are in this respect very much disposed to disregard the injunctions of their parents and have sufficient address to elude the vigilence of their guards. After marriage they are more circumspect and the Husband if an Indian severely punishes the infidelity of his Rib if discovered, but a price will command the Princess of Wales downwards. When married or allied to the Whites they are under little restraint and in most cases gain such an ascendency that they give law to their Lords, indeed this observation applies to the whole Indian Country on both sides the Mountain and I am sorry to say that even Members of Council are not excepted which is more injurious to the Comp^ys interests than I am well able to describe; but to return to the Chinooks.

They are in general exceedingly filthy in their habits, their persons and habitations swarming with loathsome vermin which they do not take the trouble of hunting except for the purpose of conveying to their mouths; they are however wonderfully healthy being rarely afflicted by any other than *Imported Diseases* and such as proceed from them viz., Scroffula Sores and a species of Leprocy and the original is so prevalent that Nine Whites out of Ten who have been resident at Fort George have undergone a course of Mercury. They have no knowledge of Simples or Medicinal herbs but are now beginning to discover the value of our Drugs and when the case is not very serious they apply to us for assistance but dangerous cases are seldom or never cured or almost invariably prove fatal as their conjurers have so great an influence over them that the patient is forthwith put under the care of one of those men of Medicine; the treatment is most inhuman and preposterous; the conjurer and his followers beat a kind of Drum & Sing making a horrible clamour for perhaps 24 hours on end, if this affords no relief, he gets all fours on the body of the Invalid (who is held down by the attendants) and presses with his hands and knees the wretched sufferer who frequently faints under this racking pain which is intended to force out the evil spirit occasioning the indisposition; this process is continued in the din of Drums, Kettles Singing and Yelling in order to drown the voice of the patient until the conjurer has wrought himself into a kind of phrenzy, he then pretends to have caught this said spirit and exhibits it in the shape of a small pebble or piece of Ivory which has hitherto been secreted in his hand or Mouth and calls for assistance to overpower this turbulent spirit when all present lend their aid to the conjurer in dragging it to the River for the purpose of being Drowned which occasions a violent struggle:—if the conjurer thinks the patient will recover he declares with triumphant shouts that he has conquered the Spirit but on the contrary he admits that it has got the better of him and made its escape back to the patient which Seals his fate. When the conjurers themselves are afflicted by sickness they undergo similar treatment. These conjurers or men of Medicine live by their profession and are much respected by all classes who never venture to question their skill and conceive that they have the power of conjuring or praying them to Death at pleasure and even from a distance. When the patient Dies, the body is placed in a canoe with his most valuable property and interred and if he is a man of consequence all the relatives go into mourning by cropping their hair allowing their beards to grow and exhibiting no ornaments for a given time; they had an inhuman practise of sacrificing Slaves on such occasions but it is now wearing away in consequence of the interference of the Whites; Concomely however killed one a few months ago on the Death of his Son before we were aware that such was his intention and excused himself by saying that the Slave was dangerously ill at the time and could not have recovered so that he did not consider it a crime as it was merely anticipating Death in its regular course by a few Days or Weeks.

Slaves form the principal article of traffick on the whole of this Coast and constitute the greater part of their Riches; they are made to Fish, hunt, draw Wood & Water in short all the drudgery falls on them; they feed in common with the Family of their proprietors and intermarry with their own class, but lead a life of misery, indeed I conceive a Columbia Slave to be the most unfortunate Wretch in existence; the proprietors exercise the most absolute authority over them even to Life and Death and on the most triffling fault wound and maim them shockingly. Several of the Flat Head Women at the Establishment keep Female Slaves and it was the practise to allow them be let out among the newly arrived Servants for the purpose of prostitution; indeed the Princess of Wales (Mr McKenzie's Woman) carried on this shameful traffick to a greater extent than any other having 8 or 10 female Slaves, it is now however broke off altho with some difficulty all the Women in the Fort having come to a resolution that they would not conform to this innovation as it deprived them of a very important source of Revenue. These wretched Slaves often change proprieters two or three times in the course of a Season and when they escape a violent Death they are brought to a premature end by Disease when they are left a prey to the Dogs & Crows as they are denied the ordinary burial. Our remonstrances with the Chiefs however begin to have the effect of ameliorating the situation of those dreadfully oppressed people and Casseno the next man to Concomely in the River shews his respect for the Whites by kind treatment of his Slaves.[158]

A most inhumane practise existed here for some time after Fort George was established of the Children of the Whites by the Native Women being murdered by the Mothers; this arose from the circumstance of the Fathers insisting that the heads should not be flattened and the Mother preferring to sacrifice her child to having it ranked as a Slave the grand distinction being in the formation of the head but the custom was held in such detestation by the Whites that I believe no instance of the kind has been known for some years past.

Gambling is a favorite amusement with all Indians but par-

[158] See Appendix B, *post*, 352-356.

ticularly so with those of the Columbia, I have never had the curiosity to see any of their Games played throughout but they appear very simple merely consisting of secreting a certain number of small sticks or stones and guessing where they are placed; these Games sometimes occupy a whole Day on which large bets depend; Slaves Beads Hyaques and Blankets form the Stakes and the Slaves go to the gambling ground as composedly to be played for as to their ordinary avocations.

I have questioned some of the most intelligent Indians as to their religious notions, and opinions in regard to a future state but could not discover that they have any idea that there is a Supreme being, they however believe that rewards and punishments await them according to their deserts in an other World; the former consists of meeting their Friends & Relatives and living in ease and comfort in a fine Country, and the latter of being subjected to hard labour and Starvation in a strong Wood Country where the Navigation is dangerous:—this other World they conceive to be beyond Seas and that they must proceed thither by Water which accounts for their being buried in Canoes. They listen with great attention to our remarks on these subjects and since we have commenced reading prayers in public on Sundays at the Establishment they attend regularly and conduct themselves with great decorum.

The principal occupation of the men during the Winter is going about among the Neighbouring Indians for the purposes of trade; preparing their canoes fishing tackle &c; the Women are employed in like manner. In Spring Summer & Autumn they are chiefly occupied in Fishing and feasting, their Slaves collect Roots and the Country affords such abundant resources that they never know what starvation is altho' they are idle and lazy to an extreme. There are Thousands of Sea Otter on their Coast but they never give themselves the trouble of Hunting them; in short they are quite a Nation of Traders and not of Hunters.

Their Fishing tackle consists of Nets made from the Stalk of a shrub resembling Hemp which they prepare in like manner and which they prefer to our Twine; with these they catch the Salmon and the Indians of the upper part of the River use Scoop

Nets attached to a pole or shaft, the mouth kept open by a hoop and with this they scoop up the Fish as they are mounting the Rapids, the Fishermen standing on a projecting Rock; the Salmon are very fine until the Fall and weigh from 15 to 30 lbs.

The Sturgeon are generally speared as on the East side the Mountain and Weigh from 100 to 500 lbs. A small Fish resembling the pilchard[159] comes into the River in immence shoals, they are very delicate and are taken by dragging a Rake through the Water after a Canoe, the teeth being sharp pointed Wooden pins or Fish bones which pass through the body of the Fish and so numerous are they that every time the Rake is drawn through the Water one or more Fish appear on each Tooth. In rainy Weather in the Fall they collect Shell Fish on the shore resembling a Lobster in shape and colour also in taste but much smaller, in fact they are the Lobster in miniature. Whales and Sea Lions are occasionally found on the coast by stress of Weather and sometimes find their way into the River where they are generally killed, but the Natives make War on them from a safe distance; the Flesh and blubber they are very fond of.

Their Canoes are neatly made from the trunks of trees say from one or more according to the size; the small Canoes are about the size and after the model of a Thames Wherry and go swiftly through the Water; the War Canoes are on the same plan, good Sea Worthy Craft and will carry 30 to 40 people.

Our Iron Works are not as yet come into general use among them; they have no occasion for Hatchets to fell timber as their shores are covered with Drift Wood which they split with Wedges; in hollowing trunks of trees for Canoes or in making boards for their Houses they use a sharp edged flint Stone which answers every purpose, indeed some of their workmanship with this tool is very ingenious and well finished. Their Cooking Kettles are Baskets made of the inner skin or rind of a small shrub which is twisted into a stout thread or cord and wove so close as to hold Water and the contents are cooked by casting in from time to time heated stones so as to keep the Water constantly boiling.

The Natives male & female bathe regularly throughout the

[159] The species referred to is the ulicon, or candlefish.

year and are excellent Swimmers; they even surpass our Sandwich Islanders and remain under Water a longer time.

The great people of the Village are constantly at variance with each other, arising chiefly from jealousy of the attentions shewn them at the Fort; these misunderstandings are never attended with serious consequences we therefore keep them alive as by that means we know all that passes and have them in a certain degree under our control. The principal personage is His One Eyed Majesty Concomely a well disposed Indian; he lost two fine young men lately one of whom was to have been his successor altho the youngest; the only remaining Son Cassicus[160] is a cruel Tyrannical blood thirsty Villain who has formed several plans to cut off the Fort; he and the old man are anxious that I should take his Son a Boy of about 9 years of age for the purpose of being Educated, but the lad looks delicate and if any accident happened to him it might be attended with unpleasant reflections & perhaps consequences I am therefore as yet undetermined on the subject; the Princess of Wales (Mrs McKenzie) is much attached to us and not only leads her Husband but the whole of the Royal Family. Calpo, the next Man is nobody as his Lady rules the Roost; she is now eating bread & molasses by my Elbow and has just been taking a great deal of pains to make me acquainted with her pedigree the old Lady being very proud of her ancestry; she is the best News Monger in the Parish and through her I know more of the Scandal Secrets & politics both of the out & inside the Fort than from any other Source; she is much attached to the Whites and has repeatedly saved the Establishment from being cut off by giving timely notice of the treacherous plans of the Indians. The third in rank is Sachla but in consequence of an alliance formed lately between Chief Facter Kennedy and his Daughter, he begins to dispute precedence with Concomely & Lady Calpo, the former knows his superiority and laughs at the presumption but the latter is quite outrageous and indignant and presses hard that I should take her Daughter (a buxom Damsel of 18 or 20 who has never yet seen Day light) even for the few Weeks I have to remain here with a Dowery of 100 Beaver in

[160] For Cassicus see Corney, *Early Northern Pacific Voyages*, 65.

order to re-establish and confirm her rank; I have therefore a difficult card to play being equally desirous to keep clear of the Daughter and continue on good terms with the Mother and by management I hope to succeed in both altho her Ladyship is most pressing & persevering tempting me with fresh offers and inducements every succeeding Day.

The Climate of the Columbia is temperate regular and salubrious; on New Years Day I have seen at Fort George Pease, Carrots and Radishes in blossom and up to that Date we had neither Frost nor Snow the Thermometer being generally about temperate; below the Cascades there is a great deal of Rain from about the latter end of November until the latter end of March the Plurometer averaging about 5 Inches p Month; the Winds at that Season blow from all the points of the Compass, I did not observe that they prevailed from any particular part and are less violent than in any other part of the World in which I have been, indeed I cannot say that we experienced a strong Gale of Wind while in the Columbia. In the course of the Winter there are occasionally falls of Snow, but they are of short duration and it melts away almost immediately; we had no Frost before the Month of January and very little afterwards. From the beginning of April until the month of November the Weather is delightful, the heat never oppressive as for three or Four hours during the height of the Sun there is always a refreshing Sea breeze.

The Soil is poor at Fort George being a mixture of Clay & Sand, it however produces excellent Potatoes Cabbages & Turnips these being the only Vegetables that have had a fair trial and altho considerable quantities of different kinds of seed Grain have been sent hither from England and the United States I cannot learn that any trouble has been taken to ascertain if it would yield returns. We have however accidentally discovered that Oats will grow as a few Stalks made their appearance last year from seed that fell into the Ground from among the Sweepings of the Fort.

Timber grows to a prodigious size say Cedar Oak Hemlock Pine &c &c there is the trunk of an old Cedar still standing close to the Fort exceeding 300 feet in heighth and 42 in. circumference without the bark. At Fort George the ground is so uneven that a Farm to any considerable extent cannot be made and there are not above 15 to 20 acres where a Plough can be used, on the contrary at the Jolie Prairie or Belle vue Point where the New Fort is situated it may be from time to time enlarged to any number of acres or even miles without the trouble of felling a tree.

I do not know any part of North America where the Natives could be civilized and instructed in morality and Religion at such a moderate expence and with so much facility as on the Banks of the Columbia River; on the East side the Mountain it does not appear to me practicable on account of the erratick Life the Indians lead changing their Encampments almost Daily and the great difficulty nay utter impossibility of procuring the means of subsistance for any considerable body of people until cultivation becomes a principal object of attention among them; but in many parts of the Columbia they are settled in Villages; the River affords ample provision and the Earth yields spontaneously nutricious Roots in abundance. The praise worthy zeal of the Missionary Society[161] in the cause of Religion I think would here be soon crowned with success; they would not only have the satisfaction of ameliorating the condition of an immence savage population but of extending Christianity to regions where there is not even the idea of the existance of a Supreme being. I have spoken to several of the Chiefs & principal men on the subject of forming Establishments on their Lands for Religious purposes and they have assured me that nothing could afford them so much delight as having Spiritual instructors among them. There are two or three places in this part of the Country which I would particularly recommend for this object viz., the Neighbourhood of the Cascade Portage on the Columbia, Spokan House, and the Forks of Thompsons and Frazers Rivers; at these three places the Indians live in Villages; the Soil is capable of the highest cultivation and the Waters produce Fish in abundance; cattle & Hogs could be reared in any number and the few European supplies that would be required could be had at a moderate Expence.

[161] Refers to the London Missionary Society.

If the Society were to determine on sending Missionaries, it would be proper that they should be engaged for a series of years certainly not less than Five as new faces and changes of system would occasion great difficulties, moreover the Comp^y could not undertake to provide interpreters as we are so ignorant of the Languages that most of our negotiations are carried on in dumb show; it would therefore be necessary for those Gentlemen to apply themselves closely to the study of the Languages and I do not think that in less than a couple of years they could make themselves sufficiently understood to convey much instruction. I shall here endeavour to form a rough estimate of the Expence that an Establishment of this description might cost the first year, viz.,

Sal^y to Clergyman supposed to be about p Annum	£150
Wages of 2 Servants for the purposes of Gardening, &c	60
40 pieces Goods necessaries Luxuries and for the purpose of bartering for provisions valued at £8 each	320
Freight from the Coast to be regulated by the distance, if to the Cascades not exceeding £5. If to the Forks of Frazers and Thompsons River and that Indians could be prevailed on to undertake the Voyage about £10 on the contrary if done by the Co^ys Servants about £100 and if to Spokan House about the same amount	100
Contingencies, Books, &c	50
	£680

All Expenses might the first year be estimated at or come up to £700 for either the Establishment of Spokan or the Forks of Frazers River, but thereafter it would not exceed half that amount and would be reducing annually to merely the Saly^s of the Clergyman & Servants with the few imported necessaries they might require; and near the Coast either on the Banks of the Columbia or Frazers River it would not even the first year exceed about £500 as being near the Co^ys Establishment we could render it much assistance without inconvenience or Expence.

The Society should place the Clergyman in a certain degree under the protection of the Coy's representative (say the Chief Facter in charge of the District) and direct him to look up to that Gentleman for support and assistance in almost every thing as a superior; on the contrary if he attempts to dictate or act independently of, or in opposition to the views & wishes of that Gentleman it is to be feared they will not draw together. The Missionary ought to be cool and temperate in his habits and of a Mild conciliatory disposition even tempered and not too much disposed to find fault severely with any little laxity of Morals he may discover at the Coy's Establishment otherwise 'tis to be feared he would find his situation uncomfortable and it might even interfere with the objects of his Mission; he ought to understand in the outset that nearly all the Gentlemen & Servants have Families altho' Marriage ceremonies are unknown in the Country and that it would be all in vain to attempt breaking through this uncivilised custom. On no other score would he have serious grounds of complaint as the conduct of our people in general is perfectly correct decorous & proper when well managed.

There may be a difference of opinion as to the effect the conversion of the Indians might have on the trade; I cannot however forsee that it could be at all injurious, on the contrary I believe it would be highly beneficial thereto as they would in time imbibe our manners and customs and imitate us in Dress; our Supplies would thus become necessary to them which would increase the consumption of European produce & manufactures and in like measure increase & benefit our trade as they would find it requisite to become more industrious and to turn their attention more seriously to the Chase in order to be enabled to provide themselves with such supplies; we should moreover be enabled to pass through their Lands in greater safety which would lighten the expence of transport, and supplies of Provisions would be found at every Village and among every tribe; they might likewise be employed on extraordinary occasions as runners Boatsmen &c and their Services in other respects turned to profitable account.

The Honble Committee I am satisfied will take this view of the subject and there are a few of the most enlightened in this Country who would do so likewise but there are others (and I am almost ashamed to say Members of our Council) who would condemn it as being wild & visionary and ruinous to the Fur Trade without even taking the trouble of thinking seriously thereon or looking at the question in all its bearings and important consequences.

The Success of this object so much depends on the character and disposition of the Missionary that the Society could not be too particular in the Selection of a Gentleman to fill the situation; if he makes himself agreeable to the principal officers in the Service all will go on well and he will be supported on all occasions but on the contrary there is much reason to apprehend that disappointment vexation and even more serious evils might be the result.[162]

Until these last two or three years the use of Spiritous Liquors was unknown among the Natives and nothing gave them such a contemptible opinion of the Whites as seeing them (the common men) deprive themselves of reason thereby on particular occasions; but I am concerned to say that as they got familiarized to those scenes they became fond of indulging themselves in like manner and are now getting as much addicted to Drunkenness as the tribes on the East side the Mountain; this baneful habit arose from the Custom of giving a Dram every time they brought Furs which at first there was some difficulty in prevailing on them to accept; it however very soon became agreeable, they were then allowed a present of a Bottle of Rum for every 10 Skins they brought and latterly they have traded Provisions and even Furs for this article which has been so injurious throughout the Indian Country. We have however put a stop to this Traffick since our arrival here and determined on prohibiting the use thereof among the Indians altogether; it may affect the

[162] Missionaries did not come to the Columbia Valley until almost a decade after this proposal was made. Then a group of Americans headed by Jason Lee established in 1834 the Methodist Mission in the Willamette Valley. It was not until 1836 that the first English missionary, Rev. Herbert Beaver, came to Fort Vancouver.

Trade for one Season but I am satisfied it will ultimately be advantageous to the Co[ys] interests and highly beneficial to the Natives. The Most and only effectual Means of preventing its being again introduced is to limit the imports to a very small quantity barely sufficient to give an occasional treat to the Servants. The introduction of Spirits was here no doubt done with the best intentions as a stimulant to the exertions of the Natives and in hopes that it would soon become a cheap article of trade but instead of its having that effect it would in a very short time be ruinous to the Fort George trade particularly as the Indians are not Hunters but Dealers or Agents to the Neighbouring tribes so that if they were allowed to Drink the Value of the Furs they bring, they would not have the Means of continuing the Barter and we should be the sufferers in the long run; but in order to ensure good & constant returns and extend the trade to advantage we must endeavour to encourage the Consumption of Woolens and other useful British Manufactures which will in due time become necessary to the Natives from habit, when they must and will work to supply their wants, viewing the subject therefore in connexion with the trade alone I consider the introduction of spiritous Liquors as the most short sighted policy that could have been adopted and no effort of mine shall be wanting to prevent its being again brought into use among the Natives of this side the Mountain.[163]

Game is so abundant at this place that we have almost lived entirely on Geese Ducks & Swans they are not however so fat & delicate as those we have Spring & Fall on the East side the mountain. I have seen no Grouse and I do not learn that there are any on the Coast they are however numerous about Spokane

[163] Simpson was able to maintain with fair consistency the humane policy of restricting the trade in spirits on the west side of the Rocky Mountains. Dr. McLoughlin at Fort Vancouver gave him in this his vigorous support. At times the competition of American traders along the coast and in the Columbia forced departures from the rule, but Dr. McLoughlin was reluctant to meet this type of opposition in kind, and on several occasions purchased the liquor stock of American competitors in the Columbia with the purpose of putting it in storage at Fort Vancouver. On the Russian frontier Simpson negotiated an agreement with the Russian American Company in 1842 not to traffic in liquor with the Indians in territories where the two companies came into competition.

and Walla Walla and of a larger kind than we have in England. Several kinds of fresh Water or Swamp & Marine Birds are likewise numerous also a great variety of Eagles & Hawks and many small Birds which I do not recollect having seen before; Specimens of all that can be collected will be forwarded to the Hon[ble] Committee by the next Ship.

There are no Deer so low down as this place but they are so numerous about the Jolie Prairie say the Stag or Red Deer and the Chevreuil or Roe that a good Cree Hunter could support a small Establishment; I expect however we shall soon be independent of the Chase in the way of living as with a little attention to our Farm we shall be enabled to rear more Beef and Pork than will be required for the business of the whole Department; had any pains been taken in that way much expence might have been saved for several years past in Imported Provisions but the good people of Fort George have been so averse to the rearing of live Stock and so dainty that they would not Eat their sucking Pigs but by way of keeping down the Stock and for want of more rational pastime actually used to amuse themselves in practising Pistol Shooting by making War on the poor little Grunters at Twelve paces distance; we shall soon however I expect turn them to better account.

Throughout the Columbia there is a great variety of wild fruits viz., Strawberries, Rasberries Currents, Cranberries, Blackberries, Gooseberries and many others the names of which I do not know. The Natives are very fond of fruits which at certain Seasons form a principal article of subsistance with them; they are Eat Raw boiled & baked and formed into a kind of thick pudding which when Cold hardens & keeps throughout the Season.

There is likewise a great variety of Roots which are used raw, Boiled Roasted & baked and are both palatable & nutricious; specimens of these will be sent home and I have no doubt will be found curious as many of them are not known in other parts of America.

The Columbia presents a wide field for botanical research as there is a very great variety of Plants to be found every where;

I regret exceedingly that my ignorance of that interesting branch of Science prevents my attempting any description of them. indeed any one of experience in the study of natural history generally would add much to his stock of knowledge therein by a visit to this part of the World. Specimens of every kind within our reach will this season be sent Home as I have given directions to that effect at the different Establishments being unable to attend thereto myself a variety of duties connected with the general business fully occupying the limited time at my disposal while in the Country.

I have examined with much attention the different charts and maps that have appeared of this Country but none of them give any thing like a correct idea thereof Rivers Lakes Mountains Plains & Forests being introduced and disposed as suited the fancy and taste of the Draftsmen and some of the writers have had the effrontery to Gull the public with the produce of their own fertile imaginations differing widely from the truth and with descriptions of Countries they have never seen and which had not been explored when their works came from the Press. Many parts then unknown have since been examined and from various Sources that can be depended on we have with much pains and trouble collected materials and in the course of the Winter made out a sketch or rough draft of all the Country that has been traversed or explored by Whites on this side the Mountain and which altho not finished so well as I could have wished gives a more correct view thereof than any that has yet appeared.

The different Establishments and points where observations have been taken are placed according to the Latitudes & Longitudes given us on Mr Thompson's Chart[164] and the relative situations in regard to distances where observations have not been taken are given and regulated according to the length of time occupied in going from one place to an other either by Land or Water. This draft will be forwarded to the Honble Committee[165]

[164] David Thompson's large-scale map covering what is now western Canada and the Pacific Northwest of the United States, a work resting on twenty years of exploration and survey (1792-1812), is reproduced in Coues, *Henry and Thompson Journals*, map pocket at the end of Volume III.

[165] No manuscript map of the kind here described could be located in the archives of the Hudson's Bay Company.

who may perhaps allow Arrowsmith[166] to correct his map thereby which in its present state is very erroneous.

Having touched on every point which appears to me interesting connected with the Indian Trade and Natives of the Columbia likewise with the adjoining Country its resources and productions I shall follow Mr McMillan in his perilous and harrassing Voyage to the Northward, which I have the pleasure to say has been accomplished greatly to his own credit and to my utmost satisfaction.

The Country North of this place as far as the Southern Shores of Pugets Sound was visited some years ago by a small trapping party one of whom an Iroquay was Robbed & Murdered by the Natives. Mr Ogden after a lapse of a few months was sent in command of a party to avenge this murder; they adopted the Indian mode of Warfare surprised a camp of the Natives and a disgusting and inhuman scene of Carnage followed, no less than thirteen of the poor Wretches being destroyed before they had an opportunity of even making an attempt at resistance; he then returned to Fort George without holding any further Communication with the Natives and up to this period no reconciliation or peace has been effected.[167]

This affair prevented our prosecuting the trade to the Northward and since that time we have never ventured beyond the banks of the Cowlutch [Cowlitz] River. The dangers of a visit to

[166] Refers to Aaron Arrowsmith, founder of a famous London family of cartographers, who for many years had the privilege of disseminating to the world the geographical discoveries of the Hudson's Bay Company in North America. He issued his first important map of North America in 1795-96 with the inscription, "A map exhibiting all the New Discoveries in the interior parts of North America inscribed by permission to the Honorable Governor and Company of Adventurers of England Trading into Hudson's Bay In testimony of their liberal communications to their most obedient and very Humble Servant, A. Arrowsmith." This map, revised to keep pace with the progress of discovery by the fur companies and others in North America, was issued in many later editions. In 1823 Aaron Arrowsmith died and his sons, Aaron and Samuel, took charge of the business. It is possible that the Hudson's Bay Company carried out Simpson's suggestion of placing the rough manuscript draft of his map at the disposal of the Arrowsmiths, but it was not until 1832 that an important new edition of the 1795 map, with corrections for the region west of the Rocky Mountains, made its appearance

[167] For another account of this affair see Ross, *Fur Hunters*, I, 190-196.

the Northward were magnified to such a degree from the treacherous & blood thirsty character we had of the Natives that it would have been considered the height of insanity to think of opening any intercourse or communication with them; but after repeated enquiries I could not obtain distinct information to justify all this alarm and seeing the importance of gaining a knowledge of Frazers River and the adjacent country before any regular plan could be determined on in remodelling this Department I resolved on fitting out an Expedition with that view of which Chief Trader McMillan was appointed to the command aided by Messrs Work Annance and McKay Clerks; the party in all consisting of Forty Two (see my Letter of instructions Dated 17th November).[168] They started from hence on the 19th November in three Boats, made various portages and fell on the Southern Shores of Pugets Sound and proceeded along shore to the Mouth of Frazers River holding communication with the Natives as they prosecuted their route. The Channel which divides Vancouvers Island from the Main land they found studed with Islands which afford a safe and well sheltered navigation for any Craft. The Shores of the Main land they found densely peopled the Natives being collected in Villages. They had not an opportunity of exploring or examining the interior country with attention as the Season was extremely unfavourable and the small stock of Provisions they were enabled to take did not admit of their devoting much time to that object, yet from the Natives they learnt that the Country abounded with Deer and that Beaver were numerous on all the small Streams with which it is so much intersected, and this report was fully confirmed by their own observation as wherever they landed they found traces of large and fur bearing animals. The Natives received them well they got guides and interpreters from tribe to tribe and succeeded in leaving a favourable impression in regard to the Whites, by distributing small presents among the principal Men and treating them with attention.

The Guides instead of going on direct to the Mouth of Frazers River conducted them by a small Stream which fell into the

[168] This letter could not be found in the archives of the Hudson's Bay Company.

Channel dividing Vancouvers Island from the Main land to the Southward of the Mouth of Frazers River. This small Stream they ascended then made a portage and fell on an other small Stream which emptied itself into the Main River about Twenty Miles above its mouth.[169] Throughout this inland communication they saw numerous bands of Red Deer and Chevreuil and vestiges of Beaver every where that appear to have been allowed the undisturbed possession of their peaceful retreats since the beginning of time. The Main River they found to be a fine large Stream navigable so far by craft of about One Hundred Tons; they proceeded up about Forty Miles further say in all about Sixty Miles from its Mouth beyond which the influence of the Tide is not much felt, and in the course of that distance they did not see a Shoal or Rapid; the narrowest part about ¾ths of a Mile Wide and expanding to a Mile and in some places 1¼ Miles with occasional Islands, but on each side of those Islands the River maintained the same character. The Natives at first sight mistook them for a War party belonging to some of the neighbouring tribes and began to prepare for defence, but when they discovered they were Whites they received them with open arms and communicated freely with them. Their Language has some affinity to that spoken by the Pescahouse tribe in the vicinity of Okenagan which enabled Mr McMillan to converse directly with the Chiefs to whom he stated the object of his visit. They appeared delighted at the prospect of having us settled among them, having often heard of Whites altho' they had never before seen them and assured Mr McMillan that Furs being the object of our research we should have abundance as their Lands were richly stocked with Beaver. They had several articles of our supplies such as Capôts Blankets Dags [Daggers] and Knives which reached them through the medium of other tribes settled on the upper parts of the River and spoke of the Kamloops tribe as their neighbours and of our Establishment at Thompsons River altho' they had never been so high.

169 The route of the expedition may be worked out in detail from the journal of John Work in *Washington Hist. Quart.*, III, 198-228. The small streams referred to in the sentence are the Nicomekl and Salmon rivers.

I had instructed Mr McMillan to proceed up to Thompsons River if practicable but which at the time appeared to me doubtful on account of the advanced state of the Season and this apprehension he discovered to be well founded as the Chiefs informed him that about Twenty Miles higher up the River had been set fast with Ice several Days and being unprovided with Snow Shoes Sledges and the means of undertaking a Winter Journey in a strange Country and among Natives with whom he was unacquainted he determined on returning by the route he went.

In the Brigade there was a Canadian "Prevost" who accompanied Messrs Frazer & Stewart to this River some years ago; he recognized every remarkable place which he even described to Mr McMillan before reaching them so accurately that that Gentleman knew them immediately which is a conclusive proof that it is the identical River called Frazers or New Caledonia River and by the Natives "Cowitchen" deriving its Indian Name from the Tribe occupying its mouth known all along the Coast as the Cowitchen Indians.

The entrance of the River he found to be situated between Point Roberts and Point Gray which he recognised by Vancouvers Chart in his possession and which would therefore place it in about Latitude 49.15 North. Near the entrance there is a Shoal or sand bank which extends a considerable way North and South, but through which there is a clear channel of from 3 to 7 fathoms Water; the land is low inside this Shoal and covered with high Grass & Willows which gives it the appearance of an extended Marsh or Swamp (in fact it is so or more properly speaking a quag mire or according to the Canadian phraseology a Ventre de Boeuf as the Weight and Motion of a person Walking thereon shakes it for a considerable distance) which accounts for Vancouver's not having discovered it, and the only indication of a large River emptying itself at this place is the freshness of the Water and the numerous trunks and roots of Trees strewed along and sticking on this Shoal.

At the mouth of the River there is a large Village the population of which he estimates at... Souls.

The Natives describe the River as far as they know or have heard of it say to the confluence of Kamloops or Thompsons River to be a fine large bold stream and not barred by dangerous rapids or falls.[170] The Banks as far as Mr McMillan ascended were clothed with a great variety of prodigious fine large Timber. The Soil appeared to be rich and fertile; good situations for the site of an Establishment in every reach and many beautiful clear spots adapted for Agricultural purposes, but the entrance of the small River falling in from the South down which he went in gaining the Main Stream he particularly recommends as there is an extensive meadow where any number of Cattle & Pigs may be kept and where the Plough can be immediately used at a little distance; and by barring up this small Stream or forming a Weir, a sufficient quantity of Salmon & Sturgeon might be taken at the proper Seasons for the maintenance of the Establishment without rendering it necessary to have recourse to the Natives for the means of subsistance. Starvation however is out of the question in this River as the Country affords abundance of Game, Fish can be had in any quantity and if every other resource failed Nutricious Roots and Shell Fish are so numerous that no one who wishes to Eat need be hungry.

Between Frazers River and the Columbia there is no large River, but there are a great many small Streams or Rivulets; and the Natives of Frazers River do not know any large Stream to the Northward yet we are aware that the Chilcotin River[171] which we suppose Sir Alexander McKenzie to have descended determining its mouth in Latitude 52.20 at Vancouvers Cascade Canal cannot be exceeding about 180 Miles distant and the mouth of the Babine River about 2 or 3 degrees farther.

Mr McMillan found the country between Pugets sound and the entrance of Frazers River to answer Vancouvers description nearly level or rather a very gentle ascent for about 30 to 40 Miles from the Coast, and Mountanous behind. The Country

[170] This is as incorrect a description of the portion of the Fraser River here referred to as it well could be. As a matter of fact the river is there altogether unnavigable. For a correct description of it see the letter of Simpson to the British Foreign Office of January, 1826, which is printed in Appendix A, *post*, 265.

[171] Present Bellaleula River.

about Frazers River bears nearly the same character with this difference that the Mountains lay further back say from 60 to 80 Miles from its Mouth. The Mountain Sheep and Goat must inhabit this part of the Country as the Natives have Blankets manufactured by themselves of the Hair and Wool; they are good substantial clothing and are wove uncommonly well. I regret he did not see the process of Manufacture, specimens of them will however be forwarded to the Honble Committee as a curiosity.

The Village before mentioned at the Mouth of Frazers River appears to me an admirable situation for a Missionary Establishment; on this subject I shall take the liberty of addressing Mr Harrison of the Honble Committee who I am rejoiced to find takes a very particular and lively interest in ameliorating the condition of the savage inhabitants of this continent and in their moral and Religious Instruction.

Messrs McMillan & Work have prepared a Journal[172] of the Voyage and Chart or rough sketch of their route and Messrs Annance and McKay have furnished similar documents which were handed to me by M^r McMillan accompanied by a Letter or general report of the Expedition which I shall have much pleasure in transmitting to the Honble Committee.

The information acquired on this Voyage will no doubt be highly interesting to the Honble Committee and important in determining the plan on which the business of this side the Mountain is to be in future conducted; the complete and masterly way in which it has been executed reflects much credit on the Gentleman to whom the charge thereof was entrusted and in justice to him I must say that since my acquaintance with the Indian Country I have seen nothing of the kind gone through so satisfactorily; it was one of the principal objects I had in view in visiting the Columbia and in the space of 42 short rainy Winter Days when the people would otherwise have been laying idle at Fort George it has been accomplished without incurring an Expence of £10.

[172] McMillan's journal appears, in extract, in Appendix A, *post,* 248 ff. Work's Journal is in *Washington Hist. Quart.*, III, 198-228.

I have already dwelt so long on the advantageous prospects which the Coasting trade holds forth if conducted with enterprise spirit and activity from Frazers River and the important savings and gains that would be realized by transferring the principal Depot from the Columbia to the same place and making but one Department of the whole West side the Mountain to be outfitted from that Depot that I have scarcely left myself room to say more on the subject I shall therefore Wind up by expressing my earnest and anxious hope that the Honble Committee may see it in the same light that I do and by adopting the plan or scheme I am about to submit to their consideration connected therewith give me an opportunity of shewing what can be done in this new and valuable country and for the labour danger and anxiety it may cost me personally if I have again to visit this coast the satisfaction of benefitting the general concern is the only recompense I aim at or look to.

Duplicates of the Invoice & Bill of Lading of the homeward Cargo of the Vigilant will be forwarded to the Honble Committee; that Vessel arrived here on the 25th of August, delivered her cargo in good order and took her departure on the 7th October. Her safe arrival here was certainly more owing to good fortune than good management as from all I am able to collect her Captain and Mate did not confine themselves to their bare allowance of Grog on the passage and the former was so much reduced by hard Drinking and Scurvy before the conclusion of the Voyage that it was necessary to carry him on Deck when ever his assistance was required. Had any accident happened to him the probability is that the Ship would never have made the Columbia, as altho' the Mate was a very good hard Working hard Drinking practical Seaman, he was totally unfit for even the temporary command of a Vessel, held Lunar and Astronomical observations in utter contempt from sheer ignorance and had no influence or controul over the Crew. Captn Davidsons talent as a Navigator I know nothing about, but his talent as a Grog Drinker I understand is without parallel and I shall be agreeably surprised if he and his Ship ever reach the Port of Destination. It is highly important that any Vessel coming on this Voyage should be well officered as in the event of a loss on the Outward passage the trade would be most seriously affected. The two last Vessels that came here, have made the Coast of America soon after leaving the Galipagos which has occasioned very tedious passages as the North West Winds are found to prevail on the Coast at that Season, but by Steering to the Longitude of the Sandwitch Islands after crossing the Line, they would fall in with the trade Winds which would sooner enable them to gain their Latitude.

The Captains should be bound down both for themselves and the Ships Company under a heavy penalty to have no Trade or Barter with the Natives; and all dealings with them for Fish or other articles of Provisions should be through us while the Ship is in Port which would prevent misunderstandings and difficulties both with us and the Natives.

It is highly important that the Ship should arrive here in the Month of June or by the 10th of July at latest as the Brigades from the Interior cannot without great injury to the Trade remain later than the middle of July at Fort George.

In the event of our Trade on this Coast increasing so as to render it necessary to have a Ship from England Annually, which I think is not improbable in the course of Two or three years hence, and particularly so if we can open any commerce with the Russians to the Northward or the Spaniards to the Southward in British Produce or Manufactures, I should in that case recommend that the Coy have two Ships of the Tonnage that may be required for the Trade; each Voyage will occupy two years and to be employed as follows. Suppose the Ship of the Season to start from London on the 1st Novemr 1825 with the Columbia Cargo, she will arrive about the Middle of May or beginning of June 1826 at the Coys Depot on this Coast take on the Furs making up the Cargo with pickled Salmon & Spars and start for Canton 1st July, deliver her Cargo, take in a Cargo of Teas or other China produce for the East India Coy and start from Canton (for London) 1st October and be in England so as to repeat the Voyage 1st Novr 1827.

If the small Furs taken on this Coast are unsaleable in China they can be sent Home via Canton by the Ship. The article of pickled or Salted Salmon I understand is in request in Canton and commands a price of 40/ to 50/ Stg p Barrel; if this be the case it might become a valuable branch of Trade to the Co[y] as any quantity may be procured in this River Annually at a price not exceeding 16/ p Barrel as p the following calculation, viz.:—

35 Salmon, contents of 1 Barrel, may be had of the Natives for	7
Barrel country made will cost	3
Salt country made will cost	3
Coopers attendance packing transport and other contingent expences will am[t] to	3
Cost p Barrel Sterling[173]	16/

[173] Salmon, as an article of export, was being experimented with at Fort George by the officers of the Hudson's Bay Company as early as 1823. Not much progress was made at first. "The Barrel of salmon sent home as a sample," the Governor and Committee write on July 22, 1824, to the Chief Factors of the Columbia Department, "will not answer, and it could not be used; the expence of keeping up an establishment is considered too great, for altho' the Fish may be taken in the highest perfection, yet by a neglect in the curing and packing it, it may, as was the case in the present instance, be unsaleable when brought to this country." Gen. Letter Book 621. Again the Governor and Committee write on July 27, 1825, "The salmon was of superior quality to that received by the Lively; we are, however, of opinion, that from the difficulty of curing this fish properly, and the length of time it must unavoidably continue in pickle, that it will not answer as an article of commerce." Gen. Letter Book 621. The difficulties of curing seem by 1831 to have been partly overcome, and a regular export had developed, as may be seen from an extract of a letter written at Fort Langley, Feb. 20, 1831, by Chief Trader Archibald McDonald. "Am now preparing from 2 to 300 Barrels to be at the salmon immediately in the commencement of the season—they say a cooper is come across for me but we saw nothing of him yet. In consequence of my Casks of last season losing the pickle, the Dr. [McLoughlin] sent none of them to market but sent his own, and kept ours for home consumption, so the end is always assured and perhaps this ought at all times to be the arrangement as the Columbia fish is acknowledged better than ours. Curious they are caught a week or two sooner at the bridge than here—last season it was approaching the end of August before they appeared here." *Washington Hist. Quart.*, I, 259. The chief market for the salmon during the fur-trade period was the Hawaiian Islands. A market in Canton was not attempted owing to the decision of the Hudson's Bay Company not to attempt a direct fur trade there.

Ship Spars is likewise a valuable article at Canton and no part of the World can produce finer than this Coast and at no expence or trouble.

Having now stated every thing that appears to me worthy of remark as connected with the Trade &c while at this place and the time having arrived when it is necessary to commence my return Voyage I shall note our progress thereon with whatever strikes me as deserving of notice from Day to Day.

Wednesday, March 16th. 1825. The business of the Season being now wound up and the Spring sufficiently advanced to admit of my commencing my return Voyage I took my departure at 12 o'clock A. M. to Day from (Fort George) the Shores of the Pacific for those of the Atlantic accompanied by Messrs Kennedy & McMillan with Four Boats, two of them intended to proceed with us to the Mountain and the other Two laden with supplies for the Snake Expedition in case it may not be enabled to come lower down than Fort Nez Percés.

All the valuable property having been transported to the new Establishment at Belle Vue Point,[174] Dr McLoughlin accompanied us to take charge thereof leaving Mr McKenzie, Cartie & Eight men at Fort George where they are to remain for two or three weeks until the few remaining articles are removed.

The poor Chinooks appeared in great distress at being deserted by us and my old Friend His Majesty "Concomely" actually shed Tears when I shook hands with him at the Water side; the fair Princess "Chowie" I have reason to believe was not less affected, but they were all somewhat consoled by my assurance that they would soon again see me among them and for various reasons I sincerely hope that may be the case. I have the satisfaction to feel that the present visit has been productive of most important advantages to the Honble Coys interests; the Work of reform is not yet however thoroughly effected and to put the whole Machine in full play I find that my presence is absolutely necessary on this side the Mountain one more Winter at least. I can scarcely account for the extraordinary interest I have taken

[174] Refers to Fort Vancouver which had been built during the winter of 1824-25.

in its affairs, the subject engrosses my attention almost to the exclusion of every other, in fact the business of this side has become my hobby and however painful dangerous and harrassing the duty may be I do not know any circumstance that would give me more real satisfaction and pleasure than the Honble Committee's authority to take a complete survey of and personally superintend the extension and organization of their Trade on this Coast for 12 or 18 Months and if they do so I undertake to make its commerce more valuable to them than that of either of the Factories in Rupert's Land.[175] Incessant Rain throughout the Day we however pushed on to "McKenzies Encamp^t" near Oak Point where we put up for the Night.

Thursday, March 17th. Renewed our March at Day break and Encamped at the lower branch of the Wilhamot at Dusk; Casseno, who is the principal Chief about this part of the River and one of our best customers visited us with a supply of Fish for Supper. Both Casseno and Cassicus (Concomely's eldest Son) offered to put a son each under my care for the purpose of being Educated at the Missionary Society's School in Red River Settlement but the Boys appeared too young & delicate to undergo the Labour and hardship of Crossing the Mountain at this early Season and as any accident happening to them might be seriously taken up by the Indians I thought it most prudent to leave them and did so in such a manner as not to give offence to their Fathers who may be considered the principal Men below Walla Walla.

Friday, March 18th. Continued our route before Sun rise and got to Belle Vue Point at 11 o'Clock A. M. The Establishment is beautifully situated on the top of a bank about 1¼ Miles from the Water side[176] commanding an extensive view of the River the

[175] The two factories in Rupert's Land were York Factory representing the Northern Department and Moose Factory representing the Southern.

[176] Fort Vancouver, as laid out by Simpson, was intended to be no more than a trading post. The main depôt of the Columbia Department was intended to be, as indicated earlier in this journal, a fort built at the mouth of Fraser River. When, however, Fraser River was found to be unnavigable, Fort Vancouver had to be accepted as the Department base. That made necessary relocating its buildings nearer the water's edge, which was done in 1828-29.

surrounding Country and the fine plain below which is watered by two very pretty small Lakes and studed as if artificially by clumps of Fine Timber. The Fort is well picketted covering a space of about ¾ths of an acre and the buildings already completed are a Dwelling House, two good Stores an Indian Hall and temporary quarters for the people. It will in Two Years hence be the finest place in North America, indeed I have rarely seen a Gentleman's Seat in England possessing so many natural advantages and where ornament and use are so agreeably combined. This point if situated within One Hundred Miles of London would be more valuable to the proprietor than the Columbian Trade. In the Evening had an interview with the Wilhamot Freemen and sounded them about joining our Expedition to the Umpqua;[177] they were rather shy on account of their numerous Families and the hostile character of the Natives, we are however perfectly independent of them and on the whole I would be better pleased that they did not go. Determined on bringing Thos McKay along with us to Walla Walla for the purpose of taking down about Forty Horses for the use of the Expedition. Sat up all Night making various arrangements.

Saturday, March 19th. At Sun rise mustered all the people to hoist the Flag Staff of the new Establishment and in presence of the Gentlemen, Servants, Chiefs & Indians I Baptised it by breaking a Bottle of Rum on the Flag Staff and repeating the following words in a loud voice, "In behalf of the Honble Hudsons Bay Coy I hereby name this Establishment *Fort Vancouver* God Save King George the 4th" with three cheers. Gave a couple of Drams to the people and Indians on the occasion. The object of naming it after that distinguished navigator is to identify our claim to the Soil and Trade with his discovery of the River and Coast on behalf of Gt Britain. If the Honble Committee however do not approve the Name it can be altered. At 9 o'Clock A. M. took leave of our Friend the Dr, embarked and continued our Voyage. Put up for the night about 20 Miles below the Cascade Portage.

[177] For the Umpqua Expedition see *ante*, 88, 89 n.

Sunday, March 20th. Started before Day break, got to the Cascade Portage about 10 o'Clock A. M. found about 100 Indians there but they were very friendly. Occupied in making the Portage until Sun Set and Encamped a few Miles above; kept watch but had no visitors.

Monday, March 21st. Raised Camp before Day break, saw a number of Natives and gave a pipe of Tobacco to the Principal Men, they all seem well disposed. Put up close to an Indian Village about two Miles below the Dalles and were visited by about 70 to 80 Natives at our Encampment. Kept watch altho' scarcely necessary.

Tuesday, March 22nd. The weather has been delightfully fine since we left Belle Vue Point, and to Day the heat was actually oppressive. On the tops of the distant Hills we see a little Snow, but along the banks of the River vegetation is in a forward state. Made a demi discharge of a Mile at the Dalles and carried the whole of the Baggage at the little Dalles. Made the Chûtes Portage and Encamped at the upper end. Surrounded by Indians all Day who assisted us on the Portage and conducted themselves with great propriety, indeed from what I have seen of the Natives on the Communication I am satisfied that if any serious evil or difference arises hereafter with them it will be our own fault as notwithstanding the bad character they bear I should not hesitate to pass up or down the River with merely the Crew of my Single Canoe.[178] The Muschetoes commenced their persecuting visitations this Eveng, they are larger than those on the East side the Mountain but their sting not so full of venom.

Wednesday, March 23d. Had a long conversation in the course of the Night (as we all kept watch) with a Chief called the "Blue Capot" who has been on the banks of the Umpqua and describes the Country very rich in Beaver the Indians peaceable

[178] Simpson's confidence in these Indians received a rude shock in 1829 when he traversed the "Chutes" portage a second time. They undertook to pillage his party, and were held off only by a narrow and exciting margin. See Simpson, *Journey Round the World*, I, 164-167.

and large Animals numerous so that I am in hopes our new Expedition will not only pick up much useful information but handsome returns; the Indian has a Woman belonging to one of those distant tribes and he agrees to accompany the Expedition with his Wife in the capacity of Guide & Interpreter. Left our Encampment at Day break, breakfasted opposite John Day's River, found the Rapids bad on account of the lowness of the Water and damaged our Boats; put up early in order to Gum & repair. The Sun very powerful to Day and much incommoded by the Clouds of Dust & Sand drifting across the River which is most injurious to the Eyes. The Country we are now passing through does not present a single Shrub & little vegetation being nothing but a Sandy desert and we have difficulty in picking up along Shore sufficient Drift Wood to Boil our Kettles.

Thursday, March 24th. Raised Camp about an hour before Day break and kept polling against a strong head Wind until Sun Set having scarcely made a Mile p Hour, and the most uncomfortable Days Travelling I recollect being enveloped in Clouds of Sand from Morning until Night. Our people are fed on Wretched fare, Pease & Beans, with no other Seasoning than a little Grease; the Pease and Beans are bad of the kind and occasion a Bowel complaint which keeps the people constantly running ashore instead of prosecuting the Voyage. The face of the Country we passed through to Day is Sand & Rock and the only symptom of Vegetation is a Solitary Wormwood bush here and there of which we can barely collect sufficient to cook our Meals.

Friday, March 25th. After noting down the occurrences of yesterday just as we were sitting down to Supper we experienced one of the most violent Storms I recollect, Strong Wind, & Rain in torrents which continued all Night and gave us a thorough drenching. Started at peep of Day, breakfasted below the big Island[179] and Encamped at the Utella River. The Weather cold and disagreeable and had much difficulty in collecting sufficient Withered Grass & Horse Dung to Boil our Kettle.

[179] Present Blalock Island.

Saturday, March 26th. Continued our route at the usual hour, breakfasted at the upper end of the Grand Rapid and reached Walla Walla about 6 o'Clock P. M. where we found Mr Dease surrounded by a Camp of about 300 Tents of Nez Percés Cai-uses, Walla Wallas & the neighbouring bands. These Indians have of late been more troublesome than usual and actually threatened to attack the Establishment arising Mr Dease supposes from the disaffection of his Interpreter who in consequence of being severely reprimanded for over intimacy with the Natives and indiscreet amours both in the Camp and at *Home* has in a fit of revenge endeavoured to incite these Tribes (over whom he has some influence) against us. I must tomorrow hold a Council with the Chiefs in order to remove this discontent and shall endeavour to dispose of the Interpreter without giving umbrage to the Indians. It is a lamentable fact that almost every difficulty we have had with Indians throughout the Country may be traced to our interference with their Women or their intrigues with the Women of the Forts in short 9 Murders out of 10 Committed on Whites by Indians have arisen through Women.

Sunday, March 27th. Occupied with Mr Dease the greater part of the Day in making various arrangements connected with the business of the Establishment. The returns have fallen off this Season about 300 Skins; this seems to have arisen from a Mortality that took place in the course of the Winter among the Cai-uses which prevented them from hunting. Sent John the Interpreter across to Spokan with Letters for Messrs Mc-Donald & Ross and directed him to meet me at the Forks where I mean to put him in Irons, bring him across the Mountain and fix him for a few years at the Coast to keep him out of harms way. In the afternoon Nine Chiefs came up from the Camp in full Dress for the purpose of holding a Council with me attended by their respective bands amounting in all to about 300 Wariors; 5 of the Chiefs were Cai-uses, 3 Nez Percés and 1 Walla Walla. I made them a speach occupying about 2 hours, gave them a Dram 2 Fathoms Tobacco 50 Ball & Powder each and about 3

Fathoms Tobacco, for the general use of the Camp. The Speech and present were well received, they promised to exert themselves in hunting, to respect the Whites, to protect us while on their Lands and begged me to assure the great Chiefs on the other side of the Water, that they had not two Mouths, one for me, an other for the Camp, that they meant what they said would act up to it and that their hearts were now exactly like those of White Men. Four Hours and many pipes of Tobacco were consumed in this Council, we parted excellent Friends, they proceeded quietly to the Camp with their followers and having finally settled with Mr Dease I at Dusk took Horse, followed the Brigade which had started about Mid Day and found them encamped near the Forks of the South branch or Louis's River.[180] Mr Dease seems most desirous to leave this Establishment but not the Deptmt and I have promised that he will be relieved next Spring, it is an anxious charge, he will then have had it Four Years and it is but fair play that some other Gentleman should now have a turn of it; he this Season remains inland with Five Men and requires no Imported Provisions in short is satisfied with the arrangements I have made generally in regard to the Post and highly approves of the contemplated extension of Trade. As an example of the Waste and extravagance of Provisions some time ago no less than Seven Hundred Horses were slaughtered for the use of this Establishment in three Years besides Imported Provisions and it has been left for me to discover that neither Horse Flesh nor Imported Provisions are at all required as the River with a Potatoe Garden will abundantly maintain the Post. Mr Dease's demands on the Depot will this Season be moderate as he has a large Inventory of remains about £400 which is a proof that no consideration or judgement was exercised in preparing his requisition of last Year and that he must have been attending to any thing except his Business; this indeed appears to have been too much the case hitherto throughout the Columbia but it must not be so in future. In order that there may be no excuse for neglecting the Gardens hereafter I brought up from Fort Vancouver Ten Bushels of Seed Potatoes

[180] South branch or Louis's River is the present Snake River.

which were delivered to Mr Dease with a long lecture on the advantages to be derived from attention to the Horticultural Deptm^t^ of the Post.

Monday, March 28th. This has been a charming Day after a Morning of Severe Frost, started about an hour before Sun rise and Encamped about half way up the Marl banks about 7 P. M. having made a tolerable Days March. Obliged to put ashore repeatedly to Day for the purpose of collecting a few Morsels of Wood to burn in the Even^g^ otherwise we could not have lighted a Fire as here there is not so much as a Willow or Wormwood Bush, in short nothing that can burn.

Tuesday, March 29th. Continued our route from before Sun rise until after Sun Set and put up about half a League below the Priests Rapid. The Weather continues fine. Myself sadly annoyed with Toothache and after many ineffectual attempts succeeded in pulling out the offender this morning with a silk thread.

Wednesday, March 30th. Started at Day break and had much labour in poling and hauling or tracking up the Priests Rapid on account of the lowness of the Water. Encamped at the head of the Rapid and were visited by the Priest[181] and his band amounting to about 100 Indians in the Even^g^ who smoked with us and went away peaceably.

Thursday, March 31st. Raised Camp about the usual hour, had a cold drizzly Rain all Day with aft Wind but not sufficiently Strong or regular to afford us much benefit. The Country still dismally barren and the banks of the River bold; on the cliff of a rock which forms the North bank of the River about 200 feet

[181] This was an Indian chief who was given his name in 1811 by a party of Pacific Fur Company trappers. Alexander Ross thought the name to be the English rendition for the Indian name *Ha-qui-laugh,* which means doctor or priest. Franchère attributed the name to the fact that the trappers saw this native performing on some others at the Rapids "certain aspersions and other ceremonies, which had the air of being coarse imitations of the Catholic worship."

above high Water Mark the trunk of a large Tree is to be seen evidently left there by the Stream but when the Cognoscenti must determine; some of our Columbia Sages will have it that it was in the Days of Noah!

Friday, April 1st. The Weather very changeable to Keen Frost in the Mong oppressive heat in the middle of the Day & heavy Rain in the Eveng. Made a poor Days Work of it having lost much time in making a portage on Isle de Pierre owing to the lowness of the Water. Saw several bands of Indians who complained of Starvation arising from their own improvidence in not laying up a sufficient quantity of Fish and Roots in the Fall. Got some fresh Meat from one of the Chiefs which is a treat as we have lived entirely on Salt Beeff and Pork since leaving Fort George. A serious accident had nearly happened through my carelessness this Eveng in firing at a Duck in the direction of the other Boats, several grains of the Shot having lodged in the Gunwale within a few inches of Mr Kennedy's Head altho at a distance of nearly 200 yds.

Saturday, April 2nd. Started at the usual hour the Weather cold & disagreeable; as we proceed to the Northward the Snow seems to approach us and vegetation is in a less forward state; put up at Dusk about a League below the Point des Bois; between the Dalles (which we passed on the 22nd ulto.) and this place there is not a single Tree of any kind and the most Sterile tract Country perhaps in North America.

Sunday, April 3d. Okanagan. We this Morning amused ourselves in the Rapids for three hours by Moon light, to the great annoyance of the Bottoms of our Craft and to us the danger of drowning in order to gain Okanagan if possible and by hard poling and paddling the Canoes reached this Post about 9 P. M. I accompanied by Mr McMillan arrived two hours earlier having borrowed Horses of Indians about 10 Miles lower down. Here I found Chief Trader McLeod who came with his people and returns from Thompson's River about a Fortnight ago; the returns are tolerable amounting to about...Skins say Kamloops producing ....& Okanagan.... The Indians of Thompsons River have conducted themselves better last Winter than the former and Mr McLeod thinks the complement of people determined on in my appropriation before mentioned sufficient altho reduced to nearly one half the number employed there for several years past. The Inventory of remains is heavy about £500 which shews that no regular estimate could have been made of the actual wants of the Post but I have so settled it that this slovenly careless mode of doing business which has hitherto been so general throughout the Columbia will not be repeated. Sat up all Night making various arrangements connected with the Posts and engaging the people who all accepted the terms proposed and are engaged for general Service not for individual Posts or to particular Masters as heretofore and with the express understanding that we are not to maintain their Families; almost every man in the District has a Family, which is productive of serious injury and inconvenience on account of the great consumption of Provisions; but by changing the men this evil will be remedied and the Women and Children sent to their Indian relatives. Mr M..... is really the most stupid useless inactive Commissioned Gentleman I have seen; his Woman and Family occupy his whole attention and the Compy's interests are become quite a secondary consideration with him; the poor (Daughter to Chief Trader P.....) is now quite deranged arising 'tis said from a fit of jealousy and the unfortunate man is nearly in as wretched a state. We must really put a stop to the practise of Gentlemen bringing their Women & Children from the East to the West side of the Mountain, it is attended with much expense and inconvenience on the Voyage, business itself must give way to domestick considerations, the Gentlemen become drones and are not disposible in short the evil is more serious than I am well able to describe, but a remedy must be applied and if I have not sufficient influence to bring it about I shall be under the disagreeable necessity of soliciting the interference of the Honble Committee; it is a lamentable fact that two Chief Traders out of Three now in the Columbia say Messrs D.... & M..... are so much under the influence of their Women and so watchful of their chastity that what they say is Law and they can not muster sufficient resolution in themselves or confidence in their Ladies to be 5 Minutes on end out of their presence and even for that short time keep them under Lock & Key altho they have more than once discovered that "Love laughs at Locksmiths." Here I found Mr Yale Clerk waiting my arrival with Letters from Messrs Brown & Connelly[182] of New Caledonia.

Monday, April 4th. Dispatched our Canoes after breakfast with the intention of following them tomorrow Morning on Horseback as many things connected with the business of the ensuing year required to be settled and adjusted previous to my departure. Wrote Mr Brown as p Letter Book assigning reasons for not complying with the demands of New Caledonia for Horses. Had a long interview with the principal Chief of Thompson's River who came hither purposely to see me; he is the most respectable manly looking Indian I ever saw, appeared much pleased with what I said to him and promised faithfully to back and support us with all his power; I made him a present of a Medal bearing the Coys arms which he seemed to prize greatly and gave him a few other triffles. We parted excellent Friends and this interview I think will go far towards the safety of the Establishment and future good conduct of the Indians; he enquired particularly if they might soon expect a "Messenger from the Master of Life" on their Lands (Meaning a Missionary because they had heard in the course of the Winter that I considered such probable) but I could merely tell him that I should represent to the "Great Chiefs on the other side of the Water" that such was their wish. There not being a sufficient number of Horses at Walla Walla to equip the Umpqua Expedition I determined on sending 15 of the Coys from this place and 11 belonging to the people say 26 which with 20 at Walla Walla and 18 at Fort Vancouver puts 64 at the Drs Disposal with which he should be enabled to re-enforce the Snake Country Expedition, equip

[182] Chief Trader William Brown shared with Chief Trader William Connolly the superintendence of New Caledonia.

the Umpqua Expedition and do all his Farming work. Had much difficulty in prevailing on Mr M. . . . . to conduct the party required to take those Horses to Walla Walla, he pleaded indisposition, the unfortunate state in which his Woman was and a variety of other excuses but all would not do; the charge appeared to me too important to be left in the hands of common Servants as in the event of the Horses being lost or Stolen the expedition must necessarily be at a stand I therefore insisted on it. Put Mr Annance in charge of Okanagan for the Summer with Two Men and removed Mr Birnie in order that he might take the Summer charge of Spokan House as Mr Finnan McDonald will be required to accompany the brigade to the Coast.

Tuesday, April 5th. Made an early start and dispatched Mr M. . . . . with his band of Horses for Walla Walla and Mr Yale with Letters for New Caledonia at same time took Horse and proceeded across the Country by an Indian track to a part of the River called the Grose Roche about 20 Miles distant from the Fort where the Boats that started yesterday Morning joined us about 1 o'Clock. Embarked and proceeded until dark when we Encamped; experienced a violent Thunder Storm in the course of the Night with torrents of Rain.

Wednesday, April 6th. Continued our March. The weather cold with a strong head Wind and clouds of Sand flying about us all Day; put up at the usual hour about a couple of Leagues below the San Poil River.

Thursday, April 7th. Made an early start; at the San Poil River found a band of Indians of whom we borrowed Horses and proceeded overland to the Forks of Spokan River a distance of about 25 to 30 Miles where we arrived about 4 P. M. and found Messrs Ross McDonald and Dears, Clerks waiting for us in charge of the Spokan returns and people; our Boats got up in the course of the Night. The remainder of to Day occupied in giving and receiving News as we could not proceed regularly to business on account of the bustle occasioned by the arrival of people and

Indians from all quarters. Found Letters from Mr Ogden dated Sources of the Missouri 25th Jany stating that all was well up to that time; the party was in the midst of Buffalo but the Snow was too deep for trapping they had however killed a few with Trenches[183] and I think it may be well to provide the Expedition next Season with the necessary Iron Works for Winter Hunting. Mr Ogden appears undetermined as to the route he may pursue coming out but Mr Ross assures me he will receive my Letters which will regulate his Motions. Here I likewise received a Letter from Mr Dease written the day after my departure stating that the Indians appeared more peaceable and well disposed than they were previous to the harangue at Walla Walla.

Forks Spokan River, Friday, April 8th. Had a consultation with Messrs Kennedy McMillan McDonald & Ross on the subject of removing the Establishment of Spokan House to the Kettle Falls; the advantages to be derived from this change are, that a very heavy expence and serious inconvenience in transporting the Outfits and returns between the Main River and the present Establishment by Land a distance of about 60 Miles will be avoided; that at the Kettle Falls an abundant stock of Fish may be secured for the maintenance of the Post throughout the Year; that the Indians in that neighbourhood and towards the Lakes will exert themselves more than heretofore and in all probability make considerable Hunts as their Lands are tolerably Stocked with Beaver; that the Post of Okanogan can be abandoned and that by a little attention to Farming a sufficient quantity of Pork Potatoes & Grain may be provided for consumption at the Post and on the Voyage so as to render them independent both of the Natives and of our Stores at the Coast. The Coutonais and Flat Head Posts may be supplied with equal facility from one place as the other if it is found that by the Flat Head and Coutonais Rivers the Water Communication is impracticable, but if practicable the use of Horses may be

[183] *Cf.* with the entry in Ogden's journal of Dec. 27, 1825, in *Oregon Hist. Quart.*, X, 345. "Some of the trappers started trenches, the rest visited the traps, returned at night with no success, their traps fast in ice, and no beaver from the trenches. The river is so wide we cannot get beaver with the ice chisel."

discontinued which would be a great Saving of Expence and trouble. The only difficulty in removing is that it may give offence to the Spokan Indians who have always been staunch to the Whites and induce them to Steal our Horses and annoy us otherwise, but those Gentlemen who are best acquainted with them think we have sufficient influence to prevent such evil. Under all circumstances it appears that the change will be attended with advantage it is therefore resolved upon and to be effected on the return of the Craft from Fort Vancouver.[184] Some doubts having arisen in my mind as to the abilities of Messrs Work and McKay for the conduct of the Umpqua Expedition and as I expect very important benefits to result therefrom if properly managed I have been induced to offer the command to Mr Finnan McDonald who is better qualified for such a charge than any person now at our disposal. This Gentleman gave me intimation last Fall of his wish to retire and it was agreed that he should cross the Mountain in the Fall but he has fallen in with my views and accompanies the Brigade to the Coast where he leaves his Family for the Year; Mr Work will therefore come back with the Brigade and take charge of the affairs of Spokan until the arrival of some Commissioned Gentlemen from the other side. Had a long interview with Eight Chiefs belonging to the Flat Head Coutonais Spokan and other tribes who assembled here for the purpose of seeing me; they appeared much pleased with all that was told them and promise well. Made them a present of a little ammunition and Tobacco. The Spokan & Flat Head Chiefs put a Son each under my care to be Educated at the Missionary Society School Red River and all the Chiefs joined in a most earnest request that a Missionary or religious instructor should be placed among them; I promised to communicate their request to the Great Chiefs on the other side of the Water with a recommendation from myself that it should be complied with.[185]

[184] *Cf.* with the entry at *post*, 139.

[185] Six years after this promise was made (see also entry for April 9) there appeared in St. Louis a delegation of Flathead and Nez Percés chiefs. They had made the immense journey from the Columbia River over the mountains and deserts and Great Plains to the American metropolis to learn of the white man's Bible. That appealing quest, effectively dramatized by the religious periodicals

Finally Settled with Mr Ross that he should undertake charge of the Missionary Society School Red River at a Sal^y^ of £100 p Annum and he accompanies me out[186] for that purpose. Mr Birnie is appointed to the Summer charge of Spokane House with Four Men and Mr Dears to accompany the Brigade to the Coast. We shall be detained two or three Days here until the accounts are closed.

Saturday, April 9th. Busily occupied with M^r^ McDonald in closing the Accounts, those of Spokan are not in a forward state, the Clerks in charge of the different Posts being unacquainted with the forms. Two Nez Percés Chiefs arrived to see me from a distance of between 2 & 300 Miles; my fame has spread far and Wide and my speeches are handed from Camp to Camp throughout the Country; some of them have it that I am one of the "Master of Life's Sons" sent to see "if their hearts are good" and others that I am his "War Chief" with bad Medicine if their hearts are bad. On the whole I think my presence and lectures will do some good.

Sunday, April 10th. Occupied all Day in writing to Messrs McLoughlin Dease and Ogden as p Letter Book.

Monday, April 11th. Our accounts are nearly wound up, they shew a profit of about £10,000 on this Deptm^t^[187] the returns

of the day, led in 1834 to the sending of the first American missionaries to Oregon, and this in turn helped to put in motion the first parties of American pioneers to Oregon, which so significantly affected the Oregon boundary settlement. Perhaps this remarkable train of events can be traced back to Governor Simpson, and to the interest he aroused in Christianity among the Columbia River Indians on this occasion and on the occasion of his second visit in 1829 when he probably reported to the Spokan and Flathead chiefs on the progress of their sons at the Red River Missionary School.

[186] Ross kept a journal while crossing the mountains with the Governor which he later used as a basis for the last chapters of his *Fur Hunters*. This record is worth comparing with Simpson's journal. There are other good contemporary accounts of the crossing of Athabasca Pass in Ermatinger, "York Factory Express Journal," in Roy. Soc. Can., *Proceeds. and Trans.*, 3rd series, VI, sect. ii, 67; Cox, *Columbia River*; Franchère, *Narrative*.

[187] Refers to the Columbia Department.

amounting to about 20,000 Beaver & Otter, but I think in consequence of the change of System I have this Season introduced that the profits will be about £15000 and the returns about 30,000 Beaver and Otter next year say an increase in the profits of at least £5000 and in the returns, of 10,000 Beaver & Otters; and if my plans are followed up and myself on the Spot Winter 1826/27 I undertake to double the returns and profits of this year.

Tuesday, April 12th. Through my Servant Tom I this morning discovered that Mr. Deases Interpreter was in league with "Cut Lip" a Cai-Use Chief to Cut off the Fort of Nez Percés and that he had determined on effecting this horrible deed on his return while the place was weak after the departure of the Brigade for the Coast by seizing the opportunity of Mr Deases momentary absence (in superintending the Butchering of the Horses) to make themselves Masters of the Fort or in other words to Massacre its Inhabitants; I therefore set myself seriously to work to get this Villain away with me without having recourse to force as he stands so high with the Indians that they would probably revenge on the Establishment any harsh measures that might be adopted in regard to him and the removal of him by fair means is no easy Matter as he is intimate with and attached to a Woman at the Fort whose Name he will not divulge but who I suspect to be Mr D...'s wife; by fair promises & flattering hopes however I have succeeded in enticing him away and he accompanies us under the impression that he is to return in the Fall, but while I am in the Country he may consider himself a Ruperts Land Man—wrote Mr Dease on the subject. On reconsidering the state of Thompsons River Deptm^{t} I do not feel easy in entrusting the charge thereof to Mr M...... who at best is nearly useless but (dogged as he is at present with a deranged Wife who even in her madness governs him) is now entirely so; I have therefore given him permission to recross the Mountain with his Family in the Fall and appointed Mr Arch^{d} McDonald to the charge. Wrote the D^{r} fully on this subject as p Letter Book. Every thing being settled here we made a start in the Even^{g} and Encamped about a League above the Forks. The

Weather Stormy with hail Showers and Rain. Baptised the Indian Boys, they are the Sons of the principal Spokan & Coutonais War Chiefs, Men of great Weight and consequence in this part of the Country; they are named Coutonais Pelly and Spokan Garry.[188]

Wednesday, April 13th. Left our Encampt at 4 A. M. and made a long Days March the Men working with great constancy until 7 P. M. We are now getting into a different Climate cold and uncomfortable as we approach the Mountains. Encamped about 3 Leagues below the Grand Rapid.

Thursday, April 14th. Keen Frost during the Night but the Sun powerful in the course of the Day. Altho' the Season is now advanced about a Month since we left Fort Vancouver vegetation is not in such a forward state here as it was there on our departure and this I do not ascribe so much to the difference in Latitude as our proximity to the Mountains which are covered

[188] Simpson's experiment in educating these boys did not turn out well. Coutonais Pelly died at the Missionary School a few years after he entered it; Spokan Garry sank back to the level of his people as soon as he returned to them. Simpson found him in 1841 on the occasion of his third visit to the Columbia under the following circumstances:

"In one tent a sight presented itself, which was equally novel and unnatural. Surrounded by a crowd of spectators, a party of fellows were playing at cards obtained in the Snake Country from some American trappers; and a more melancholy exemplification of the influence of civilization on barbarism could hardly be imagined than the apparently scientific eagerness with which these naked and hungry savages thumbed and turned the black and greasy pasteboard. Though the men who sold the cards might have taught the use of them, yet I could not help tracing the wretched exhibition to a more remote source—a source with which I was myself, in some measure, connected. In this same hell of the wilderness, I found Spokan Garry, one of the lads already mentioned as having been sent to Red River for their education; and there was little reason to doubt that, with his superior knowledge, he was the master spirit, if not the prime mover, of the scene. On his return to his countrymen, he had, for a time, endeavoured to teach them to read and write; but he had gradually abandoned the attempt, assigning as his reason or his pretext that the others 'jawed him so much about it.' He forthwith relapsed into his original barbarism, taking to himself as many wives as he could get; and then, becoming a gambler, he lost both all that he had of his own and all that he could beg or borrow from others. He was evidently ashamed of his proceedings, for he would not come out of the tent to shake hands even with an old friend." Simpson, *Journey Round the World*, I, 144-145.

with Snow. Passed the Grand Rapid about 10 A. M. where a Portage was made with Craft and Cargo of about 100 Yards. At 2 O'Clock got to the Kettle Falls where we made a portage of about a Mile with Craft and Cargo. While the people were carrying I went to the Chiefs Lodge about a Mile above the Carrying place; had an interview with him and some of his principal followers and intimated my wish to form an Establishment on his Lands provided he undertook to protect it and assured us of his Friendly disposition. He received the proposal with much satisfaction and offered me the choice of his Lands in regard to situation or quantity. We selected a beautiful point on the South side about ¾ths of a Mile above the Portage where there is abundance of fine Timber and the situation elegible in every point of view. An excellent Farm can be made at this place where as much Grain and potatoes may be raised as would feed all the Natives of the Columbia and a sufficient number of Cattle and Hogs to supply his Majestys Navy with Beef and Pork. My reasons for abandoning the Establishment of Spokan House and forming one here in its stead are explained under Date the 8th Inst. Lined out the Site of the Establisht 150 feet Square on a bank facing and commanding a view of the River and I have taken the liberty of naming it Fort Colvile[189] as both the Establishments that bore that Gentlemans Name were abandoned at the Coalition; likewise marked out the Garden and wrote Mr Birnie to Spokan House directing him to send a couple of Men across immediately to plant 5 or 6 Bushels of Potatoes, and to make the necessary preparations to remove the property on the arrival of the Brigade from Fort Vancouver. The Spokan Chief known by the name of "Mr Frazer" came here to meet me hearing of my fame and previous to parting with him and the Kettle Fall Chief I made them a present of Ammunition and Tobacco with a Speech of about an hours length as they estimate harangues by measurement; they said in return every

[189] Fort Colvile was built in the autumn and spring of 1825-26, and Spokane House was immediately after dismantled. Andrew Colvile, the person after whom the fort was named, was a director and later a governor of the Hudson's Bay Company.

thing that was satisfactory. Put up at Dusk and narrowly escaped upsetting in a strong rapid the boat being forced broadside on a Stone in consequence of the Bowsman's pole breaking. We have still 5 Men labouring under the "Chinook love Fever" altho 7 were sent back to the D^r^ from Spokan Forks; one of our poor fellows is in a horrible state and it requires all the professional Skill of Mr Ross & myself to keep him at his duty; that Gentleman has no contemptable opinion of his own surgical talents having once performed a wonderful cure on himself in the *Short* space of *Two Years*.

Friday, April 15th. Severe Frost again last Night but the Day fine. Started at ½ past 3 A. M.—passed the little Dalles at 8 and the Mouth of the Flat Head or Ponderais River at 4 P. M. Put up at ½ past 7 having made an extraordinary Days March considering the Strength of the Current and number of the Rapids; this hard marching is owing to an animated opposition between my Foreman and that of the Consort Canoe who are reckoned the two most adroit in the River.

Saturday, April 16. Our people were at their Poles and paddles 16 hours to Day and wrought with great Spirit. Breakfasted at the Coutonais or McGillivrays River and Encamped about the middle of the lower Columbia Lake. The Weather very fine. We are now getting into a thick Wood Country no red Pine to be seen but the Hemlock White Pine & Cedar are from hence Lords of the Forest until we reach the height of Land. Wrote to Mr Work at Spokan House from our Encamp^t^.[190]

Sunday, April 17th. The Weather continues remarkably fine, made a very long Day and put up near the middle of the Second Lake; our marching since leaving the Forks of Spokan River beats any thing of the kind hitherto known in the Columbia notwithstanding the invalided state of our Crews and their Wretched fare Horse Beans and Grease.

[190] This letter containing directions as to the building of Fort Colvile and the management of the trade of the district of Spokane is to be found in the journal of John Work in *Washington Hist. Quart.*, V, 98-99.

Monday, April 18th. In order to avail ourselves of a calm in passing the Lake we started soon after midnight and got to the upper end to Breakfast and as we were looking out for an Encampment in the Eveng two Red Deer very opportunely made their appearance within Gun Shot, the first fell to my Lot and the second to that of Mr Kennedy; all hands were immediately at Work preparing for the Feast (as we have lived wretchedly since leaving the Coast) and I suspect the fragments will be very small by Day break as altho we have been now Four Hours ashore roasting and Boiling is still the order of the Night and our voracious Canadians seem disposed to make but one "pipe" of it in the eating way until the signal is given for being under weigh. The Weather oppressively Warm to Day and since Sun Set the Muschetoes have been very troublesome. The Water rising rapidly.

Tuesday, April 19th. The paddles & poles were kept constantly and vigorously employed 16 hours to Day; large patches of Snow on the banks of the River and to all appearance we shall have no sinecure in crossing the Mountains. Put up about 3 Leagues above the little Dalles.

Wednesday, April 20th. A good Days Work, fine Weather and the Water rising; made a demi decharge at Rapid aux Morts where I picked up some curious specimens of Stone to be sent home. Encamped about 3 Leagues below the Crooked Rapid.

Thursday, April 21st. Long Faces, much Snow, the Water rising and no Encampt the banks being covered with soft Snow to the Waters edge.

Friday, April 22nd. Started as early as it was possible to distinguish the Stones in the Rapids, found the Water had risen about 3 feet in the course of the Night. Saw large quantities of Beaver Cuttings which had drifted down the various streams falling into the Main River, indeed I never beheld such numerous vestiges of Beaver and am satisfied that if a party of 20 good Trappers would pass a year in this neighbourhood and employ their time well they would make great hunts. Arrived at the Boat Encamp[t] west end of the [Athabasca] Portage at 10 A. M. where I found a few lines from M[r] Laroque dated East end of the Portage 2nd Inst. That Gentleman might have saved himself the trouble of writing for all the information his Letter conveys as I never saw a document in which there is such a dearth of news or interesting matter; this is very thoughtless inconsiderate and disobliging as he must have been well aware of my anxiety to know what has been doing for these last Six Months on the West side the Mountain the little he does say is by no means cheering; in the first place he can give us no Provisions so that we must have to fast 4 or 5 Days; in the second place the Horses will not start from the other side the portage until the latter end of the Month altho I had directed that they should be at Camp[t] Fusil on or before the 25th so that instead of Riding half the Journey as is usual we shall have to make use of our Legs, no joke after the labour & hardship we shall undergo in getting across the hundreds of Channels of Iced Water through the Battures[191] and the Mountains of Snow we have to scale and wade through with heavy loads; but what concerns me more than either is to learn that M[r] D. Finlayson one of the finest and most promising young Gentlemen in the Service has by the last Accounts from Peace River been mortally Wounded by the accidental discharge of a Spring Gun lodging the contents in his body; also that one of our Clerks at Dunvegan has been Wounded by an Indian and that the latter was immediately put to Death by the people of the Establishment. This last affair I think calls for particular investigation and if it is found that the Indian was to blame I think it will be a favorable opportunity of giving Peace River a few years respite by withdrawing the Establishments which will be attended with important benefits to the concern and effectually punish the Beaver Indians for their late atrocities.[192] About 12

[191] *Batture* is the French-Canadian name for a sand or gravel flat in a river bed, which is dry or submerged according to season.

[192] Refers to the murder by the Beaver Indians of five men at St. Johns on Peace River in the fall of 1823. The Council for the Northern Department of Rupert's Land voted on this account and because of the affair at Dunvegan to abandon Dunvegan and the Rocky Mountain establishment.

O'Clock sent Cadotte and Grande Louis light ahead across the Portage in order to have the Canoes repaired and Gummed by the time we arrive so that we may not be delayed there as our people will be so much reduced by Hunger as to be unable to proceed if any detention takes place. Put the Boats en Casche on the Island and distributed our Baggage among the people amounting with their own property and provisions to about 60 lbs. p Man. Left the Boat Encamp[t] at 2 P. M. proceeded through a Swamp of about 3 Miles in Iced Water then across the first point of Woods 6 Miles the walking exceedingly bad; forded the River twice and Encamped on the Bature at Sun Set. Four of our people fell behind and Encamped in the Point of Woods being unable to keep up with us.

Saturday, April 23[d]. The people who were left behind last night arrived about Sun rise this morning when after giving the Camp a Dram (which they now frequently require on account of the extreme coldness of the Water we have to Wade through) we all started; after having made about 4 Miles on the Batture or Flats we halted for some of the people who had fallen behind and when they made their appearance we discovered that the Blackguard Iroquois had on our departure broached the Keg of which all partook except a few of my own Crew and about half a Doz. of them were so drunk that they could not come on. We proceeded about 3 Miles further and stopped for Breakfast. M[r] McMillan was sent back to bring up the rear and I led the advanced party but had not gone a mile when one of the people informed me that *Isaac* the Iroquois Chief (the leader of the Mutinous Dogs who were discharged from the Snake Expedition and one of those I had sentenced to transportation for Life from the Columbia for his uniform bad conduct) was the person who had broached the Keg in the Morn[g] and had that moment in a fit of drunken rage sent his Provisions down the Stream to lighten his burthen; this information irritated me exceedingly and particularly so on account of the low state of our Provisions as we must either give the fellow a share of our own little stock or leave him to perish in the Mountain and seeing the dangerous consequences of allowing an offence of this kind pass unnoticed I was on the impulse of the moment induced to descend to the disagreeable duty of chastising him on the spot with the first Stick that came to hand, he will feel it for a few Days and recollect it while in the Indian Country and it will have a good effect on the whole of our Columbians who are by no means in a good state of discipline; and further to mark my displeasure of the conduct of our people this Day I knocked a Hatchet into the head of our Rum Keg and dashed the contents into the River which I have no doubt drew lamentations from some of them. Passed about 9 Miles of Battures the upper point of Woods 6 Miles and Encamped much fatigued at Sun Set. We forded the River 41 times in the course of to Day. Mr McMillan and his Drunken Squad not come up by the time I am writing this and 'tis not probable they will join us to night as it is now Dark.

Sunday, April 24th. Keen Frost during the Night and the Still Water & edges of the River covered with thin Ice; we had notwithstanding to renew our fording Work which is certainly the most disagreeable I know; passed about 9 Miles of Battures and had to Ford the River 17 times before 6 A. M.; some of the people were so benumbed with Cold that on getting out of the Water they actually could not stand; entered the Woods of the big Hill[193] and found the Snow deep and soft we however with great labour made a couple of Miles and put up for breakfast drenched with perspiration altho' the Morng was very severe. In the face of the Hill for about a couple of Miles the Snow was about 18 Inches deep but as we advanced it deepened to 6 feet; the labour of Walking without Snow Shoes was dreadful during the heat of the Day sinking every Step 18 Inches to 2 feet we however by great exertion got to the top of the Hill at 5 P. M. having Walked 12 hours with three Indian Shoes on rough Shingle & in deep Snow; every Man in the Camp lame & exhausted. In the Morng I was surprised by a rumbling sound which at first we mistook for distant Thunder but on looking in the direction from whence it came I saw it arose from a prodigious avalanche from

[193] Grande Côte, a long steep ascent to the summit of Athabasca Pass.

the top of a very high Mountain which swept down the Valley beneath like an overwhelming torrent and sending forth Clouds of drift resembling immense volumes of Smoke.

Monday, April 25$^{th.}$ Left our Encamp^{t} at ½ past 3 this Morn^{g}, the Snow very deep and the Walking most laborous. At 6 A. M. got to the Committees Punch Bowl where the people had a Glass of Rum each and ourselves a little Wine & Water which was drunk to the Health of their Honors with three Cheers. At 9 got to the Camp^{t} Fusil where we put up to breakfast and rested until 12 A. M. Lesperence and François were from hence sent off light to assist in repairing the Canoes and hasten the Horses. Proceeded through deep Snow and along the Bed of the River in some places Waist deep in Iced Water until 6 P. M. when we put up on the Grande Batture; every Man of the party knocked up. The Avalanches have been sounding throughout the Day like Thunder.

Tuesday, April 26$^{th.}$ Never did exhausted travellers turn out less disposed to renew a toilsome Journey than we did at 3 o'clock this Morn^{g}, every man of the party requiring the aid of a Walking Stick our feet being much blistered and Lacerated by the rough Travel on the Battures and in the Bed of the River; we however improved as we got Warm upon it and continued a Steady pace until 10 O'Clock having by that time forded the River 27 times when the joyful shout was given by one of the people that the Horses were in sight; we immediately put up for Breakfast. By the men who conducted the Horses I received a Letter from Mr Laroque conveying the distressing information of the total destruction of Norway House, the Stores and property therein contained by accidental Fire; a loss of about 3 to £4000—no further particulars are given. This truly unfortunate accident I fear will put us to most Serious inconvenience independent of the loss and I must if possible increase the Speed of our Journey in order to get to Cumberland House and from thence at all hazards to Norway House by Ice to the end if possible of lightening the evil by timely arrangements.

Relieved the people of their burdens and continued our route in the course of which by an unlucky stumble of the Horse carrying my Baggage it was precipitated into the River and thoroughly drenched:—the damage sustained by my own things I care little about they like their Master are accustomed to such refreshing dips, but I am concerned to find that my papers have got a share; this occasions the loss of a few hours in order to dry them and we accordingly put up at 5 P. M. at the Grande Traverse. Passed a few Tents of Shewhoppes on their way to the Post, they had very few Skins appeared Wretchedly poor; were in great dread of the thick Wood Assiniboines[194] and half breeds and had not a Gun among the whole party to defend themselves with.

Wednesday, April 27th. We were on horseback this Morng a few Minutes after 3 A. M. and got to the Mountain House at 6 O'Clock Chief Trader Laroque in charge who handed me a large bundle of Letters from all parts of the Country; they generally convey satisfactory accounts of the Trade except in regard to the article of Provisions which is more scarce than ever known, the Buffalo Hunts having entirely failed throughout the plains. There are no Letters direct from Red River Settlement but 'tis reported that the Indian Corn Crop has failed; if this be true I am at a loss how we shall get through the business of the Season as the demands of the Land Arctic Expedition are heavy and must be met whatever inconvenience the Service may experience. Here I likewise received the Honble Committees Despatch of June last by which I am rejoiced to find that in some of my arrangements in the Columbia I have anticipated their Honors wishes and met their views. The accounts conveyed by this Despatch are most cheering & satisfactory. When Mr Laroque left York last Fall it was determined that he should Winter at Cranberry Lake in the heart of the Mountain but his craft was set fast by Ice in the Athabasca River which rendered it impos-

[194] Assiniboines are a branch of the Siouan family who became separated from the main body shortly before the advent of the whites and began moving northwestward, allying themselves with the Crees. The Thickwood Assiniboines are the Assiniboines of the Rocky Mountains.

sible for him to get beyond this place; he however took a Winter excursion in that direction and finds that no Establishment can be maintained further in the interior of the Mountain than where now situated large Animals being scarce and the Lakes producing no Fish which together with the improved footing on which I have placed Thompsons River District completely changes my views in regard to this Post [Rocky Mountain House] being meant to draw the Shewhoppes to the Neighbourhood of the Mountain in order that the returns of the North branch of Thompsons River might be brought to York instead of being sent to the Columbia; it was likewise expected that considerable hunts would be made in the Mountain by those Indians and the Freemen of Lesser Slave Lake; this may still be done by a small outfit being given to two trusty men from Thompsons River who would pass the Winter with Indians instead of keeping up a regular post with an Establishment of a Commissioned Gentleman Clerk and Eight Men as has been done this Year; in short viewing the subject in all manner of ways I think it will be to the Coys interest that this post be withdrawn altogether as the Furs will assuredly find their way either to Fort Assiniboine or Kamloops[195] without incurring the Expence of an Establishment which this Year will be little short of £800; I have therefore directed its being withdrawn. The Columbia Gentlemen may complain of this measure as exposing them to personal hardships in crossing the Mountain by being deprived of the usual facilities; one good consequence will arise from this change which is, that it will effectually put a stop to the practise of Gentlemen transporting their Families and heavy luggage across the Mountains; the Coy require no transport it is therefore quite unnecessary to keep a band of Horses, Horsekeeps and Hunters as Single Gentlemen can or ought to be able to Walk; my wardrobe does not exceed 20 or 30 lbs which my Servant can carry on his back and I do not see why their's should be more weighty; cases Baskets Tents Cassets and other heavy unnecessary Luggage may be dispensed with in the

[195] Kamloops is another name for Fort Thompson at the junction of North Thompson and South Thompson rivers.

Mountain and therefore the Co[y] should be at no expence in affording such indulgencies; half a Doz Pemicans is all that is required for the Voyage Westward which the Crew can carry on their backs and coming East a couple Bags may be transported in like Manner and instead of Gentlemen consuming 10 Days or a Fortnight in the Mountains studying their own comfort and that of their families 5 Days are quite sufficient even on foot, I have done it in that time and at an earlier and more unfavorable Season than it was ever undertaken, furthermore I am ready to do it again and our Chief Factors & Chief Traders ought to learn to do as I do or if incapable through Age or infirmity of doing their duty and meeting the hardships & privations to which the Service exposes them, they ought in my opinion to withdraw and enjoy themselves on their retired Shares. After getting our Canoes repaired we embarked at 12 A. M. and proceeded to the foot of Mayots Rock where we put up at Dusk.

Thursday, April 28[th.] Embarked at 3 O'Clock A. M. got to Jaspers House at 8 where we found Mich[l] Klyne who goes to take the Summer charge of Lesser Slave Lake in the course of a few Days; remained there a couple of hours and continued our route, found the Athabasca River very low and were obliged to put up early to repair our Consort Canoe which was much injured in running Rapid au Mort.

Friday, April 29[th.] The Weather extremely cold; made a very long Days March, collected a number of Eggs and Killed several Geese. Saw about 50 Moose & Red Deer, but time was too valuable to amuse ourselves in hunting I however shot one of the former of which we only took the Tongue & Nose.

Saturday, April 30[th.] Got to Fort Assiniboine at 9 O'Clock this Morn[g] Mr Deschambeaut in charge, Chief Factor McIntosh having gone with his returns across Land to Edmonton agreeable to my directions of last Fall; it was intended that M[r] Frazer should have passed the Summer here, but learning by the York Factory Despatches that M[r] Ermatinger would not be at Edmonton in sufficient time to conduct the Arctic Expedition Boats,[196] I have ordered Mr Frazer thither for that purpose and intend that either M^r^ [Patrick] Small or Mr Fisher from Edmonton shall exchange places with Mr Deschambeaut as I do not consider him to have sufficient experience for even the temporary charge of a Post. Wrote to the Commissioned Gentlemen passing Isle a la Crosse (from hence as p Letter Book) on the subject of Provisions and other assistance required for the Expedition. At 3 O'Clock P. M. left Fort Assiniboine for Edmonton on Horseback and put up at...having gone about 12 Miles, the road tolerably good considering that it has been opened since I passed here last Fall through thick Woods.[197]

Sunday, May 1st. Reached Burleigh's Lake[198] through a similar track to that passed Yesterday which is sufficiently good for transport of property on Horseback but not fit for Wheel carriage or Sled and I am now from experience enabled to say that New Caledonia and Lesser Slave Lake can be supplied by this route instead of Athabasca and the Beaver River which will be a very great Saving in Men's Wages Provisions &c &c; indeed the change of routes I have determined on will on these two Districts alone yield a saving to the Company of at least 12 to £1500 p Annum if the Company determine on continuing the transport business of New Caledonia with York Factory and further I am satisfied that this discovery of Mine (as I alone can claim the

196 The Arctic Expedition to which Simpson refers was that of Captain John Franklin, already mentioned in this journal, *ante*, 6 n. It had been provided during the autumn and winter with supplies and transport by the Hudson's Bay Company, and it lay at the time of this writing at Cumberland House on the Saskatchewan awaiting the arrival of pemmican from Edmonton and the opening of navigation to the northward. The pemmican boats, to which Simpson refers, reached Cumberland House on June 2, and the expedition under the command of the clerk Fraser proceeded northward to Methye Portage, where Captain Franklin, who had come from England, overtook it and assumed charge. *Cf.* Franklin, *Narrative of a Second Expedition*, ix-xxiv, 1-6.

197 This is the road cut under Simpson's orders by Cardinal, the freeman. See *ante*, 22, 25-28.

198 Burleigh's Lake (Berland's Lake as correctly rendered by Edward Ermatinger or Lac de Bourlon as it appears on the Canadian Department of the Interior map of 1884) is the present Deadman Lake.

merit thereof it never having been even dreamt of by any other) will enable us to do the Peace River business at a reduction of one third on the usual expences of that place as the Peace River outfits & returns can be taken by Horses in 5 Days between Dunvegon & Lesser Slave Lake, by Boats in 4 or 5 Days between Lesser Slave Lake and Fort Assiniboine, by Horses between the latter place and Edmonton in 3 or 4 Days and by Boats between that and York Factory and the difference of Expence between Boat and Canoe transport is at a fair estimate 33⅓d p Cent.

Monday, May 2nd. Reached Edmonton at 12 A. M. having come from Fort Assiniboine in about 2 Days the distance being about 80 Miles; found Mr Rowand up to his Ears in business as usual and without exception he is the most active and best qualified person for the troublesome charge he has got of any man in the Indian Country. The Provision Trade has entirely failed the two Posts (Edmonton & Carlton) barely producing 200 Bags Pemican and many plain Indians having Starved to Death in consequence of the absence of Buffalo. The Rat hunts have likewise failed in consequence of the lowness of the Waters, but the returns in Beaver are very fair about 3,000.

Wednesday, May 4th. Occupied throughout the Day in various arrangements and gave the people a Danse in the Eveng.

Thursday, May 5th. I am concerned to find that serious differences have taken place this Season between Messrs Clarke McIntosh and Laroque; there is a good deal of abuse and recrimination on all sides but I cannot exactly get at the merits of the case as yet; dissentions among the Gentlemen of neighbouring Posts are most injurious to the general interests and to prevent a repetition of them among those Gentlemen this ensuing Season I shall endeavour to remove them out of the reach of each other. Family Matters I believe to be the cause of those misunderstandings, Mr Laroque is a single man, the other two are Family Men; the Coys interests Mr Laroque thinks are made subservient or secondary to private or Family considerations and altho there may be some other grounds for animosity between them, he lays hold of the former; he does not exactly charge them with fraud or misapplication of property, I can however discover that he has strong suspicions on that head and he makes no secret that the Co^{ys} affairs are entirely lost sight of in maintaining the dignity, self importance and domestic comfort of the one (Mr Clarke) and that the other (M^r McIntosh) to indulge his ill nature, low cunning and the fancies of his Wife and Daughter (who in reality govern both him and the affairs under his Management) would and does sacrifice his own and the Co^{ys} interests.

Closed all my arrangements with Mr Rowand in regard to the affairs of his Establishment.

I have every inclination to indulge my poor crew with a few Days rest at this place as they are quite Worn out by the long and harrassing Voyage they have made and a little repose would not be unwelcome to myself being a good deal jaded but my anxiety occasioned by the deranged state of our affairs owing to the Norway House Fire, scarcity of provisions failure of the Indian Corn Crops in Red River together with the assistance required of us by $Capt^n$ Franklins Expedition quite unhinges me so that every hour will appear an Age until I get into the scene of action have therefore determined on being off immediately. The Brigade[199] does not start for 10 or 15 Days and it is not considered safe to pass down the Saskatchawaine with merely the Crew of One Boat we are however prepared for the Worst and must take our chance.

Thursday, May 12th. Carlton. Our Voyage from Edmonton to this place was very tedious owing to the lowness of the Waters and continual head Winds occupying 8 Days in which nothing of interest occurred. We were not molested by Indians. Killed a few Buffalo Red Deer and abundance of Feathered Game.

Altho' this River (Saskatchawaine) has been unremittingly hunted for nearly 100 Years, it is still tolerably well stocked with Beaver and if it was possible to let it have 5 Years rest or respite

[199] Refers to the flotilla of boats that annually took out the returns of Edmonton and neighboring posts, and brought back from York Factory supplies for the ensuing season. According to Alexander Ross the brigade of 1825 comprised twelve boats.

would be as Rich in Beaver as ever. In all parts we saw cuttings and other vestiges of that most industrious and valuable animal. These Beaver are not natives of the River but are carried down the Stream from the Mountain every Spring; they have not time to settle or Multiply as before the close of the navigation in Fall every one is destroyed by the innumerable Indians that frequent its banks during the Summer; there are no possible means that we can divise to remedy this evil as the Natives are so numerous and independent that persuasion has no effect and we cannot venture to dictate. Withdrawing the Establishments would of course partially withdraw the Indians and the banks of the Main River and of its feeders would as a matter of course become a valuable Field of Beaver in the course of a short time but that cannot be done as every District North of Norway House is at present dependent on it more or less.[200]

When I left Edmonton it was my intention to have proceeded direct to Norway House (either by Ice or across Land from Cumberland [House] on foot as the Navigation would not be entirely open so early) for the purpose of making various arrangements previous to the passing of the different Brigades. From Fort Assiniboine I had written to the Commissioned Gentlemen of the Northern Depts to meet me there (Norway House) as early as possible in order to hold a Council on Columbia affairs and other matters requiring immediate consideration; and on my way to the Columbia last Fall I wrote Govr Pelly of Red River[201]

[200] Edmonton and Carlton produced the pemmican which maintained the transport service of the Hudson's Bay Company.

[201] R. P. Pelly was governor of a special district in Rupert's Land (the district of Assiniboia) extending from Red River and Lake Winnipeg westward to the junction of the Red and the Assiniboine rivers, and embracing what is now southwestern Manitoba and southeastern Saskatchewan. This district had been obtained by Lord Selkirk from the Hudson's Bay Company in 1811, and he had founded in it the Red River Colony in 1812. In 1825 it was administered by the Hudson's Bay Company, partly in virtue of the terms of Lord Selkirk's will, and partly by reason of rights of jurisdiction reserved at the time of the grant. Lord Selkirk had been permitted by the Hudson's Bay Company during his lifetime to name the chief magistrates of the district—the governor and the councillors—but this right, together with the right of confirming the appointments, was exercised after his death by the Hudson's Bay Company. Nominations, as a matter of fact, were made in 1825 by Simpson as Governor of Rupert's Land. Simpson had the right

begging he would if possible meet me at Norway House this Spring in order to compare Notes and determine our plans respecting the Colony business of the Winter conceiving it probable that either he or I would visit England in the Fall. On my arrival at Carlton it was my intention to have sent Despatches across Land to Red River by a party of Indians with the object of pointing out to Govr Pelly the propriety nay almost necessity of my going to England this Season if the Colony affairs would admit thereof, as the state of Mrs Pelly's health and other circumstances made me apprehensive that he would not meet me at Norway House and to prevail on him if possible to defer his going home until the following Season as also to give him my best advice and assistance in regard to the management of his Government. Likewise with a view of purchasing a sufficient quantity of Grain to make up the deficiency occasioned by the failure of our Provision Trade and in order to hire a sufficient number of people for the Settlement transport business from York as owing to the loss of property in Depot at Norway House I did not expect that the Co^ys^ Servants could in addition to the transport business of their respective Districts accomplish that of the Colony. These different objects appeared to me of too much moment and importance to be entrusted to a Written communication p Express I therefore formed a plan the boldness of which induced the people to believe my senses had taken leave of me no other than that of starting forthwith personally across

in addition, as Governor of Rupert's Land, to attend the Council of Assiniboia, and when he did he presided over its sessions. He did not exercise this right during the incumbency of Governor Pelly. "I think it better," he wrote in 1823, "that I should *not* attend the Council at all because when present it would be necessary for me to preside which must in some degree affect the consequence of Mr. Pelly in the eyes of the lower classes. In order to command due respect he must on all occasions be the great man and head of the Colony and as such I shall always treat him." The proceedings of the Governor and Council of Assiniboia, like the proceedings of the Council for the Northern Department of Rupert's Land, were subject to review by the Governor and Committee of the Hudson's Bay Company in London. After the retirement of R. P. Pelly from the governorship of Assiniboia in 1825, the Hudson's Bay Company combined his office with that of the chief factorship of the fur-trade district of Fort Garry. For a good collection of documents on the early constitutional history of Assiniboia see Oliver, *Canadian North-West*, I, 154-263.

Land to Red River Settlement a distance according to our route computed at 800 Miles[202] through plains infested by the Most Warlike and hostile Tribes in North America which would occupy Twenty Days constant Travelling. On my arrival at Carlton at 11 O'Clock A. M. this Day I made known my intentions to Chief Factors Kennedy & Stewart[203] and to my Staunch & Manly Friend and Fellow Traveller, Chief Trader McMillan, they saw the importance of the object and the two former were lavish in their commendations but they would not venture the offer to accompany me (altho' they might have done it with safety as I should not have accepted it knowing their inability to meet the fatigues of the Journey) McMillan however altho' Worn down to a shadow began to pack up instantly. To my Crew I intimated my intention but would require none of them to undertake this laborious and dangerous trip as they were all nearly exhausted. Four of them however would not be denied and entreated permission to follow me say my own Servant Tom, Lesperence, Hogg & Sherkie, the other Six would not venture being dead beat, I therefore selected Four half breeds from Carlton our party in all including myself and McMillan amounting to Ten. From hence I sent Letters to Messrs Leith[204] & McTavish as p Correspondence Book, got every thing in readiness for my Journey and started from Carlton at 2 O'Clock having remained there only 3 hours for repose & preparation. We were furnished with 12 Horses the best at the Fort but scarcely able to Walk light far less to carry; for Provisions we had to depend on our Guns. Our Guide was not at home in the route having only passed twice the last time Eleven Years ago in short never did a party undertake a dangerous Voyage so ill prepared and never was such a Voyage considering all the circumstances thereof undertaken in the Indian Country. Just as we were on the eve of starting information was brought to the Fort that a War

[202] Simpson exaggerates the distance. It is not much over 525 miles by the route he took.

[203] John Stuart was in charge of Carlton, recently transferred there from New Caledonia.

[204] Chief Factor James Leith in charge of Cumberland House.

Camp of Fall Indians[205] was in ambush about a Mile distant in the Woods. When Messrs Stewart & Kennedy and all the other good folks of the Garrison prayed that we would not venture from the House until the "Coast was clear" but on examining the informants they could give us nothing but vague conjectures sufficiently alarming, it does not however do for a Governor to appear shy I therefore wished our Friends good bye and pushed off and at Dusk encamped on the borders of a small Lake about Ten Miles from the House.[206] To guard against surprise we have determined to keep constant guard, myself and two of the people took the first Watch.

Friday, May 13th. Started at ½ past 2 found Mr Stewart in the track, he had ascertained that the Fall Indian reports were false and followed us last night in order to communicate on some points connected with the Summer arrangements of his post but could not fall on our Encampt; he accompanied us to the South branch of the Saskatchawaine or Bow River where we breakfasted crossed and struck through a beautiful country consisting of small plains, hillocks clumps of poplar and ponds or Lakes. Encamped at the Cross Lake having crossed the Birch Hills.

Saturday, May 14th. Continued our route at ½ past 2, crossed the Next Hills and Encamped at the borders of the Buffalo Robe plain. Our guide to Day got quite bewildered and lost much ground by not keeping in the proper direction. Our course is South East making however numerous turns to avoid Woods & Lakes; the order of our March is to start at dawn travel 5 hours, breakfast and give the Horses two hours rest, then travel 3 hours, lay by until 4 O'Clock and then go on until Dusk. Our rate is a steady Walk of about 3½ to 4 Miles p Hour all hands on foot except Mr McMillan and myself and we do not ride above 3 hours p Day and the object of bringing so many Horses is to carry our little Baggage, live on them if Game fails and make

[205] Fall Indians are a detached branch of the Arapaho family of no great importance historically.

[206] Simpson's route is in general southeast toward the Quill lakes. It is too indistinctly described here to permit of its exact location.

Skin Canoes of their Hides if we find it necessary on account of Indians Sickness or any other cause to go down the Assiniboine River after reaching its heads instead of Crossing the Red River plains. My Servant Tom and George Bird act in the capacity of Hunters for the party & supply us w^t abundance of Swans Ducks & Geese.

Sunday, May 15th. Got into a very thickety country intersected with deep Swamps and small Lakes to avoid which we are compelled to Wind about in all directions. A circumstance occurred to Day which gives me much uneasiness and is likely to expose us to much inconvenience; soon after Breakfast while on the March a Red Deer appeared close to the track; the Hunters asked if they might follow to which I replied in the negative as we could not afford time, they however (my servant Tom & George Bird) struck off the Road to have a shot and we proceeded on our route for about a couple of hours conceiving they were in the rear until the usual resting time 12 O'Clock; after turning the Horses loose and lighting a Fire to smoke the muschetoes which assailed us in clouds I missed the Hunters but was informed by our Guide that the track was perceptable in the Grass and that they would immediately be up w^t us; after waiting about an hour we heard 3 Signal Shots to Windward which were immediately answered by myself & Mr McMillan (the people being asleep) but as we were by the Sound about a couple of Miles to Leeward and blowing fresh they could not of course hear the reports. We were now satisfied that the Young Men had lost our track and I dispatched our Guide, La Plante and Laverdure in various directions in search of them it being unsafe to trust the other people from the Camp as they have not the talent of finding their way through the Woods; those who were sent returned after a fruitless search of 3 hours and had some difficulty in finding their way back to us the country being quite a labyrinth so that I am obliged to give them up as lost to us for this Voyage. We however remain where we are for the remainder of the Day in case they may cast up by Morn^g; it is quite unnecessary to stop longer as there is no chance of their falling in with us. Their

Lives are not in danger as by keeping in a North West direction they must fall on the Bow River which they can cross by Raft or Swimming and get to Carlton or they can make a Raft & drift down to Cumberland; they have plenty of Ammunition and cannot Starve, but they will suffer much as they have but one pair of Indian Shoes each and no other cloathing than their Shirts & Leather Trousers. If I was even alive & similarly situated I should be under no apprehension in regard to my safety and therefore feel very little uneasiness about theirs unless they fall in with hostile Indians in which case they will lose their scalps as a matter of course but that is not likely as we have not as yet seen any trace of Natives.[207]

Monday, May 16. Our Guide has been at fault for these last Days having gone further to the Southward than our course and I was about to make up my mind to return to Carlton fearing we might get bewildered in the Sea of plains we this Morn^{g} entered upon when he fortunately fell on Salt Lake which he immediately recognised; this piece of Water is about 60 Miles in length and 3 to 10 Miles broad quite salt.[208] Proceeded along this Lake all Day having the Touch Wood Hills in sight on the other side. Hitherto the Weather has been very Warm and the Muschetoes more numerous and troublesome than I ever knew them to be but this Even^{g} to our great relief it has become extremely cold.

Tuesday, May 17. At 12 A. M. to Day got to Rocky Lake the South side of which we followed until Sun Set when we put up near the Dogs head[209] and for the first time since we left Carlton

[207] See Appendix B, *post*, 356.

[208] This lake appears on present-day maps as a pair of lakes known as the Quill lakes.

[209] Simpson's route beyond the Quill lakes was a trail running along the south bank of Whitesand River to a crossing near an elevation called Dog Knoll, thence northwest to Fort Pelly on the upper waters of the Assiniboine, thence southeast along the east bank of the Assiniboine to Fort Ellice, and thereafter due east to Fort Garry. There is today in the region of Simpson's "Rocky Lake" no body of water of sufficient size to fit his description of it, but Fishing, Whitesand and Dog lakes differ in their elevation only slightly and the ground separating them is low

our Guide found himself perfectly at Home on the route. Found a number of Swan Goose & Duck Eggs this afternoon; they were too highly flavoured for my taste but considered a great treat by the people; our allowance of provisions has been very scanty since the loss of our hunters and if we are not more successful tomorrow one of the Horses must suffer.

Wednesday, May 18th. The Country we have passed these two last days is a succession of plains Lakes & Hummocks of Poplars but to Day we have travelled Waist deep in Mud & Water and obliged to Swim the Horses in many places; the Weather very unfavorable, bitterly cold for the Season, blowing hard and occasional hail Showers we however kept close at our Work and got to the head of the Assiniboine River within a Mile of the old Establishment of Fort Alexandria[210] or Hibernia at Dusk; Fort Pelly[211] cannot be above 15 or 20 Miles distant from this place but none of our people know the exact spot and as it might occupy more time to find it out than we can at present afford I have determined on proceeding direct for Q'Appelle.

Thursday, May 19th. Severe Weather, a little Snow on the ground & freezing hard with strong N. W. Wind. Left our Encampt on the South bank of the Assiniboine River at Dawn and struck out towards the plains in a Southerly direction; there being no track had much difficulty in getting through the Swamps and Underwood. Breakfasted at the Riviere Blanche[212]

lying, with saline lakes, deep sloughs and marshes predominating along Whitesand River, so that it is likely that, in a period of slightly greater precipitation than at present prevails there, an extended shallow lake covered the whole area. There seems to have been considerable shrinkage generally in the lakes of this region during the last century. See, for the trail, "Papers relative to the Exploration of the Country between Lake Superior and Red River Settlement" in *Brit. Parl. Papers, 1859* (sess. 2), XXII, 649; also Simpson, *Journey Round the World*, I, 68-76.

[210] Fort Alexandria was an old North West Company post located (David Thompson's map) on the west bank of the Assiniboine River in what is now Township 32, Range 3, west of the Second Meridian. It was abandoned in 1805. There is a brief description of it in Harmon, *Journal*, 59.

[211] Fort Pelly was located on the north side of the Assiniboine River at the Second Meridian.

[212] Rivière Blanche is the present Whitesand River.

an awful Thunder Storm and were drenched with Torrents of Rain and in the Morn^{g} we could scarcely force our way through the Muschetoes; at 10 A. M. got to the Forks of Q'Appelle & Assiniboine Rivers where we fell in with a couple of plain Crees; I pressed those indolent rascals to Guide us to Brandon House and offered them the value of 100 Skins for that Service but they declined it with a variety of excuses, such as the danger of being cut off by War parties which they represented as very numerous, the risk of losing their Horses in crossing the Rivers &c &c so they left us with the most hearty curses from every one of our party. Made several ineffectual attempts to cross the Assiniboine River owing to its high state & the Depth of Mud at its edges, we had therefore to retrace our Steps a little way up the Q'Appelle River and at length found a place which we considered passible but here we had a variety of difficulties; the Water was too Deep to Wade, there was no wood of any kind to make a Raft several of our people could not Swim and the bottom & banks so soft that there was the utmost danger of drowning or miring our Horses; in this dilemma we had nearly resolved on killing our Horses & making Skin Canoes of their Hides for the purpose of going down to the Settlement by Water I however being more at home in the Water than any of my fellow travellers and anxious to save the lives of the poor animals, stripped & Swam across with a few things 3 others followed my example and by making several crossings in this way we got the whole of our little Baggage over; the Horses were driven across those people who could not Swim holding on by their Tails and with the assistance of Cords we hauled the poor Animals out of the Mud; in like manner we got across the Assiniboine River having been occupied 5 hours in effecting our passage over these two Rivers nearly the whole of which time myself and those with me being naked in the Mud & Water exposed to the blood thirsty assaults of Miriads of Muschetoes, in short I believe there never was an unfortunate Govr in such a Woeful plight as that of the North^{n} Deptm^{t} of Ruperts Land this Day. In the even^{g} saw a Grizzle Bear, his sense of smelling must be very acute as from the distance of more than a Mile he came towards us at a canter; we concealed ourselves behind some Bushes anxiously waiting his approach but the rogue discovered us and retreated before we could make sure of him, he was the largest I ever saw. Put up at Dusk much fatigued.

Monday, May 23d. Got under Weigh at 3 A. M. crossed several small Rivers of which our Guide could not give me the names. My people and Horses are getting so low upon it that I am almost afraid we shall stick on the way; three of the men lame & obliged to Ride in turns altho our Wretched Cattle are more Dead than alive.

Tuesday, May 24th. The Weather fine and the Track generally good except where intersected by streams which either great or small give us a vast deal of trouble owing to their muddy banks and rendering necessary for us to haul the Horses out of the Mire with Cords. The muschetoes as usual most tormenting.

Wednesday, May 25th. Our Guide expecting to shorten the route by cutting across some points of the River Wandered into the plain this Morng and it occupied us until 9 P. M. to regain the River when we found ourselves within a Mile of the old Establishment of Brandon House[215] which I meant to have visited but was alarmed by the appearance of a band of Horses Grasing on the skirts of the Plain which from the trimming of their Mains & Tails I conjectured to belong to some straggling War party who might probably be encamped at the House, we therefore took possession of a small clump of pines for the Night where we could defend ourselves against all the Indians of the Plains if necessary. All hands on guard to Night.

Thursday, May 26. Started before Day break and was very much inclined to give the Indian Horses the benefit of a few Miles exercise in order to relieve our Weary limbs but ascertained the proprietors could track us and not knowing their Strength

[215] Brandon House, on the north bank of the Assiniboine River, opposite or nearly opposite the mouth of the Souris, was built by the Hudson's Bay Company in 1794.

thought it was as well to let be for let be. Incessant Rain throughout the Day and so foggy we could not keep our Land Marks; lost ourselves among the "Sandy Knowls" for about 3 hours and having separated in various directions in search of the track had some difficulty in collecting our small party. Put up at the old Pine Fort.[216] The Settlement is still three long Days March distant, considering our Worn out condition and finding that we could not all get that length without assistance I dispatched the two best Men of our party Burassa & Cadotte with a Note to Cuthbert Grant[217] at the White Horse Plain begging he would immediately send us relief in provisions and Horses.

Friday, May 27th. Passed a dismal Night, Soaked with continual Rain and unable to light a Fire our touchwood having got Wet, we were therefore obliged to lay shivering in our drenched Leather hanging about us so much Tripe until Day light when we continued our route and got to Portage la Prairie at Sun set.

Saturday, May 28th. Seeing this Morng that our people and Horses could scarcely crawl and our Provisions being entirely out Yesterday morng I proposed to Mr McMillan that he and I should push on ahead on foot in hopes of reaching the White Horse plain but we had not gone far when we found the low Grounds near long Lake inundated we had therefore to pass through a Swamp of 9 Miles in length frequently up to the Waist in Mud & Water; the suppressed sighs & groans of my poor Friend McMillan convinced me that he was fully as low upon it as myself we however persevered and got to the White Horse Plain at Dusk. Grant was not at home otherwise we should have had

[216] Pine Fort was a post of the North West Company built in 1785 and abandoned nine years later. It was located on the north bank of the Assiniboine River near the entrance of Pine Creek.

[217] Cuthbert Grant was the leader of the *mêtis* or half-breeds congregated at the White Horse Plain some fifteen miles above the present city of Winnipeg on the north bank of the Assiniboine River. He was a prominent figure in the armed collision between the North West Company and the Hudson's Bay Company, which culminated in the Battle of Seven Oaks in 1816 in which he led the *mêtis* in the attack on the Selkirk settlers. He was later "Warden of the Plains" and a councillor of Assiniboia.

earlier assistance, but our Messengers being unable to proceed themselves hired an Indian to go to Fort Garry[218] with my Note which by a few hurried lines from Govr Pelly & M^{r} McKenzie astonished them beyond measure, they instanter dispatched Men, Horses, Eatables, Drinkables and dry cloaths for our relief but I was so anxious to get once more among my much valued Red River Friends that without looking at the contents of their Saddle Bags (altho' furnished with an excellent appetite) I got across my old charger "Jonathan" gave him the Rein with a smart cut across the haunches and commenced a furious attack on the Gates of Fort Garry at 12 P. M. which was immediately answered by a most hearty welcome from Mr McKenzie and every person at the Garrison and here I purpose taking a rest of Eight Days after having performed one of the most dangerous and harrassing Journeys ever undertaken in the Country through which thank God I have got with no injury or inconvenience worthy of Notice.

Tuesday, June 7$^{th.}$ Since my arrival at this place I have been constantly occupied with Govr Pelly on various matters connected with Colony affairs and am most happy in being enabled to say that he appears to have gone through the troublesome Duties of his Government with much credit to himself and great benefit to the Settlement which is in a state of the most perfect tranquillity; the Colonists would not be contented if even Manna & Gold Dust were Showered down upon them, the Govr however is sufficiently popular, and the well disposed and thinking part of the Community have at length discovered his worth.[219] Chief Factor McKenzies uniform and powerful support was always at hand and his sound judgment and advice invariably forthcoming and if Red River Settlement does not improve under management combining so much Worth and talent its ultimate fate is

[218] Fort Garry at the junction of the Assiniboine and Red rivers was the fur-trade center of the Red River and neighboring districts. Fort Douglas, a mile to the north of it, was the administrative center of the district of Assiniboia. For a brief description of Fort Garry see Ross, *Fur Hunters*, II, 261, 262.

[219] Governor Pelly was thought by his contemporaries to lack firmness and decision. See Oliver, *Canadian North-West*, I, 45, 46.

hopeless indeed! As I anticipated, Govr Pelly could not give me the meeting I requested at Norway House owing to Mrs Pellys delicate state of Health and had determined on returning to England with his Family by the Fall Ship; I pointed out to him the necessity of my going Home for the purpose of communicating with the Honble Committee on business by shewing him my Columbia Dispatch, but his Mind was unalterably made up Dr Hamlyn having intimated that if Mrs Pelly did not go to England this Season for the benefit of Medical advice her Life was in danger, but if that was saved it was more than probable she would be attacked with palsy and not only lose her corporal but mental faculties; Dr Hamlyn moreover stated that he did not think Mrs Pelly could with any degree of safety undertake the Voyage unless attended by Govr Pelly and these statements he made to me in his professional capacity in the presence of Govr Pelly; under those circumstances they take their departure from hence for York about the 20th July. The next point to be considered was who would be the fittest person to take charge of the Settlement during our absence; this did not require a Moments hesitation our Eyes being simultaneously directed to Chief Factor McKenzie[220] and we have but one opinion on the subject which is that no Man in Ruperts Land is so fit for it; his judgment is sound, his coolness and determination proverbial, the whole of the population is under his influence and he is both feared and respected by Indians as well as by Settlers, in short I consider our choice as a most happy one; Mr McKenzie is much averse to being placed in such a prominent situation but knowing the importance and necessity of both Govr Pelly & myself going home he saw there was no alternative and accordingly undertook the troublesome & laborious duties of superintending the Colony for the Current Year in addition to those of the Honble Coy and I do congratulate all interested, in seeing it in such able and competent hands.

It was my intention to have started tomorrow for Bas de la Riviere[221] to meet the Montreal Express Canoe, but I was agreeably

[220] See Appendix B, *post*, 358.

[221] Bas de la Rivière is the name given to the mouth of the Winnipeg River.

surprised by the arrival of Mr Joseph McGillivray[222] with the Packet about 11 P. M. of the 5th; he reached Bas de la Riviere on the 3d and hearing of my being at this place continued his route immediately. By him I have received the Honble Committees Despatches up to the 11th March; their contents are most highly gratifying, conveying the pleasing accounts that the Coys affairs are in a state of great prosperity and rapid improvement, likewise their unqualified approbation of all my proceedings and arrangements which they are pleased to mark in the handsomest manner by an expression of their satisfaction with my conduct, a gratuity of £500 for past Services and an increase of £200 p Annum Saly; these proofs of their approbation flatter me exceedingly, they cannot be repaid or acknowledged by greater zeal or devotion to the Coys interests than I have already manifested but have laid me under obligations which I trust are duly appreciated and for which I shall ever entertain the deepest Sense of gratitude. I am also proud to say that several members of the Committee have honored me with private communications expressive of their Friendly desposition to and good opinion of myself. My heart overflows with gratitude and while I have health & Strength if I know myself they will not have occasion to alter their Sentiments towards me.

Having finished my arrangements with Govr Pelly and being anxious to get to Norway House as early as possible I took leave of the Settlement this afternoon accompanied by Messrs McKenzie McGillivray & McMillan; the first goes to Norway House for the purpose of receiving official instructions in regard to his temporary charge of the Colony and in order to give his opinion on the projected arrangements connected with the business of the West side the Mountains being more conversant on that subject from his knowledge of and experience in the country than any of the Gentlemen with whom I am likely to meet at Norway House.

The Winnipeg River was part of the Rainy Lake route from the Great Lakes to the West.

[222] Joseph McGillivray was in 1825 a chief trader of the Hudson's Bay Company assigned to the Severn River district. He was a son of the famous William McGillivray of the North West Company.

Monday, June 13th. Norway House. Our passage across the Lake was most boisterous and occupied us until this afternoon; we parted with the Montreal Express Canoe and two of the Compys Boats in a Storm on the Morning of the 11th saw them in distress and making for a Harbour which I trust they gained while we kept driving under close reefed Sail shipping sufficient Water to keep two Men constantly baling at length it became necessary to give up the contest and we put ashore under the Lee of Rabbit Point from whence we started yesterday afternoon, kept at our Oars all Night had the benefit of a fair breeze in the course of the Day and got here at Sun Set where I found Messrs Stewart McIntosh McDonell Rowand & Laroque with their respective Brigades. Here I received the Honble Committees despatches p the Ship of last Fall, my private Letters from England by the same conveyance and communications from all parts of the country which are highly satisfactory.

Tuesday, June 14th. The Canoe and Boats with which we parted on the 11th made their appearance to Day likewise Messrs Leith & Kennedy with the Columbia Brigade. Those Gentlemen met Capt Franklin and Dr Richardson[223] on the 12th Inst. wind bound in Cedar Lake; they expected to have fallen in with me coming down the Saskatchawaine and appeared disappointed that we had taken different routes, they had however nothing particular to communicate and appeared much pleased and gratified by the arrangements which had been made for them all along the route; they expect to reach Fort Chipwyan in sufficient time to send back their Canoes to Montreal this season which can be done with perfect ease; Mr Back[224] in charge of two half laden Canoes was coming on behind. Those Gentlemen will

[223] Dr. John Richardson was surgeon and naturalist to the first and second expeditions of Captain John Franklin to the Arctic. He led the search expedition which in 1847 was sent out in the vain hope of tracing the lost explorer.

[224] Lieutenant George Back was an officer on Franklin's first and second expeditions to the Arctic. He himself was the leader of two famous Arctic expeditions, for his services in which he was knighted in 1839 and raised to the rank of admiral in 1857.

have no ground for complaint on the present occasion;[225] we are all endeavouring & anxious to anticipate their wishes and whatever support assistance and Co-operation they may require of us will be cheerfully afforded. It was my intention to have assembled a Council at this place for the purpose of getting through the principal arrangements of the Season so as to be enabled to proceed to England via Canada in hopes of getting there about the latter end of August before the departure of the Columbia Ship and thereby have an opportunity of communicating fully with the Honble Committee so as to enter upon the extension of Trade on the West side the Mountain without delay if such met their Honors approbation; all the Gentlemen I have had an opportunity of communicating with on the subject saw the propriety of this measure but on looking over the correspondence of Mr Sect^{y} Smith with Messrs McGillivrays Thain & Co.[226] of Montreal I find by that Gentlemans Letter of 8th Dec that the Columbia Ship of this Season was intended to have Sailed early in the Summer; in which case no benefit but serious inconvenience to the Service generally would result from my absence as it would have been impossible to have got to London before the end of August. I have therefore altered my plan deferring it until the Fall when I shall proceed agreeably to their Honors instructions but in order to give them the earliest intimation of our proceedings I purpose dispatching a Light Canoe for Canada with dispatches for England as soon as a sufficient number of Gentlemen assemble to form a regular Council.

My Columbia Voyage being now considered as terminated I shall conclude this Journal which any person who may glance at it will perceive was never intended to have gone out of my own possession, but as there is not a thought, word or action connected

[225] On the occasion of Franklin's first expedition to the Arctic the Hudson's Bay Company was engaged in its desperate trade war with the North West Company, and the explorer had to leave Fort Chipewyan in July, 1820, with inadequate supplies.

[226] Messrs. McGillivrays Thain & Co. was the company organized on Nov. 30, 1822, to wind up the affairs of the North West Company and to act as agents of the Hudson's Bay Company in Canada. See G. C. Davidson, *The North West Company* (University of California, *Publications in History*, VII), 184-193.

with my duty which I can have any object in concealing from the Honble Committee, it is my intention to hand it to the Dep^{ty} Govr *in Confidence* knowing that he will make the proper use of whatever it contains worthy of remark and be so indulgent as to excuse any blunders that may have crept into it, and this I am satisfied he will readily do when he knows that many parts of it were scrawled off on the Voyage under circumstances not favorable to study and that my time does not now enable me to reperuse, far less to revise or correct, it.

Names of the different Tribes inhabiting the Banks of the Columbia from the Cascades Portage to the Rocky Mountain 1824-5.

Soteaux	South	side	River Cascades
Cathlieye-ach-eachs	“	“	“ above Cascades
Lamlepams	North	side	Elk River
Wapamthla	South	side	Below Dalles
Necutamechs	North	“	“ “
Wascopam	“	“	opposite Dalles
Yampam	“	“	“ Chutes
Lowhum	South	side	above Chutes
Day's River	“	“	above Lapum River
Sapa	“	“	Small River
Youmatalloni	“	“	“ “
Walla Wallas	“	“	Walla Walla R.
Cassispa	“	“	Lewis's R.
Eya Kimu	North	“	Small River
Nasputsemacks	“	“	Eyakima River
Ispipichimacks	“	“	“
Scam-nam nacks	“	“	“
Iscamoomacks	“	“	Priests Rapids
Incomicanatook	“	“	above Priests Rapids
Piscowes	“	“	River same name
Intiatook	“	“	above “ “
Tsillani	“	“	River “ “
Meatuho	“	“	“ “ “

Okinagan	North side River same name
Samilkumeighs	" " " " "
Nispellum	" " " " "
Simposllechach	" " " " "
Spokane	South side River of this name
Isnihoyelps	" " below Kettle Falls
Sinwhoyelpetook	North side River same name
Callespellum	South " " " "
Arcduplatte	South side Kootoney Lake
Calsiulk	" " Kootoney River
Sinachicks	Lakes of Main River
Skeechhues	Lake of same name
Paloosh	Lewis & Clarkes River
Shahaptains	Forks of Lewis & Clarkes River
Snakes	South branch Lewis & Clarkes River
Shewhoppes	Tho[s.] River south branch
Sintencutiacuti	" north "
Younahanus	Frazers River below Alexand[a]
Stlemuhoohnuhoos	" " towards Tho[s] River
Lilowit	North & West Frazers River
Necutamuchs	Forks Frazers River
Cayouse	Between Walla Walla & Blue Mts.
Flat heads	Flathead River.

Rough estimate of the Population on the Columbia River from the Coast to the Cascade Portage as far as the influence of the Tide is felt, a distance of about 120 miles, 1824-25.

Tribes	Situation of Villages	Principal Chiefs	Free		Slaves		Total
			Males	Females	Males	Females	
Clatsops	Point Adams south side	Waphoola	50	50	20	10	130
Chinooks	Chinook Point north side	Concomely	350	200	100	70	720
Chinooks	Point George south side	Calpo	50	50	50	40	190
Wakycomes	Grays Bay north side	Skinaguia	100	60	30	20	210
Cathlamet	South side	Ashwallax	50	50	15	10	125
Chillwitz	River same name south side	Killakina	60	60	20	10	150
Upper Chillwitz	River north side	Wasalsal	50	50	20	15	135
Clatskaneyes	Upper Chillwitz north side	Illhachwa	70	70	20	15	175
Wacumap	Mouth lower branch Willamot River South	Kasseno	100	100	50	40	290
Catleapcotle	Small River North Side		30	30	20	15	195
Twotillacome } Namuit }	Two villages on an Island in the River opposite the Willamot		80	80	20	10	190
Wasoughalles	North side		40	40	10	10	100
Canhooks or Catlatla	Cascade Portage north side		60	60	20	10	150
			1140	950	395	275	2760

STANDARD OF TRADE COLUMBIA RIVER 1824-25

Returns	Skins Made Beaver	
	Ft. George	Spokan House
1 Large Prime Beaver	1	1
1 Small " "	½	½
1 pup " "	¼	¼
1 large Beaver coating	1	1
1 large land otter	1	1
1 small " "	½	½
1 prime sea otter	12	
1 com. large sea otter	10	
1 med. " "	7	
1 small " "	3	
1 large piece coating	2	
1 pup	¼	
1 musk rat	1/10	1/10
1 mink	¼	¼
1 martin	¼	⅓
Dressed Leather Etc.		
1 prime deer skin	2	2
1 prime chevx	1	1
1 large wooden canoe native work	15	
1 small according to siz	8	
1 good working horse	15	15
1 Chinook Hat 1st quality	4	
1 " " common	1	
1 large Chinook mat	2/5	
1 " " double	½	

STANDARD OF TRADE COLUMBIA RIVER 1824-25—Continued

Goods	Skins Made Beaver	
	Ft. George	Spokan House
Awls Indian p. doz.	1	1
Axes Com. Half ea.	2	2
" " small ea.	1	1
" Square-headed half ea.	3	2
" " small ea.	2	1
Blankets Plain 3 points ea.	6	6
" " 2½ " "	5	5
" " 2 " "	4	4
" " 1½ " "	3	3
" " 1 " "	2	2
" Green 4 " "	10	2
" " 3 " "	8	2
" H.Bay 3 " "	8	2
" " 2½ " "	7	6
" Rose 9/4 "	5	6
" " 8/4 "	4	6
Balls Musket & Trading p. lb.	1	
Beads Sky Blue Enam[d] p. lb.	5	
" Transparent Canton "	5	10
Buttons Y & W metal p. doz	1	1
" " " List p doz.	½	1
Cloth Blue List p. fathom	6	6
" Com[n] Scarlet fathom	8	10
Combs Com[n] Horn pr doz	3	6
Coating Bolt, Blue, Grey & Red pr fathom	4	
Capôts Woolen 3½ ells ea.	4	5
" " 3 ells ea.	3	4
" " 2½ " "	2½	3
Dags Plain 7 inches ea.	1	1½
" Eyed 8 " "	2	2
" " 12 " "	3	2
Duffles Blue pr yd	3	
Files flat 6 & 7 inches pr doz	6	12

STANDARD OF TRADE COLUMBIA RIVER 1824-25—Continued

Goods	Skins Made Beaver	
	Ft. George	Spokan House
Files flat 8, 9 & 10 inches pr doz	12	12
Flints, Gun pr doz	1	1
Guns Com. N. W. each	20	18
Guns fine half stocked ea.	30	
Gartering pr. Roll	3	4
Glasses looking oval gilt ea.	1	1
" " pocket cased ea.	½	1
Gun Powder per lb.	3	4
Hats Beaver ea.	6	
" Com^{n} Wool ea.	3	
Hooks Large cod p. doz.	1	1
" Small Kerb p doz.	½	
Horns Powder ea.	1	1
Knives Scalping ea.	1	1
" Folding ea.	½	½
" Clasp	1	1
Kettles brass & copper pr lb.	2	2½
" Tin pr Gall.	2	
Needles assorted p. 20	1	
Pistols Com. American ea.	3	4
" Engl. brown barrels	4	4
Rum reduced ⅓ p. bottle	1	
Rifles American ea.	30	
" English twist Barrels ea.	40	30
Rings plain brass per doz	⅓	1
Strouds com^{n} blue b^{d} cord p. yd	2½	3
Strouds H Bay blue b^{d} cord p. yd	3	3
Scissors women pr. pair	½	½
" large shop pr. pair	1	1
Shot Beaver & Duck p. lb.	½	1
Tobacco Twist p. lb.	1½	2
" Leaf p. lb.	1	1½
Thimbles brass p. doz	½	1
Vermillion p. lb.	4	8
Wire Brass Collar p. lb.	2	

STANDARD OF TRADE COLUMBIA RIVER 1824-25—Concluded

Provisions	Skins Made Beaver	
	Ft. George	Spokan House
1 Red deer Fresh	4½	
1 Chev[1] "	3	2
1 Beaver "	1	1
1 Black Bear "	1	2
1 Sturgeon fish mdlg size	2	
1 Salmon large 30 lbs.	1/3	1
1 Gall. Smelts or Pilchards	½	
1 Seal	3	
1 Gall Wapanoos or Columbia Potatoes	½	
1 Gall Berries of all sorts	1	3
1 Gall Fish oil	2	
1 Gall. Hazle Nuts	1	
Sturgeon Glue well prepared per lb.	2	
Swans ea.	1	
Geese "	½	
Ducks "	¼	
Cranes "	½	

APPENDIX A.

GOVERNOR & COMMITTEE TO GOVERNOR SIMPSON[1]

London 27 Feb. 1822

9. We understand that hitherto the trade of the Columbia has not been profitable, and from all that we have learnt on the subject we are not sanguine in our expectations of being able to make it so in future. But if by any improved arrangement the loss can be reduced to a small sum, it is worth a serious consideration, whether it may not be good policy to hold possession of that country, with the view of protecting the more valuable districts to the North of it; and we wish you to direct the attention of the Council to this subject and collect all the information which you can obtain from individuals acquainted with the country.
11. We consider the charge of freight will be less than the allowance hitherto made to Mess[rs] Perkins & Co. and that if we are disappointed in obtaining a proper price for the furs here, we can at a very small expence ship them from hence to Canton, and that at all events it is not desirable under present circumstances to continue the arrangement with Mess[rs] Perkins & Co.
12. Should the result of all your enquiries be unfavorable to the plan of continuing the trade of Columbia it will be proper to consider, whether it will be better to continue the trading establishments there until the goods are nearly all expended, or to transport those remaining after the business of the winter 1823/24 is finished to New Caledonia.
13. The Russians are endeavoring to set up claims to the North West Coast of America as low as Latitude 51, and we think it desirable to extend our trading posts as far to the West and North from Fraser's River in Caledonia, as may be practicable, if there appears any reasonable prospect of doing so profitably. It is probable that the British Government would support us in

[1] H. B. Co. General Letter Book No. 620.

the possession of the country, which may be occupied by trading posts, and it is desirable to keep the Russians at a distance.

JOHN L. LEWES TO GOVERNOR SIMPSON[2]

Ft. George 2 April 1822

....The trade from the Interior, has this year far exceeded any thing hitherto, or what could be expected from the most sanguine hopes of the Gentlemen at the head of the affairs last fall this plainly proves that the Natives are now become so much accustomed to the produce of the Civilized world, that they find it necessary to exert themselves to procure their wants and this they know can only be done by their hunting the beaver.

Hitherto the Columbia department has been but a losing Concern to the N. W. Company, owing to the great number of people setting themselves free, but it is to be hoped, as measures are taking to discharge them gradually that the profits of the Concern will augment in proportion, for it is immence the money these people have hitherto spent for little or nothing. The total amount of the returns for this year, you will see by the accounts, will exceed Fifteen Thousand Skins, the prospects for the ensuing year are by all accounts of the most encouraging aspect.

Immence tracks of Land to the North of Fort George remain still unexplored, abounding as I am giving to understand with Beaver, as also the Snake Country, which has hitherto been looked upon with rather to high a glance, that is if the present Company wishes to extend the trade in those quarters, and find that the Canton Market will bear an increase in what is at present annually sent, but upon this head I must refer you to Messrs Haldane and McKenzie, both of whom I presume you will see this Summer, and whom are by far more qualified to give you all the requisite information, especially the latter Gentleman, who has passed several years in the Snake Country, and who knows every particular Concerning it, both with respect to its recourses, and

[2] H. B. Co. Journal No. 589. John L. Lewes was a chief trader in the Columbia Department in 1822.

the great hazard attending those who go there, as the Natives are of a most Hostile disposition towards the whites.

The Posts in the Interior from Fort George are first the Wala Wallas, second the Thomsons River Department, consisting of two posts, the third and last is the Spokan Department consisting of three Posts, it is from this last mentioned department, that the greatest number of Furs are made, and which are of the best quality procured in the Columbia, as part of the Beaver killed are on the borders of the Mountain, the returns from there are One Hundred & Thirty four Packs, being an increase on the last years trade of about forty. The returns of Thomsons River is Two Thousand four Hundred Beavers, an increase on the last years returns of Six Hundred, and the returns of the Wala Wallas Twelve Hundred Skins, an increase here also on the last year of Four Hundred. This as I have already said before will shew that the general trade is improving; and it is to be hoped that by our urgent exertions, that the ensuing year will be still more favourable....

WILLIAM SMITH TO MESS^rs PERKINS & CO.[3] CANTON

London 10 April 1822

I am directed by the Governor and Committee to acquaint you, that the Consignment of Beaver which you will receive this Year from the Columbia by the Houqua is on account of the Hudson's Bay Company, and that it is made to you on the same terms as those on which you have for some years received Consignments from the same place on account of the late Northwest Comp^y of Montreal.

I am therefore to request that you will not sell the above mentioned Beaver at a lower rate than Four Dollars p Skin, and that you will keep it on hand until you can obtain that price or until you hear further from me on the subject. I understand, that when acting for the Northwest Comp^y you made on receipt of the Beaver a Shipment to your house at Boston on account

[3] H. B. Co. Gen. Letter Book No. 620. William Smith was secretary of the Hudson's Bay Company.

that the Ship might not be detained, and the Governor and Committee have no objection to the same practice being adopted in the present instance if necessary or convenient and they expect that the return cargo to Boston will consist of articles likely to meet a Market there, that the Account may be closed within a reasonable time.

It is not intended to send any further Consignments of Beaver from the Columbia to Canton; but as it may be found advantageous to send Beaver of a finer description, and also Otter and other Skins better adapted to the China market, than such Beaver as is procured at the Columbia; I have to request you will furnish me with all the information you can procure on this subject and give me your opinion of the prices which you think they would fetch at Canton, as the proper description of Skins could be selected here and shipped to you by the Vessells of the East India Company. I have also to request you will inform me on what terms you will receive and sell such Consignments, and remit the Proceeds in Bills of the East India Comp^{y} or in China produce through Boston.

GOVERNOR SIMPSON TO A. COLVILE[4]

Ft. Garry 20 May 1822

....Mr. McTavish joined me at York about the middle of Octr. and with him I was busily occupied in making various arrangements for the business of the ensuing season, until the Rivers and Lakes set fast early in December, when I took my departure for the interior, making a circuitous journey of about 1500 miles by Norway House, Cumberland, Swan River, Qu'Appelle and Brandon House and arrived at this place early in March, much gratified by my trip as it gave me a thorough knowledge of the Country and Trade, and introduced me to the acquaintance of some of our fresh allies,[5] who received me with much politeness and attention.

[4] Dominion Archives, Selkirk Transcripts, XXIV, 7587.

[5] Refers to former wintering partners of the North West Company who in consequence of the coalition had become field partners in the Hudson's Bay Company.

I am sorry to say that the prospects of Trade in the Districts through which I passed, were by no means flattering; the late arrangements have given mortal offence to the Indians, a settled and sullen melancholy seems to have arrested their exertions, and altho' the Factors and Traders have used the most conciliatory measures to cheer them, they are as yet unsuccessful. Their immediate wants have been fully supplied, but of course the scenes of extravagance are at an end, and it will be a work of time to reconcile them to the new order of things. I have made it my study to examine the nature and character of the Indians and however repugnant it may be to our feelings, I am convinced they must be ruled with a rod of iron, to bring, and keep them in a proper state of subordination, and the most certain way to effect this is by letting them feel their dependence upon us. In the Woods and Northern barren grounds this measure ought to be pursued rigidly next year if they do not improve, and no credit, not so much as a load of ammunition given them until they exhibit an inclination to renew their habits of industry. In the plains however this system will not do, as they can live independent of us, and by withholding ammunition, tobacco and spirits, the staple articles of trade, for one year they will recover the use of their Bows and spears and lose sight of their smoking and Drinking habits; it will therefore be necessary to bring those Tribes round by mild and cautious measures which may soon be effected....

Little or no provision has been made for them [Swiss emigrants to Red River Colony] here, indeed the crops were so unproductive, and the Provision Trade during the Summer so triffling, that nothing of consequence could be collected, and the unprecedented and almost total failure of the Buffalo with the encreased population, has made this Colony the most distressing scene of starvation that can well be conceived. I have not heard that any persons connected with the Settlement, have actually perished through hunger, but soul and body have been kept together on next to nothing, chiefly by a little musty Grain which Mr. McDonell[6] served out with great economy and an esculent

[6] Alexander McDonell was at this time Governor of Assiniboia.

root called "Indian Potatoes" resembling a horse raddish in appearance but very insipid; this root which is plentiful here they eat either raw or boiled, but possesses little nourishment....

On their arrival Mr. McDonell sent the greater part of them to Pambina for the purpose of being near the Buffalo, where they chiefly remained until the opening of the navigation; they did through Freemen and Indians pick up a triffling supply of animal food, but how they have spun out the Winter and Spring is unexplicable; Horses, Dogs, Bears, Buffalo in short whatever came in their way was devoured.

The Company's establishments from this place to the source of the Assiniboine have even been at times in a state of Famine and several of our people have deserted in consequence. The failure of the Buffalo may be attributed to two causes, one is that the plain Indians finding the coalition had taken place conceived that the sole object was as they express it "to render them pitiful," and by way of having revenge determined on Starving the Traders by keeping the Buffalo off in the Summer and Fall, which was easily effected by obstructing them at their usual passes to the Northward, setting fire to the Plains, etc. The other cause was that in this part of the Country and to the Northward we have had an unusually severe Winter with an extraordinary quantity of snow nearly 3 ft Deep, whereas to the Southward the Season has been mild and little or no snow so that the unfavorable state of the season prevented the Cattle from taking their usual Northern tour: a few straggling bands and solitary Bulls were however to be met with occasionally but so much hunted that it was impossible to pound them. The Indians have met with their deserts as many of them have starved to Death and they now consider it a judgement from "the Father of Life" (to use their own words) for their wickedness in driving the cattle away.

Mr. McGillivray[7] last year took much pains to impress on the

[7] Refers to Simon McGillivray, the North West Company partner, who was active in 1821 in arranging the terms of the coalition with the Hudson's Bay Company. For his activity in putting the agreement into effect in the field see the "Diary of Nicholas Garry" in Roy. Soc. Can., *Proceeds. and Trans.*, 2nd series, VI, sect. ii, 73-182.

information in case the subject should come before the Committee, if they were known by the very pious I might be looked upon as a true North Wester. The Committee I understand are desirous that Mr. West should attend at York Factory during the business months, this visit will not only interfere with our operations, but may be injurious in other respects, the Transport Season is so very limited that the best use must be made of our time, our Stores, Shops, Counting Houses etc must be open on Sundays as on Week days; from the Governor downwards we must closely attend from 4 A. M. till 10 P M, otherways things will revert to their former irregularity; the men of each District must have their two or three Days Drinking bout, and Brigades must start as they can be dispatched without respect to Days; the Parson will be the only idle man about the place, and he will have an opportunity of seeing the whole routine of our business which may be converted to an improper use at some future period, or he may feel it a point of Duty to give information of our immoral conduct (according to his doctrine) to people who might afterwards make a handle of it to the injury of the concern. Mr. West I believe to be a very good well meaning man and strictly correct in his conduct, but as the Hudsons Bay Compys Chaplain or Servant, inclined to deal too freely in politicks. In a conversation with him the other day I understood it is his intention to lay before some of the pious societies with whom he corresponds an expose of the baneful consequences of the use of Spiritous Liquors among the Indians and hopes that through their interference and that of some members of the Committee that it will be prohibited. It is not my province to go into this subject in a moral point of view and shall therefore confine my opinion thereon as to the effect such restriction might have on our Trade. If the quantity of Spirits given to Indians was calculated I am satisfied it would not amount to a pint p man annually on an average, which may give some idea of the extent of crime likely to result therefrom; and I'll venture to say there are not three murders committed annually on the average of the last Ten Years in the whole tract of country occupied by the Hudson's Bay Coy from ebriety. As an article of trade it is not generally used and I do not suppose we make Ten packs of Furs p annum by it: it is however the grand Stimulus to call forth the exertions of the Indians and I have often heard them reason thus, "it is not for your Cloth and Blankets that we undergo all this labor and fatigue, as in a short time we could reconcile ourselves to the use of Skins for clothes as our forefathers did, but it is the prospect of a Drink in the Spring to enable us to communicate freely and speak our minds to each other that carries us through the Winter and induces us to Work so hard." This I really believe to be the case, and that if Spirits were withheld it would materially discourage them and produce a lassitude which Weight of other property could not remove.

In the Provision Countries it is however a very principal article of Trade and indispensibly necessary: the Plain Indians are a bold independent race, Dress entirely in skins and with them Tobacco and Spirits are the principle commodities; a Quart of Mixed Liquer will at times procure more Pounded Meat and Grease than a Bale of Cloth, indeed our whole profit in that Trade is upon those articles, and if Provisions were paid for in Dry Goods they would eat up all the gains of the Fur Trade. I therefore sincerely hope the Committee will take due time to examine this subject and that they will not prematurely determine thereon, as it might be very injurious to the interests of the Concern; this last year I find they have been inclined to commence the Work of reform as they have limited us to about 40 to 42 puncheons Rum, less than half the quantity we require, and the consequence is that the people will not have an opportunity of disgorging their heavy Wages, that we are unable to give the European Servants their usual allowances, which may produce a Mutiny, that we cannot rectify a single Gallon on account of the waste it would occasion and in many other respects it will seriously interfere with our business. In a very short time we may despense with it as an article of Importation as the Colony will produce more than we can take off their hands, but some very strict regulations must be kept in force to prevent its becoming too general an article of Manufacture and Sale, otherways it may be ruinous to the Settlement; in less than Five Months, I am certain that Distillation will be commenced here and that all the present influence of the Company and Colony will not be able to suppress it. Some of our principal Settlers I suspect are even inclined to turn their attention that way and I should not be surprised that Mr. Bird[11] did under the Rose show their example. . . .

The North or Nelson River Track I shall say little further about until I have seen it on my way to York in about a month hence; when I first talked to Mr. Williams and the old hands about carrying on the northern business (say north of the English River) through that route they laughed at me, and I could scarcely get Mr. Williams to give me a patient hearing thereon until he knew I intended mentioning it to the Committee, it will now however beyond all doubt save about three weeks in the Season to those Northern Districts which is very important. . . .

With Mr. Williams I passed several days at Cumberland and can see that he is a little hurt at being removed to the Southward, but had the choice been left to himself he certainly would have gone thither as it is a more comfortable place and a sinecure compared with this Department. I think he will endeavour to lay aside his domineering manner, if not the business will not go on smoothly, all parties seem pleased with the change altho' a degree of soreness exists among our first allies that a Governor was not taken from their own side of the question.

Governor Simpson to Governor & Committee[12]

31 July 1822

8. From the result of Columbia Outfit 1821/22 the prospect is rather more flattering than hitherto, however large profits can scarcely be expected, yet by aeconomy and perseverance and following up measures which are found to be practicable, combined with a favourable Market for the Furs, the Trade might

[11] James Bird was a chief factor of the Hudson's Bay Company stationed at Red River. For many years after his retirement from the fur trade he was associated with the government of Assiniboia.

[12] H. B. Co. Journ. No. 588.

support itself, provided always, that no formidable opposition from the Americans assail us, in that quarter, for in that case, 'tis more than probable that all parties would loose Money by the Trade.

11. It is presumed that a Vessel direct from England to the Columbia, will be attended with much less Expense, than the mode hitherto followed through the Agency of Messrs Perkins & Co. of Boston. It might be supposed that the change respecting the Messrs Perkins & Co. would induce them to oppose us in the Columbia yet from their habits of business it is more than probable they will not enter into a speculation so doubtful as one to the Columbia from their knowledge of the state of things in that quarter.

12. Under existing circumstances in the Columbia it might be premature to relinquish that Trade as it appears the quantity of Furs from the Indians is encreasing and in several places capable of increase, and should a peace amongst some of the Tribes be effected a proportionally greater improvement in the Trade might still be expected.

GOVERNOR SIMPSON TO A. COLVILE[13]

York Factory 16 Aug. 1822

....Bird (in the background) has endeavoured to sow seeds of dissatisfaction in regard to the reduction of the N. W. Tariff of remains Spring 1821, as he feels that his capital is thereby materially depretiated; it bears rather hard on the H. B. Factors and Traders, but the N. W. have no cause of complaint as they brought the stock in trade to a good market; they entered into the Engagement with their eyes open, & it is but right that they should conform to it. The Equipments the N. W. I think had a right to expect from the wording of the Deed Poll and, Messrs Garry & McGillivray making no objection to their taking them last year at Fort William they now feel disappointed. Yet if these Gentlemen who mean to retire the third year, know their own interest they would be gainers by not having them as by

[13] Dominion Archives, Selkirk Transcripts, XXIV, 7757.

taking them they must be given to others which brings it nearly to the same thing in the long run as regards themselves, yet would be a heavy expence to the Coy in which I think they should not be indulged. Respecting the Clerks Salaries I had nearly come to an open rupture with them, but at last gained my point; they wished to make £100 the highest & the others proportionally low, but the terms now left for the consideration of the Committee I think are fair & liberal say £150, £100, £75, £60, £40 and Apprentices eligable to enter on the 2nd, 3rd & 4th Classes according to ability & merit; they are aware that they have no voice in the business & do not object to the scale handed to us by the Committee but merely submit their opinions in order that that subject may be reconsidered before acted upon. They have written me a Letter on those and a few other triffling grievances which I shall transmit to the Committee but I do not see that they have a right to expect much relief. Bird is the framer thereof & original cause, Haldane who is a sensible man but very selfish and illiberal backs him in it but if you once begin to give way there will be no end to their demands and some of those useless old people will never think of withdrawing from the concern but keep more enterprizing Young men in the background....

On the whole those who are collected here are reasonable well meaning men and I feel that we shall understand each other very well; they seem pleased with the interest I feel in the general concern and have no room to grumble about hardships and trouble as I make light of and am always ready to meet them myself and in regard to the general and particular arrangements of the business & Country I just know as much as themselves so that things go pretty much my own way....

P. S. The Nelson River Track is good, plenty of Water for Craft of any size but the current very strong; the Brigades North of Portage Fort du Trait will gain 3 Weeks on the passage out and in to York.[14] I came down in 5½ days p. Light Canoe, the Navigation when known will be perfectly safe and I am still of opinion

[14] Portage Fort du Trait is Frog Portage, for which see *ante*, 10 n. See also *ante*, 14 n.

that it will answer better for the Colony transport than the old Track. There are not more than 17 to 20 Portages, many of them but a few paces in length and none exceeding one mile. Not more than 40 miles Lake Way so that no danger of detention arising from bad weather exists, but if a road is not made across the Isthmus from York to the River it may at times be difficult to get round the head land.

GOVERNOR & COMMITTEE TO JOHN HALDANE AND JOHN D. CAMERON[15]

London 4 Sept. 1822

[Paraphrased]

The two men are requested to transmit to London a detailed statement of the trade of the Columbia Department, an opinion as to the possibility of extending it, and of bringing other articles than peltries to a profitable market, also whether a vessel can be beneficially employed on the coast in collecting furs and procuring provisions from California or elsewhere for the service of the Department, "and in the event of it being considered in future advisable to forward the Trade of the Columbia Department direct to Canton, you will state whether there is any officer in the department competent to take charge of the Goods and proceed with the ship as supercargo to Canton."

6. The Russian Government has published a ukase prohibiting any other nation trading within certain limits. This is a subject of negotiation between Russia, the United States and Great Britain. The two men are instructed to secure information concerning the Russian establishments to the north.

7. An extract from an American paper is enclosed which states that a party of 150 Americans have left the Missouri for an expedition across the Rocky Mountains towards the Columbia. The Governor and Committee have learned also of the intention of the American Government to form a settlement at the Columbia. Information is requested concerning these developments. "And we depend on your strenuous exertions to secure the Fur

[15] H. B. Co. Gen. Letter Book No. 620. John Haldane and J. D. Cameron were the chief factors in 1822 in charge of the Columbia Department.

Trade to Great Britain by your liberality to and kind treatment of the Natives.''

GOVERNOR SIMPSON TO A. COLVILE[16]

York Factory 5 Sept. 1822

....The price at which these Goods [from Y. F. to Colony] are to be furnished should be settled with the Committee at Home and not left to the Council and I think the 33⅓ p cent advance would be a very fair charge and leave a moderate profit. If the Council have any thing to do in the Settlement of price they will not be inclined to exhibit great liberality. All Goods however bought by Colonists or others at Red River should I think be charged at the same rate of advance as to our own Servants.

I regret exceedingly that it is not in my power to visit Red River this winter as my presence there might be very important to Captn. Bulger;[17] in the course of a few days hence I proceed for the Interior—round by Athabasca, Peace River, Lesser Slave Lake, and the Upper Posts of the Saskatchawain, the object of this immence Journey is if possible to check abuses which nothing but my own presence can effectually stop; and get rid of several Establishments which are a heavy burthen on the concern & may in my opinion be abandoned with perfect safety; this will not only relieve us of very heavy expences but Enable exhausted tracts of Country to recruit.

You will be pleased to learn that the business of this Season was got over smoothly & pleasantly without any feeling of party spirit arising from old grievances, there was however an attempt made by some of the indolent inactive Chief Factors on both sides to form a party for the purpose of keeping each other in their ''snug comfortable places'' & have things their own way. Bird and Haldane were the Leaders and as these sapient Gentlemen are about to meet in London it may be well to receive their

[16] Dominion Archives, Selkirk Transcripts, XXIV, 7766.

[17] Captain Bulger was the successor in 1822 to Alexander McDonell as Governor of Assiniboia.

opinions in many points with caution as both have their prejudices, are fond of ease and comfort, and the most selfish and illiberal altho' perhaps among the best informed of our Chief Factors. In the Southern Department (where there is a great want of talent) I think Mr. Haldane might be useful particularly at Temiscamagne but here he devotes himself more to Legislating than to business and has the entire lead of McDonald, George Keith and Leith his old XY partisans.[18] Bird is quite superannuated and I think will retire immediately—it is high time that some of these indolent men should make room for our more active enterprising Chief Traders who are far superior to them in every point of view.

A. Colvile to Governor Simpson[19]

London 10 March 1823

I have received your letters of the 20th May 16 July & 5 September, and am much obliged by your giving me such frank and detailed accounts of all that was going on at the Settlement.... Your doing so, I mean coming home, will of course depend in some measure on your being satisfied that your absence will not be attended with any serious mischief and I should hope you will have got the machine into good order by that time. The Committee are very much pleased with all your proceedings with the Council and with the correct view which you have taken of the powers of the Council and of the mode of arranging all the business. The only deficiency has been in the [form of the] accts....

The low price of the furs and the great amount of wages with the reduced value put on the remains must make a bad account this year, but I have no idea at present how much the loss will be; whatever it may appear to be on the face of the accounts the real balance will be shewn by allowing for the difference in the

[18] The X Y Company was a group of North West Company traders which broke away from the parent organization in 1795 and for some years engaged it in severe competition. The two groups were reunited in 1804.

[19] Dominion Archives, Selkirk Transcripts, XXV, 7825.

estimation of the remains. There is no question however even with lower prices for the furs that it will be a profitable concern in the future....

The business in the South has not been commenced so well as with you, partly I suspect from the Council having been left to themselves without any Governor. They seem to suppose they have the whole power and controul in their own hands and that the Governor and Committee are only their agents and commission merchants!! but I hope our letter by this dispatch will settle all that in a proper way. Haldane will go there and take charge of the Lake Superior department which requires a man of arrangement & firmness & I hope he will be of use in the Council there....

The Govr & Comm^{e} & the Gent^{n} of the 2^{d} part[20] however are quite convinced of the necessity of establishing an efficient Governor there [Red River Colony] with the means of exercising jurisdiction when required. They are all convinced that a well managed & governed settlement will be of service & if ill managed it will be an injury to the trade, and they consider it will be the means of the trade being relieved of the heavy burden of women and children & men with large families at the trading posts. These people, however, will require tight management & it is not just that Lord Selkirk should be put to expense for such people. Your proceedings at the Council with Mr. Halkett[21] in withdrawing the Pembina post and employing & empowering Mr. Clarke to assist & manage the people have been approved by all parties here, and you will perceive that the Co^{y} is to assist in paying the Govr. I do not see that there is any trade to be got at RR. in furs, and if from the failure of their Crops the settlers were in

[20] Refers to the signers of the coalition agreement of which the Gentlemen of the 1st part were the Governor and Committee, and the Gentlemen of the 2nd part, the McGillivrays and Edward Ellice. By the terms of the agreement the Gentlemen of the 2nd part retained certain rights in the reorganized Company, which were, however, in 1824 purchased by the Governor and Committee.

[21] John Halkett was an executor of Lord Selkirk's will and long a member of the Honorable Committee. He came to Rupert's Land in the summer of 1822 to counsel with Governor Simpson over the reorganization problems of the Company and the Colony. He presided at that time as president over the Council of the Northern Department of Rupert's Land at York Factory.

want of provisions & clothing it was natural and to be expected that they should endeavour to induce the Indians to supply them with meat & leather, in fact from your own account the Indians drove away the Cattle [Buffalo] out of spite to the Coy on the Coalition & thus deprived the settlers of their accustomed resources for food; it is therefore not fair to put all the blame of the distress of last winter on the Settlement.

GOVERNOR & COMMITTEE TO GOVERNOR SIMPSON[22]

London 13 March 1823

With reference to the 33 par. of your Letter of the 1st Sept. on the subject of the Beaver skins found in a hole in the Snake Country, we have agreed to allow the North West Compy Two dollars p. skin for the large and one dollar for the small which will be adjusted.

WILLIAM SMITH TO MESSrs PERKINS & CO.[23]

London 9 April 1823

I am directed by the Governor and Committee to acknowledge your letters of the 10 September and 23 Novbr, advising the arrival and sale of the Furs from the Columbia river by the Houqua, and I am happy to learn that you obtained a better price for them than you at one time expected. I have now to inclose Invoice and Bill of lading for a quantity of beaver and Otter Skins which have been shipped on the Lowther Castle and consigned to you on account of the Company.

The Beaver skins have been selected with considerable care, and are much superior to those imported from the Columbia, and I have to request you to draw the attention of the dealers, to the different qualities and trust you will endeavour to procure the best information you can on the subject for the guidance of the Governor and Company in future Shipments.

[22] H. B. Co. Gen. Letter Book No. 620.
[23] *Ibid.*

You may be surprised that Beaver of a superior quality should be sent to your market after the very decided opinion which you have given that the inferior kind only would answer, as the dealers would not pay above a certain price. But the Governor and Committee finding that the quality now sent, could not be sold here without submitting to a greater reduction of price, compared to what it used to fetch, than the lower qualities, have been induced to make the trial. They have further been induced to do so from the interruption to the export to Russia, given by the late regulations of that Government.[24] For many years past there has been a regular trade of fine beaver and fine Otter skins from this market to Russia, which it is well known found their way to China through Kiachta. This shows that there must be a regular and constant demand for fine furs at high prices in some of the provinces of China. I annex the prices for several years at which those Skins have been sold in this market for that destination, and I know that the Shipment made last year to Russia sold at St Petersburg in February last at 73¼ Roebles for full grown Beaver skins, 30½ R^{s} for Cubs and 51½R^{s} for Otters, equal at the present rate of Exchange to about 61/St^{g} p Skin for the first, 25/6 for the second and 43/ for the Otters, and that they were intended for the Kiachta trade.

No Shipment will take place this year to Russia, and I understand from good authority that the Fur Company of Russia have procured very few Beaver or Otter Skins. The Consumers in China therefore must either do without these articles, or get them through Canton, and the Governor and Committee conceive that it would be very advantageous both to the Company and to their agent at Canton, if that place could be made the channel of the trade in fine Beaver and Otter skins in place of Russia. The supply could be regulated accurately to the demand, and the charges on the transport must be much less.

I annex a List of the Beaver and Otter skins imported into S^{t}

[24] In the interest of the Russian American Company the Imperial government in 1822 prohibited the import of beaver, otter, and other furs from foreign countries into Russia.

Petersburg for the last Six years, and it is understood these all found their way to China vizt.

	1817	1818	1819	1820	1821	1822
Beaver Skins	7068	5289	4599	4489	4878	4851
Otter Skins	8547	9189	4236	9305	7661	5559

For many years fine Beaver and Otter were shipped from London, and met a ready Sale at Canton, till the prices were so high in England, as to render it no longer profitable.

The Governor and Committee conceive that the Skins now ship'd should fetch not less than 6 or 7 dollars each, if the view they have taken of the subject is correct, but they leave it to you after making due inquiry, to sell at such prices, without limiting you, as can be obtained, or as you may think advisable, at the same time it is probable, that for the usual demand of Canton the price must be higher as the Columbia Beaver of this year will all come to England, and the Governor and Committee will be guided by your letters, as to their Shipments by the China Ships of next Spring.. . .

ALEXANDER KENNEDY TO GOVERNOR SIMPSON[25]

Spokan 12 April 1823

. . . . As the Snake Country is the Source from which we draw the Major part of our Returns, my attention to this Branch of the Trade has been more particularly applyed, and from the information received from Michel Bourdon last fall I have been induced to send a stronger Party along with the Freemen going to that quarter this Season, in hopes of being able to get out all the Skins that may be procured there as the freemen when left to themselves become so indolent and careless, that often after they have been at the trouble of procuring Furs at the risk of their Lives, they are too lazy to come in with them and the Consequence is that their Furs are either lost or damaged before they reach this place. At this time there are Seven Hundred Skins

[25] H. B. Co. Journ. No. 606.

remaining in the Snake Country owing to this cause, and in Order to Guard against the evil the ensuing Season, I have fitted out Mr [Finan] McDonald accompanied by Michel Bourdon and five men with Horses &c to accompany the freemen who leave the Flat Head Post this Spring for the Snake Country.[26] The Plan is so arranged that Mr McDonald is to be back again at the Flat Head Post next Fall in time enough to take charge there and it is expected he will be able to bring out all the Furs that are procured in the Snake Country with him. A Part of the Freemen are to accompany him as far as Fort Providence in order to assist in bringing out the Furs, and to get fresh supply's with which they are to return again immediately to their associates when by passing the Winter in the Snake Country they will be able to Kill the Beaver in better Season, than they have hitherto had an Opportunity of doing; accustomed as they were always to leave the Flat Head Post late in the Spring and returning again in the Fall with their Hunts where they Generally passed the Winter, by which means the best Season for hunting was always lost. Previous to my arrival here last Fall a party of Freemen with their Families had arrived here from the Saskatchewin, they brought a few Skins which they Traded for Necessaries, and were fitted out with little Supply's to enable them to prosecute their intentions of making a hunt this Season in the Snake Country. They have passed the Winter near the Flat Head Post, doing little or nothing and this Spring they accompany Mr McDonald to the Snake Country, where it is hoped they will make Good Hunts.... I have found the men whose times are out here very backward in coming into the new terms offered them, and I am determined not to go beyond it till I see Mr Lewis and Know what disposable men he may have to spare, when I hope some of those who are standing on for the Old terms may find themselves taken in. A list of the men in the District is herewith sent specifying those who are engaged as well as those whose times are out. Upon the whole the General returns of this District will not be far short of last year (notwithstanding a number of Skins are still remaining in the Snake Country)....

[26] See Ross, *Fur Hunters*, II, chaps. x, xi.

Governor & Committee to Governors Williams and Simpson[27]

London 28 May 1823

We have ship'd to Canton, consigned to Messrs. Perkins & Co. 3600 Beaver skins and 2400 otter skins, and we enclose you copies of our Correspondence with them on the subject of the sale of Fur articles in that market...and should there not be a demand for otter and the fine Beaver skins for the Russia Market, we intend to send a further quantity by the first direct vessel for Canton expected to sail in about two months.

We have insured £20,000 at 50s/ p ct on the investment from Canton to Boston, made with the sale of the Furs from the Columbia, and from the present price of China goods in America we anticipate favorable returns.

Governor Simpson to Governor & Committee[28]

Norway House 23 June 1823

27. Messrs Lewes and McMillan are arrived from the Columbia and the accounts from thence are very satisfactory the utmost harmony prevails between the Whites and Natives, and a respectable increase has taken place in the returns, amounting to 18790 Beavers & Otters, besides 700 Beaver collected by the hunters in the Snake Country which Mr Finnan McDonald had been sent in quest of. That neglected but rich part of the country is likely to come under the consideration of the Council this season and 'tis probable some encouragement will be given to prosecute the trade in that quarter. Repeated attempts have been made by Mr Cameron to extend the trade along the Coast to the Northward, a tract ascertained to abound in Furs, but without success on account of the implacable revenge of the natives for a supposed outrage committed on them by the Whites some years ago, and time alone can reconcile them to the traders. The natives however are getting rapidly into the way of collecting Skins in all parts, and when the present redundency

[27] H. B. Co. Gen. Letter Book No. 62c.

[28] H. B. Co. Journ. No. 603.

of useless and expensive articles will be exhausted and the establishments cleared from the heavy burden of families, and the produce withal brought to a fair market, it is not only probable that the Columbia will clear itself, but yield respectable profits, its returns in the course of one or two seasons are expected from the increase of the last few years to amount to about 20,00[o] Beaver & Otters. The Ship arrived in safety on the 12th May delivered her cargo in good order (a few casks of Rum Molasses Provisions &c excepted) and proceeded on her voyage on the 16th of June.

GOVERNOR SIMPSON TO A. COLVILE[29]

Norway House 24 June 1823

....Several of our Gentlemen last Season appeared to feel that they possessed more influence and authority in the general arrangements of the business than I considered was their due, which occasionally places me in delicate and unpleasant situations, but I find that by adopting calm and conciliatory measures generally and showing a little firmness when necessary they are to be managed; thus we go on smoothly, they feel that I am alive to their interests, that none of my proceedings are influenced by Private or selfish considerations, and the example I show them of a total disregard to personal ease and comfort does much good. The liberal view which the Committee take of every subject connected with the business and the favorable impressions made by the individual members thereof they have seen contrasted with the intrigue, roguery & pillage they have been accustomed to and the domineering conduct of the late Agents[30] has quite altered their nature; they are no longer the suspicious dissatisfied men they have been and I am convinced that even should the first year or two of the business not come up to their expectations, there will be little grumbling and that they will accommodate themselves to the views and wishes of the Committee without a murmur....

[29] Dominion Archives, Selkirk Transcripts, XXV, 7922.

[30] Refers to the directing eastern partners, or agents, so-called, of the North West Company.

Since last Fall I have made a very extended Tour by Athabasca, Gt. Slave Lake, Peace River, Lesser Slave Lake and the Saskatchawene; it cost me a good deal of personal hardship but I have the satisfaction to feel that it will be productive of lasting advantages to the concern. My remarks on those Dept$^{mts.}$ enclosed to the Committee by this conveyance will show my general views and arrangements but in addition to what appears there I have ferritted out & checked a vast number of malpractices and little disreputable proceedings which from motives of delicacy I have not made public but are effectually stopped; in short I conceive that my last winters services are of the first import to the business and were my presence not required elsewhere, I intended devoting this ensuing winter to a similar tour in the Columbia where the broom & prooning knife are I believe much required....

Mr. Bulger by the enclosed Letter seems determined on leaving the Settlement in the course of the Summer and he has requested me to appoint a person to take the charge off his hands, he recommends Kemp but he is likewise fond of *Grog* and I cannot think of entrusting it to him;[31] it is therefore my intention to propose to the Council that either Mr. Don^{d} McKenzie or Jas. Keith, Chief Factors, be appointed to the Lower Red River Deptmt and that one of them be forwarded by the earliest opportunity to undertake the management of the Compy & Colony business until my arrival in the Fall, the former is the preferable man as he is cool, decisive, reflecting and determined and the most enlightened of the Class; they all dread the charge and there is not a man in the Country who would not prefer a polar Voyage to this situation in the present state of affairs. I am the more anxious to get McKenzie placed there as he is a liberal minded honorable man possessing no vain empty dignity and who will devote his sole attention to the business and as tis probable I shall go home next winter 1824 I could with ease of mind leave him to follow up any plans or measures that may be

[31] On account of disturbances in the Red River Colony in the winter of 1822-23 Governor Simpson found it necessary in spite of this unfavorable opinion to entrust William Kempt with the charge of the Settlement until the arrival of a new governor. See Oliver, *Canadian North-West*, I, 247-248.

deemed most conducive to the general interests; moreover he has a warm side to the Colony, you may recollect it was him that gave the information as to the intended destruction of it in 1814 on which occasion Pritchard was sent up and in consequence has been looked upon as a black sheep ever since; he is much attached to myself personally and would be influenced by my wishes....

Governor Simpson to the Chief Factors Columbia River District[32]

12 July 1823

[Paraphrased]

The Columbia District trade is improving; it may not only defray its expenses, but yield moderate profits if strict economy and exertion are exercised and there is no opposition. The Snake Country Expedition has been fitted out under Mr. Ross, who should be cautioned against opening a road for the Americans.

Donald McKenzie to Governor Simpson[33]

Ft. Garry 27 July 1823

....The Red River Settlers from the portrait I have of them are a distinct sort of beings somewhere between the half Indians and overgrown children. At times they need caressing and not unfrequently the discipline of the birch, in other words the iron rod of retribution. But in the present instance the latter not being within our reach, it behooves us to attempt by stratagem what we cannot compass by force. In the first place therefore all former scrapes and barefaced practices should be carefully avoided by every person holding a conspicuous station and the bottle and the girls so late the bane must with monastic strictness be forborne. Order and religion likewise to be held in veneration; therefore with faces long and minds most pure and delicate shall you & I regularly attend the chapel in the coldest as well as the warmest weather, even should we slip a passage or two & ponder

[32] H. B. Co. Journ. No. 604.

[33] Dominion Archives, Selkirk Transcripts, XXV, 7951.

in mind the next resolves of Council at times; with the Priests we will hold discussions from the era of that directing old prototype who ruined us all, down to the passing date, ever mindful of giving no kind of umbrage to their dearly beloved bigotry, else make our account to extenuate our offences by mortifications, fasting and watching, with the Scotch and Irish let us scour up our rusty Erse, and loudly extol that prince of heroes old Fingal, with the French and the Swiss we will be frenchified, et vive la bagatelle, with the Canadians we can pass their voyages over again, with the Brules listen to their feats against the Scioux, and with the indians you know we shall be indians still. By accommodating ourselves somewhat like this to the manners & customs of this degenerate heterogeneous mass, we may insensibly gain their confidence and secure a key that unlocks their inmost recesses thereby reclaiming them to that principle of exertion & simplicity which alone can establish their future welfare. There are certainly too many refuse of different nations huddled together in this distant corner, with very little mixture of the better ranks of society among them. Those of our Chief Factors, Chief Traders and clerks, who are burthened with families that tie them to the country would probably retire after a while to Red River, could proper inducements be held, and they saw the place in a prosperous posture. Their removal would also facilitate promotion, of course diffuse a necessary spirit of Emulation in the trade, and though they be not all of them men of our enlarged ideas, yet the presence of persons comparatively independent in Circumstances, and of a thorough-going turn, would not fail to put industry in motion.

GOVERNOR SIMPSON TO A. COLVILE[34]

York Factory 8 Sept. 1823

....He [Gov. R. P. Pelly] was unprovided with necessaries or Luxuries as we call them, vizt Butter, sugar, Flour, Tea, Wine etc, and left it to me to make up the quantity of those articles that I might consider necessary. I explained to him how myself

[34] *Ibid.*, 8011.

was situated in regard to those matters, which is that I take the same allowance that the Coy grant to Chief Factors or Chief Traders and anything exceeding that quantity goes to my private account; but as he has a Family & might be expected to see strangers at times, he would require more, and it was arranged that he should take four times that quantity with a few additional articles....

Mr McKenzie I consider a host of strength, he is of all others the fittest man in the Country for the situation he holds, and by his Letters you will see that he takes no common or luke warm interest in the business; he is a cool determined man, conciliatory in his manners, æconomical & regular and privately attached to the Colony; our object is to keep him where he is, altho' it will cost me some difficulty, as there is a strong party in our Council against him, arising in some degree from his being in Days of opposition a partizan of Lord Selkirk and the Colony which my Letters from Norway House would have explained; by keeping this Gentleman at the Settlement he will become so devoted to the interests thereof, and so perfectly master of the business that in the event of Mr. Pelly's retiring or any change taking place, you can be at no loss in regard to a manager, either as a temporary superintendant or regular Gov[r] as he has both ability and respectability enough for either....

[Governor Simpson explains why he had not wintered at Red River Colony.] The fact is that I was placed in a very delicate situation, the year preceding I had requested the Committee to fix my winter residence expecting they would have said Red River as a matter of course but instead of that there was not a syllable on the subject; from having passed the preceding spring there all eyes from the parties of the second part downwards were upon me, and if I had gone thither of my own accord at a time when my services were so much required in other parts of the Country, it would have given our fresh allies room to suspect that the Coys interests were a secondary consideration, and neither the Committee as a body nor any individual thereof having expressed a wish that I should proceed thither, I did not feel that under existing circumstances I should have been justified in doing so of my own accord. I therefore volunteered on the severe and arduous duty which I undertook, and performed very much to my own satisfaction and that of all who have a correct view and proper interest in the business in this Country, and to the regret of some whose maladministration I discovered and was obliged to check very much to their confusion; it did however give my constitution a shake from which I am now perfectly recovered.[35] . . . .

I am afraid I have worn out your patience with these unsatisfactory remarks on the late administration—shall therefore now take the liberty of drawing your attention to the feelings of the Council in respect to Colony affairs. Nearly every member thereof is hostile to the Settlement, both Hudsons Bay and North West, and this principally arises from the expense it entails on the concern and the continual fever in which the Colonists keep us. By the Deed Poll or rather the Original Deed between the Contracting parties it is provided that no expense relating to Colonization will affect the Fur Trade. The salys to the Governor and Clergyman therefore gave them a handle to break out violently; it kept them in a ferment the whole season, and altho' I used every means to bring them into good humour it was for a length of time impossible; they looked upon me with suspicion, had private meetings in Councils day after day, and were about to have written the Committee in a strain which must have given offence. Robertson[36] was one of the leading malcontents, but his blustering folly knocked the whole on the head, and in order to make himself pass for a man of weight came out with all their secrets which gave me an opportunity of bringing them to their senses; in short I found it necessary to show my power and authority and in full Council gave them a lecture which had the desired effect, made them look on each other with suspicion and restored their confidence in myself.

[35] During Governor Simpson's absence from Red River Colony the famous Bulger-Clarke feud occurred, which wrought the Settlement to a dangerous pitch of excitement. See Oliver, *Canadian North-West*, I, 232-244.

[36] Colin Robertson was a chief factor formerly in charge of the Saskatchewan district but removed to the Churchill district.

Instead of writing themselves they left the whole to me and attended to their other business. No man ever took greater pains or labour to please and give satisfaction than I have done, but some of our Chief Factors are so much accustomed to grumble that a Saint could scarcely keep them in humour. This last season however I found it necessary to act with firmness, convinced them that I could talk loud also, and made an example of Robertson to begin with. He was more noisy about the Colony than any other, talked of rights and previledges, getting Councils opinion on the Deed Poll, in short wished to be a Leader, but I have made such an exposure this season of his maladministration in the Saskatchawine and told him so many home truths in presence of the whole Council that he is quite crest fallen and will I think give no more trouble. McDonald (one eye)[37] was likewise inclined to be violent about the expenses incurred on account of the Colony, and was to have given me a set down or prepared speech thereon at the close of the sittings, but the lecture to Robertson had the desired effect, none seemed inclined to enter the Lists with me again, and on the whole we all separated on excellent terms and I believe they have now a greater respect for me than ever. It is extremely desirable to keep our Factors and Traders in good humour until the accounts look a little better than they at present do; the state thereof this year has annoyed them very much and until the Bal^ce^ is on the right side I think it would be advisable to say as little as possible in the public Despatches on Colony affairs, as it is a galling subject; it will be my business to watch its interests privately, and nothing shall escape my observation and your knowledge. In regard to the £200 to Mr. Pelly they were most clamorous, and would have protested formally against it, had I not smoothed the thing over through private channels, but finding they could not help themselves they wished to make a merit of necessity and thrust a compliment upon me by recommending to the Committee that it should be added to my saly, but I saw through the object of this bribe and treated it & them with the merited

[37] John McDonald was a chief factor in charge of the Winnipeg district.

contempt. With these men I find nothing does so well in the long run as candour and plain dealing, it may not be palatable at times, but must ultimately prevail, and finesse should never and will not be resorted to by me except in extraordinary cases....

[Form of the accounts] No blame could certainly attach to me last year as we had neither proper Books nor Clerks for all the writing that was necessary and it required time to bring the North West people into our forms.

The admission of Black, Ogden & Grant[38] has given great satisfaction and I feel highly flattered that so much attention has been paid to my recommendation, they will be very useful men and will prove they are worthy of the indulgence that has been shewn them. Black could at first scarcely look me in the face, he recollected my Athabasca Campaign, and never will forget the terrors in which he was kept that Winter; we met and parted excellent Friends. I have started him on an Expedition which excites some interest and will be no sinecure, to explore the Country on the West side of the Mountain north from Babine Lake in New Caledonia as far as practicable; it has occupied my attention for these last two years but could not succeed in procuring any one to undertake it. Ogden has gone to the Columbia and determined to do great things; he does not want for ability. Grant is to winter with me at Red River and through him I shall have the entire controul over the half breeds, in this respect he will be most useful.

The Southern Council I observe are desirous to show their powers or rather to assume authority which they can have no right to. Vincent and Bethune are at the bottom of it and Mr. Williams has not sufficient knowledge of business to take a lead in the arrangements. The fact is they seem to have made a party against Williams, and are determined that he shall merely have the nominal management; they opened a private correspondence

[38] These three former Nor'Westers, Samuel Black, P. S. Ogden and Cuthbert Grant, had been outstanding figures in the fur-trade war, and had been left unprovided for in the coalition. On Governor Simpson's recommendation they were admitted to the Hudson's Bay Company in 1823, Black and Ogden as chief traders, and Cuthbert Grant as a clerk.

with our Council this year which I found means to discourage. Copies of these Letters are handed to Mr. Garry. Both Councils would be desirous to open a correspondence with the Committee and the Northern malcontents as I formerly remarked would have followed the example of the Southern had I not dealt firmly by them; if such correspondence was countenanced there would be no end to the private councilling and party work, which might be most injurious to the general interests....

A great number of discharged servants with their Families have this season gone to the Settlement which will relieve our Establishments greatly, but I imagine it will be necessary for us to assist many of them this winter....

The tract of Country alluded to in Mr. McPherson's[39] Letter to Mr. McGillivray is little known and I had directed my attention thereto last Winter while in Athabasca; Mr. McLeod was to have sent a small party to explore it this season, but if it is not done I have arranged with Mr. Smith that it will be attended to next year. Mr. Black will be able to give us some information on this subject, as he is likely to fall in with the Nohanus, and you will observe by my correspondence with McLeod that I have turned my attention very particularly to the affairs of McKenzies River generally, as there is a greater Field for the extension of Trade there than in any other part of the Country. I am not acquainted with Mr. McPherson, but have a very high character of him, and he is sure to get forward if merit is now the Road to promotion. On the subject of promotion generally I have written to Mr. Garry shall not therefore trouble you with any remarks thereon....

I have requested leave of absence of the Committee agreeable to your kind suggestion, but have left it to Mr. Garry privately whether I go to England or to the Columbia next season, and it is probable he will consult you on the subject; in this I have no choice or request to make; you know the object of my visit to England and I have pointed out where my services and presence

[39] Murdock McPherson was a clerk at this time in the McKenzie River district. He became a chief factor in 1847.

may be useful, and have no desire that my private views should interfere with the interests of the service....

GOVERNOR & COMMITTEE TO THE CHIEF FACTORS IN CHARGE OF THE COLUMBIA DEPARTMENT.[40]

London 12 Nov. 1823

The Houqua, Capt. Nash, arrived at Whampoa on the 28th Sept. and the cargo which escaped the conflagration that destroyed great part of Canton fetched as follows.

Beaver skins	one with the other	$4	p. skin
Land otters		$3.20	"

and the 28 Sea otters and 35 foxes produced $360, averaging from $10 to $12 for the former.

A. COLVILE TO GOVERNOR SIMPSON[41]

London 11 March 1824

....I notice what you say of the feeling of the gentn of the Council towards the Settlement which must give you some trouble at present, but it will subside. The Govr & Comee will at all times act upon fair & liberal principles to the Chief Factors & Traders, and will not charge to the Fur Trade expences that do not belong to it, but they will not suffer the Fur Trade to oppose or oppress the Settlement, & if it be attempted, the expence of redressing the evil must & will fall on the Fur Trade as in justice it ought.

It is incumbent on the Company if there was no settlement to have a chaplain in their country & at least to allow missions to be established at proper places for the conversion of the Indians, indeed it wd be extremely impolitic in the present temper & disposition of the public in this Country to show any unwillingness to assist in such an object. By uniting with the Missionary Society & the Settlement these objects are obtained safely, conveniently & cheaply. As to Mr. Pelly's salary, I would most

[40] H. B. Co. Gen. Letter Book No. 620.

[41] Dominion Archives, Selkirk Transcripts, XXV, 8148.

decidedly have objected to the locating the savage, halfbreed families at R. R. unless the Company had assisted in paying a proper Governor (for we only require an Agent—the jurisdiction being with the Coy) & also unless they provided the means of the people settling themselves—and means for civilizing & instructing them. These are not in fact objects of colonization, though they happen to be united with & assisted by the Colony, but part of the necessary establishment of the Company & the cheapest mode of relieving the fur trade of a ruinous expence.....

As to your coming home, particularly with the object which you have in view, I think it will be better to postpone it both on your own account & that of the Company. A wife I fear would be an embarrassment to you until the business gets into more complete order & until the necessity of those distant journies is over & if it be delayed one or two years you will be able to accumulate something before the expences of a family come upon you. I think that having taken the Settlement in hand that you should not leave it until you see it is in the right road—then the Columbia & McKenzies river will require your examining & arranging, particularly the former, where improved management might do a great deal; perhaps in McKenzie's river & near Caledonia it is only necessary to direct active and discreet chief factors or traders to push their Examination of the Country & to extend the trade. As soon as you are satisfied that the business the home country including the Settlement will admit of your absence, I think you ought to visit the Columbia, but it appears to me that your plan of starting 10 Sept & making the whole from Cumberland a winter journey is exposing yourself to needless inconvenience & fatigue, & your life & health to needless risk. Perhaps it would be better to delay the journey until Summer 1825, when you may have your business & correspondence in such a state of forwardness that you may leave it to Mr. McTavish to ship the furs & finish the other details, & start with the light canoe for Columbia, say 20 June or 1 July, pass the winter there & come out as early as possible in the light canoe of 1826. You might then after arranging the business of the Season proceed to Montreal by the return of the Express Canoe....

GOVERNOR & COMMITTEE TO GOVERNOR SIMPSON[42]

London 12 March 1824

40. We have after some negociation entered into a Contract with the East India Company to sell to them 20,000 Beaver skins and 7,000 Otters for the present, and the same quantities for the next year, as you will perceive by the inclosed Copy of the arrangement N° 14. Our object in this was to relieve this market of a part of the importation of Beaver, particularly of the inferior quality, and to endeavor to make Canton the Channel for supplying the North of China, with the fine Beaver and Otters, which used to reach them through Russia by Kiachta. Without the assistance of the East India Company we should have had great difficulty in obtaining a Remittance from Canton, and there would have been much time lost before the Proceeds could have been realized, we were also anxious to secure the assistance of the Company's Factors at Canton, in persuading the Canton Merchants to purchase the fine Beaver until they could ascertain their market for it in the North of China. We therefore did not wish to fix too high a price, because if the transaction is attended with loss we cannot expect the East India Company to repeat it, and from what passed in the course of the negociation, we have reason to believe they will give as high a price in future as the state of the China Market will justify—their object being to discourage the Russian and American Trade with China, while at the same time they assist and encourage the British Fur trade. We therefore fixed the prices at the same rate as we got in the Bargain made last year with Messrs Borradaile & Co.--and tho' at the recent Sale we have obtained higher prices for the seasoned parchment and the heavy Beaver, yet some fine Beaver which remained after the Selection for the contract with the East India Company, did not produce more than we got from them, and there is no doubt that the Price of the whole quantity at the Sale was enhanced by this Contract which we had previously made.

The Russians do not allow either Beaver or Otter skins to be

[42] H. B. Co. Gen. Letter Book No. 620.

imported we could therefore have had no Market for fine Beaver but that for the Hatters, for whose use it is of little more value than the ordinary Parchment Beaver, if the East India Company had not acceded to our proposition, and which they have done in the most liberal and friendly manner. From the non-arrival however of the Ship from the Columbia we shall not be able to deliver the whole quantity this year.

Governor & Committee to Governor Simpson[43]

London 12 March 1824

We are certainly anxious that you should either before visiting this country or after your return, make a visit to the Columbia and place the arrangements there on a proper footing, but perhaps it would be better to postpone this until early in the summer of 1825 when you could go in the Columbia light Canoe after making all the arrangements for that season, leaving the details to be compleated by Mr. McTavish. We should think it would be attended with needless risk and fatigue to make it a winter journey, and would leave you too little time while in the Columbia Country.

Governor & Committee to Governor Simpson[44]

London 12 March 1824

We observe that your attention is directed to the Columbia, we think the trade should be extended in the Snake Country, and also along the Coast to the Northward. The Russians are endeavouring to obtain all that Coast and the subject is now under discussion between the two Governments.

We hope that the valuable part will be secured to this country but the actual occupation by traders will go far to establish the rights of the respective nations which is an additional inducement to extend the Posts westward towards the Coast from New

[43] *Ibid.*
[44] *Ibid.*

Caledonia and if possible to establish upon the Coast as far North as may be practicable.

GOVERNOR SIMPSON TO A. COLVILE[45]

Ft. Garry 31 May, 1824

....The Coys old servants, Canadians, are the least troublesome and most attached to us, either in starvation or in plenty— we can do anything with them; if they have but a hatchet and hoe, a little ammunition and a few hooks and lines they can shift for themselves, and are of that happy thoughtless disposition that they are never discontented or out of humour, when any plots are on foot they give us intimation and altho' they will not fight for us they always have a warm side to their old Bourgeois, in fact consider themselves under the Coys protection and look up to their representatives as Fathers, they generally gain little more than a few fair words thereby, and are perfectly satisfied; all other descriptions of settlers look for more substantial favors and would insist on having them if they dared.

DISTRICT RETURNS

May 31, 1824

Outfit 1823.[46]

	Cr.		
By Athabasca	7,110.	15.	0.
By Western Caledonia	4,827.	7.	11.
By Lesser Slave Lake	4,635.	12.	0.
By English River	4,093.	1.	5.
By Saskatchewan	6,613.	16.	10.
By Cumberland	4,140.	13.	11.
By Swan River	2,325.	3.	1.
By Upper Red River	2,673.	5.	11.
By Lower Red River	333.	3.	5.
By " " " shop	503.	1.	5.

[45] Dominion Archives, Selkirk Transcripts, XXVI, 8218.

[46] Huntington Library MSS. H. M. 2152.

By Lac La Pluie	1,530.	18.	5.
By Winipeg	740.	15.	7.
By Island Lake	880.	3.	1.
By Severn	1,761.	15.	10.
By Nelson River	1,251.	6.	6.
By Churchill	1,379.	17.	8.
By Columbia	11,274.	1.	10.
By Profit & Loss A/c	1,871.	19.	0.
	£57,946.	18.	10.

GOVERNOR & COMMITTEE TO GOVERNOR SIMPSON[47]

London 2 June 1824

In this vessel the indent for the Columbia will be shipped, and we shall send the Bricks and Tiles as the cost is trifling. We shall instruct the officers in charge however to make no new buildings or expensive repairs at the present Fort, which belongs to the Americans but to endeavour to find a good situation for a Fort on the North side of the River to which our Establishment may be removed at a convenient opportunity. There seems no necessity for our keeping in repair the present Fort when the Americans have the right of taking possession of it when they please.

MINUTES OF A TEMPORARY COUNCIL held at Y Factory Northern District of Ruperts Land this first day of July one thousand Eight Hundred and twenty four.[48]

Present

George Simpson Governor
Alex[r] Stewart Chief Factor
John Geo McTavish "
John Stewart "
Edward Smith "
James Keith "
Joseph McGillivray Chief Trader
James McMillan "

[47] H. B. Co. Gen. Letter Book No. 620.
[48] Huntington Library MSS. H. M. 2164.

It being expedient to determine upon a new scale of wages together with a new Tariff for Sales to Servants in order to be enabled to meet without further delay any application for Advances and the Honble Committee having in various despatches more particularly in that of the twelfth month last signified their intentions on this subject

Resolved 1st That the following be the scale of wages to be allowed to all districts in the Companys Territories

Steersman	£22 Stg
Bowsman	20
Milieux	17

For Athabasca McKenzies River and Lesser Slave Lake

Steersman	£ 24
Bowsman	22
Milieux	19

Western ci devant New Caledonia Canoe System

Boutes[49]	27
Milieux	22

Columbia River

Boutes	22
Milieux	17

Together with an Augmention when employed out and in to and from York Factory of per Boutes £4 St[g] and for Milieux £3

Guides to be allowed £5 in addition to the Wages [of a Steersman] of the District. Interpreters when absolutely required [MS. torn] from assisting as Summer men or at other Districts [MS. torn] upon Wages not to exceed Twenty five pounds....

Mechanics at the Depot to have their wages regulated by the Council and those inland not to

[49] *Boutes* is the general term for the end men in a boat or canoe. See *ante*, 13 n.

exceed the wages of the Steersmen of the District to which they belong unless hired in a double or triple capacity in which case they will be allowed an augmentation by way of extra service money

Resolved 2nd That all those hired last winter below the foregoing scale of wages and under bona fide of being allow'd the current wages and advantages of their Respective Districts be permitted to reap the benefit of such augmentation and that all those hired on higher wages than those already specified and under a perfect understanding of having their supplies continued at their then existing Tariff used at the period of being hired have their advances priced conformably thereto, till the expiration of their contract such distinction being considered Expedient to prevent jealousy and dissatisfaction with those on the reduced scale of wages, as also to induce those on a higher scale to come into its terms

Resolved 3rd That the following be the terms for Advances to servants throughout the Northern district

To Clerks and other Servants on the foregoing scale of wages 50 per cent on the prime cost of all imported and 12½ per cent on the York stock of all Country made articles taken during summer at the Depot, Spirituous Liquors excepted, to be continued at fixed prices, viz Madeira Wine 30/ Port and all other wines at 24/ Shrub Gin and Brandy at 18/ Jamaica spirits 15/ and Rum not beyond Proof Strength 12/ per Gall, and all subsequent advances without distinction of Articles whether taken at the Depot or Inland, to be charged 50 per cent on the York Inventory Tariff with the exception of Spirituous Liquors to be sold 50 per cent on the Depot summer sale [tariff] to servants, and also with the exception of Country produce [torn] of Dress[d] Leather, Buffaloe Robes, Provisions etc. etc. which [will] be sold throughout the year at 50 per cent on Inventory Prices [such] advances being found expedient to prevent too frequent application or abuse. For all servants or Engages on old Canadian terms the late North West Tariff for all advances taken during the Summer at the Depots, Spirituous Liquors excepted to be continued as follows: Rum not beyond proof strength 72 livres, Shrub Gin and Jamaica Spirits 90 Livres, wine and Brandy 150 Livres per Gall., and all subsequent advances without distinction of Articles whether taken at the Depot or Inland to be 50 per cent on the Depot Summer sale Tariff with the exception of Country produce to be continued at fixed Prices throughout the Year viz large ordinary Moose Skins 24 livres, prime select 26 Livres, Small Do 16 livres, large Red deer Skins 18 livres, Small Do 12, Rein deer Prime Skins, 9 livres, small do 5, Buffaloe Robes prime 30, Shoes, Mittens, dress[d] per pair 2, Tallow Pounded meat or Pemican 2, Shaganape[50] small per lb. 6#, Pack Cords per lb. 2 Liv., dried meat per lb 1 livre, Fresh per lb 10 Sols, salted meat per lb 1 livre, Salt per quart 2 livres, Buffaloe Hides dressed 12 livres, Parchment do 6 livres, and for Servants or engages on reduced terms 25 per cent deduction from the above specified prices for those on old Canadian agreements conformably to the tenor and Intention of their existing contracts. It is however understood that in consideration of the peculiar living and mode of Journeying at York as also at Fort George, Columbia River, Spirituous Liquor will be allowed to Mechanics or Engages on whatever scale of wages at the Depot Summer sale Tariff throughout the year.

[50] *Shaganapie* is the Indian term for rawhide thongs or cords.

Resolved 4th That the foregoing Tariff for sales to servants unless disapproved of do remain fixed and only subject to revision or alteration whenever any considerable change takes place on the prime cost of the Articles sold.

Resolved That this Council do adjourn Sine die

3rd July 1824

It being also deemed urgent and important [MS. torn] patching part of the Western Caledonia [MS. torn] at which place that Brigade is now supposed arriving

Resolved 6th That Mr. Joseph McGillivray Chief Trader be appointed to take his departure thither for that purpose and that he be directed to equip and dispatch four loaded Canoes having about 100 p[iece]s with part of the current Outfit, leaving the remainder to be made up and forwarded from thence by the person to be appointed by the Council for the management of that district as soon as the number of hands required to complete the deficient Crews arrive from the Interior

Resolved that this council do now adjourn

George Simpson Gov

Alexr Stewart C. F. J. George McTavish C. F.
John Stewart " Edward Smith "
James Keith " J. McGillivray C. T.
James McMillan C. T.

5th July 1824

Every means having been used to remove the existing prejudice and aversion entertained by the majority of unhired Canadians against the European scale of wages, and the advanced season and imperious necessity of completing the defective Establishments particularly those of the Northern Districts and the Columbia River rendering it indispensably to take immediate steps for facilitating the rehiring men for the current year and moreover conceiving that the most effectual mode of producing conviction would be by affording them an opportunity of perceiving the advantages it secures to others

Resolved 6th That it be left discretionary to endeavour rehiring for only the Current Year on reduced Canadian terms conformably to the scale of wages, and price of Goods [MS. torn] last year those who will not accept of the new [scale of] wages of the Current Year

Resolved that this Council do now adjourn

George Simpson Gov	Edward Smith C. F.
Alexr Stewart C. F.	James Keith "
John Geo. McTavish C. F.	Josh McGillivray C. T.
John Stewart C. F.	James McMillan C. T.

Minutes of a Council held at York Factory Northern Department of Ruperts land this tenth day of July one Thousand Eight hundred and twenty four for the purpose of establishing such rules and Regulations as may be considered expedient for conducting the business of said Department and in order to investigate the result of the trade of last Year and determine the Outfit and arrangements of the Current Year conformable to the provisions of a deed Poll under seal the Governor and Company bearing date the Twenty sixth one Thousand Eight hundred and twenty one at which the following members were present

George Simpson	Gov.	J. George McTavish	C. F.
James Leith	C. F.	John Clarke	"
Colin Robertson	"	George Keith	"
Alexr Stewart	"	John Dougal Cameron	"
James Sutherland	"	John Charles	"
John Stewart	"	John McLaughlin	"
Edward Smith	"	James Keith	"

Resolved 1st That the Chief Traders be invited to attend during the sitting of Council in compliance with which the following immediately appeared viz: Thomas McMurray, John Rowand, John Peter Pruden, James McMillan, Allen McDonell.

2nd That the rotation of Furlough of Chief Factors for the Current Year being in favor of John Charles, George Keith and John D. Cameron and the said Gentlemen having notified their intentions of not availing [themselves thereof that] John Charles, George Keith and John [D. Cameron be] therefore considered disposable for the current year

3rd That the rotation of furlough of Chief Traders for the Current Year being in favour of John Spencer and Hugh Fairies the former having exchanged his Rotation of Furlough [with] Jos. Felix LaRocque and the latter not having signified [his] intention of availing himself thereof

4th That it be optional with Jos. Felix LaRoque [to accept] of the Rotation of Furlough of John Spencer

5th That J. P. Pruden C. T. be permitted leave of absence [for a] Year on account of ill health agreeably to a [certificate of] this date from William Todd Surgn

6th That Jos. McGillivray Chief Trader be permitted leave of absence for a year for the benefit of his health [agreeably to] a certificate of this date from Wm Todd Surgn

7th That the following appointments take place

Athabasca	James Keith C. F.
	Hugh Fairies C. T.
	Robert McVicar C. T.
McKenzies River	Edward Smith C. F.
	Alexr R. McLeod, C. Trader

New Caledonia	Wm Brown Chief Trader
	Wm Connolly Chief Trader
Lesser Slave Lake	John Clarke Chief Factor
	W^{m} McIntosh Chief Factor
English River	George Keith Chief Factor
	John Spencer Chief Trader
Cumberland House	James Leith Chief Factor
	John Lee Lewes Ch. Trader
Saskatchewan	John Stewart Ch. Factor
	John Rowand Ch. Trader
Swan River	Allan McDonell Ch. Trader
Red River Colony	Donald McKenzie Chief factor
Winipeg River	John McDonell Chief Factor
Lac La Pluie	John D. Cameron Chief factor
	Thomas McMurray Ch. Trader
	Simon McGillivray Ch. Trader
[mss. torn]	to be abandoned as a district
[Island Lake]	Alex Stewart Chief factor
[Severn]	James Sutherland Chief factor
[Nelson] River	John Charles
	Roderick McKenzie C. Trader
Churchill	Colin Robertson Chief Factor
York Factory	J. Geo. McTavish Chief Factor
Columbia River	Alex^{r} Kennedy Chief Factor
	John McLaughlin Chief Factor
	John W. Dease C. Trader
	John McLeod C. Trader
	P. Skeene Ogden C. Trader
Rocky Mountain	Expedition Samuel Black Ch. Trader
[To] accompany Gov. Simpson [to the] Columbia	James McMillan
Leave of absence on account of ill health	John P. Pruden C. Trader Joseph McGillivray C. Trader
Rotation of Furlough	J. F. Larocque C. Trader exchanged with John Spencer

[Government] having requested the Honble Company to render Captain Franklin any assistance he may require in the prosecution of a voyage of discovery about to be undertaken via McKenzies River and that Gentleman having made application for the services of P. Warren Dease Chief Trader

Resolved 8th That Mr. Dease be requested to enter upon the necessary arrangements connected with that Expedition agreeably to Captain Franklin's desire and conformable to the directions of the Honble Committee and that he be considered as attached thereto from the Receipt of this Instruction.

9th That the following Arrangements take place

ATHABASCA

Fort Chipewyan	James Keith C. F.
	Colin Campbell Clk.
	F. W. Wentzell Clk.
	Robert Clouston Clk.
Great Slave Lake	Robert McVicar C. T.
	Robert Harding Clk.
Dunvegan	Hugh Fairies C. T.
	Wm. McGillivray Clk.
	—Mittleberger Clk.
Fort Vermilion	Duncan Finlayson Clk.

That 6 Boats containing 330 pieces manned by forty two men constitute the Current Outfit including freight

That James Keith Chief Factor be authorized to take his departure from Fort Chipewyan for the Depot the 1st June Proximo

MCKENZIE RIVER

10th Winter Arrangements

Forks	Edward Smith C. Factor
River au Liard	A. Roderic McLeod C. T.

		Fort Norman	M. McPherson & Jno McLeod
		Fort Good Hope	Charles Brisbois and Jno Hutcheson clerks
			Jno Bell to go in
			C. J. Dease Clk. coming out

Discretionary with Edward Smith and Alex^r^ R. McLeod to regulate the appointments on account of the existing ferment among the Indians.

Res. 11th That five canoes containing 115 pieces manned by twenty six men form part of the current outfit and that the remaining pieces be carried in on freight by the six Athabasca Boats

Summer Arrangements

Forks	a clk and two men including Interpreter
River au Liard	a clk and three men including Interpreter
Fort Norman	a clk and two men including Interpreter
Fort Good Hope	two clks and three men including Interpreter

12th That Edward Smith Chief Factor be requested to remain in land and that A. R. McLeod be permitted to visit the Depot, that 120 ps for McKenzie River outfit 1825 be transported on freight this season to Split Lake

NEW CALEDONIA

13th Winter Arrangements

McLeods Lake	Wm. Brown & W. Connolly
Frasers Lake	Js. McDougal & Jno McDonald
Chilcothe Country	Jno Todd & G. McDougall

Alexandria	James Murray Yale and Wm. Scott McBean clks
	Charles Ross clk to go in
	P. C. Pambrun to go in

of the above W[m] Brown chief trader and Charles Ross clk to be appointed to winter in the Babine country and W[m] Connolly chief trader and the remaining clks to winter where most required.

Res. 14 That 6 canoes containing 130 ps manned by 36 men constitute the current outfit

Summer Arrangement

Babine Country	William Brown C. Trader Clerks & men
McLeods Lake Chilcothe Country Alexandria	Clerks and 21 men constitute the Establishment of the whole District.

It being represented that there is a considerable field for the Extension of Trade to Advantage in the Babine Country as also to the Northward and Westward thereof

15 That William Brown be requested to remain inland and assisted by clerks & men be directed to take such steps as his means may safely warrant to prosecute the discoveries already begun in that quarter; that William Connolly be directed to accompany the loaded canoes of the District to Fort Chipewyan from whence he is to be allowed a passage in the Athabasca light canoe to the Depot

16th That the projected new Post in the Chilcothe Country situate about 150 miles north west of Frasers River and which circumstances prevented establishing this summer be Established this Ensueing season.

Res. 17th Serious differences and insubordination being understood to have lately existed among the Gentlemen in New Caledonia without any Satisfactory or conclusive evidence having been produced from what cause they originated and it being considered highly essential and important to the Good Government and successfull management of the trade that such matters should undergo a thorough and impartial investigation in order to prevent a recurrence

18th That the Gentlemen entrusted with the management of that or any other district wherein such Evils are found to Exist be directed to use every justifiable means for suppressing the same and when this cannot be done that they be directed to order out the Individuals concerned and to produce every requisite information in order that the case may be brought under the Investigation of Council for their determination and the particulars thereof transmitted to the Honble Committee for their final judgement and decision

Lesser Slave Lake

19th Winter Arrangement

Smoky River — Jno Clarke C. F.
Slave Lake — Paul Fraser Clk & Jno Allen Clk

Discretionary with Mr. Clarke to fix his winter residence

That 3 canoes containing...ps manned by... men constitute the current outfit

Summer Arrangements

Smoky River — an Inr & 2 men
Slave Lake — a clk & two men

Discretionary with Jno Clarke C Factor to abandon the last Post if considered expedient and that he be desired to provide the requisite supplies of provisions and other facilities for keeping up the communication with Columbia River

ENGLISH RIVER

Res. 20th Winter Arrangements

Isle a la Crosse	Geo Keith C. Factor
	James Douglass Clk
Lac La Ronge	Jno Spencer C. T.
Green Lake	James Heron Clk
Deers Lake	Lach McLean Clk to go in

21st That 2 Boats containing 120 pieces manned by 15 men constitute the current outfit

Summer Arrangements

Isle a la Crosse	a clk and 3 men incl Interpreter
Lac La Ronge	a chief trader & 2 men inclg Intr.
Green Lake	a clk & 2 men inclug Interp
Deers Lake	a clk & a man

22 That 220 Bags Pemican be provided at Isle a la Crosse for the outcoming and ingoing ensueing season of the Athabasca and New Caledonia Brigades and that each Bag contain 85 lb net

CUMBERLAND

23 Winter Arrangements

Cumberland house	James Leith C. F.
	Thomas Isbister Clk
Moon Lake	Jno Lee Lewes C. T.

24 That 2 Boats containing 80 ps manned by 11 men constitute the current outfit and that two new Boats of 27 feet keel be built in course of the winter

25th Summer Arrangement

Cumberland house	a C. Trader, clk, & 3 men or
	a clk and 3 men
Moon Lake	a clk & man if kept up

But left discretionary to abandon it for the summer

SASKATCHEWAN

Res. 26th Winter Arrangements

Carlton House	Jno Stewart C. F.
	Jno Harriott Clk
	George Bird Clk
Edmonton	Jno Rowand C. T.
	Pat Small Clk.
	Henry Fisher Clk.

27th That 4 Boats containing about...Pieces manned by 36 men constitute the current outfit and that an additional containing...Pieces and manned by 6 men accompany the above with the current outfit for Athabasca or Elk River and that William McIntosh be appointed to the management thereof for the winter

28th That the requisite quantity of Provisions be supplied from Carleton House to make up any deficiency at Isle a la Crosse of the requisition for Athabasca and New Caledonia Brigades ensuing season and that the same be forwarded to Green Lake

29th That Carlton House be directed to communicate with Swan River in the Event of any apprehension of Scarcity of Provisions in order that the latter District be enabled to supply any deficiency of the former District

30th That about 2000 Wolves be traded and 8 new Boats of 27 feet keel be brought out to York Factory

31st Summer Arrangement

Carlton House	2 clks & 10 men includingIn. Intr.
Edmonton	2 clks & 12 men including In. Intr.

SWAN RIVER

Res. 32nd Winter Arrangements

Fort Pelly	Allan McDonell C. T.
	Cuth Cummings Clk.
	Anty Feistol "
	Thomas Swaine "
	George Linton "

33rd That 3 Boats containing about 150 Pieces and manned by 19 men constitute the current outfit that Mr. McDonell be directed to build 4 new Boats of 27 feet keel and that any of his indebted freemen be employed to furnish about 20 Kegs Salt and as much sugar as they can supply

Summer Arrangements

Fort Pelly to be abandoned during Summer and a Clk and 3 men including an Interpreter to pass the summer at or in the vicinity of Lower Swan River

RED RIVER

35th Winter Arrangements

Fort Garry and Colony Shop	Donald McKenzie C. F.
	Francis Heron clk.
	Jas. Hargrave "

36th That 2 Boats and 12 men be provided containing such part of the annual requisition for the Colony Shop as can conveniently be embarked and that the remaining part of such requisition be forwarded on freight by returning servants and such other means as may hereafter be deemed most Expedient That the Post of Pembina be ~~abandoned~~ withdrawn and that of Netly Creek transferred and attached to Winipeg River and that Donald McKenzie be empowered to furnish supplies conformably to Tariff of Colony Shop to retired servants and petty traders on prompt payment for the purpose of collecting any furs in possession of the Indians of the more adjoining ~~districts~~ sections; in the valuation of such furs he is to be regulated by the accompanying Price List and that in issuing those supplies he be directed to impose such ~~restrictions~~ conditions and restraints on the Individual purchasers as circumstances may warrant to secure and protect the trade of the surrounding Districts and that sales for cash to colonists be continued as heretofore at Inventory Prices excepting the Article of Spirituous Liquor which must be sold in limited quantities and at the Depot summer Tariff to servants.

Res. 37 That Mr. McKenzie be directed to purchase from the Colony the following supplies made up in sound and transportable packages at the Rates thereto annexed 200 cwt best kiln dried flour at 20/ cwt, 12 cwt Hulled Barley 16/6, 100 Bushels pease at 5/6, 100 Bushels unhulled Barley 4/9, 1000 Bushels Indian corn at 6/6 and 20 Kegs well cured Butter at 60/ per Keg of 60 lb net and that he take the necessary steps to get the same conveyed to Norway house so as to be depended on and thereby be the means of curtailing the requisition from England.

38 That the freight to be allowed to carriers and the Districts for the current year for the transport of Pieces from the Depot to Red River colony be 25/ per actual piece and to Norway house 15/

39 That no District or Post be allowed to have any dealings or Barter account on behalf of the Company with Red River Settlement, including the Buffaloe Wool Company, Red River district excepted, without the authority of Council and that no sales be made by that District to colonists in-

cluding the Buff. Wool company excepting for cash or approved Bills.

Res. 40th Summer Arrangement

Fort Garry and
Colony Shop a Clerk and 4 men

Donald McKenzie C. F. be requested to remain at that place for the summer in the Event of Governor Pelly's taking his departure thence or in the Event of Donald McKenzie considering his presence absolutely necessary.

WINIPEG RIVER

41 Winter Arrangements

Fort Alexander John McDonald C. F.
Jno Robertson Clk

42 That a Post be established at some convenient situation in Lake Winipeg between Berens River and Jack Head

43 That a Boat containing...ps manned by 6 men constitute the current outfit and that a part of the outfit and men required for the new Establishment be delivered over to Mr. Robertson on the way and that the remaining outfit proceed to Fort Alexander

44 Summer Arrangement

Fort Alexander a clk and two men
New Post between Fort Alexr and Berens River } to be abandoned for the Summer

LAC LA PLUIE

45 Winter Arrangements

Lac La Pluie	J. D. Cameron C. F.
Lac des Bois Blanc	J. McGillivray C. T.
White Fish Lake	Thomas McMurray C. T.
	C. W. Bouck Clk
	Wm Clouston Clk
	Wm Sinclair Clk

Res. 46 That 2 Boats and 17 men be provided to take in the current outfit and that the deficient loading be made up with freight for other districts That five new Bark canoes be built next spring three of which to be brought to Fort Alexander and the remaining two together with about fifty fathoms Best Bottom and side Bark to be brought out to Norway house

47 Summer Arrangements

Lac La Pluie a C Trader 2 clks & 5 men

NORWAY HOUSE

48 Winter Arrangements

Norway House Alex[r] Robertson Clk

49 That 4 men be provided and that an outfit of about...ps to be taken up thither on freight constitute the current outfit

Summer Arrangements

50 Norway house a Clk and two men

ISLAND LAKE

Winter Arrangements

Island Lake Alex[r] Stewart C. F.
New Post Jas. Robertson Clk.
Oxford house Donald McKenzie Clk.
Thomas Fleming Clk.

52 That 8 men be provided and that a Boat containing 50 ps constitute the current outfit
Summer Arrangement

53 Island Lake a Clk and two men. That Alex[r] Stewart C. F. be directed to remove the Post to Manitou Lake
Oxford house a Clk and man

Severn

Winter Arrangement

Res. 54 Severn fort James Sutherland C. T.
Trout Lake Francis Ermatinger Clk

55 That 10 men be provided and that the necessary outfit be conveyed to Severn in Boats

Summer Arrangements

56 Severn Fort a Clk and man
Trout Lake two men

57 That the remainder of the men be Employed in conveying the returns to and taking the outfit from York Factory in the event of no vessel being provided for that purpose

Nelson River

Winter Arrangement

58 Nelson H[s] Jno Charles C. F.
Split Lake Rod McKenzie C. T.

59 That nine men in two Boats containing the requisite outfit be provided and that the men of that District make an Extra trip on freight to Split Lake

60th Summer Arrangement

Split Lake a ch. T. clk. and 2 men
Nelson House Two men in[g] Interpreter

Churchill

Winter Arrangement

Churchill Fort Colin Robertson
Hugh Leslie

62 That 10 men be provided and that the requisite outfit be conveyed thither in Boats

Res. 63 Summer Arrangement

Churchill Fort

In the Early part of the Ensueing season the men to be Employed about the procuring of oil and that Mr. Robertson endeavour to prosecute the trade to the northward and that it be understood that he sends out his returns and the same men be Employed to take in the outfit for the Ensueing season

York Factory

64 Winter Arrangement

York Factory	J. G. McTavish C. F.
	Robt Miles Accountant
	William Todd Surgeon
	Richard Grant Clk
	Edward Ermatinger Clk
	George Barnston "
	George Taylor "

65th That the following men be provided 2 Blksmiths 2 asst Blksmiths 4 carpenters or joiners 2 Coopers 4 Sawyers 1 Feeder of live stock—1 Cook—1 waiting man 4 Wood Cutters 2 Wood Carters—6 Labourers and Express men 2 Balers and 1 cook for the people = 32 Total

66 That Mr. McTavish be directed to forward such proportion of outfit 1826 for New Caledonia as his means permit

Columbia River

67 Winter Arrangement

Fort George	Alexr Kennedy C. F.
	Jno McLaughlin C. F.
Fort Nez Percés	J. W. Dease C. T.
Spokan House	P. S. Ogden C. T.
Snake Country	Alexr Ross Clk

Thompsons River	Jno McLeod C. T.
Okanagan	James Birnie Clk
	Alex^{r} McKenzie "
	Ard McDonald "
	Jno Work "
	Finan McDonald "
	William Kittson "
	Thomas McKay "
	Thomas Dears to go in

Res 68 That 2 canoes and 14 men be provided for that district. That Alexander Kennedy be permitted to come out next spring and that Jno McLoughlin C. F. assumes the management of Fort George on his departure and that the Chief traders above named be also considered appointed for ensueing Year 1825/6

Summer Arrangement

69 That Governor Simpson aided by the Advice and opinion of Chief factors and Chief traders make the necessary Arrangements

70 Rocky Mountain Expedition Samuel Black C. T.
Donald Manson Clk.

71 That Mr. Black be directed to prosecute the original object of the Expedition in and westward of the Rocky Mountain towards the Frozen Ocean in the discovery of whatever may tend to promote Science and encourage Mercantile speculation and that he be provided with such assistance and facility as he may require and the means may warrant

72nd In the Event of unforeseen circumstances occasioning Mr. Blacks return prior to his having attained the object of his Expedition he is to be directed together with Mr. Manson to Fort Chipewyan and there to wait the determination of Council

Res. 73rd In consequence of J. F. LaRocque not wishing to avail himself of the Rotation of Furlough transferred to him by Jno Spencer C. T. that he be accordingly appointed to the management of Smoky River Establishment for the Ensueing Winter and summer to be supplied from Lesser Slave Lake and that Jno Clarke C. F. fix his residence at the latter post

74th That the winter post of Athabasca River under the Management of William McIntosh C. F. be kept up for ensueing summer attached to the Saskatchewan District and that George Deschambault Clerk & 2 men remain in charge thereof

75 That the following clerks whose Engagements expire or Resignations have been accepted of be permitted to retire this season viz

Andrew McDermot	Louis Pion
Cuthbert Grant	Jno McLeod
William Smith	Alex Douglass
J. R. McKay	Ranold McDonald
Robert Henry	Jno Stewart
Joseph Cook	Alex Fisher
J. P. Bourke	William Shan
J. M. Brown	Vital Bourassa

76 That of the above Jno McLeod Alexr Douglass Ranold McDonald apprentice clerks be each allowed the sum of 20£ Sg as a donation from the concern and that Robert Henry be allowed 60£ being his salary for the current year

77 That the following clerks whose Engagement expires this year be re-Engaged for a term of three Years viz

Robt Harding	60£ Stg per Annum
Jno Bell	60
Paul Frazer	60
James Hargrave	75
Thomas Dears	60
George Taylor	50

Res. 78 That all Clerks and other servants under Engagement after the first June Prox° be bound to give one Years previous notice of their intentions of retiring from the service and that without such previous notice their services at the Expiration of their existing contracts will be considered disposable for the following Year at the Salary of the Preceding Year

79 That all clerks wintering Inland whose Engagements expire ensuing season and whose services may be required for the summer have the terms of their new Contracts left to the discretion and impartiality of Council till such time as a regular classification and new scale of wages be prepared

80 That in all new Contracts to be Entered into subsequent to the business of the present season it be particularly and distinctly specified therein that the person hired be at the rate of so much per Annum wages and duly to commence and be computed from the date of his Embarkation from England or Canada and be continued to his reęmbarkation and departure from York factory subject however to work his passage from thence when required in any of the companys craft or vessels whether light or laden without any compensation to his Arrival in England or Montreal where his Engagement will cease

81st That great detriment and inconvenience having been experienced from the circumstance of clerks appointed to distant Establishments returning to the Depot the following season under plea of family affairs or ill health

82nd That in all such cases for the future it will be necessary that the Council be provided with every satisfactory information touching the propriety or urgency of such application otherwise the person so ~~applying~~ coming out will be considered as retiring from the service and be provided with his discharge accordingly

Res. 83 That no commissioned Gentleman be hereafter allowed to purchase either Horses or Dogs on his own private account or as agent for another nor to dispose of any except his present Stock But that all such dealings be for and on account of the company each commissioned Gentleman to be nevertheless permitted to keep a saddle Horse or a train of Dogs for his own use when considered necessary on paying the surplus cost thereof over and above the Established Indian or Inventory price of the District and that no Clerk or other servant be permitted to purchase either Horses or Dogs beyond what is necessarily required for their own use nor to dispose of the same to any who are not in the companys service it being understood that in the event of any removal or retirement of the Individual the Company will estimate and assume such property on a fair and equitable valuation as if constituting part of the Inventories of the current Year

84 The Better to prevent the further continuance of further abuses practised by persons leaving the Country That no servants or others Retiring from the Country be permitted to Embark beyond two dressed Skins or Buffaloe Robes or their Equivalent in made up leather but that all such property be subject to search and Examination at such places along the communication as may be deemed expedient and where any willfull contravention or Evasion of such regulation is satisfactorily detected the same to subject the property to seizure and confiscation accordingly

85th That Joshua Hales Clerk be allowed twelve months

leave of absence to England on account of ill health and passage free of Expense be provided him

Res. 86th That Lodsuuk Osterlog Surgeon to the Red River settlement be allowed the sum of 50£ Stg for Medicines and attendance and Advice at the Companys Establishment at Red River Colony and neighboring districts during the last twelve months.

87th Great delay and Inconvenience having arisen this season from the late arrival at the Depot of members of the Council

88th That all commissioned Gentlemen superintending districts comeing out to the Depot be permitted to precede their loaded craft hither and that they concert Measures for leaving their winter Grounds sufficiently Early to Enable them by comeing out two or more in one of the outgoing craft to reach the Depot on or about the 1st July at which period it is intended hereafter that Council will commence Business

89th The Better to prevent any deception abuse or loss of freight inwards that those superintending or in charge of loaded Boats from the Depot previous to their Departure give in to the Person appointed for that purpose a correct account for the purpose of being enterred, of the Bills of Lading thereof which must not be under 60 actual real Packages allowing a deduction therefrom to cover the private luggage and voyageing apparatus of passengers as follows

To Each commissioned Gentln 10 Packages
" " Clerk........from 2 to 5 Packages

and for Each of the same class remaining in land one half of above with a Distinct understanding that such proportions are to be strictly observed throughout the voyage inwards

Res. 90 That regular and correct accounts of supplies furnished along the communication or of property transferred from one Post or District to another be delivered or forwarded accompanying such supplies or transfers of property otherwise no charge thereof can afterwards be brought forward by the district furnishing against the district receiving the same

91 That the Tariff of Sales for commissioned Gentlemen throughout the Northern District for any supplies taken subsequently to those during the summer at the Depot be at 20 per cent on the Depot Inventory Tariff for all Goods without distinction, spiritous liquors excepted to be at 100 per cent on the Depot Tariff, and country produce to remain at Inventory prices throughout the Year

92 That all Furs received from retired servants and petty traders attached to Red River in payment of supplies furnished be valued during the current year conformably to the average net sale price of Returns of 1821 and that all debts for furs or other articles incurred by freemen and other trappers in General having funds in the Companys hands and for which they have no furs to tender in payment be valued at the rate of a Dollar or 4/6 stg made Beaver

93rd That all Gentlemen in Charge of Districts or Posts on the communication be directed to afford every requisite facility and assistance which the means permit to Captain Franklin and the Gentlemen and men connected with his Expedition during their passage Inwards ensuing summer

94th That in the Event of Captain Parry commanding an Expedition fitted out for the purpose of exploring a North West passage or Captain Lyon commanding an Expedition for the purpose of Exploring to the Northward of Churchill touching at any of the Companys Establishments that Every assistance and attention be afforded them

Res. 95th That for the purpose of transmitting corrected Accounts from the Depot of the summer transactions as well as conveying information relative to ~~such~~ the state of the Districts in General—that a winter Express from the Depot and the Interior be appointed to meet at Carlton house about the close of February the one to proceed northward via Isle a la Crosse and Lesser Slave Lake and the other southward via Cumberland and Norway house that steps be also taken by means of Indians or others to forward from the Depot to Norway house or Cumberland House before the closing of the navigation any private letters conveyed by the Ship in order that the same may reach their respective destinations before the departure of the craft and returns in spring

96th That all those in charge of Districts be directed to afford every assistance in order to facilitate and promote the humane and benevolent intentions of the Church Missionary Society towards procuring, for the purpose of Christianizing, the children of such of the Indians as the parents may be induced to part with for which purpose the Society authorize to the value of 3£ to be expended in Goods for outfiting of such Children

97th That the Indians be treated with lenity and forbearance and every mild and conciliating means resorted to for to Encourage industry repress vice inculcate morality and that the use of Spiritous liquors be gradually discontinued.

98th That they be discouraged from hunting beaver in

Summer by convincing them of the injurious effects thereof to themselves and the country at large

Res. 99th That the following Resolves no 100, 101, 102, 103, 104, 105, 106, 107, 108, 109, 110, 111, 112, 113, 114, 115, 116 containing the substance of certain Resolves passed in Council during the sitting of 1822 and of last year and part of which was comprehended and particularized under no 138 of the minutes of last Summer be considered till rescinded as forming part of the General regulations for the management of the trade viz

100 That to prevent any misapprehension in regard to the Rotation list of Chief factors and Chief traders who may wish to avail themselves of Furlough conformably to the provisions of Articles 20 & 21 of Deed Poll that such rotation for Furlough be invariably understood according to the order of seniority expressed in said deed Poll

101st That Chief factors Chief traders or clerks in charge of Districts or posts be directed annually to furnish Registers of the number of Indians attached to ~~each post~~ their respective Districts or Posts particularizing the tribes—number of Chiefs and followers with the district of Country they inhabit and hunt on together with their General character and habits of life also the same to furnish annually exclusive of a regular Journal a General report conveying every requisite information in regard to the present state resources and mode of conducting the trade—the number of hands Employed—Families supported—Posts occupied, means of subsistence conduct and character of officers and men—climate Soil and vegetable productions, accompanied with a comparative statement of returns—together with such further suggestions in regard to Amelioration or improvement as may occur

Res. 102nd That the practice of allowing servants to trade Provisions leather or other Articles be discontinued and that no traffick or barter of any kind be permitted with Either freemen or Indians under penalty of a fine to be imposed by Council for Each offence

103rd In order to draw a line of distinction between Guides Interpreters and the Gentlemen in the service no Guide or Interpreter—whether at the factory Depot or inland be permitted to mess with commissioned Gentlemen or Clerks in charge of posts but while at the Depot they shall be allowed per week four days ordinary rations as issued to Engages besides three loaves of Bread three pounds of Pork ¼lb Tea 1½lb sugar and one pint Rum and have an Allowance delivered them on departure for the voyage inland of 1lb Tea 6lb Sugar 10lb Biscuits and 10lb Beef or Pork besides an Extra allowance for the Wintering Grounds of 25lb Flour and 20lb Sugar and 10lb Grease in addition to the ordinary rations of Engages at the place where they winter

104 That all servants having full wages and who may be Employed as fort Hunters or permitted to hunt furs dureing the winter be allowed in Goods half the price paid to Indians for their hunts and that all servants having full wages and not Exempt from the ordinary public duties of the place and who may Kill furs by trapping or otherwise be allowed in Goods the full price paid Indians

105th That any augmentation of wages extra service money or remuneration allowed servants over and above their contract wages be particularized and satisfactorily accounted for in the statement of annual wages and Balances of the district, otherwise all such extra wages service money or Remuneration be placed to the account of the person authorizing or ordering the same

Res. 106th That Gentlemen in Charge of districts upon arrival at the Depot deliver in for the inspection of Council the District account complete accompanied by their respective order or indent for the current and next succeeding outfit

107th That no transfers of Money from one account to an other for bargains or otherwise be allowed among servants under the rank of clerks excepted from Monied to Indebted servants at the close of the Year and that no money transactions—Barter—traffic or Exchange between clerks and other servants be allowed without the special permission of Council

108th That servants oweing large Balances to whom are allowed the current wages of the districts be permitted to have advances in course of the year not exceeding ¾ of their current wages ~~of the~~ viz one half at the Depot and ¼ inland

109th That no servant be transferred from one District to another without being accompanied with a satisfactory statement of his account and that no servant belonging to one district and sent to another be furnished any advances by the latter without an order from the former district unless the person making such advances has a statement of his account or assumes the Responsibility thereof

110th That all property remaining on Inventory and classed or considered as unsaleable or which on that account it may be found advantageous to transfer to another district be got off hand by every favorable opportunity meantime that it be valued at the prime cost of the place where the same was originally manufactured or procured and that damaged property be valued in proportion.[51]

GOVERNOR & COMMITTEE TO THE CHIEF FACTORS IN CHARGE OF THE COLUMBIA DEPARTMENT[52]

London 22 July 1824

6. By an arrangement made with the East India Comp^{y} we have contracted to supply them for this and the succeeding year with 20,000 Beaver and 7000 Land otter skins.
7. The Barrel of Salmon sent home as a sample will not answer, and it could not be used, the expence of keeping up an Establishment is considered too great, for altho' the Fish may be taken in the highest perfection, yet by a neglect in the curing and packing it, it may, as was the case in the present instance be unsaleable when brought to this country.
10. As the Americans are to have possession of Fort George whenever they please, you will immediately proceed in erecting a Fort on the North side of the River taking care to select the most convenient situation and remove from the South side of the River with everything belonging to the Company: we are likewise desirous that the Establishment at Walla Walla and any other Post on the North bank of the Columbia should be put in good repair, and by the Ship send home Plans and particulars of all the Posts and Establishments in your district.

GOVERNOR & COMMITTEE TO J. D. CAMERON[53]

London 22 July 1824

In the general dispatches you will receive Instructions that as soon as the William & Ann has discharged her outward Cargo she is to be sent to the Northward and that you immediately

[51] The manuscript breaks off at this point, but the substance of Resolutions 111-116 is probably to be found in Resolutions 120 and following of the "Minutes of Council 1825," *Can. Hist. Rev.*, VII, 317-319.

[52] H. B. Co. Gen. Letter Book No. 621.

[53] *Ibid.*

proceed in building a Fort on the North side of the Columbia River. It has not been thought prudent in the public letter to detail the reasons which have induced the Governor and Committee to give these directions, but they feel it right to communicate to you some particulars, that by knowing the object, you will better understand how to carry these views into effect.

You are aware that the Russians have laid claim to almost the whole West Coast of America and forbid vessels to approach within 100 leagues any of the Shores in the Pacific, this has consequently been resisted by our Government and it is expected that a treaty defining the limits of Territory of the respective Powers will be the result and we anticipate that we shall have the Coast exclusively to the North West as far as the Portland Canal with the territory within it and likewise the territory to the North of the Canal to the Sea with a right of shipping goods from any place between that Canal and Mount Elias;[54] it is therefore very desirable that it should be ascertained, whether there is any good Roadsted or Harbour in the Portland Canal or between it and the Columbia, and if there are any and what Rivers communicating with the Interior and how and by whom the Coasts are inhabited. [The vessel might go as far north as Sitka.]

The next point to which we wish to call your particular attention is the building of a Fort on the North side of the Columbia, this is likewise connected with a probable arrangement with the Americans. You are aware that by the Treaty of 1818 the Lands

[54] The Convention of Feb. $\frac{16}{28}$, 1825, established a line of demarcation between the possessions of Russia and Great Britain in North America which was to run from the southern tip of Prince of Wales Island in latitude 54°40′ to the Portland Canal, up that canal to latitude 56°, thence along the summit of the mountain range parallel to the coast (but never farther inland than ten marine leagues from the coast) to the intersection with meridian 141 near Mt. St. Elias, and thence along meridian 141 to the Frozen Ocean. Subjects of Great Britain were to be permitted to navigate the streams flowing to the Pacific across the strip of coast left by this line to Russia; they were to have the right for ten years to engage in trade or in fishing in the gulfs, havens and creeks along the coast, and the right of free commercial access for the same period to the port of Sitka.

In the negotiations preceding this settlement the Hudson's Bay Company was consulted freely by the British Foreign Office, and the Governor and Committee had seven months foreknowledge, as our letter shows, of the main terms of the agreement.

on the West of the Rocky Mountains are free to ourselves and the subjects of the United States for 10 Years from the date of it which will expire 1828, but that at any time they can demand possession of Fort George, if it were alone on this account, it would be very desirable to have one of our own to which we could move, but in the present day occupying the soil is considered as the best title; it is therefore of great consequence that we should have buildings of our own, and those built before the Americans take possession.

You should therefore without delay commence a Fort on the North side of the River, selecting a spot which will command the entrance of the River convenient to the vessels frequenting it, sufficiently elevated if possible to be well seen from the sea and in a dry place with good water.

It appears to us from the accompanying Plan that the Point on Cape Disappointment would be the most desirable, and next to it point Ellice, but we have not sufficient information to give a decided opinion.

In the William & Ann are three carpenters, two of these could be spared to assist in the erection, and if any of the Seamen could be beneficially employed in removing the Guns across the River etc. they might be exchanged for other men to accompany Capt. Hanwell to the Northward....

It is likewise very desirable that the Post at Walla Walla should be made as respectable as possible, as well as any others on the North side of the River, and as we cannot expect to have a more Southern boundary than the Columbia in any Treaty with the Americans (altho' we are entitled to it from occupancy) it will be very desirable that the hunters should get as much out of the Snake Country as possible for the next few years.

Governor Simpson to A. Colvile[55]

York Factory 9 Aug. 1824

....On perusal of the Dispatches I immediately returned thither (Red River Colony) and after having given the subjects

[55] Dominion Archives, Selkirk Transcripts, 8326.

they embraced connected with my future proceedings due consideration laid my plans open to him [Gov. R. P. Pelly] for the benefit of his opinion and advice; he previously knew of my intention of visiting England and the principal object thereof, likewise my wish to cross the Mountain, and his intention of going Home the following year was so fully understood between us that both he and I were at liberty to communicate thereon with you and the Committee. I perceived the desire of the Committee that I should cross the Mountain either this year or next and that if I did not go thither this season it would be impossible to get away the following as Mr. Pelly's visit to England would render my presence necessary in Red River. I therefore in order to accomplish both objects determined on going to the Columbia this Fall which he likewise seemed to consider a judicious arrangement (altho' he would have preferred my Coy at Red River) and with that understanding and determination I took my departure for the Coast. This appropriation of my time and services I trust will be satisfactory to you....

I am highly gratified to find that my general conduct is approved by the Committee and can assure you that no exertion of body or mind shall be wanting on my part to merit a continuance thereof. In visiting the Columbia this Season instead of next year as you suggest I have alone consulted the welfare of the Company & Colony interests and laid aside all feeling or consideration in respect to my own ease and comfort as by starting so late as the 15 Inst I shall be exposing myself to great hardships and fatigues, having determined in the event of being obstructed by ice in the Athabasca River (which is not improbable) on going across land to Edmonton and crossing the Mountain at Kootonais Portage to the Flathead Post on Snow Shoes and from thence on foot or horseback as may be necessary to the Coast. This I am induced to do from the certainty that I cannot go next year in the event of Govr. Pelly returning with his family to England, and the affairs of the Columbia are now in such an unsettled state that my presence there is absolutely required either this year or the following. Our Council know little about that Country having confined their attention to the mere trafficking with

Indians and not taking an enlarged view of its affairs either in regard to political or commercial prospects indeed there is a general feeling against it and I believe they would gladly throw up all interest in the trade on the West side of the Mountain (New Caledonia excepted) if left to themselves. On this subject I have addressed the Committee both publickly & privately as also Mr. Garry who will probably show you my letter. That Gentleman seems to take a very lively interest in the Compys affairs generally, and having honored myself individually with much kindness and attention I have communicated with him unreservedly on all points; it may therefore be unnecessary for me to go over the same ground again.

On our present uncertain tenure of the Columbia I could not recommend any experiment or deviation from the established course that would involve expence. If the Americans settle on the mouth of the Columbia it would in my opinion be necessary for us to abandon the Coast and come into some arrangement respecting a division of the trade & move to the Northward as I conceive an opposition would be attended with a ruinous sacrifice of money. The mouth of Frazer's River appears to be the only point at which we could establish with advantage as from thence we could supply the whole interior by Thompsons and Okanogan River, but my information respecting the navigation is not yet sufficient to authorize a distinct opinion on the subject. If there was a division of the trade, say the Coast to be given up to the Americans and the Interior kept by us it would be practicable to conduct the business either by the Saskatchawaine, say Kootenais Portage or Athabasca River Portage (at Jaspers House) as far as the Willa Wallas or Nez Percés Fort. By the Kootenais Portage there is some danger from the Piegans and other Plain Tribes at war with the Flatheads & Snakes, but that 'tis probable might by negotiation be obviated and I think by making a Depôt at Cumberland the craft of that District & Carlton managing the transport from thence to the Depôt at York the returns and outfits might be taken the same year; but by the Athabasca Portage it is my opinion that it would be necessary to have a Depot at Isle a la Crosse and keep the Goods and returns on hand for one year as is now done with the trade of McKenzies River at Athabasca.

From all the information I am able to collect I do not think we could risk either provisions, outfits or returns from or at any of the Spanish Settlements north of Cape Horn, the Spaniards on that Coast are not to be depended on or trusted and ready to take any advantage and the Guarda Costas little better than Licensed Pirates at least it was so under the old Regime. We might possibly find them honorable and well disposed for one or two years but treachery and caprice is their characteristic and they might take an advantage to suit their own ends which might be ruinous to all our plans and prospects. You must however be better informed as to our relations with the existing Government and whether it would be safe to trust them; if safe a small vessel on the Coast æconomically sailed might answer as I think by good management a profitable coasting trade might be carried on and she might be sent to China direct with the returns; it is but a short voyage of Four Months out & home that can be performed in the Winter when she could not otherwise be employed on the Coast, and the interest of money saved by bringing the Furs so early to market might nearly clear her Expences and the Freight thus saved together with that of a return cargo of China goods to be transshipped for England by the vessel that goes with the outfit or sold to the Spaniards on the Coast, would assist in clearing the Expence of Freight on the outfit, as according to this plan there would be no return cargo of Furs. These are merely undigested ideas of my own drawn forth by your remarks and which our Council would think I was mad if I advanced, but I shall give them further consideration and probably advert to them in my report of the Columbia. I have suggested to Mr. Garry the propriety of the Ship going out this Fall surveying the Coast from the Columbia to the mouth of Frazers River in Latitude 49 a distance of 2½ or 3 degrees in order to ascertain if it would be practicable to form an Establishment there; in the meantime I shall endeavour to gain accurate information respecting the Inland Navigation from thence but at present my ideas in connexion with the subject generally are so crude, unconnected and irregular that I do not venture any opinion thereon with confidence. I shall however devote my attention exclusively thereto this winter on the Spot and hope to be able to give more information thereon generally than has yet been collected by any of the visitors from this side of the Mountain. . . .

After My present Journey is completed I do not see that I shall have occasion to undertake any more Winter Trips as the trade and country is now brought into a regular and organized state. My attention has for these last two years been particularly directed to New Caledonia & McKenzies River and everything that can be done is in progress in those countries. I do not therefore consider my presence could be attended with any material benefit, if you or the Gentlemen of the Committee however think otherwise I am disposable and as ready to pass the winter on Snow Shoes as in Red River, England, or Montreal, altho' after Winter 1825/26 I am of opinion that I could be of more service to the general interests at the latter place than anywhere else.

GOVERNOR SIMPSON TO JOHN McLEOD[56]

Okanogan 1 Nov. 1824

I am disappointed in not having the pleasure of seeing you here and sorry that the advanced state of the Season does not admit of my visiting Thompsons River, but hope to fall in with you at this place about the latter end of March on my return to the East side of the Mountain.

Herewith you will receive a copy of the Minutes of Council to which I need scarcely request the favor of your particular attention; there are likewise forwarded some letters to your address which were entrusted to our care by your friends at the Bay.

The returns of Thompsons River, I am concerned and surprised to learn have fallen off while at the same time the expences are considerably increased within the last year or two; this may have arisen from circumstances beyond your controul, but which I doubt not you will be able to account for, and I am satisfied is

[56] Dominion Archives, McLeod MSS.

not occasioned by any want of zeal or exertion on your part. I however sincerely trust things will assume an improved appearance next spring:—if its affairs do not look better, my opinion as also that of Mess[rs] McLoughlin, McMillan & Ogden is that it should be abandoned as 1700 Beaver will do little more than cover the interest on the capital employed, whereas in many other parts of the Country it can be turned to much greater advantage. The complement of people intended for the District this season appears to be greater than necessary and than the trade can afford we have therefore reduced it from 21 Gentlemen & Servants to 18 in all which we hope you will find sufficient. Mr. Annance is particularly required to accompany Mr. McMillan on a very hazardous expedition to the mouth of Frazers River in the course of the Winter and from the report we have of Jacco La Fontese, there can be no doubt that he is competent to all the Duties in which Mr. Annance was last season employed. In the course of this Winter we shall at Fort George determine whether the Post of Thompsons River is to be continued or not, in the meantime you will be pleased to make the necessary arrangements for abandoning it by removing every valuable article in Spring in case it may be deemed expedient to adopt the latter measure.

It is probable an establishment may be formed at the Mouth of Frazers River if the reports from that quarter are favorable and I have to request you will be pleased to make particular inquiry among the Natives as to the Navigation, numbers & disposition of the Tribes on that communication as also the means of subsistence and general character of the Country.

While at Spokane House we recd Letters from Mr. Ross and the report he gives of the Snake Expedition is favorable; it has been reenforced by a Clerk, Interpreter and 13 Men and Mr. Ogden proceeds immediately to the Flat Head Post in order to outfit and conduct it back to the Hunting Grounds. Mr. Ross will be left in charge of the Flat Head Post, Mr. McDonald of Spokan House, Mr. Kittson of the Kootonais, and Mr. Work accompanies us to Fort George.

The complement of people for the Spokane Departmt being reduced it will be necessary for yourself & people to proceed to the Forks of Spokan River in order to assist in taking down the returns and a larger supply of Fish than usual will be required at this place as the extra men who accompany the Express canoe in Spring so much earlier than customary will remain here a considerable time.

In renewing the Engagements of your people it is necessary that they be hired for the Columbia generally and not for particular Districts or Posts and the terms prescribed by the Minutes of Council will I hope be adhered to strictly.

Enclosed I beg to hand you an average price List of Furs which will regulate You in regard to the Trade, if you find that Swan Skins, Swan Quills or Bear Skins will pay it might be well to encourage the Indians in procuring them.

I shall expect the pleasure of seeing you here about the latter end of March and with best wishes.

P. S. Mr. Ogden is to write me from the Flat head Post & his Dispatches will be at the Nez Percés early in Decb: if you address me soon after rect of this it may be in time to reach Spokane or Nez Percés Fort for that Conveyance.

Extracts from Mr Chief Trader MacMillan's Report of his Voyage and Survey from the Columbia to Frazer's River

Columbia 31st December 1824[57]

In 28 days from our departure hence we reached Frazers River and ascended it about 60 miles, the intervening country is densely peopled along the Coast, we communicated with several tribes of the Natives, were received kindly and as far as we are able to judge, a favorable impression was made on them in regard to the Whites. The Country is said to abound with Red deer and Chevriel and Beaver are represented as very numerous, but the decreasing state of our provisions and various other circumstances did not render it expedient to occupy time in examining the country en route.

[57] British Public Records Office, F. O. 5/208.

The mouth of Frazers River we found to be situated between Point Roberts and Point Gray, in about latitude 49.15 north per Vancouvers Chart, it is a fine large River emptying itself by various channels, but in none of which do I conceive there is a draft of Water for a Vessel exceeding 150 to 200 tons burthen.

The Tide runs up about 60 Miles and at the narrowest part it is about three quarters of a mile in width.

The Natives are very numerous, and collected in Villages along its banks, they were overjoyed to see us, and entreated that we might settle among them, they have heard of but never saw Whites until we fell in with them. They have a few articles of British manufactures, which reached them through the medium of other Tribes occupying the country between them and Thompsons River which I conceive to be situated about ten days march higher up. They speak a language that has such an affinity to that of the Piscahouse Tribe or Okinagan, that I was enabled to maintain a conversation with them. The upper part of the River as far as Kameloops (beyond which they are unacquainted with it) they represent as being navigable with a strong current.

I should have proceeded to the post of Thompsons River had I not been informed that it was set fast with ice, so that being unprovided with snow shoes and other means necessary for undertaking a winters journey in a country of which we were ignorant, I found myself reluctantly constrained to retrace my steps.

No question can exist as to the stream we ascended being Frazers River called by the Natives Cowitchens as one of our Men ''Proveau'' who accompanied Mess[s] Frazer and Stewart described several parts of it before reaching them and those parts I recognised afterwards by his description particularly the points from whence those Gentlemen returned which is situated about 20 Miles above the entrance of the River.

The Indians moreover made me understand that there is an Establishment on the Kameloops River, which is our part of Thompsons River. I distributed a few presents among the natives which were gratefully acknowledged, and by every word and gesture they evinced their anxious wish, that we should settle among them, holding forth as an inducement the assurance of their bringing us large quantities of Beaver with which I have ascertained that their Country is richly stocked.

It appears extraordinary that Vancouver should not in the careful survey he made of the Coast have discovered a River of such magnitude and I could only account for it by the flatness of the shores at its mouth, which being covered with high grass has much the appearance of a marsh or swamp and it must thus have escaped his observation.

I ought to observe that there is no such River as that called New Caledonia in Arrowsmith's Map, indeed there is no large or navigable River between Frazers River and the Columbia.

[Endorsed] Extract from M^r McMillan's Report of Voyage and Survey from Columbia to Frazers River, 1824, In Mr Pelly's 9 Decr 25.

GOVERNOR & COMMITTEE TO GOVERNOR SIMPSON[58]

London 11 March 1825

[Paraphrased] You and the Council seem to think that the Governor and Committee intend to use the funds of the Fur Trade to further colonization at Red River. This leads us to state the principles which govern us in the administration of Red River Colony. We think the Colony will be of no small importance in furnishing provisions for the Fur Trade and will serve as an asylum for retired servants of the Company who must otherwise be maintained at heavy expense at the different inland posts. Consequently the Colony ought to be supplied with the goods which it requires at prices just sufficient to repay the costs of importation. The Governor and Committee have no interests in the Colony other than as it may be connected with the interests of the Fur Trade; they will therefore not apply the funds of the Fur Trade to objects relating solely to colonization. But the Company is responsible for the government of the Colony since in granting the soil jurisdiction neither was, nor could be, transferred. The Colony ought to pay its own expenses of government, but since it cannot in its infant state, troubled as it has been by

[58] H. B. Co. Gen. Letter Book No. 621.

the contests of the Fur Trade, and with a numerous half-savage population thrown upon it to the great relief of the Fur Trade, the Fur Trade should in equity contribute the moderate sum of £200 to the salary of a resident Governor. Likewise the Fur Trade ought to contribute £250 for the salary of a missionary and £260 for the building of a schoolhouse, as the exclusive license to the Hudsons's Bay Company requires that provision be made for the moral and religious instruction of the natives. There is another view to be taken—in the event of hostilities with the United States the settlers, if well treated, would help to defend the trading establishments.

12. [Paraphrased] No word has been received as yet from the East India Company as to the result of the shipment of beaver to Canton. Shipment is now being prepared of

5000 fine beaver skins
5000 seasoned beaver skins
4000 heavy beaver skins
4000 otter skins.

The arrival of the vessel from the Columbia is awaited to complete the contract by shipping 6000 heavy beaver in addition to the above.

45. Having taken into consideration the important service which you have rendered to the Fur Trade more especially your arduous Journey in 1822/23 and the advantages derived from it in the shape of the great and immediate improvement in the arrangement of the Posts and Establishments for carrying on the trade, considering also the very spirited manner in which you last year undertook the Journey to the Columbia at so late a period of the season when very great personal fatigue and privation, as well as some risk was to be encountered, and that we may reasonably expect much benefit will be derived to the Trade of that district, we have voted you a Gratuity of Five hundred Pounds and resolved to increase your salary two hundred Pounds per annum, to commence from 1st June next, and which we feel satisfied will meet with the unanimous approbation of every Chief Factor and Chief Trader in the Country.

JOHN McLOUGHLIN TO THE CHIEF FACTORS AND CHIEF TRADERS[59]

Ft. Vancouver 20 June 1825

....The Snake Beaver was full of sand and evidently had not been beaten since the Freemen gave them in; this ought not to be in a Country like this, we ought to be very particular and beat our furs from time to time, however there were no moth in them, and the only furs in which we found moth were the Okanagan Rats and Nez Percés beaver and small furs. It is certainly difficult to keep moths from Rats, but if when traded they were hung in a Cellar, the skin would get pliable and they could be turned without injuring the Skin and then kept free from moths as easily as any other furs, 'tis a pity the Indians cannot be got to keep their Furs clean and stretch them better; I am of opinion they would bring 25 p C^t^ more if we could get them in the same state as we get them on the other side of the Mountain....

GOVERNOR & COMMITTEE TO THE CHIEF FACTORS COLUMBIA DEPARTMENT[60]

London 27 July 1825

4. The Salmon was of superior quality to that received by the Lively; we are, however, of opinion, that from the difficulty of curing this fish properly, and the length of time it must unavoidably continue in pickle, that it will not answer as an article of commerce.

7. We also notice Mr. Ogdens observations respecting the Trade of the interior, and as you are already in possession of our views as far as regards the Americans, we have merely to observe that it will be advisable to work the southern portion of the Country as hard as possible, while it continues free to the subjects of both Nations. It is possible that an arrangement may be made with the American Government to define the Limits of the respective Powers, as has been done with Russia, and we expect to hear by return of this Vessel that the whole of the Establish-

[59] H. B. Co. Journ. No. 762.
[60] H. B. Co. Gen. Letter Book No. 621.

ments have been removed to the North side of the River as directed last year, it being probable that the course of the River will be the Boundary to a certain degree of North latitude.

JOHN McLOUGHLIN TO THE GOVERNOR, CHIEF FACTORS AND CHIEF TRADERS[61]

Ft. Vancouver 10 Aug. 1825

When I last had the pleasure of addressing you I expected long before this to have sent off Mr F. McDonald, but I have been obliged to detain him in the first place to enable us to send a party to salt our Salmon as we would be too weak to have done so after his departure.

But while this was going on, hostilities broke out between Cassino and his father-in-law, Concomley, which threatened to put a stop to nine tenths of our Trade, however we think we have succeeded in bringing them to agree to make peace, indeed as far as words go they seem extremely anxious to come to terms, the old Man and his Son are now here and have brought a good lot of Skins, to morrow they are to start and we are to escort them down, when they and Cassino will have an interview about making up their disagreements.

You will find the first account of hostilities breaking out between them in my letter to Mr Dease of the 23d July, and untill matters were some how settled it was necessary to have a Strong party to protect those who came to trade. Cassino in my opinion makes it up, because he sees we are determined and able to escort them up and down the River, and as this would increase their importance which he does not wish, he prefers to leave the navigation of the River free, at the same time we distinctly told him, we would protect those who came to us with Skins, and if he fired on any of our Craft, we would not allow him to do so with impunity and there the business stands, however these wars and quarrels amongst them, have been the cause of our trade being for some time at a stand, at present it is improving. I certainly was very much disappointed when I learned the disasters we suffered

[61] H. B. Co. Journ. No. 762.

in the Snakes[62] it was impossible to take more pains in every way to insure their getting their Supplies in due time, to enable them to hunt, and all these precautions and care are blasted by the Villany of these rascals. The amount of Debt due by those deserters is seen in the inclosed account, by the desertion of these Men we will loose Furs to the amount of about Three thousand pounds and their future Services. The accompanying letter will show you what I have advised to be done in the present state of our affairs, and referring you to the documents accompanying this for any further information regarding what we have done.

JOHN McLOUGHLIN TO CHIEF FACTORS AND CHIEF TRADERS[63]

Ft. Vancouver 10 Aug. 1825

Yesterday evening Mr. Deares messengers arrived with the dispatches conveying the mortifying intelligence of the desertion of our Freemen in the Snake and the threats made by a Mr. Gardner that the Americans would be at the Flat heads and Kootenais this Fall and would drive us from their Territory. On the latter subject I have only to observe, that the Committee write "that by the Treaty of 1818 the Lands on the Westside of the Rocky Mountains are free to ourselves and the subjects of the United States for Ten Years from the date of it which will expire in 1828" and by this you will see we are justified in resenting to the utmost of our power any attack on our persons and property or any assumption of authority over us by the Americans.

Indeed so confident am I of our being justified in this, that had we a party sufficiently strong to defend itself from the Natives and that could be depended upon—I would have no hesitation in making another attempt in that quarter if it was merely for one year to defy them to put their threats in execution, and to counteract the evil impression the vaunting words of Mr. Gardner and the desertion of our Freemen will have on the In-

[62] Refers to the desertion in the Snake Country of the freemen attached to P. S. Ogden's Snake Expedition of 1824-25.

[63] H. B. Co. Journ. No. 762. Johnson Gardner was the leader of the party of American trappers to whom the freemen of the Snake Expedition deserted.

dians and remaining Freemen; however Mr. Ogdens party is I am afraid too weak and cannot be sufficiently depended upon, as I infer from their behaviour at the time the Iroquois walked off with their Furs—horses and traps all which were certainly our property, I think the Engagees evinced the most disgraceful I might say criminal neglect, of their bounden duty in not supporting Mr. Ogden to the utmost of their ability which had they done I am of opinion we would not have suffered the losses we have nor the indignities of seeing people going off with our property and at the same time insulting us with the most approbrious Epithets they could express.

There is not a Man of the party then those present who does not full well know that no Man was ever induced to buy a single article, and that they were in debt much against our will and inclinations, and their advances had been made to oblige and accommodate them, when at the time we ran the risk of loosing our property by their death, and in return if they did not murder Mr. Ogden and pillag'd him of the property in his possession, it is not from a want of will....

JOHN MCLOUGHLIN TO GOVERNOR & COMMITTEE[64]

Ft. Vancouver 6 Oct. 1825

....As I consider our object ought to be if there is a strong opposition on the coast as this year to allow them to exhaust themselves; as they have only this market for their goods they will sell for what they can get, while having an extensive inland trade we would be certain of disposing of ours and would be always ready to take every advantage in the market.

JOHN MCLOUGHLIN TO JOHN MCLEOD[65]

Ft. Nez Percés 9 Nov. 1825

"....You will also receive ten horses and by the winter express we hope to be able to forward sixteen more to make up the number to one hundred for New Caledonia [transport service]

[64] H. B. Co. Journ. No. 1323.

[65] Dominion Archives, McLeod MSS.

and you will have to write to the Gentlemen here if more are required that they may be forwarded if we can purchase them, if the number intended to be sent is considered not to be required you will direct some to be left at Okanagan as Horses will be very scarce next year and we will require yet a certain number for our trappers. We are most anxiously looking out for Mr. Ogden—he was to have been here most positively by the 20th Oct.[66] and since that time we have no accounts of him from Indians or others. The vessel only traded 400 skins and only visited Observatory Inlet where they were detained near a month, and touched at Nootkat and were about a month about Frazer's River though I expressly stated to the Captain that he ought only to visit that place after he had examined Skittegats etc and only if he had *time*. There were six vessels on the Coast—one had fifteen hundred otters. Our trade at Ft. Vancouver is less than last year at this time, but as we were not able to send about and have now more time I expect we will yet be able to turn out as much as last year. Messrs McDonald & McKay are only four days march from this[67]—they had met with a good many difficulties, and were only then on the Borders of the Beaver Country, they find themselves weak in numbers and Mr. [A. R.] McLeod with Mr. Dears and twelve men start from this to join them.

I have this moment been called off to receive Mr. Ogden his men are to be here in two days. His Horses are so knocked up that we cannot send you any until he is supplied however his will remain to recrüit and by the Express in the winter we will send you all that can be spared though I am of opinion by sending a trip in winter with all your Horses Loaded with provisions or furs, in the spring you could spare twenty of your horses for New Caledonia....

[66] Dr. McLoughlin had heard from Ogden from the region of the upper Missouri during the summer and had sent him instructions in return by an Indian messenger. See "Journal of John Work" in *Washington Hist. Quart.*, V, 83-115; also *Oregon Hist. Quart.*, X, 331-335.

[67] Finan McDonald and Thomas McKay were returning from their unsuccessful Umpqua Expedition. They were probably at the Des Chutes River waiting to be joined by P. S. Ogden. See *ante*, 253; also *post*, 281.

Gov. J. H. Pelly to Hon. George Canning[68]

London 9 Dec. 1825

....By the Convention 20th October, 1818, between Great Britain and America the Trade of the Rocky Mountains is left open to subjects of both Nations for ten years without prejudice to the claim of either Nation; but no American subjects have as yet availed themselves of this privilege. The British Fur Traders however have never withdrawn from the Country since they first entered it; on the contrary they have gradually and at much risk and expence increased their Settlements which now amount to thirteen in number (besides temporary Stations which are occasionally changed) and extend over a Country exceeding fifteen degrees of Latitude, say from Lat. 45° to North of Lat. 60°.

In the year 1821 the Hudson's Bay Company made an arrangement with the North West Company of Montreal by which they acquired possession of all the trading Posts and Stock of that association, and now under their Royal Charter and His Majesty's License the whole Indian Trade of British America to the North West of Canada is carried on by the Hudson's Bay Company. In order to acquire more correct information respecting the Country on the West of the Rocky Mountains and for the purpose of carrying into effect some measures connected with extending our Trade on the North West Coast, Governor Simpson was directed to proceed thither last Season, and after an arduous and fatiguing journey he accomplished an extensive Survey of the Company's Trading establishments, and is now in London. He will remain here until the beginning of February, and will attend any appointment, that you may be pleased to make should you wish to be possessed of any further information respecting that Country. Whilst at Fort George, Govr Simpson fitted out an

[68] H. B. Co. Correspondence with Government No. 721; also F. O. 5: 208. Canning had this letter before him on July 7, 1826, when he wrote his often-quoted communication to Lord Liverpool, the prime minister, outlining the policy of Great Britain with regard to Oregon. See E. J. Stapleton, *Correspondence of George Canning* (London, 1887) ,II, 71-75. This letter has been printed, though without the endorsement by Canning, in *Oregon Hist. Quart.*, XX, 25-34.

Expedition under the direction of an intelligent Officer Mr Chief Trader McMillan for the purpose of exploring the Coast to the Northward. In the course of his Survey, he discovered the entrance of Frazer's River between Capes Roberts & Gray in about Lat. 49.15. The Mouth of this River was not discovered by Vancouver nor by the Subjects of any civilized Nation, untill Mr McMillan visited it last Winter, but the Upper part of the River and down to within 20 Miles from the Sea, was explored by Messrs. Frazer and Stewart, partners of the North West Company in the Year 1808. I annex extracts from Mr McMillan's report[69] and as this Country appears to be rich in Fur bearing Animals, we have it in contemplation to form permanent Establishments therein next Summer; to push our discoveries to the Northward both in Land and on the Coast, and to embark a considerable Capital in endeavouring to secure to Great Britain the benefits arising from an exchange of British Manufactures for the Produce of that Country with its numerous inhabitants.

In compliance with a wish expressed by you at our last interview, Governor Simpson, when at the Columbia, abandoned Fort George on the South side of the River and formed a new Establishment on the North side, about 75 Miles from the mouth of the River, at a place called by Lt Broughton Belle Vue point. Governor Simpson named the new Establishment "Fort Vancouver" in order to identify our Claim to the Soil and Trade with Lt Broughton's discovery and Survey. He considers the Soil and Climate of this Place, to be so well adapted for agricultural pursuits, that in the course of two or three years, it may be made to produce sufficient Grain and animal Provisions, to meet not only the demands of our own Trade, but to almost any extent, that may be required for other purposes, and he considers the Possession of this Place and a right to the navigation of the River Columbia, to be quite necessary to our carrying on to advantage not only the Trade of the Upper parts of the Columbia River, but also that of the Country interior from the mouth of Frazers River and the coasting Trade, all of which can be provisioned from this Place.

[69] See *ante,* 248. The Strait of Georgia was reached by Fraser.

Under existing circumstances, I respectfully submit to your Consideration whether it might not be adviseable to endeavour to arrange a Boundary line between Great Britain and the United States, in that Country to the West of the Rocky Mountains, more especially as the attention of Congress has been called to the Subject and in an American Map, lately published, the Line of Lat. 49 is continued from the Rocky Mountains to the Sea-coast and the Country to the South of that Line is described to be United States Territory, which at some future Period might be made use of by the American Government. This Line would deprive Great Britain of a valuable Country now occupied and traded by the Hudson 's Bay Company and would occasion many practical inconveniencies in carrying on the Trade of the Country which would be left to us.

But as I have already stated it does not appear that the Americans can establish a just Claim to any part of the Country either to the South or North of the Columbia River, and as the free navigation of that River is necessary to our carrying on the Trade, I have endeavoured to fix on a Boundary, which would answer the views of the Hudson 's Bay Company, without pushing the Claims of Great Britain to their full extent. I have therefore to suggest that starting from Lat. 49 at the Rocky Mountains the Line ought to be continued Southward along the height of Land to the Place where Lewis and Clarke crossed the Mountains, said to be in Lat. 46° 42 thence Westerly along the Lewis 's River, until it falls into the Columbia, and thence to the Sea, leaving the navigation of both these Rivers free to the Subjects of both Nations. This Line would leave to America the Trade and Possession of an extensive and valuable Country, and would furnish fewer opportunities of collision between the Traders of the two Nations, than any other Line that could be suggested.

I send herewith a Map on which the Line which I have taken the liberty of suggesting is coloured and on which the trading Posts now occupied by the Hudsons Bay Company are marked.[70]

[70] This map could not be located in the archives of the Foreign Office.

[Pencilled endorsement]

This is a very important Paper. The Map which accompanied it should be carefully preserved & the whole placed among the Papers belonging to the negotiation with the U. States. Did Mr. Addington see Gov. Simpson & take a memo. of his communication? G. C.

H. U. Addington to Governor Simpson[71]

191 Regent St., London 28 Dec. 1825

Mr. Henry Addington presents his compliments to Mr. Simpson, and having received Mr. Secretary Canning's directions to communicate with Mr. Simpson on the subject of the Columbia River and North West boundary, with a view to the final adjustment of those important questions with the Government of the United States, he is desirous of arranging an interview with Mr. Simpson and in so doing wishes to consult Mr. Simpson's convenience equally with his own. . . .

Governor Simpson to H. U. Addington[72]

Hudson's Bay House, London 29 Dec. 1825

Mr. Simpson presents respectful compliments to Mr. Addington, will have much pleasure in communicating with and giving him all the information he possesses in regard to the Columbia River and North-West Boundary; for which purpose Mr. Simpson will do himself the honour of waiting on Mr. Addington when and where he may be pleased to appoint, Mr. Simpson's time being quite at Mr. Addington's disposal.

H. U. Addington to Governor Simpson[73]

191 Regent Street, London 30 Dec. 1825

I inclose herewith the set of queries on which I wish for more particular information.

71 H. B. Co. Correspondence with Government No. 721. H. U. Addington was the permanent British under-secretary for foreign affairs in this period.

72 *Ibid.*

73 *Ibid.*

The answers to them may be as concise as is consistent with perfect perspicuity. The more matter of fact they are, the better. That to Query IX, I wish to be as strictly conformable to fact and history as possible.

GOVERNOR SIMPSON TO H. U. ADDINGTON[74]

Hudson's Bay House, London 5 Jan. 1826

Mr. Simpson presents respectful compliments to Mr. Addington, begs to hand him answers to his list of Queries, likewise a corrected chart of the Country on both sides of the Rocky Mountains; should Mr. Addington require further information on this important subject Mr. Simpson will do himself the honour to wait upon him at any time he may appoint.

1. Query.

What is the nature of the Soil, its capability of production, and general character in the Vicinity of the Columbia and Lewis's rivers? What the Climate?

Answer.

The banks of the Columbia on both sides the River from Capes Disappointment and Adams to the Cascade portage a distance of from 150 to 180 Miles are covered with a great variety of fine large timber, consisting of Pine of different Kinds, of Cedar, Hemlock, Oak, Ash, Alder Maple and Poplar with many other kinds unknown to me. The Soil of the low grounds is alluvial and found very productive, that of the high grounds a rich black mould, chiefly composed of decayed vegetables. Some of the points formed by the windings of the River are extensive and beautiful with sufficient Timber for use and Ornament and where the plough may be used immediately and the Point on which the Companys Establishment of Fort Vancouver is situated is, from its extent and the fertility of its Soil, capable of producing large quantities of Grain of every kind, of pasturing

[74] *Ibid.* For a discussion of the relation of this communication to Oregon diplomacy, see my article on the "Oregon Pioneers and the Boundary" in *American Historical Review,* XXIX, 697 ff.

numerous herds of Cattle and nutricious roots are so abundant that almost any number of Hogs may be reared.

The Climate delightfully temperate from the Month of April until the Month of October and from November untill March rainy, with little or no Frost or Snow. From the Cascade portage to the entrance of Lewis's River, the banks are sterile, the Soil very sandy producing stinted grass and willows, and little or no timber. The Country in the vicinity of Lewis's River I understand is level and generally fertile, but I cannot speak with certainty on this point, not having had an opportunity of visiting it personally except at its junction with the River Columbia.

2. Query:—

Are the natives on the Northern bank of the Columbia warlike or pacific, inclined or averse to intercourse with the Whites? Is the Country between the Rocky Mountains and the Columbia densely or thinly inhabited?

Answer:—

The different Tribes on the banks of the Columbia are generally bold and warlike as regards each other and extremely jealous of any encroachments on each others Territorys or privileges but peaceable and well disposed towards the whites, with whom they are very anxious to maintain a friendly intercourse. Occasional differences I understand took place when we first entered the Country, in which some lives were lost on both sides, but at present the best understanding exists between us and them. The Country is densely inhabited, on account of the great abundance of its resources in the way of living.

3. Query:—

Is there a good hunting ground immediately on the Northern bank of the Columbia?

Answer:—

The Hunting grounds immediately on the Northern banks of the Columbia are nearly exhausted in respect to Fur bearing

Animals but the back Country is still productive and Beaver are found in all the small Rivers & Lakes.

4. Query:—

What, on a rough calculation are the annual profits of Trade in the district of Columbia, and do they arise from the Northern or Southern portion of that district principally?

Answer:—

The Trade of the Columbia is yet in its infancy and the Countries to the Northward and Southward produce about an equal quantity of Furs amounting together in value to between 30 and £40,000 p Annum.

5. Query:—

Have the Americans any Post or trapping parties on the Columbia or to the West of the Rocky Mountains in that direction?

Answer:—

The Americans have not had a Post on the West side of the Rocky Mountains since the Year 1813 and I am not aware that they ever had any Trapping parties on the West side of the Mountains until last year, when the Hudson's Bay Companys Snake Country Expedition fell in with five Americans, who had straggled across from the sources of the Missouri.[75]

6. Query:—

Is the Country northward of the Columbia favourable for Land and water communication?

Answer:—

The Country to the Northward of the Columbia is not favorable for Water communication with the Coast on account of the impetuosity of the current at particular Seasons in the different Rivers, and frequent chains of Rapids and dangerous falls, and the communication with the Coast by Land is quite imprac-

[75] Alexander Ross permitted this group, of which Jedediah Smith was the leader, to accompany his Snake Expedition to the Flathead Post. See Alexander Ross, "Journal of the Snake River Expedition, 1824," in *Oregon Hist. Quart.*, XIV, 369 ff.

ticable, on account of the mountainous character of the Country, which is covered with almost impenetrable Forests.

7. Query:—

For what extent of Country does the Columbia River furnish an outlet for Trade? Specify this exactly and according to the latest and most accurate accounts.

Answer:—

The Columbia is the only naviagable River to the Interior from the Coast, we are acquainted with, it is therefore the only certain outlet for the Companys trade west of the Mountains, comprehending that of thirteen Establishments now occupied:

1. Ft. Vancouver
2. Nez Perce
3. Okanagan
4. Colvile House
5. Flat Head
6. Kootenais
7. Kilmany
8. Fraser's Lake
9. Ft. St. James
10. McLeod's Fort
11. Chilcotin Fort
12. Thompson's Fort
13. Alexandria Fort

8. Query:—

What time is required for communication between Hudsons Bay (York Fort) and Fort Vancouver?

Answer:—

I was last year occupied 84 days in travelling from York Fort, Hudsons Bay, to the mouth of the Columbia, but I think the Journey can be performed in the height of the Season in a light Canoe, unincumbered with baggage for the Water communication and with good horses for the Journey by Land, which may be about 1/6th of the whole distance, in 2 Months or 65 Days by a different route to that which I took.

10. Query:—[76]

What comparison does Frasers River bear in magnitude and capacity for the purposes of Trade with the Columbia? Is the

[76] Query 9 concerns the question of British priority in trade and discovery in the region about the mouth of the Columbia River. It elicits from Governor Simpson a partisan reply, which may be found in *Oregon Hist. Quart.*, XX, 336-338.

native population on its banks dense or not, well disposed or not, warlike or pacific?

Answer:—

Frazers River is not so large as the Columbia and not to be compared with it for the purposes of Trade, the depth of water found at its entrance was about 3 fathom: the banks are generally high and steep covered with Timber and such places as are sufficiently low and clear for the site of an Establishment bearing marks of having been overflown in the Seasons of high water.

About 70 Miles from its entrance the navigation is interrupted by Rapids and Falls, so as to render it nearly impassible and according to the best information I have been able to collect, the banks of the River about 150 Miles up, form precipices where the towing line cannot be used, and the Current so impetuous at certain Seasons, as to render it impossible to use, either the setting Pole or Paddle; Canoes being the only craft that can attempt to stem the Current at any Season. The natives treated our Party with civility and seemed *anxious* that we should settle among them. They assemble from the back Country to the banks of the River in great numbers during the Fishing Season (from April until October) when the population is very great, and at all Seasons the Country may be said to be densely peopled, and their character much the same as that of those inhabiting the banks of the Columbia, I should not however consider it safe to form an Establishment there, with a Smaller force than 60 to 70 Men and Officers, until we are better acquainted with them.

11. Query:—

Could the Fur produce to the North of Frazers river and West of the Rocky Mountains be conveniently transported by means of this River for Shipment to other Countries?

Answer:—

From all the information I have been able to collect respecting Frazers river, it is not my opinion that it affords a communication by which the interior Country can be supplied from the Coast, or that it can be depended on as an outlet for the returns of the interior. I will further altho' unasked take the liberty of giving it as my opinion that if the Navigation of the Columbia is not free to the Hudsons Bay Company, and that the Territory to the Northward of it is not secured to them, they must abandon and curtail their Trade in some parts, and probably be constrained to relinquish it on the West side of the Rocky Mountains altogether.

GOVERNOR & COMMITTEE TO GOVERNOR SIMPSON[77]

London 23 Feb. 1826

6. [The Governor & Committee approve of Governor Simpson's arrangements for raising grain, cattle, hogs, potatoes etc at various posts.]
10. [They approve of attaching New Caledonia to the Columbia Department and of the plan of extending the trade on the coast as well as in the interior.] "If well managed we expect that it will become an important branch of the business, and we direct that a vessel of 50 or 60 tons be fitted out and employed in the Coast trade."
11. We are apprehensive that the China market will not take off the whole of our returns from this Coast, particularly as the Skins procured there are not the best adapted to the China Market; we do not therefore think of employing a Vessel to trade with Canton more especially as there is no probability that the East India Company would allow us to take a return Cargo from thence. They seem to be liberally and well disposed to the British Fur trade, but are tenacious and jealous of their exclusive right to the China trade.
12. We approve of the removal of the depôt from Fort George to Fort Vancouver, and expect that much benefit will be derived from raising here all the provisions that can be required for the whole of our trade West of the Mountains.
14. As your Services will be required elsewhere during the ensuing Winter it will be necessary to communicate fully with Mr Chief Factor McLoughlin who we do not doubt will be able to carry into effect all your views which we approve of. It is highly

[77] H. B. Co. Gen. Letter Book No. 621.

gratifying to us to know that such a good understanding exists among the Gentlemen in this department, as the contrary would be productive of the most injurious consequences; but the great distance from the seat of Council renders it necessary that the Gentleman in charge of the Department should be invested with discretionary powers in respect to its management, it is therefore our wish that such arrangements as he may direct may be carried into effect, and in these arrangements he will of course be regulated by such instructions as he may from time to time receive from you in Council.

15. We think it probable that a profitable trade may be carried on with the Russians and recommend that the small Vessel employed in the coasting trade may visit their principal Settlement at Norfolk Sound in order to open a communication and make further inquiries.

16. [Commendation of C. T. McMillan for his Expedition to Frazer River.] "We wish Frazers River to be established next season if possible, and that Mr. McMillan should be appointed to the charge of it, as his re-appearance among the natives may have a good effect. From the central situation of Frazers River we think it probable that it will be found to be the proper place for the principle depot, but not until we have passed at least one year there and acquired a knowledge of the character and disposition of the Natives and ascertained whether the navigation of the River is favorable to the Plan of making it the principal communication with the Interior. If Frazers River cannot be established this year we wish the people intended to be sent thither to be employed as last year in trapping in the country to the Southward of the Umpqua, as it is desirable to obtain from that Territory as large a present supply of Beaver as possible and to allow our other Country to recruit."

19. [Approval of economies and concentration of posts] "whereever it can be done with propriety and consistently with the reasonable convenience of the Natives who must be supplied with absolute necessaries, altho', from bad seasons, disease or other causes they may not be able to pay for them, and care must

be taken that the Trade is not endangered by too great a reduction of officers and men.''

20. [Red River Colony. R. P. Pelly does not return as Governor in consequence of the ill health of Mrs. Pelly. Chief Factor McKenzie is given charge, by which the allowance of £200 for Governor of the Colony is saved.]

25. The first shipment of Beaver &c to China by the report which we have received from the East India Company appears to have been a losing concern to them, even at the low price at which the Skins were charged to them. The result of the second years shipment is not yet known here, but we do not expect that it will prove much better than the first, or that the East India Company will be disposed to take any quantity this year. However unless we can dispose of our whole importation at good prices here, we may probably send a small adventure to Canton and possibly one to Singapore on account of the Fur Trade with the view of keeping open the China market.

At Singapore the China vessels from the Northern ports come to trade and they may perhaps be disposed to speculate in a few skins which would be the means of opening a direct communication with the part of China where the furs are used.

36. [Long argument in favor of permitting beaver to recruit.] ''The importation of Beaver from our own home Territories was Seventy years ago as large as that received this last Season from the whole of British North America, and at the period the Company had not a trading post more than 300 miles from the shores of the Bay. The country is peculiarly favorable to the Beaver and by good management it may be brought again to produce as large returns as formerly. . . .''

''In the meantime the deficiency might be made up by keeping all the frontier country hunted close, and by trapping expeditions in those countries likely to fall within the Boundary of the United States.''

JOHN McLOUGHLIN TO GOVERNOR, CHIEF FACTORS AND CHIEF TRADERS[78]

Ft. Vancouver 20 March 1826

[The William and Ann as soon after her arrival from England as possible undertook a coasting voyage northward in accordance with the instructions of the Governor & Committee of 22 July 1824 q. v.]

4. At Skettegats[79] on their way back our people saw two Vessels, one the Owhyhee Captn Kelly[80] from Boston was just coming out of the harbour, the other was her consort who brought the supplies to the Owhyhee. Captn Kelly was on board the William and Ann, said he had been five years on the Coast, that in general he took his supplies at Owhy-hee where he deposited his Furs and had passed last Winter on the Coast—and had Sixteen hundred Sea Otters on board. That a few days previous to our people entering Observatory Inlet he had at Nass on the North side of the entrance, traded One thousand Beaver and Land Otter skins. From this and the documents we have on the Coasting trade stating more Land Furs are traded at Nass than at any other place along the Coast (at that time exceeding those traded at the entrance of the Columbia) and by the Water appearing muddy opposite that place I would not be surprised if the entrance of Simpsons River was found to be there,[81] but the best mode of ascertaining the communication between the Interior and the Coast is by descending the Rivers as the Company has Establishments on their Sources and certainly it is much to be regretted since Mr Brown's[82] state of his health prevented his proceeding on the intended discovery last year, that some of the young Gentlemen were not sent by Mr Brown, the Indians at

[78] H. B. Co. Journ. No. 762.

[79] Present Skidegate Inlet in Queen Charlotte Islands.

[80] Captain Kelly was a trader in the service of the Boston merchant Josiah Marshall.

[81] Simpson's River is the Nass River of present-day maps. The port of Nass lies at its mouth.

[82] William Brown was a chief trader in charge of the Babine district in New Caledonia.

Nass have the under lip split with the piece of wood in it just in the same way as the Babines.

5. Captn Kelly was very communicative the short time he was on board the William & Ann told our people their vessel was not well arranged for the purpose of trade and defence, invited them on board his Vessel, and offered to shew them how she was arranged, and to shew them his Furs, but they did not avail themselves of his invitation, the Owhy-hee is of about Two hundred Tons burthen, and had a crew from Appearance of between thirty and Forty Men. Capt. Kelly also said there were then six vessels on the Coast, I send you a Copy of M^{r} McKenzies report.

16. Our farming is coming on as well as we could expect, except in Pigs of which we have lost four large since last Spring poisoned by eating a kind of poisonous Camas; we have not killed a single calf, and have a stock at present of twenty seven cows, five three year old heifers, three bulls, eleven Steers two oxen, Eleven year old heifers—two this Spring calves, and we expect this Fall to have between eighty and ninety head of Cattle of all sizes; we succeeded in raising nine and a half Bushels seed pease from those imported, and we expect with this to be able to raise a sufficient Stock of Pease to dispence with importing any corn in future, we have also succeeded in raising a few beans for seed and had a crop of nine hundred barrels of Potatoes, of the latter I will endeavor to put two hundred barrels in the ground, so as to have a sufficient supply for this place and Frasers River.

25. [Ft. Vancouver employs 20 men, Spokan 16, Thompsons River 12, Walla Walla 7, Snakes 34, 20 to establish Frazer River and for contingencies, *total* 109]

27. As to the Snakes though the desertion of twenty three Men was a great Drawback on its Returns, yet you will see by the accounts sent out that its gains are very handsome and though this year in consequence of the Men being under engagements the Furs will be dearer, on a supposition their hunts equalled those of the three last years would clear about Two thousand five hundred Pounds.

28. I make the observations in the preceding paragraph to call your attention to this subject as after all it depends on circum-

stances with which you are better acquainted than I am, whether it is our interest or not to keep up the Snake Expedition, perhaps we are on the Eve of being obliged to withdraw from it.

GOVERNOR & COMMITTEE TO A. L. JOHNSTONE & CO. SINGAPORE[83]

London 31 March 1826

[The Hudson's Bay Company are shipping three puncheons containing 1000 beaver skins, and two containing 1000 otter skins]

These Goods have been forwarded to your care at the recommendation of Mess[rs] Palmers Mackillop & Co. and I am to acquaint you that they have been selected of the finest quality from the whole of the Companys last years importation, and are similar to the Skins that were purchased at the London Sales (prior to the prohibition of such goods being admitted into Russia by the Imperial Ukase of 1822) for the Petersburgh market, and for which much higher prices than the goods now consigned to you are charged at were obtained; from Petersburgh the Skins were forwarded by Land carriage a distance of nearly Five thousand English miles, which must have added greatly to the cost of them, by way of Moscow Tobolsk and Irkutsk to Kiachta and there disposed of in barter trade with the Chinese.

Subsequent to the prohibition the China market has been principally supplied with Otter and Beaver skins by shipments from hence; in 1823 a small consignment of 3600 fine Beaver skins and 2400 fine Otter skins was made by the Company to the very respectable Firm of Perkins & C° at Canton; who had for several years disposed of Furs for the late North West Company of Montreal now combined with the Hudsons Bay Company, and which produced moderate prices. These Shipments averaged annually from 15 to 17,000 Beaver skins and 1,000 Otter Skins of inferior quality and were imported direct from the Companys establishments on the North West Coast of America. In 1824 an arrangement was made with the Hon[ble] East India Company

[83] H. B. Co. Gen. Letter Book No. 621.

and shipments were made to their Establishment at Canton—in that year

5,000 fine Beaver Skins similar to those p Bonavista
5,000 2nd quality about 20 p Ct inferior
10,000 3d quality North West direct and
7,000 Otter Skins of different qualities

were sent. In 1825 the same quantity of Beaver skins were sent, but only 4,000 Otter skins; the first years consignment did not turn out so well as was anticipated and of the disposal of the Second there has not yet been received any Account. This Year the Hudsons Bay Company intend to ship only 4,000 fine Beaver and 2,000 Otter skins rather inferior to those consigned to you, and none other will be sent from this market; as it appears by account Sales of Shipments 1824 that the Fur Merchants of Canton do not fully appreciate the quality of the Goods or that the rate of transport between that port and the Northern provinces where the Skins are principally used, combined with the Transit duties is so heavy that they cannot afford to give better prices.

The Governor and Committee being however informed that Merchants from the Northern ports of China are in the habit of trading to Singapore, some of whom it is not unlikely may be fully acquainted with the quality and value of Beaver and Otter skins, have been induced to send the present outfit by way of experiment, and in the event of it turning out advantageously, they will be induced to make an annual Shipment to a larger extent. The Skins are invoiced at low prices taking into consideration the quality of them and the returns that were made for a parcel of similar goods, which had been sent to Petersburgh prior to the Ukase of 1822 taking effect and were disposed of there in July 1823; for instance 60/4d Stg p Skin was obtained for Skins of the same mark and quality as those packed in puncheons N° 1 @ 3 containing 1,000 Skins, wt 1251 lb. Nt @ 37/6 p lb. making the price of those now sent as near as possible p Skin 46/11d Stg.; 52/3d Stg p Skin was obtained for skins of the same quality as those packed in puncheons N° 4, 5 containing 1,000 Otter Skins which are charged at 42/6d Stg p Skin.

J. W. Dease to the Governor, Chief Factors and Chief Traders[84]

Spokan 7 April 1826

[He has traded 250 horses since April last up to the date of leaving Fort Nez Percés.]

I succeeded last Summer in sending the Kayouiks and a band of Nez Percés to make peace with the Snake Indians, which was effected, and the result of which enabled those I had sent to hunt on the Snake frontiers as they came back in which they were pretty successful, having brought me in nigh Eight hundred Beaver skins in about Six weeks.

William Smith to Messrs. Perkins & Co. Canton[85]

London 19 April 1826

[Paraphrased] The Governor & Committee have shipped to your house 4000 beaver and 2000 land otter skins all of the first quality. They have also sent to Johnstone & Co. at Singapore 1000 beaver and 1000 otter skins with instructions if these should not prove saleable at a fair price to forward them to Perkins & Co. at Canton. The foregoing are all the furs that will be sent this year to Canton from the London market, the East India Company not shipping any on their own account.

P. S. Ogden to Governor Simpson[86]

Burnt River 1 July 1826

Finding it necessary from the low state of our horses want of Provisions to send Messrs McDonald, McKay and Dears with the Furs we now have, I beg leave to refer you to them for all my news; having sent a party of my Trappers to trap last February in the F^t Vancouver route with 8 Men and 30 horses [I am going] to find them; at the same time it will enable me to see the road

[84] H. B. Co. Journ. No. 762.
[85] H. B. Co. Gen. Letter Book No. 621.
[86] H. B. Co. Journ. No. 812.

from whence I joined M^r^ McDonald last Fall to Fort Vancouver.[87] In case the inclosed proposal[88] should meet with your approbation, I shall not be at a loss what route to take, as I know full well now we can place little or no reliance on Canadian or Indian report. The trappers with us have succeeded in taking 2 M Beavers and this from a Country that has already been trapped, and I have yet to learn and receive the hunts of 18 Men if they have escaped with their Scalps, but of this number I seriously apprehend 4 have lost theirs. From the Country we explored this year we obtained only 100 Beaver not from the want of Streams but there were none and the privations we endured were great, however we have the satisfaction to know that the Southside of the South branch of the Columbia[89] has been examined and now ascertained to be destitute of Beaver. My party is small, my horses weak, but I trust if no accident should happen to us to reach F^t^ Vancouver by the 1st August, where I trust I shall have the pleasure of seeing you in health,[90] and I trust altho' I have not been so fortunate the last two Years as formerly you will not attribute it to want of exertions on my part, and I must only hope that I may be more successful hereafter.

P. S. Ogden to Governor Simpson[91]

Burnt River 1 July 1826

I offer for your consideration the following statement.

From the lateness of the Season last year when the expedition started from Fort Vancouver for the Claminitt Country,[92] want of information of the country destitute of provisions, also hunters, are the principal causes of its failure; at the date I reached F^t^ Vancouver expedition, it would have been folly if not madness to

[87] For a clear account of this expedition, Ogden's second to the Snake, see his general letter of 10 Oct., 1826, at *post*, 281. Ogden's day-to-day journal of the expedition is also available in *Oregon Hist. Quart.*, X, 331-365.

[88] See for this proposal the letter following.

[89] The south branch of the Columbia is the Snake River.

[90] Governor Simpson did not again visit the Columbia after his first trip until the autumn of 1828.

[91] H. B. Co. Journ. No. 812.

[92] Present Klamath Country.

have attempted it,[93] there was no other alternative left from the information I obtained but to proceed to the South branch of the Columbia and endeavor to reach the Lake on which so much *Stress* had been laid, and which I have since ascertained beyond a doubt both from the Americans as well as from many Indians who are in the habit of resorting to the Clammitt country is the same Lake I saw last year on the Spanish waters[94] and within 6 days march of the Spanish Settlement (called Taas)[95] and as I have every reason to believe that a party of Americans who started from the Lake in May last for the purpose of penetrating to three large Rivers, which are said to be in the Vicinity of the Claminitt Country and rich in Beaver were obliged from starvation to retreat,[96] that the Country still remains unexplored, but will not long remain so, as I am of opinion now that the Snake Country is fast on the decline, from this I conclude the Americans will soon make another attempt better provided now that they know as well as us do from experience that provisions are required to reach it. I now beg leave to propose and in lieu of a better volunteer to lead a party to that quarter provided you should consider it worthy of a trial, at the same time I beg leave to observe that it is only from the information obtained from the Natives and a Slave of the deceased Nipising that it is a

[93] Ogden is explaining why the Umpqua Expedition under Finan McDonald failed to penetrate farther into the Klamath region, and why a second attempt was not made after the Umpqua and the Snake parties had joined.

[94] Refers to Great Salt Lake, which Ogden reached in the spring of 1825 on his first Snake Expedition. The lake was apparently first discovered by James Bridger or Etienne Provot, employees of William Ashley, in the winter of 1824-25. Ogden shared the view of these early explorers regarding the location of the lake, the mysteries of the enclosed Basin having not yet been disclosed. For an excellent account of the exploration of this region see H. C. Dale, *The Ashley-Smith Explorations* (Cleveland, 1918), 95-109. Professor Dale believes that Ogden did not penetrate to the shores of Great Salt Lake on his first expedition (1824-25). But Ogden's statement here will dispose of this much mooted point.

[95] Taos.

[96] Ogden is mistaken in thinking that a party of Americans attempted to explore the country westward of Great Salt Lake in 1825. The only American trappers at that time in the region were William Ashley's men, and they did not make the attempt. They may, however, have represented to Ogden that they intended to try, in order to discourage him from doing so. See Dale, *Ashley-Smith Explorations*, 152-158.

Country rich in Beaver and the greatest obstacle to surmount, as the Beaver country is far distant, is the want of Provisions, as none can be obtained from the poverty of the Country on our going to it, not even a days allowance, the expedition should one be undertaken would therefore require a supply of 50 days otherwise it would be folly to attempt it, so far as Mr McDonald proceeded last Year he found the Natives very friendly, but they represented the Tribes beyond them as hostilely inclined towards all, but it is a common remark that it is an invariable custom of every tribe to represent their neighbours most particularly so when at variance with each other as hostile, at all events I should not consider it safe to visit the Country with less than 30 Men and an assistant, with 4 hunters engaged for the express purpose; in the number of Men required it is to be understood that Indians Slaves and Islaweens[97] should not form a part.

I have this year experienced too much trouble and anxiety with them and proved beyond a doubt their unfitness to explore a new Country. It is also my opinion if an Expedition should be undertaken, it should start from Fort Vancouver as early as possible after the arrival of the present party by that means it would be enabled to cross the Mountains ere the Fall commences by so doing the Spring hunt would not be lost and Winter quarters could be found with the assistance of our Hunters to join the party and proceed at the opening of the Season to the Country beyond the Claminitts from whence Mr McDonald returned; by not starting before the Spring it is impossible from the quantity of Snow to cross the Mountains before late in June and even then with difficulty. In all the different expeditions to the Snake Country two thirds of the time is lost in travelling to and from headquarters, far different is the mode the Americans conduct their trapping expedition, their trappers remain five and six years in their hunting grounds and their equippers meet them annually secure their furs and give them their supplies and although great the expence and danger they have to encounter to reach the Missouri, still they find it to their advantage to conduct their

[97] Refers to Hawaiians.

business in this way,[98] and surely there is a wide difference in the prices they pay for their Furs and sell their Goods compared to us a difference of 200 p C. I would further request if we should be so far fortunate as to discover a Country rich in Beaver, to be allowed to remain for Two years, I am fully aware the sooner the Beaver reach a market less loss is sustained; and I think it probable, but this I cannot possibly assure you will be the case, that when we become acquainted with the Country, I might send ⅓ of the party with the Returns, and the Trappers might remain to work. I shall now only add that if you feel inclined to send an expedition to that quarter no time should be lost[99] as you may rely on it the Americans will not loose sight of it, and altho' they were not successful in their first attempt, they will not abandon it without giving it a few more trials, altho' they have the same obstacles to encounter in reaching it that we have, the only difference between us they take their departure from a Buffaloe country, whereas unfortunately if we go we must take a Supply of Provisions from the Establishment we start from.

JOHN MCLOUGHLIN TO THE GOVERNOR, CHIEF FACTORS AND CHIEF TRADERS[100]

Ft. Vancouver 16 July 1826

Mr. Ogden suggests in his letter of April last the propriety of sending an officer with an outfit to follow the Flatheads, but I am afraid this would be running too great risks as the Flatheads hunt on the East side of the Mountains, if a party of Americans fell on our people, there would be a chance of our people being taken.[101]

[98] Ogden is describing here the institution of the mountain rendezvous which had recently been developed by the St. Louis traders, Andrew Henry and William Ashley. The rendezvous took place in midsummer, in the off-season for trappers, so that no valuable time was lost by it. A classic account of such a mountain meeting is in Washington Irving, *Adventures of Captain Bonneville* (New York, 1895), I, chap. xx.

[99] Ogden's third Snake Expedition was to the Klamath Country in accordance with this recommendation.

[100] H. B. Co. Journ. No. 812.

[101] Hudson's Bay Company parties had no right, of course, to trade east of the Rocky Mountains as that was American soil.

Gov. J. H. Pelly to Hon. Wm. Huskisson[102]

Hudson's Bay House, London 25 July 1826

4. Quaerie:—

In what year was the first English ship sent to the Columbia for the purpose of collecting Furs, and carrying supplies to the Company's agents, and trading with the Natives on the Columbia river? has a Ship been sent every year since the first?

Answer:—

The Isaac Todd which sailed from England in 1813 and arrived at the Columbia River in April 1814 was the first Ship that took any Produce of the North West Companys trade collected on the West side of the Rocky Mountains and carried it to China from whence she brought a Cargœ of Tea to England for account of the East India Compy: all that had been collected in former Years having been sent by the Interior to Canada, (but as early as 1786 the East India Compy had Vessells on the Coast and purchased Land of the Natives as related by Meares in his Memorial see State papers annual Register 1790 page 287) The Isaac Todd took at the same time all that had ever been collected by the American Fur Company at the Establishment of Astoria. The Americans arrived in the Columbia as before observed, Summer 1811, the Furs that were collected the following Winter they were not able to send away, the Ship which was to have conveyed them having been destroyed by the Natives on the Coast and the whole of the Crew massacred. No Ship arrived in 1812 and in the Fall of 1813 (it was that) the North West Company purchased of the American Traders all they had collected the preceding two years, therefore no American Ship ever took away, or have the Americans ever taken any produce of their

[102] H. B. Co. Correspondence with Government No. 722. Hon. Wm. Huskisson was one of the commissioners entrusted by George Canning with the Oregon negotiation of 1826. Governor Pelly's letter to him should therefore be read in conjunction with the documents of the negotiation which appear in Stapleton, *Correspondence of George Canning*, II, 71-115. Queries 1, 2 and 3 of the letter relate to the question of British priority in the interior trade of the Columbia. They may be found, together with the answers made to them, in *Oregon Hist. Quart.*, XX, 339-342.

Trade from the Country and when they established themselves in 1811 on the South side of the River, they had no Establishment on the North side, and from the terms of the Treaty for the purchase it appears that they had one subsequently on Thompsons River, but abandoned it when they left the Country, and they have never been there since.

In 1814 the Schooner Columbia was sent out which arrived at Fort George in the Spring of 1815, and having delivered her supplies, proceeded with Skins to Canton from whence she returned to the Sandwich Islands and to the Columbia river in order to carry the Skins of the following Season to Canton.

The Supplies sent from England in 1815 and which reached Fort George in the Spring of 1816 were sent in the Brig Colonel Allan, which Vessell returned from the Columbia to England.

All these were British Vessels belonging to and fitted out by the Agents of the North West Comp[y] with supplies for their Traders at the Columbia river.

The Outfits of these Vessels having been found expensive and unproductive in consequence of the restriction of British subjects from trading in China except under License from the East India Company, which Company refused to permit the Agents of the North West Company to carry away Tea in return for the Skins sold by them at Canton, whilst American Ships and Traders not being under similar restrictions had the benefit of freight for the whole voyage to China and back. Under these circumstances in the year 1815 an arrangement was made with a house at Boston under which the Supplies of British manufactures required for the Establishments at the Columbia were sent from England to Boston, from whence a Ship was dispatched to convey them to the Columbia, to take the Skins from the Columbia to Canton and to carry the proceeds of their Sale in Teas and other Produce of China from Canton to Boston, where the American House retained a certain proportion of the net Proceeds as a compensation for the Freight.

In this manner Annual Supplies were sent to the Columbia River in each year from 1816 to 1820 and in 1821 the Establishments were transferred to the Hudson's Bay Company, since which time the Proceeds have been brought by British Ships to England.

5. Quaerie:—

How many Posts and Settlements has the Company now on or near the Banks of the Columbia or its tributary branches; when, as nearly as can be ascertained, were they first formed and how many are North and how many South of the River or of its branches.

Answer:—

The Company have now six Settlements on the Columbia and its tributary branches exclusive of Fort George and thirteen Settlements in the whole on the north side of the River in New Caledonia. The Company have none on the South side, but parties have been fitted out from Fort George to hunt the Country on that side....

JOHN McLOUGHLIN TO THE GOVERNOR, CHIEF FACTORS AND CHIEF TRADERS[103]

Ft. Vancouver 8 Aug. 1826

....I have also the pleasure to inform you, that the Snakes beaver of this year is much better dressed than it has hitherto been, and that it will in this particular bear comparison with the best stretched and cleanest Pelts on the Eastside of the Mountains; the Servants attached to the Snake Expedition brought Two thousand one hundred and eighty eight plus in Beaver weighing Two thousand eight hundred and seventeen pounds, and Seventy nine plus in Otters making a total of Two thousand two hundred and sixty seven and a half plus and these cost including wages to Officers and Men, reduction of Debt gratuities &c &c Fifteen hundred and thirteen pounds nine shillings and five pence being an average cost of thirteen shillings and four pence and a fraction each made beaver, allowing it to sell 20/ p lb it would clear 100 p C....

[103] H. B. Co. Journ. No. 812.

JOHN McLOUGHLIN TO JOHN WORK[104]

Ft. Vancouver 10 Aug. 1826

....In case the Americans come to the Flat Head Country, they must be opposed as much as we can, but without a waste of property because the right to remain there will be decided between the two Governments. As an opinion, I think from discovery & occupancy we will have that part of the Country, therefore it is not our interest to spoil the Indians, however we must do so if necessary and treat them as liberally as the Americans.

As to our right on this side the mountains the Committee write "that by the Treaty of 1818 the lands on the West side the Rocky Mountains are free to ourselves and the subjects of the United States of America for Ten Years from the date of it which will expire in 1828." By this you will [see] the Americans have no right to assume any authority, or claim this Country as part of their Territory and I feel confident the Company will abandon none of their Establishments until they are informed our Government has given up its claims to the Sovereignty of the Country on which they are situated.

P. S. OGDEN TO THE GOVERNOR, CHIEF FACTORS AND CHIEF TRADERS[105]

Borders Snake Country 10 Oct. 1826

The result of my first expedition to the Snake country and serious losses attended on it you are already in possession of. In consequence of instructions received from Chief Factor McLoughlin I conducted the remainder of my party to Fort Nez Percéz, having equipped the trappers I lost no time in joining Mr Finan McDonalds party who I found encamped on the River of the Falls of the Columbia, about four days march from the Main stream, this was in December, the Season was then too far advanced to explore the Country he had been obliged to return

[104] H. B. Co. Journ. No. 762.
[105] H. B. Co. Journ. No. 812.

from, finding his party too weak and the Natives too numerous to explore it; so far as he advanced the Indians were friendly towards his Party but represented the Natives beyond them as hostilely inclined. Finding myself thus situated without Guides or any one who had the slightest knowledge of the Country, rather than return to the Columbia and the Season lost I resolved on penetrating across the Country, so as to make the Snake River or South branch of the Columbia which early in February I effected but not without suffering a loss of horses and severe privations from the want of food, not an animal to be seen, the cold severe, and we had no less than six feet snow to wade through, with horses nearly reduced to skin and bone ere they commenced their journey.

I had flattered myself on reaching the Snake River our privations would have terminated, but unfortunately it was covered with ice, it was there I found it absolutely necessary for the preservation of the lives of the party to divide it into three and proceed with the remainder to explore the different Rivers which discharge on the South side of the Snake River which I effected and in Fur only we found Beaver sufficiently to supply us for a short time, and while so employed we met with a party of Americans and some of our deserters, in all 28, who had but shortly left their winter quarters on Bear River but found themselves disappointed as we had already trapped the River ~~but~~ consequently their Spring hunt was lost, the few Beaver they had I obtained from them from our deserters in part payment of their debts and the remainder in trade with the Americans, we then parted, shortly prior to this we were visited by a War party of Blackfeet, they made one attempt on our horses but fortunately without success—in July I again reached the vicinity of Fort Nez Percéz, when Mr Finan McDonald took charge of the party, and I proceeded with some Men to cross the country and to reach the Williamette by land and from thence by water to Fort Vancouver, in this I succeeded in nineteen days in the mountains which separate the Snake Country from the Williamette River altho' at the latter end of July we had on an average seven feet of Snow and in my opinion with loaded horses the only Season they can be crossed without sustaining a loss of property in horses would be in September and in Six days it could be effected, the road is fine for horses. On my arrival at Fort Vancouver I had the satisfaction of finding all my party safe arrived there; and considering the severity of the winter and obstacles we had to surmount which only left us three out of eight months to trap, my returns certainly exceed my expectations amounting to Three thousand eight hundred Beaver and Otter which yields a profit on the expedition of Two thousand five hundred pounds. I have now to observe that the conduct of the Party was the same of last year, altho' great were the Offers and temptations held out to desert, not one expressed the slightest inclination this I presume however must be attributed to ⅔ of the party being engaged Men which gave me a decided advantage over the remainder on all occasions.

Having anxiously waited the arrival of Governor Simpson untill the 12th Septr I again took my departure from Fort Vancouver with 35 Men including Mr Thomas McKay and myself with the intention of exploring a River discovered last Spring by a party of my trappers,[106] who from their horses being stolen and Indians troublesome and numerous could not trap it, nor ascertain if it discharged in the South branch of the Columbia or elsewhere. The present party is composed of nearly half freemen and the remainder Servants, and from the advantages they have this Year will I am convinced not only increase their gains but also that of the Concern, should we be so far fortunate as to discover a Country rich in Beaver and it is to be regretted that the present Plan had not been adopted many years since, for from the exorbitant price the Trappers paid for their Goods and horses is solely to be attributed their desertion and former misconduct, indeed from the enormous prices they have been charged with, the difficulties they had to encounter and subject

[106] Ogden had a twofold program for this third Snake Expedition—to trap the river of which he speaks, the Silvies, discovered by Antoine Silvaille in the Malheur Lake region of Oregon the preceding spring, and to complete the work of exploration which the Umpqua Expedition of Finan McDonald had left undone. Both of these objects he effected. See for his day-to-day journal of the expedition, *Oregon Hist. Quart.*, XI, 201-222.

to so many losses, it was almost impossible however industrious a Man might be to clear his annual expences, in fact his four horses and traps alone cost him One hundred fifty large Beaver, nor could he depend on the latter for the year as they have been of late years of an inferior quality, and seldom could a Trapper return to the depot without being obliged to renew both and the former at an advanced price, and as we now have every reason to suppose not only from the information I have obtained from the different American traders and other sources, that the Americans will soon establish themselves in the Columbia, it was full time *if we are allowed to remain* on the North side of the River to reduce the Freemens tariff, otherwise how can we expect to retain one of them in our Service, and under their present terms it is doubtful we shall; although some articles are sold by the Americans higher than we now sell, still there is a wide difference in the price they pay for Beaver say three dollars p lb delivered in the Snake Country and three and a half to four at St Louis and although it may appear to many of you as almost exceeding belief, still I can assure you the Americans transport their property to Yellow Stone River from thence, by land in waggons, over a mountainous Country to the Spanish Settlement called Taas,[107] this establishment is not more than fifteen days march from Bears River, where they equip their trappers, and pay for their Beaver at the prices already stated and from the number of their trappers it is no small quantity they collect in the course of the year, when they have so decided an advantage over us, not loosing two third of their time in travelling to and from Headquarters, this however I trust from my present understanding with Chief Factor McLoughlin will in future be avoided, and I am confident had this plan be adopted sooner we should have taken more Beaver out of the Snake Country than we have, and altho it is now some years since trapping expeditions were first sent to the

[107] Taos was the northern outpost of Santa Fé, and served, after the opening of the Santa Fé trade, as an outfitting center for trappers of the southern Rockies. For the trade of the northern Rockies it did not displace St. Louis as a base, and Ogden was deceived as to the advantage American trappers possessed in the matter of transport. American trappers had but one important advantage over British in the mountains, that derived from their institution of the rendezvous.

Snake country, it is a fact the trappers have not yet made a fall hunt, and only the last two years were Spring hunts made, prior to this the Beaver taken in this Country were trapped in June, July and August and consequently were of a much inferior quality, and it was generally the opinion of all that no other could be procured, but by trapping at the proper Season it is as good as any Beaver procured in the Columbia, of this in my last returns I have given a most convincing proof, altho many American Trappers are scattered over the Snake Country it is still an object worthy of attention the Headwaters or Sources of the South branch of the Columbia and its environs are still rich in Beaver, but a party less than Fifty could not trap with safety, it being in the vicinity of the great War road in fact of all the War tribes; an American party attempted to reach the Crow Village by that route in Fall 1824 but all with the exception of one and he was wounded *were killed*[108] and since that period no attempt has been made, the severe loss the American trappers have sustained within the last three years, has caused them to act more prudently than formerly, no less then 32 Men have been killed with the loss of all their Traps, horses and Beaver, the greater part of this number have been killed by the Snakes who appear determined to destroy and annoy them whenever an opportunity offers, last Spring I was encamped three days with a Camp of fifteen hundred Men, we met and parted as friends, they had no Beaver altho' no Scarcity of American traps amongst them, the great value they lay on their horses prevented my obtaining any, we saw many places where they had taken Beaver, but I am of opinion they prefer the more speedy mode of singeing than skinning....

Governor & Committee to Governor Simpson[109]

London 24 Dec. 1826

We consider the Fur Trade is very much indebted for its prosperous state to your talents for distinct businesslike arrange-

[108] Ogden is probably misinformed concerning this massacre or has confused it with some other. The Crow Indians were normally friendly to the whites.

[109] H. B. Co. Gen. Letter Book No. 621.

ment, and to your indefatigable zeal and perseverance in making yourself master of all the minute details, as well as of the general arrangement of the business, indeed we consider that you have acquired a more perfect knowledge of the Indian Trade than perhaps was ever possessed by any one Individual or even by any body of Men who have been engaged in it, and it affords us great pleasure to find that your merits are duly appreciated by the Northern Council, as appears by their address annexed to the Minutes of Council for 1825.

[Paraphrased] Having placed the business of the Northern Department of Rupert's Land, including the country west of the Rocky Mountains, on a proper footing, you are put in charge of the Southern Department and the Canada Posts, and your salary is raised to £1800. Governor Williams is recalled to England.

GOVERNOR & COMMITTEE TO GOVERNOR SIMPSON[110]

London 12 March 1827

5. It was with the most painful feelings that we read your account of the inundation at Red River, and we fear that the possibility of the recurrence of a similar calamity will deter any number of people from settling there to form a Colony as originally proposed, but if the people who returned there determine to remain, we would wish the same conduct to be pursued towards them that we have heretofore directed.

....[Snake Expedition] We can afford to pay as good a price as the Americans and where there is risk of meeting their parties it is necessary to pay as much or something more to avoid the risk of a result similar to that of Mr Ogden. By attempting to make such expeditions too profitable the whole may be lost and it is extremely desirable to hunt as bare as possible all the Country South of the Columbia and West of the Mountains, but the parties must have positive instructions not to cross to the East of the Mountains South of 49 degrees North latitude. In the event of our trapping party falling in with any Americans in the Country common to both, the leader ought to have instruc-

[110] *Ibid.*

tions to endeavor to make an amicable arrangement as to the parts of the Country which each will take to avoid interference, and to be careful to avoid giving just cause for accusing our people of any aggression against the Americans or violence except in a clear case of self defence.

7. We are sorry to observe that Mr Chief Trader Black had received orders to persevere in removing the Establishment of Walla Walla to the North side of the River, even at the risk of being opposed by force by the Natives. It would have been wiser to incur the expence of two Establishments, keeping the principal one on the North side until by establishing a convenient ferry the Natives become reconciled to it. As there is no immediate prospect of the boundary being settled this matter does not press but it ought to be kept in view and arrangements made to reconcile the Natives to the change if not already accomplished.

22. We cordially approve of your views and arrangements for the management of the Saskatchewan district, a liberal price ought to be given to those Indians who bring Furs from the American territory and the freemen who now hunt in the northern part of the district should be employed as far as possible in the Columbia trapping expedition.

John McLoughlin to Governor Simpson[111]

Ft. Vancouver 20 March 1827

3. I have perused the documents you sent relating to the Boundary line and beg to observe by the Boundary demanded in Governor Pellys letter[112] the Americans will have it in their power to intercept the Flathead trade, as these Indians hunt principally on the head waters of the Missourie and towards Henrys fork, and if we are prevented sending to Indians and sending trappers on the Southside of the Columbia, we shall be deprived of the whole of the Snake trade, nine tenths of the Walla Walla, Willameth and a fourth of that of Spokane, in short will leave

[111] H. B. Co. Journ. No. 812.
[112] See *ante*, 257.

us with only the Kootonais trade, three fourths of that of Spokane and the trade of this place, which in the event of an American opposition being here and the post of Frasers River cutting off our trade from the North will reduce the trade of this place to a mere trifle, and I know no place on the North side of the Columbia between Walla Walla and Cape Disappointment that will pay the expence of keeping up an Establishment when there is a Post in opposition on the South side except a small post in the Chichilese River,[113] which if the Columbia is the Boundary would not be opposed and would prevent the Establishment at Fort George having any Trade with the Country North of the Chichilese and with that about the head Waters of the Cowlitz and Pugets Sound provided we could afford to sell as cheap as our Opponents, and though it is mortifying to be obliged to abandon a business after such pains have been taken and such expences incurred to organize and establish it, yet it is preferable to do so than to carry on a loosing concern, and moreover I am certain the trade of the Columbia under no circumstances will support competition and it is this conviction that made me request (after giving their Honors all the information I possessed relating to the Columbia) their directions in the 45 par. of my letter to them of 6th Octob. 1825, Copy of which letter I forwarded you, and to which I beg to refer you and in case my meaning is not sufficiently and distinctly expressed or that their Honors have not replied to it, I beg to state that I would wish to know if an opposition establish themselves here whether it is wished we should oppose them to the utmost by underselling them or if you would approve of our making an arrangement not to spoil the trade (in doing which we must be guided by circumstances) your directions on the subject if their Honors have not already given theirs will relieve us from a deal of anxiety and enable us to conform to what is wished.

7. You say you think the allowances for extension of Trade and Frasers River in the Scheme I sent out liberal in the Outset, if we are to rely on the information we could collect from the documents we have and from the trip of the William and Ann, the Coasting

[113] Present Chehalis River.

trade is of that nature that we must expect to sell at a low price and to gain more from the quantity we sell than from the price we sell at, and the annual outfit for the coasting trade is only calculated on a Scale under Five hundred pounds prime cost. To secure our Inland trade we must endeavor to destroy competition on the Coast, as these Coasters trade with Indians who in their turn trade with the Natives of the Interior some of these get Skins annually even from the vicinity of the Babine Lake.
10. [A strong hunting party would find employment in the Country about the Trois Tettons for three years.] If such a party was sent they ought to go direct to the Trois Tettons and hunt up that place, then turn North and hunt all the head branches of Missouries[114] in the vicinity of where Mr Ogden was in Summer 1825, in three years they would do this which would destroy the Inducements the American trappers from the other side have to push to the Head waters of the Columbia and by hunting the Head branches of the Missouries where I state diminish the inducements the Americans might have to equip hunting parties from this side of the Mountains and to interfere with our Saskatchewan trade sooner than they otherwise would. I said 80 Men would be required so as to accomplish this object as soon as possible, and without fail; none of the several Snake expeditions either from not being sufficiently strong or from their Men not being in such a state as they ought, have had it in their power to penetrate to the Country I allude and which is the place they intended to go when this business was begun (except Mr Finan McDonald and he was obliged to abandon it after losing several of his Men) this Country lies in the track of all the war-tribes from the Eastside of the Mountains, and this is the reason why the party should be so strong, the number you state of the intended party will be too few to go there. The best place for them if they come to this side of the Mountains is to come to

[114] This is a curious recommendation. The head branches of the Missouri lie in American territory and the right to hunt there was not open to British subjects, as Dr. McLoughlin must have known. Still he was not the man who would ordinarily have suggested unlawful procedure, particularly in the face of the known attitude of the Governor and Committee. Compare this suggestion with the vigorous letter of Governor Simpson of 18 Feb., 1829, at *post*, 307.

where Ross hunted in 1824 about River Malade, River Payette &c where such a party as you state, would stand their ground, find sufficient employments. . . .

12. [On August 18 Mr. A. R. McLeod[115] returned from his trapping excursion along the coast, south of the Columbia. He brought 285 Beaver, 36 land and 3 sea otters; one third of this was procured in trade. He reports beaver very scarce along the coast.]

15. Mr. Ogdens Men are all Freemen and engaged Trappers, the last on the same terms as last year, say their wages £17—all the expences of the hunt charged at Inventory prices to be paid in Beaver at the rate of 4/ p Skin, the half of the remainder to go to the Concern and the Servant to be paid the other half at the rate 4/ per made Beaver.

16. As you have allowed the necessity we were in of reducing the Tariff to Freemen I can only say that urged by the necessity of the Case and in anticipation of your approval I have promised the Freemen 10/ for every large Beaver and half that sum for a Cub and I beg to observe as I said in my letter to the Honble Committee that I consider the measure will be advantageous to the Concern, and if we wished to retain these Men we had no alternative left; the price these Men paid for their supplies formerly was enormously high as you will see by Louis Vallé's account which I forward, his is a sample of the rest, to have put so high a price on the supplies to these Freemen when this expedition was set a going was certainly bad policy as we always have held a precarious tenure of that part of the Country and the Natives will not hunt Beaver, and it is well known all the difficulties, disappointments and losses this Expedition has suffered have been caused by the high price the Trappers paid for their Supplies, which when we consider the personal dangers they were exposed to (last year is the first Season none of their number were killed) the losses they suffered, the inducements held out to them by the Americans, it is more surprising in my opinion that any of them remained than that any run away. It may be

[115] A. R. McLeod was a chief trader in the Columbia Department, attached to Fort Vancouver. See *ante*, 90.

asked but why was not this looked into when Governor Simpson was in the Columbia. To this I beg to observe that the Snake Expedition account was so blended with that of Spokan, that unless a person had been on the Spot, it was impossible to make the two accounts out and it was only in the Spring of 1825 after we had received by the Brigade the necessary documents that we were able to make an approximation to the cost of a made Beaver from the Snakes, and Mr Ogdens returns fall 1825 are the first on which we could ascertain the costs of a made Beaver and by the accompanying account it will be seen it was 10/2/2, but if you look to the freemens a/c you will find their Furs paid in goods at the rate they were charged cost 2/ each made Beaver, valuing the goods at an advance 70 p C, and the difference between this and their actual cost is caused by losses incurred by desertion and by expences in sending clerks and servants to watch over them. It is certainly much better—much more effectual to allow the expences we are obliged to incurr at once to the Hunters, it secures their fidelity equips them more completely and stimulates them to exert themselves, and is only paid after we have value in our hands; by the former mode the cost was in expences laid out before any returns were made.

22. [Capt. Kelly of the Owhyhee, told our people he had passed five winters on the Coast.]

26. Our Potato Crop failed, from two hundred barrels which we planted we only got Six hundred barrels—one hundred and fourteen bushles pease from nine and a half, twelve bushles wheat from two, twenty seven bushles barley from Two, and Six of Oats from one, and one and a half bushel of Indian Corn from the Seed you sent, which was at first very bad and with the Wheat and Oats got greatly injured in bringing here; we will sow all the Wheat and Oats we have, half the Barley and plant all our Indian Corn, and sow all the pease we can if possible we will sow all.

27. Our Cattle thrives well, we lost no Pigs by poison since last year, but the Wolves have destroyed several of them. It is a pity the Pumpkin seed I requested was not sent, potatoes and Turnips in this warm Climate are subject to fail; if we could raise a sufficiency of Pumpkins it would enable us to feed our

Pigs, in house all Winter they would thrive better and none would be devoured by the Wolves.

30. But it is impossible for me to say what number of Men we may require as that depends on how we are situated when the Boundary line is drawn; even if we have the Boundary Govr Pelly suggests in his letter to the R^{t} Honble. George Canning, and are prevented sending to Indians on the South side or sending Trappers to the Snakes—and are opposed here, the best we can do if the Americans cannot pass the Columbia in my opinion is to abandon this place and Walla Walla, establish a post in the Chichilese and Outfit the Interior from Frasers river. If this Plan should be adopted it would be necessary, either the provisions we want were sent us or an arrangement made with the Spanjards at Monterrey to supply us untill we raised what we required.

34. I beg to observe that the advance of 70 p C on the prime cost put on the Goods in this department seems to me too high. The additional requisition for Outfit 1826, and the requisition for Outfit 1827 which you took from this amount to £5874.12.8^{d}, the advance on this at 70 p C is £4812.4.10¼ the requisition for 1828 amounts to £3960.13.11 the advance on this is £2772.9.8¾ the requisition for Outfit 1829 amounts to £4530.13.8 the advance to £3171.9.6¾ that for 1830 to £5400.15.2 the advance to £3780.10.7¼. What may be real costs of bringing Goods here I cannot say but certainly the present rate of advance is too high....

Whatever may be the decision you may depend if we have to compete for the trade the cheapest shop will ultimately carry the day.

41. The rule is with Servants to deduct all the expenditure of ammunition and hunting implements from the Hunt at the rate of 4/ p. made Beaver, the remainder is divided between the Servant and the Company, allowing the servant 4/ for every skin of his half.

William Smith to Messrs James P. Sturgis & Co., Canton[116]

London 12 April 1827

I am directed by the Governor and Committee to acknowledge the receipt of your esteemed communications of the 14th Novbr and 10 Decebr and to acquaint you that the information respecting the state of the Canton Fur market is very interesting, still the price you expect to obtain for the Beaver skins is so low in comparison to that now given in the London market for Skins of a similar description that the Governor and Committee do not consider it advisable to ship any to China this season, they have however forwarded to your address by the Duke of Sussex 5 Puncheons containing Two thousand Eighty five Otter skins of a very superior quality. Enclosed are Bills of Lading and Invoice valued at £3101.16.6d and although you are not limited in price, they trust you will be able to procure not less than 7 Dollars p Skin for this Consignment as you will observe there are 245 of the E. M. mark none of which were in last years shipment; at the time the Russian market was open upwards of Four Pounds Stg p Skin was frequently given for goods of this description which afterwards incurred the expenses of freight to St Petersburg and land carriage &c from thence to Kiachta (which must greatly have added to the cost of them) before they were disposed of in Barter trade....

John McLoughlin to Governor Simpson[117]

Ft. Vancouver 17 April 1827

I am of opinion, if a Post is established [by Americans] on the South side of the Columbia, we can establish no post on the North side in the Nez Percéz or Walla Walla district that will pay the Expence of keeping it up....It is true we could certainly annoy those on the South side much but we never could expect any benefit from it, except that the dread of our establishing a

[116] H. B. Co. Gen. Letter Book No. 621.
[117] H. B. Co. Journ. No. 812.

Post on the North side would induce our opponents to purchase our forbearance—the district accounts of that place [Ft. Nez Percés] will shew how much it ought to be estimated at—but the most advantageous arrangement for us would be if they would agree to carry on the trade of the place jointly with us, each furnishing half the Goods and Men and to divide the returns, as the Furs procured from the Northside bear no comparison for quantity to those got on the South side.

GOVERNOR & COMMITTEE TO GOVERNOR SIMPSON[118]

London 16 Jan. 1828

5. ....The Country on the West of the Mountains remaining common to the Americans and us for an indefinite period, terminable by a years notice from either Government, it becomes an important object to acquire as ample an occupation of the Country and Trade as possible, on the South as well as on the North side of the Columbia River, looking always to the Northern side falling to our Share on a division, and to secure this, it may be as well to have something to give up on the South, when the final arrangement comes to be made.

[118] H. B. Co. Gen. Letter Book No. 621. A new vigor pervades the correspondence of the London Committee and of Governor Simpson with regard to the Columbia Department from this point forward, reflecting the breakdown of the Anglo-American negotiations of 1826-27 for a partition of the Oregon Country. So long as the Hudson's Bay Company was faced with the possibility of British concessions to the United States in the lower Columbia Valley it was naturally hesitant about committing itself deeply there. But with the adoption of the Convention of 1827, which extended indefinitely the old agreement of joint occupation, the Company was assured of a fairly long tenure of the country and could calculate on receiving the benefit of any mastery of the trade it might gain there. The new energy permeates every phase of the business, but particularly that along the coast, where the campaign to drive off American competitors begins now in sober earnest. Dr. McLoughlin was less aggressive in this contest than his superiors. He would have been willing to make arrangements with opponents, at least with the more powerful of them, on the river and in the interior. He wished "not to spoil the trade;" he was eager that the Columbia Department should show gains on the Company's books; he had the short-term outlook. But the Honorable Committee and Governor Simpson viewed the struggle in a larger light, and the policy upon which they insisted, and which prevailed, was one of inexorable competition. See *ante*, 257 ff.

If the American Traders settle near our Establishments, they must be opposed, not by violence, which will only be the means of enabling the Traders to obtain the interference of their Government, but by underselling them, which will damp their sanguine expectations of profit, and diminish the value which they at present put upon that Trade. It will be useful to give the Americans full occupation by active and well regulated opposition on the South of the river to prevent them advancing towards the North, and the general arrangement of this part of the Country and the proper regulation of the Trapping parties call for your best attention and we think merit your devoting a year of your time to it as you have proposed; but we desire that you do not attempt to accomplish too much within a fixed Period of time, so as to involve great fatigue by rapid travelling or risk to your health and life, by your having to perform those journies too early or too late in the Season, when bad weather and bad navigation are to be expected.

30. We are sorry to inform you that the Consignment to Singapore of 1826 did not find purchasers at our limits at that market, altho' there were many Chinese from the Northern provinces there; and the Furs have been forwarded to Canton. We have not yet received any information respecting the small Consignment of 1827 but hope to do so before the sailing of the Ships in June.

We are not sanguine however respecting the China market and apprehend that unless where the trade can be carried on in the way of Barter and the profit be obtained in the sale of China produce, it will not answer to send Furs to China, and that it will be better for the Company to sell their Furs here, to those who can carry on such a Trade with the Chinese.

GOVERNOR & COMMITTEE TO GOVERNOR SIMPSON[119]

London 27 Feb. 1828

32. We think it very important that you should have the means of gaining a firm footing in the Coast trade, and in all the country

[119] H. B. Co. Gen. Letter Book No. 621.

on the West of the Mountains before the Americans arrive there in greater force; as if they are met with a systematic and well regulated opposition on the principle of underselling them, they will be less likely to persevere in their attempts, than if they are allowed at first to make large profits.

35. If you should consider it proper for you to remain another season in the Columbia for the purpose of visiting the Russian settlements and acquiring information of the Coast trade, and of more fully organizing the business generally we leave it in your own discretion to do so.

WILLIAM SMITH TO MESSRS J. P. STURGIS & CO. CANTON[120]

London 15 April 1828

[He makes acknowledgement of information furnished concerning the state of the Canton fur market]. It is not likely that any Beaver will be sent from hence this season, the prices that have been obtained at the Companys public sales being much higher than for some years past. Skins of similar quality to those shipped to China in 1826 & 1827 having produced upwards of 35/ stg per lb.

R. W. HAY TO HON. EDWARD ELLICE[121]

Downing Street 2 May 1828

Mr. Hay presents his compliments to Mr. Ellice and will feel greatly obliged by any observations which Mr. Ellice may have to offer upon the enclosed Memorial of Citizens of the United States, praying for a Grant of Land, and the aid of their Government in forming a Colony on the Northwest Coast of the United States.[122]

[120] *Ibid.*

[121] H. B. Co. Correspondence with Government No. 722. R. W. Hay was British under-secretary for Colonial affairs in 1828. Hon. Edward Ellice was a member of the Honorable Committee and for a time deputy governor of the Hudson's Bay Company. He was one of the guardians of the Company's interests in Parliament, where he long held a seat for Coventry.

[122] For the text of this Memorial, which Hall J. Kelley prepared and Congressman Floyd presented, see *House Docs.*, 20 Cong., 1 sess., no. 139.

Dep^ty^ Govr N. Garry to R. W. Hay[123]

London 7 May 1828

....No American Citizens have had any trading Establishments Westward of the Rocky Mountains since 1814 and very few if any casual wandering parties have crossed the Mountains; but the Hudsons Bay Company have fixed Trading Posts on the Columbia or Oregon River and to the Northward as far as the Russian Boundary Line, and Parties are sent from their principal Establishments on the Columbia, who trade several hundred Miles to the South of that River so as to command the Indian Trade of all that Country. The principal Fort or Establishment used to be at the mouth of the Columbia River on the South side, but by the desire of Mr Canning the Hudson's Bay Company to avoid all risk of collision with Citizens of the United States, whose Government by some ambiguity of the Treaty of Peace claimed this scite as a public Fort removed their principal Establishment to the North side of the River about 80 Miles from the Sea where at very considerable expence a Fort and trading Establishment have been erected, now called Fort Vancouver, being at that part of the River called by that Navigator Point Vancouver and in about 46° North Latitude....

N. P. The other papers refer to territory to the South of 49° North Latitude and East of the Rocky Mountains and within the Boundary line of the United States as settled by the Treaty of Ghent, but no part of that Line West of the Lake of the Woods has yet been agreed upon by mutual observatiõns.

I must remark however on the incorrectness of several statements in these papers respecting the Hudsons Bay Company havg Agents or Traders within the American Lines; the Factors and Traders of the Company have pointed instructions not to intrude on the United States Territory, and from the Report of the Governor of the Companys Territories I have reason to believe these instructions are strictly obeyed, though possibly the native Indians and some of the mixed breed people who live like Indians may hunt on both sides of the Line and traffick with both Parties.

[123] H. B. Co. Correspondence with Government No. 722.

Governor Simpson to Captain Aemelius Simpson[124]

"Cadboro" [No date c. October 1828]

....Now that our Saw Mill is in operation we can supply timber of various kinds in such quantity as to meet all demands either in the Sandwhich Islands, or at the Spanish Missions, and if the prices are so high as they have been represented to us, the Timber Trade as a distinct branch of business would yield us large profits in proportion to the Tonnage employed therein—at the lowest quotations given us say 60 Dollars p^r M feet we can furnish 200,000 feet annually by the shipping employed in our Coasting Fur Trade, & realize handsome profits & even at 40 Dollars p^r M it will be an object worthy our attention, but if 200 Dollars the highest quotation can be had we shall undertake to supply any quantity required for a term of Years provided ample security be given us....

Salted Salmon of such quality as the Cask Shipped we can supply at 4^d St^g p^r lb so as to yield a moderate profit, and for 6^d p^r lb we should undertake to supply 2 to 300 Barrels of 300 lbs each annually....

[N. W. Coast Survey] It is desirable that three or four of these hands, [for the crew of the Cadboro] should be men who have been employed on board different American Fur Trading Ships, and understand the Language of the Natives about the Ports of Nass and Kigarnie[125] and can [furnish] information as to the mode of dealing with those Indians, indeed in the selection of your people we consider American preferable to British Seamen as they are in general more easily managed and being less indulged in regard to Fare and not accustomed to any particular routine of Duty but "Servants of all Work" are more suitable for our purpose. We likewise require two good stout active Sandwhich Islanders who have been to Sea, for 1, 2, or 3 Years as they can be got and on the most reasonable terms you can procure them.

[124] H. B. Co. Journ. No. 950A.

[125] Kigarnie or Kaigani was an Indian village at the tip of Cape Muzon in Dixon Entrance.

GOVERNOR SIMPSON TO WILLIAM SMITH[126]

Ft. Vancouver 17 Nov. 1828

On the 25 Ult. I arrived at this place after having passed through English River, Athabasca, Peace River, New Caledonia and visited the Establishments of Thompsons River and Fort Langley from the last place passing inside Vancouvers Island through Pugets Sound and down the Cowlitz River.[127] The Honble Co^y's^ affairs at the different places I visited, were in a prosperous state, and the Natives on this side the Mountains are I am happy to say more quiet and orderly than heretofore, this favourable change in their conduct towards us, arises more from the fear of punishment should they continue their outrages, than good will or improved disposition as their whole character is marked by crime of the Blackest Dye, and their conduct towards each other as well as towards Strangers hostile and treacherous in the extreme. The appearances of Trade are favorable at all the Establishments and the expeditions under the direction of Mr Ogden and M^r^ McLeod promise well. The American Trappers have been exceedingly unfortunate, as during the past Season, independent of the 15 Men of Mr Smiths Party, cut off by the Natives of the Umpqua, Mr Tullock & his party of (we understand) 12 in all were destroyed by the Snake Tribe within 200 Miles of Walla Walla.[128] M^r^ McLeod has been directed to pass with his party by the place where Mr Smiths People were cut off to recover the stolen property if possible and to punish the Murderers if when he acquires further information on the subject he considers it expedient to do so.

In the Coasting Trade we have as yet done little, as no less than five American Ships were employed therein this Season,

[126] H. B. Co. Journ. No. 950A.

[127] For a journal of this expedition by one of the Governor's travelling companions see McLeod, *Journal of A. McDonald, 1828*.

[128] Samuel Tullock was leader in 1828 of a detachment of trappers in the service of the St. Louis firm of Jedidiah Smith, Jackson and Sublette. The disaster which Governor Simpson inaccurately describes was the destruction by Blackfeet of half his party of six men, with a loss of furs worth $40,000, in addition to forty-four horses, and a quantity of merchandise.

before the duties with which the Cadboro was occupied were completed. Lieut. Simpson however has collected much valuable information which will be conveyed to their Honors in the General Dispatch of next Summer as I do not consider it prudent to enter into particulars at present. From his report we have little doubt of acquiring the Command of the Trade; it may however cost in the first instance a considerable sacrifice of money but the prospect it holds out in point of returns, and the necessity which appears to exist of our being firmly established on a navigable communication between the Coast & the Interior we conceive fully to warrant the expence we propose entering into. Frasers & Thompsons Rivers which never were passed, until this Season by my Canoes, are found exceedingly dangerous even to perfectly light Craft under the most skilful management, & in the most favorable state of the water, & cannot under any circumstances be attempted by loaded Craft; it is therefore necessary for the Salvation of our interior Trade in the event of our being excluded from the Columbia, that we should have a Settlement on the Babine[129] (or Simpsons River) situated in Lat. 54 at the Port of Nass which is the grand mart of the Coast both for Sea Otters and Land Skins. The establishing of this Post will be a Work of great danger, and great expense on account of the number and hostility of the Natives and of their powerful means of offence, indeed it cannot be attempted with a smaller force than One Hundred Officers and Men say 50 for the Establishment and 50 for the two Vessels to protect and act in concert with the Land Party while building. A strong establishment at this point would collect the Land Furs that come down from the Northern parts of New Caledonia which forms the principal returns made by the Americans on this coast, it would likewise enable us to settle the Country to the eastward of the Russian Boundary Line running parallel with the Coast which is now drained by their Establishment at Norfolk Sound, and in co-operation with our Shipping would in the course of 2 or 3 Years compel the Americans to relinquish the contest.

[129] Babine River appears on contemporary maps as the southern tributary of Simpson's River, the present Nass River.

The whole line of Coast, likewise the Islands, Inlets and Rivers, from Cape Disappointment northwards are very numerously peopled, murder and pillage are the principal occupations of the natives, and the further north we go the more formidable we find them. The Americans supply them abundantly with Arms and Ammunition, they frequently attack Shipping and on several occasions have captured Vessels and did at one time even make themselves masters of the Russian Fur Companys principal Establishment[130] altho' equipped and maintained as a regular Garrison. The "Cadboro" is quite unfit for the Trade, there are hundreds of War Canoes on the Coast longer & higher out of the Water than she is, carrying from 40 to 50 men each.

Our crops this season were very abundant and we have now a two years stock of Grain on hand, so that we shall not require either Flour or Grain from England in future, but the Salt Provisions ordered will be required as we do not mean to kill any Cattle until our Stock which now Exceeds 150 Head amounts to 400.

GOVERNOR SIMPSON TO JOHN WORK[131]

Ft. Vancouver 17 Nov. 1828

[Paraphrased] The Flathead Post requires superior management. The freemen who are there must be skilfully dealt with. We are anxious that they should join either Mr. Ogden's or Mr. McLeod's party. If they should agree to do this and should accompany Mr. Ogden's people hither, it would be best for all concerned; if not they should deliver their hunts to you and come down by land with their horses and baggage.... "They need not be apprehensive of harsh treatment from us,[132] we shall deal liberally by them as regards their old debts, sell them our supplies cheap (say on Servants prices) & give them large prices for their Furs, their savings will be paid by £Stg. either in England or Canada as they choose, in short we can afford and are disposed

[130] The Sitka garrison was surprised and massacred by the Kolosh Indians in the summer of 1802. Governor Baranof could not effect a reconquest until the autumn of 1804.

[131] H. B. Co. Journ. No. 950A.

[132] Refers to the desertion of these freemen from the Snake Expedition of 1824-25.

to give them most advantageous terms, so advantageous that any saving industrious man may clear from £60 to £80 Stg per annum. If they have any desire to see me on the subject & that they conceive they would be more secure by treating with me personally than in any other way—I shall be ready to confer with them at Colville on my way out."

Governor Simpson to Jedediah S. Smith[133]

Ft. Vancouver 26 Dec. 1828

As you have had a great deal of communication with Mr McLeod on the subject of your affairs in this quarter in the course of your late Journey to the Umpqua and as that Gentleman is now on the eve of taking his departure hence on a Voyage which may occupy him from 12 to 16 Months I consider it proper that we should come to a final understanding or Settlement on all matters relating to business while he is on the spot and in order to guard against any misapprehension that our communications thereon should be in writing instead of Verbal.

You are aware that previous to your arrival here in the Month of Augt last Mr McLoughlin the Honble Coys principal representative at this place had determined on sending a party under the command of Mr McLeod on a Trapping & Trading Expedition in a Southerly direction from hence & that the equipment of this party was nearly completed when you to our great surprise appeared at this Establisht.

The melancholy report you brought of the destruction of 15 Men out of your party of 19 a few days previous on your way from St Francisco to the Columbia by the Natives of the Umpqua and of the pillage of your property excited in the minds of the Gentlemen here the most lively feelings of Sympathy and commiseration and [moved] by those feelings towards you and your unfortunate companions Mr McLoughlin instructed Mr McLeod to proceed with his party to the Umpqua to communicate with the Natives, to ascertain the cause of their atrocious conduct, to punish them should it have been considered expedient & found practicable and to endeavour to recover your property.

[133] *Ibid.*

He accordingly went thither, his party consisting of 38 Servants and Indians and accompanied by you and your surviving followers. While on the spot he learnt that the Melancholy catastrophe was occasioned by some harsh treatment on the part of your people towards the Indians who visited your Camp some of whom they said had been beaten, and one of them bound hands & feet for some very slight offence, which treatment they further said corroborated in their Minds a report that had preceded you from Indians that your party had been conducting themselves with hostility towards the different Tribes you passed in your way from the Bona Ventura (for which it appears there were some grounds) and that as a measure of Self Preservation they determined on the destruction of your party which its injudicious conduct and unguarded situation enabled those savages to accomplish with little difficulty or danger to themselves.

Mr McLeod under all circumstances found that it would be unsafe and unpolitic to take any hostile steps against the Tribe but endeavoured to recover of the property of which you had been pillaged and with some trouble and difficulty succeeded in getting nearly the whole of it restored.[134] The property he has thus recovered consists of about 700 Beaver Skins, 39 Horses and a few other articles of little value.

When Mr McLeod and his party took their departure Dr McLoughlin did not conceive that any inconvenience or delay would have been occasioned by their visit to the Umpqua he did not therefore intend to have made any charge against you for the Services of Mr McLeod & his party in the recovering of your property but the time occupied in visiting the different Camps on the River & Coast with that object we now find has occasioned the loss to us of the Services of this Expedition for the whole Season thereby subjecting us to an expense of exceeding £1000 independant of the loss of Profits we had reason to calculate on from the services of the Expedition.

Had you been in the condition of discussing terms with us, we should as a matter of course have insisted on your defraying the expences, that the recovery of your property might have

[134] See Appendix B, 359.

occasioned to us, but you was not in that condition consequently nothing was said on the subject, and altho' we are well aware that either in Law or Equity we should be fully entitled to Salvage, we make no claim thereto, on the contrary place the property which we have recovered at your disposal without any charge or demand whatsoever.

In order to suit your own convenience, you left 38 Horses at our Camp on the Umpqua which the Expedition had not the least occasion for as M[r] McLeod having independent of them about 150 being more than sufficient we conceive to meet his demands; these and a few others expected to be received in order to accommodate you we are willing to take off your hands at 40/ St[g] p head, which is a higher price than we ever pay for Horses and the same we charge to our Servants & Trappers, but if you are not satisfied with that price, they are still quite at your disposal.

In conferences you have had with me both to Day and two days ago, you told me that you was desirous of taking your Furs up by Water immediately to our Establishment of Walla Walla, that there you wished us to give you Horses in exchange for those left at the Umpqua and that in the event of our complying with that wish you would leave Horses & Furs at Walla Walla while you proceeded across from thence to your Depot on Salt Lake from whence you would in the course of next Summer send for both.

In reply I now beg to state that we should consider it the height of imprudence in you to attempt going up the Columbia with only your two followers either light or with property. We altho' perfectly acquainted with every Indian on the communication rarely venture to send a party even with Letters, and with property never less than from 30 to 40 Men; such a measure on your part would therefore in our opinion be sporting with Life or courting danger to madness; which I should not consider myself justified in permitting without pointing out to yourself and followers in presence of witnesses the desperate hazards you would thereby run.

I should consider it equally imprudent to attempt a Journey from Walla Walla to Salt Lake on many considerations, the most prominent of which are, the great danger to be apprehended from roving War parties, your total ignorance of the Country, the difficulty you would have in finding your way across the Blue Mountains, the inexperience of your people in Snow Shoe Travelling (one of whom I believe never saw a Snow Shoe) and the danger from Starvation as it is impossible you can carry provisions such a distance and the chase in some parts of the country through which you would have to pass is at this Season even to a hunting party a very precarious means of subsistance. In reference to your demand upon us for Horses at Walla Walla it cannot be met by any possibility as by the last advices from thence we [have] none at that Establishment and our own business in the Upper parts of the Columbia requires at least five times the number we are likely to be able to collect in the course of next Season.

You are well aware that we have already experienced much inconvenience incurred many sacrifices, and exposed the Concern to heavy loss through our anxious desire to relieve, assist and accommodate you we are willing nevertheless to do whatever else we can without subjecting ourselves to further loss or expense in order to meet your wishes, I shall now suggest what I conceive to be the safest course you can pursue and the most eligible plan you can adopt.

Your Beaver which is of very bad quality the worst indeed I ever saw, having in the first instance been very badly dressed & since then exposed to every storm of Rain that has fallen between the Month of April & the 22nd Inst. consequently in the very worst state of Damage, I am willing to take off your hands at 3 Dollars p Skin payable by Bill at 30% sight on Canada, which I conceive to be their full value at this place, and your Horses I will take at £2 St[g] p Head payable in like manner. But if these terms are not satisfactory to you the Furs may be left here until you have an opportunity of removing them & the Horses are at your disposal where you left them.

In either case yourself and followers shall be made welcome to a continuance of our hospitality while you choose to remain at our Establishment—and if agreeable you shall be allowed a passage free of expense to Red River Settlement with me in the course of next Spring & Summer from whence you can proceed to S[t] Louis by Prairie du Chien or you may accompany our Snake Country Expedition next Autumn by which means you will in all probability have a safe escort until you fall in with your people at or in the neighbourhood of Salt Lake.

After you have fully considered these suggestions which are dictated by the best feelings towards you and an intense anxiety for the safety of yourself, followers & property I have to request the favor of a reply thereon in Writing previous to M[r] McLeod's departure.

Governor Simpson to Jedediah S. Smith[135]

Ft. Vancouver 29 Dec. 1828

In reference to your valued communication of 26th Ins[t] and to our subsequent conferences I beg it to be distinctly understood that we do not lay claim to, nor can we receive any remuneration for the services we have rendered you, any indemnification for the losses we have sustained in assisting you, nor any Salvage for the property we have recovered for you, as whatsoever we have done for you was induced by feelings of benevolence and humanity alone, to which your distressed situation after your late providential escape & the lamentable & melancholy fate of your unfortunate companions gave you every title at our hands. And I beg to assure you that the satisfaction we derive from these good offices, will repay the Hon[ble] Hudsons Bay Comp[y] amply for any loss or inconvenience sustained in rendering them.

I am exceedingly happy that you have consented to abandon the very hazardous Journey you contemplated and that you have allowed yourself to be influenced by my advice to pursue the safer yet more circuitous route by Red River, which notwithstanding the increased distance, will in point of time be the shortest, as thereby you will, barring accidents, be at S[t] Louis in the month of July next.

With regard to your property, we are willing in order to relieve

[135] H. B. Co. Journ. No. 950A.

you from all further concern respecting it, to take it off your hands, at what we consider to be its utmost value here, say Horses at 40/ each which you know to be a higher price than we ever pay for any, and Beaver at 3 $ p Skin Land Otters at 2 $ p^r^ Skin and Sea Otters at 10 $ p^r^ Skin which from their damaged state I conceive to be their utmost value here, fully as much as they will net to us in England, and after making a fair deduction for risk and expence of transport hence to St Louis, more than they would yield you if taken to and sold in the States.[136]

But if these prices be not satisfactory to you, and that you prefer leaving your property here until a favourable opportunity should present itself for removing it, we shall with pleasure retain it for you, and deliver it when and to whom you may direct.

GOVERNOR SIMPSON TO MAJOR PILCHER, Flathead Lake[137]

Ft. Vancouver 18 Feb. 1829

I am favored with your communication of 30th December and hasten to reply thereto lest delay might interfere with your plans or operations.

I am aware that the Country watered by the sources of the Missouri, usually known by the name of the "Black feet Country" is a rich preserve of Beaver, and that a well organized Trading and Trapping Party would in all probability make valuable returns therein (altho' perhaps the most dangerous Service connected with the Indian Trade) would therefore readily entertain your proposition with the attention which its importance merits as regards capital, if a difficulty of a formidable character did not present itself, which is the Territorial rights of the United States Government to that Country. These rights, we as British Subjects cannot infringe openly, and although the protecting Laws of your Government might be successfully evaded by the plan you suggest still I do not think it would be

[136] **Jedediah Smith accepted this offer and received from Simpson a draft for £550. 2. 6 payable to Messrs. Smith, Jackson & Sublette.**

[137] ***Ibid.* Joshua Pilcher was a representative of the old Missouri Fur Company and a considerable figure in the fur trade.**

reputable in the Honble Hudsons Bay Co^y to make use of indirect means to acquire possession of a Trade to which it has no just claim. Under those circumstances I cannot fall in with your views and as regards Mr Ogden he cannot without acting in direct opposition to his instructions cross the height of Land.[138]

GOVERNOR SIMPSON TO JOHN MCLOUGHLIN[139]

Ft. Vancouver 15 March 1829

....Your whole administration is marked by its close adherence to the spirit of the Govr & Committees wishes and intentions, and is conspicuous for a talent in planning and for an activity & perseverance in execution which reflect the highest credit on your judgement and habits of business, I do no more than my duty to you to the concern at large and to myself.

The opposition with which we are at present assailed all along the South side of the Columbia and at its entrance, renders our utmost exertions necessary for the protection of our own interests, and to prevent our rivals in trade from profiting by their encroachments. It is highly satisfactory to find that hitherto these important objects have been attained and if we do not relax there is little doubt that we shall soon be left Masters of the Field, as those people we know to be needy adventure[r]s existing on a bad credit who cannot afford to follow up a losing business. Let us therefore lay ourselves out for active, well regulated & animated Opposition, and while we meet them fairly and openly as competitors in Trade, let us studiously avoid any violent or discreditable proceeding which might tarnish the reputation of the Honble Co^y and of ourselves, in the estimation of the public, and from which no permanent benefit would be derived.

[Paraphrased] Mr. Dears at Flathead Post is to sell to Indians

[138] Governor Simpson no doubt relished the opportunity to read this Missourian a lesson in business ethics, for the bitterest critics of the Hudson's Bay Company in the American government were the Missouri senators, Benton and Lynn. Pilcher's offer may also have seemed to him a trap. See in this connection, H. M. Chittenden, *History of the American Fur Trade of the Far West* (N. Y., 1902), I, 154 ff.

[139] H. B. Co. Journ. No. 950A.

at the American tariff; also to have on hand a larger stock of luxuries than usual to meet the demands of the American trappers, with such little necessaries as they are likely to be deficient in; in that way a considerable part of their hunts can likewise be secured....

[Paraphrased] P. S. Ogden's impaired health makes necessary appointing Mr. Work to the command of the Snake Expedition. The Expedition should be increased to from 40 to 45 trappers if the Freemen expected from the Flat Heads can be induced to join—otherwise kept at 30....

[Paraphrased] Mr. Work should endeavor to draw off any of the late deserters found attached to American camps—also if any respectable American trappers wish to join the Expedition there can be no objection if they deposit skins to cover the supplies they receive....

[Paraphrased] Next spring a post will be established at the mouth of Simpson's River falling into the harbour of Nass, the grand mart of the coast for land skins. This post must be strong as the natives are formidable. P. S. Ogden is to be in charge. He is to adopt the American tariff or an even lower one so as to make an immediate impression.

[Paraphrased] The "Cadboro" or "William & Ann," whichever arrives in the Columbia first is to be sent at once for the returns of Frazers River, touching, within the Gulf of Georgia, wherever skins are likely to be, so as to anticipate the Owhyhee, Capt. Dominies,[140] now lying at the mouth of the Columbia.

"The timber trade promises to become a valuable branch of business combined with the Fur Trade of the Coast as the latter cannot afford employment all the Year round, and as the officers and Crews of two Vessels on the Northern are sufficient to navigate Four or even Five Vessels"

[Dr. McLoughlin is directed to build two vessels of 200 tons each for this purpose.]

The Saw Mill will require Eight Men and should be kept constantly at Work, as I expect that fully as much advantage

[140] Captain Dominis was a trader in the service of the Boston merchant, Josiah Marshall. He was for years a thorn in the flesh of the Hudson's Bay Company.

will be derived from the Timber as from the Coasting Fur Trade and if you find that in its present situation it cannot produce the quantity required, it will be well to remove it to the Falls of the Willhamet where the same Establishment of people can attend to the Mill, watch the Fur & Salmon Trade, and take care of a Stock of Cattle, indeed the sooner you remove it to the Wilhamet I think the better.

The Farming operations at this Establishment are of vital importance to the whole of the business of this side the Continent, and the rapid progress you have already made in that object far surpasses the most sanguine expectations which could have been formed respecting it. That branch of our business however cannot be considered as brought to the extent required, until our Fields yield 8000 Bushels of Grain p Annum, our Stock of Cattle amounts to 600 head and our Piggery enables us to cure 10,000 lb of Pork p^{r} Annum. I am aware that some little dissatisfaction has been occasioned by your refusing to Slaughter Cattle for the Shipping from England, but when both you and I can say that so anxious have we been to increase our Stock, that neither of us have ever indulged ourselves by tasting either Beef or Veal, the produce of Vancouver Farm, they have no cause to complain and particularly so when they get as much fresh Fish, Pork & Game as they can consume, with the run of our Gardens & Fields in Fruits and Vegetables. Let me therefore beg that you follow up our determination on that head, whatever the consequences may be, and if any of the English Seamen put their threat in execution of killing Cattle in defiance of your authority, do me the favor to send the offender across the Mountains to be dealt with as may be considered advisable....

[The complement of the Columbia Department will be: Vancouver 32, Langley 12, Nass 46, Walla Walla 5, Thompson's R. & Okanagan 10, Colvile, Flat Heads & Coutonais 18, Snake Expedition 30, Buena Ventura Expedition 32, vessels 39,— total of officers and men 224.]

Governor Simpson to the Governor of the Russian American Company Archangel[141]

Ft. Vancouver 21 March 1829

[Lieutenant Simpson is proceeding Northward to survey the harbour of Nass, with a view to erecting an Establishment there for trade next year.]

3. Our attention on this side the Continent has been hitherto directed to the business of the Interior Country, but we have it now in view to extend it to the Trade of the Coast, and to connect therewith the discovery and Settlement of the interior Country up to our most Northern limits. This will place us so near each other as to afford frequent and facile opportunities of communication, and will I trust enable us to cultivate to Friendship, an acquaintance which we have long been desirous of forming, our wish being to establish with you an intercourse which may have for its end, the promotion of each others interests, while we are exceedingly anxious that our proximity should not give rise to any feelings of Rivalship or Competition in Trade which could not fail of being highly injurious to the interests of both parties.

4. The Service of the Coast we know to be one of great danger from the daring and formidable character of its numerous savage population, but a strict adherence to the terms of the convention of 28th Feby 1825 between our respective Governments with regard to the Sale of Arms, Ammunition & Spiritous Liquors, together with our own means of defence and means which may grow out of a good understanding between both Concerns are I think likely to render our respective dealings with the Natives less hazardous than they have heretofore been, and consequently enable the Russian Fur Compy & Hudsons Bay Compy to conduct their business on a less expensive Scale than could with safety be done if such measures were disregarded.

5. Our Imports from & exports to England employ one Ship annually and occasionally two Ships, and our supplies are laid in on the most favourable terms directly from the Manufacturers. We learn that you have not any regular or direct communication

[141] *Ibid.*

with England, it may therefore be convenient or desirable for you to have a regular supply of British Manufactures through us which we should be willing to furnish annually to the extent of 50 or 100 Tons or even more if necessary on a Moderate advance on Prime Cost to cover charges and yield us a reasonable profit and in payment we should be willing to take Furs at a saving price, or your Bills on St Petersburgh or London, or Specie as you may find convenient, and as may be agreed on.

6. We can likewise undertake to furnish you annually with from 4 to 5000 Bushels of Grain of various descriptions and 8 to 10,000 lbs of Salted Pork & Beef, for a term of years, at moderate prices, if you require such supplies.

8. [Any arrangement entered into with Dr. McLoughlin or Lieutenant Simpson will be confirmed and fulfilled.]

WILLIAM SMITH TO J. P. STURGIS & CO. Canton[142]

London 16 May 1829

[Acknowledgement of information relating to the state of the Canton fur market.] "Very good prices have been obtained this season [in London] for the Company's importation of 1828, about 11 $\frac{1}{m}$ otter skins having met with a ready sale at prices varying from 7/ to 26/ Stg p skin and about 60 $\frac{1}{m}$ Beaver Skins at from 23/ to 43/ p. lb. w^{t}.

CAPTAIN SIMPSON TO A. GORMAN, British Consul at Mexico[143]

"Cadboro" 16 Sept. 1829.

[Request to the Consul to forward an enclosed letter.]

It conveys the result of a proposal made by the Company to form a commercial connexion with the Russian Fur Company: and if entered into will I hope aid very much in depriving the Americans of their present monopoly of the Coasting fur trade, which they retain by a system of Trade quite opposed to the terms of the Treaty existing between our respective Governments

[142] H. B. Co. Gen. Letter Book No. 622.

[143] H. B. Co. Journ. No. 955.

in the sale of arms, ammunition and spiritous liquors, and these being the articles held in the greatest estimation by the savage population of this Coast, they will always have a superiority over the Trader who abstains from the Sale of these articles, and will be the means of keeping the natives of this Coast in their present demoralized and barbarous state.

CAPTAIN SIMPSON TO GOVERNOR & COMMITTEE[144]

"Cadboro" New Archangel 16 Sept. 1829.

....He [Captain Chistiakoff] rigidly complys with the terms of the Treaty existing between our respective Governments, in not furnishing the Indians with Arms, Ammunition or Spirits, tho' at a great sacrifice to his concern. An infringement of which in our dealings with the Indians (more especially on the Russian Frontiers) may I fear involve the Honb[le] Company in some unpleasant discussion, and to oppose the American Traders without a sale of these articles will be a fruitless contest. If therefore arrangements could be speedily entered into with our respective Governments and a connection formed with this Company, it would more speedily suppress opposition and overthrow the present bad system than a direct trade which must be carried on at a great sacrifice. I merely take the liberty of offering these hints to Your Honors, not with a view to damp any operation you may deem necessary in carrying on the business on the Coast. I have learned here that the Coasters have done little or nothing in the way of trade this Year, some of these Vessels called here. One the Volunteer was oblidged to come for medical assistance for her Chief mate, who in a scuffle—or rather an attempt by the Tribe of Kigarnie Indians (those visited by me last year) to take the Vessel was dangerously wounded. The Russian Government appear to take a lively interest, and give great encouragement to the Company in carrying on their business on this Coast, and have appointed Officers of rank in their Naval Service to the principal Situation. Capt. Chistiakoff is a Port captain in the Russian Navy, and their Vessels are commanded by Lieutenants

[144] *Ibid.*

and officered by Gentlemen of that profession, and martial law is established on board of them; at present there is a very fine Ship in this Port direct from Cronstadt with supplies for this Establishment and brings home their Furs, and will sail in a short time thence.

This Establishment is upon a very respectable footing more resembling a military Post, than that of a civil body—this they find necessary; the tribes of Indians in this Vicinity being formidable and well stored with arms which they procure from the American traders, of which the Governor complains very much, and has made representations to his Government as the Treaty directs.

Captain Simpson to John McLoughlin[145]

"Cadboro" 1 Oct. 1829

....Nothing particular transpired on our voyage to New Archangel, in which Port we arrived on the 10th Septbr when I waited upon the Governor, Capt. Chistiakoff of the Russian Navy, and delivered to him Govr Simpsons letter which he received in the most polite manner.

On the following day I had the honor of a confidential Interview with the Governor, who expressed himself pleased with the overtures from Governor Simpson, but stated his want of authority to enter into any definitive arrangement with the Honble Compy which I represented, untill he had first consulted the Russian Fur Compy for whom he was acting, and suggested that the most expeditious and direct method to accomplish the ends proposed would be by our respective Companys in London & St Petersburg; that he would forward by the earliest opportunity a Copy of Gov. Simpsons letter to the Russian Fur Compy and would in his communication which will accompany it, recommend their forming the connection desired[146] in preference to their

[145] *Ibid.*

[146] This overture by Governor Simpson met with the refusal of the Russian American Company to enter into a barter trade, "and as we do not consider it expedient to deal with them on any other terms, we do not suppose that there will

carrying on a Trade with American Adventurers who have infringed the Treaty existing between their respective Governments in their mode of Traffic with the Indians much to the prejudice of his employers, of which he had already complained to the Russian Government who had in consequence made remonstrances upon the subject to the Government of the United States, who either did not appear inclined to restrain these Adventurers, or had not the power to do so, as no Guarantee could bind such Adventurers as were in the habit of visiting the N. W. Coast,[147] whereas with such a respectable body as the Honble Hudson's Bay Company he anticipated cooperation in such measures as would improve the present system of Trade and state of the Indians generally with the view of rendering our respective situations more secure against Indian hostility. With respect to Goods, he said they were amply stored for at least three years as their Store ship then anchored in the Port had but a short time previous arrived from Cronstadt with large supplies, independent of large purchases from American Traders: Wheat, other Grain and Provisions are articles they would readily purchase from the Company if they could supply it in any quantity and at a moderate price, as they find their supplies from California very precarious, so much so that he intended to send a Vessel to Chile for Grain this year; on concluding this Interview

be an opportunity of doing anything of importance with their Trading settlements at present." Governor & Committee to Governor Simpson, 23 Feb., 1831.

Some years after this interchange, after a period of controversy with the Russian American Company, Governor Simpson and the London office resumed the negotiations for a commercial agreement and in 1839 obtained a lease from the Russian American Company for ten years of the strip of coast from 54°40′ to Cape Spencer. The Hudson's Bay Company was to pay for this an annual rental of 2000 seasoned otter skins, and to sell at a stipulated price to the Russian American Company further furs and a quantity of provisions. This contract was renewed with modifications when its term expired, and the Hudson's Bay Company remained in control of the coastal strip until Alaska passed into the possession of the United States.

[147] The Russian government in 1834, under the fourth article of the convention of 1824, withdrew the privilege of free navigation of the waters of the Alaska coast from American traders on the ground of their continued sale of arms and spirits to the natives. The American minister at St. Petersburgh protested but without avail.

he expressed his intention of making a reply to Govr Simpson's letter, in which he would state his Sentiments on the points proposed at his earliest convenience. On the 15th the Governor handed me a letter to your address in reply to Govr Simpsons which I beg leave to hand you. Having learnt that one of the Russian Fur Companys Vessels was soon to sail for Monterrey, I thought it offered a favorable opportunity to forward a duplicate of the Governors reply to the Honble Comp^{y} in London under cover to the British Consul at Mexico, a copy of my letter to that Gentleman, also of that addressed to their Honors in London, I also beg leave to hand you.

On my arrival the Governor expressed his confidence that I would not infringe the Treaty by opening any trade with the Indians while in their Port, which I pledged my honor not to do and requested that he would direct their interpreter to acquaint the Indians that I did not wish them to be coming alongside the Vessel as I had no intention of trading with them but notwithstanding the measure, several Chiefs visited us, and offered to trade about forty Sea Otter Skins at different times. On my acquainting the Governor with the circumstance he remarked that American Vessels visiting the Port had occasionally carried on a Smuggling trade, which led the Indians into an Idea, that I would do so also. I feel much pleasure in acknowledging, that I received the most polite attention from Governor Chistiakoff and the other Gentlemen at the Establishment, they shewed a disposition to be communicative; the want of a knowledge of their language and theirs of the English rendered it difficult to acquire information; I may here remark that this Port and their business generally appears to be under excellent management, and to judge from the extent and manner in which it is carried on, you would infer it yields great profits, as it bears more the appearance of a military establishment than that of a private body. The number of shipping attached to it (about twelve) shews, they must carry on a considerable business, and must have a number of establishments, as these Vessels are principally occupied in bringing supplies to, and the Furs from their several Trading posts, and in protecting their hunting parties who procure their principal Supply of Furs, as they do not appear to collect many in their trade with the Indians, especially of Sitka, owing to the American Vessels being in the habit of trading in their close vicinity. It appears singular that the Russians have hitherto given such encouragement to these American Adventurers, as by making large purchases from them of Goods, and giving them Furs in exchange, they furnished them with the means of carrying on an opposition against themselves, they now appear to view it in that light, as the Governor informed me, they did not intend for the future, to make any purchases from them, nor furnish them with the Fur Seal as before, as they find they can dispose of them to much greater advantage in Russia, where he says they bring $4 each and they were in the habit of giving them to the Americans for $1.75 Cents.

I found in the Port of New Archangel an American Schooner from the Coast of California, she was undergoing a repair by the Russian Ship Carpenters, of whom they appeared to have about Twenty, the greatest part of them appeared to be Natives, the offspring of Indian Women & Russian Servants of the Comp^y and bear the Character of being good workmen, and had when I was there a Ship of 280 Tons nearly ready for launching of their building.

Governor & Committee to John McLoughlin[148]

London 28 Oct. 1829

16. We have duly considered Governor Simpsons remarks on the advance to be laid on the Columbia shipments and have determined to reduce the same to 33⅓ p. c. on Invoice cost, by which means all goods exported from hence will be delivered at the three Depots of York, Moose, and Vancouver at the same cost, which will simplify the accounts, and do away with the nominal losses which arise on Sales. And in like manner will be charged any supplies or stores which may be transferred to the Establishments by the annual ship from England. This advance will not probably cover the charges, but whether it does or not,

[148] H. B. Co. Gen. Letter Book No. 622.

is a matter of little real importance as the expenses actually incurred, be they more or less are of course charged to the Fur trade.

18. [Dr. McLoughlin is commended for the attention he has given to the trapping expeditions and for the improved footing on which they are placed.] We are desirous that those Parties should be kept in constant and active employment, should they even do no more than clear expences, as the impoverishment of the Country situated to the Southward of the Columbia, we consider the most effectual protection against opposition from the Americans.

19. We are much gratified to learn that every hospitable attention and assistance were afforded to Mr. Smith the American and his Companions in distress after the horrible massacre of his party by the natives of the Umpqua, and from the humane feeling you have already manifested it is scarcely necessary to desire, that you will on all occasions render any protection in your power to Americans, Russians, or any other strangers who may be in the Country against the treachery or violence of the natives whatever may be the objects of the visits of such strangers, be they competitors in trade or otherwise, as all feeling of self interest must be laid aside when we can relieve or assist our fellow creatures.

20. [When it is necessary to punish Indians for murders or other crimes it should be done as mercifully as possible. Clemency and forbearance should be exercised wherever possible. But when punishment is undertaken there must be no chance of defeat, as that would endanger all establishments.]

21. [We approve of the increased price for Beaver in the interior of the Columbia as leading to greater exertion on the part of Indians and diminishing the chance of their changing sides when opposition appears. At Fort Langley the tariff should also be moderate to induce natives of the Gulf of Georgia and Puget Sound to bring in furs instead of holding them for opposition.]

22. [Dr. McLoughlin is commended for success in agricultural pursuits] ''indeed your whole management is marked by a degree of energy, zeal and activity highly creditable to yourself, impor-

tant to the interests of the service and meeting our warmest commendation."

RICHARD CHARLTON TO JOHN MCLOUGHLIN[149]

British Consulate, Woahoo 7 Nov. 1829

There has never been so large a quantity of Boards brought to these Islands at any time as at the present, there being two large American merchant vessels, besides three or four whalers with a large quantity on board: as those vessels must sell for the purpose of realizing their funds, I have determined not to sacrifice the boards p. Ganymede, but to hold them at least until the Spring.

The Cargo p. Cadboro is sold with the exception of a few of the short boards....

I have sold a few thousand feet of the boards p. Ganymede at one hundred dollars p. thousand.

A. MCDONALD TO JOHN MCLOUGHLIN[150]

Ft. Vancouver 14 Nov. 1829

"The vast deal of duty now to be attended to in this neighborhood [Ft. Vancouver] owing to the opposition" [induces him to agree to the suggestion of reducing Ft. Langley to a clerk, 12 men and two apprentices. That necessitates confining attention at Ft. Langley to the fort; speculations in salmon and timber, and extension of the trade must be given up. He proposes reducing his tariff to the standard of the Americans *before* they visit the Gulf next season.]

GOV. J. H. PELLY TO SIR GEORGE MURRAY[151]

London 4 Dec. 1829

Mr. Pelly presents his compliments to Sir George Murray, and sends him herewith that part of Mr. Simpsons Dispatch which

[149] H. B. Co. Journ. No. 955. Richard Charlton was the British consul at Honolulu (Woahoo Island), employed by the Hudson's Bay Company during the first years of its trade there as its agent. With the growth of the Company's activities in the Islands a full-time agent became necessary and George Pelly was appointed to the charge in 1833.

[150] *Ibid.* Archibald McDonald was the chief trader in charge of Fort Langley.

[151] H. B. Co. Correspondence with Government No. 722. Sir George Murray was secretary of state for the Colonies in the Duke of Wellington's cabinet.

refers to the Country west of the Rocky Mountains in Ruperts Land for his private perusal, and with it he begs to call Sir George Murray's attention to the proceedings in the last Congress of the United States; a printed Copy of the part to which Mr. P. alludes he has likewise enclosed, and respectfully submits, whether, as it is therein proposed amicably to establish a Line of Demarcation,[152] the subject might not now be discussed. Mr. Simpson is now in England and will remain a few weeks, and Mr. P. or Mr. S. will have much pleasure in waiting on Sir George Murray, and giving him every further information in their power that he may require.

A. McDonald to John McLoughlin[153]

Ft. Langley 25 Feb. 1830

[Refers to Americans being all over within the Sound.]

"With such means we could not of course think of underselling the Rival, nor indeed would it even have been good policy in us, when we had not the wherewith to satisfy them, to invite here Indians that received a blanket at home for a Beaver skin, while with ourselves the same article still fetched from two to three."

William Smith to William B. Astor[154]

London 3 March 1830

I am directed by the Governor and Committee of the Hudson's Bay Company to acknowledge receipt of your letter dated 15th Decbr last addressed to James Keith Esqr a Chief Factor in the Companys Service, stating that you had been informed the Company were desirous of stopping the introduction of spirituous Liquors among the Indians on the line of demarcation between Great Britain and the United States and proposing to pledge yourself that the People of the American Fur Company shall not

[152] Refers to the Senate "Report on the Fur Trade" presented in 1829 by Senator Benton. See *Sen. Docs.*, 20 Cong., 2 sess., no. 67.

[153] H. B. Co. Journ. No. 955.

[154] H. B. Co. Gen. Letter Book No. 922. William B. Astor was president of the American Fur Company. His father, John Jacob, took the more active part in the business.

in future carry in, or in any way give ardent Spirits to the Indians of that Region or vicinity, provided the Hudsons Bay Company pledge themselves to the same effect, and that the United States Indian Agent at Sault S[t] Marie has promised, that if the two Companies agree on the subject, he will not permit any Individual trader to take any Liquor into the Country. And I have to inform you that the Governor and Committee are most anxious to see such a measure carried into effect, having already accomplished this most desirable object in a large portion of the Interior with the most beneficial results to the Indians and to the Trade. The Governor and Committee have this Season confirmed and repeated the Orders given last year by Gov[r] Simpson, that in the event of the American Traders discontinuing the practice, those in the Service of the Company should do the same. But the Governor and Committee do not feel justified in leaving their trading Posts on the Frontier totally deprived of Spirits, at the same time I am directed to assure you, that the Governor and Committee have the means of strictly enforcing the instructions given to their Traders; the discontinuance of the Practise will therefore entirely depend on the conduct of the American traders, to which I am to call your attention.

Governor & Committee to Governor Simpson[155]

London 5 March 1830

[Paraphrased]

15. The great exertions made to gain a share of the Northwest coasting trade have been attended with success, though the outlay of money in the face of powerful opposition has been large. Other branches of trade such as timber and salmon, together with the returns of the furs have defrayed all expenses, so that what has usually been regarded as the regular trade of the Columbia Department has not been affected. The latter has been favorable considering the annoyances which trapping and trading parties of the United States who wander over the interior

[155] H. B. Co. Gen. Letter Book No. 1823.

in such numbers occasion. The unhealthy state of Fort Vancouver, and its distance from the sea, renders it by no means well adapted for the main depot of the West Side the Mountains, now that the trade is extended to the coast; therefore it is thought the depot should be situated in Pugets Sound, where there are good harbors, fine timber, and opportunities for agriculture.

16. A clergyman is to be sent out by the Company as a missionary for the West Side the Mountains at a salary of £100 per annum. He is to be stationed where we may hereafter determine, "and we desire that measures may be concerted to carry this object into effect with the least possible delay, as we consider it a duty both owing to ourselves and the natives, in a serious point of view, and a highly expedient measure under existing circumstances in a Political light."

17. Chief Factor McLoughlin's important services are appreciated, and satisfaction is felt "that he is succeeded in that important charge by an officer of so much zeal and ability as we have reason to expect Chief Factor Finlayson will prove himself to be."[156]

John McLoughlin to Governor Simpson[157]

Ft. Vancouver 20 March 1830

4. The Convoy, Captn Thompson passed the Fort on the 4th Ap^{l} & proceeded to the foot of the Cascades. On the 13th of the same she repassed on the way down & remained between the Cowletz & falls of the Willamitti from that time until September, when she proceeded to Fort George & in Octr sailed as is said for Owhyhee to procure a supply of Indian Guns & re-entered the river on the 24th February.[158] Captn Dominis in the Owhyhee

[156] Dr. McLoughlin did not cross the Mountains in 1829 as he seems to have intended; in fact he continued at Fort Vancouver until his retirement from the service in 1845.

[157] H. B. Co. Journ. No. 955.

[158] Captain Thompson was associated with Captain Dominis in the service of the Boston merchant, Josiah Marshall. On March 26, 1829, he wrote his employer: "They [the H. B. Co.] are determined to drive us from the River. I have at present

sailed from Cape Disappointment on the 14th April proceeded to De Fucas Streights thence to Kegarnie Point, Nunez, & re-entered the Columbia the 1st Octr & after leaving a small party at Fort George alongside of Mr Manson,[159] brought his Vessel to Cassino's Camp, where he has remained ever since & sent a party to the Dalles which obliged us to keep a party of a Clerk & Eight Men to oppose them, in short ever since your departure we have never had less than 20 Men, one Clerk, the Interpreter & a runner constantly on the go & since Octr we have had 32 Men 2 Clerks, the Interpreter & One Runner employed in that way & a few days after your departure the Tariff fell to One Beaver p Blanket.

Captain Dominis having expressed to Mr. Manson that he wished to sell out, I took the opportunity when he was here to ask him what terms he would sell; he replied at the rate of Four Dollars p Blanket & to be paid in Beaver at the rate of 4½ Dollars pr Large Beaver. This I told him could not be thought of, but that we would purchase the goods he had suitable to the Columbia trade at prime Cost to be paid in Boards at Ten Dollars Pr M feet; he said he could not accept my offer as he must proceed direct from this to Canton. Since then he has paid me another visit, & talking on the subject he says he could not carry in his Vessel payment for his Goods, but would take payment in Bills, & Guarantee us from opposition for two Years from his employers, but that I made him no proposal. To which I replied the quantity of Goods we expected was so great, he also had so much (his Invoice leaving Boston was 25 M Dollars) & he had asked so high an advance that it was impossible for us to think of such a proposal. I am aware I am not authorized to buy up an opposition & that buying up induces others to follow. But in the Columbia we are peculiarly situated & I conceive we

made a stand at the mouth of the River Cowletz about 50 miles up the Columbia, which I consider the best place for the present, but shall make proper examinations farther up the River soon. On our arrival here the English were getting six large beavers for one Blanket and twenty for a musket, but opposition has reduced it to 1/4 of the former price." Harvard College Library, Josiah Marshall MSS., 121.

[159] Fort George was maintained by the Hudson's Bay Company as a minor outlook station after the removal of the Company's headquarters to Fort Vancouver. Donald Manson was the clerk in charge there.

ought not to incur Expences (if possible) to break down an opposition in the hope of securing a Trade of which we may be deprived by treaty & situated as we are Our Stores nearly empty, dependent for a supply on the arrival of the Vessel to which if an accident happened, our Trade on this side of the Mountains would be ruined. I would for these reasons have purchased his Goods for the Columbia Trade & paid them in Boards, if he had agreed to my terms as it would have put a stop to the further disorganization of the Indians, would have enabled me to recall our trading parties & employ them to advantage in erecting our intended Saw Mill & at other work about the place.

8. Our Returns at this place as you must be aware cost much higher than usual though if deals sell as well as what Captain Simpson sold, the quantity we have sent to market say...M feet will pay for the encreased expenditure of goods, but the timber cannot appear to our credit till the proceeds are received in London, & though our returns are less than last year which is certainly in part owing to the opposition, still it must be observed that for the first time since the trade with these Indians was established we have not one single freeman attached to the place & last year we got Five Hundred Skins from Mr Smith & it is certain the Indians (from the reduced Tariff) have exerted themselves more to procure furs.

Our Farm yielded about

1500	Bushels	Wheat
396	"	White Pease
191	"	Grey do
200	"	Barley
250	"	Indian Corn
20	Tierces of Pork	

9. It is impossible to say what we will do this Year as we must regulate our proceedings by those of the Opposition, but you may depend our first attention will be directed to the Collecting of furs & then if we can spare a party, we will set about building a Saw Mill in the Willamitte on the spot you & I fixed on & every exertion will be made on my part to accomplish the plans settled

on & as soon as the Vessel arrives from England we will enter on the Coasting trade as extensively as our means will admit, for this purpose we have sheathed the Vancouver & it is intended that one of the Schooners accompany Captn Simpson.

JOHN MCLOUGHLIN TO JAMES BIRNIE[160]

Ft. Vancouver 28 May 1830

I am told Bach (who seems to have set up opposition at the Dalles) has a good deal of property. If he comes under arrangements to us he must not trade his property with the natives as that would be interfering with the Trade. But we would take it off his hands at a fair valuation, and allow him trade it at the old Tariff, allow him ¼ of the skins he trades at freemens prices to pay him for the trouble of trading them.

JOHN MCLOUGHLIN TO SAMUEL BLACK[161]

Ft. Vancouver 29 June 1830

One of our vessels from England, the Isabella, was wrecked on the same place the W & A was last year. A great part of the cargo is saved.[162]

JOHN MCLOUGHLIN TO SAMUEL BLACK[163]

Ft. Vancouver 29 June 1830

We were last year and this assailed by opposition which by reducing the price of goods 1/5 of what they previously were has greatly injured the trade of this quarter, but by your firmly keeping up the price at W[alla] W[alla] as settled upon, in spite of all the means employed by the natives to make you lower them, you prevented the trade of the interior being spoilt.

[160] H. B. Co. Journ. No. 1039.

[161] *Ibid.* Samuel Black was the chief trader in charge of Fort Nez Percés or Walla Walla.

[162] These two supply vessels were wrecked at the entrance to the Columbia River opposite Clatsop Point. The danger to navigation here was one of the reasons for moving the headquarters of the Columbia Department to Vancouver Island in 1844, and it was the reason also for American insistence on obtaining in the Oregon negotiations a share in the harbors of Puget Sound.

[163] H. B. Co. Journ. No. 1039.

JOHN McLOUGHLIN TO CAPTAIN SIMPSON[164]

Ft. Vancouver 7 July 1830

[Captain Simpson is instructed to proceed to Nass to examine its harbour and the river that flows into it. Enclosed is a] "priced account of your outfit, and if paid in furs at the annexed prices you can dispose of your Goods at 150 p. cent advance on Invoice valuation."

Large Beaver	20/	Musquash	6^{d}
Small "	10/	Land otters Large	10/
Fishers	4/	" " Small	5/
Cross Foxes	11/	Sea otters Large	£6 to 8
Red "	5/	" " Small	40/
Silver "	30/	Large Blk Bear	10/
Martens	5/	Small " "	5/
Minks	1/6	Large Bro. "	10/

GOVERNOR SIMPSON TO JOHN McLOUGHLIN[165]

10 July 1830

....Had the Masters of the American Vessels fallen in with your proposition to sell their Outfit at a moderate advance and taken Boards in payment it would have been a very advantageous arrangement, but the terms on which they offered to withdraw were quite inadmissible. We are of opinion that it is bad policy to buy out opposition, as in most cases in which this has been done we found it was merely getting rid of an evil for the moment, and had the effect of encouraging fresh competitors. We cannot, under any circumstances short of the loss of our annual supplies, and to save the lives of our people, authorise purchases from our opponents for Bills or Furs, but if you can at any time make an advantageous purchase for Boards, Salmon, or Provisions we have no objection thereto.

We are concerned to find that the Indian Tariff has been reduced so low, but are aware that it could not have been avoided with an opposition at the Doors of your Establishments, and are

[164] *Ibid.*

[165] H. B. Co. Journ. No. 954.

satisfied that very great exertion must have been used to secure to us so large a proportion of the Trade as it appears we have got. When our Opponents withdraw, which we suppose they have done before now it will be necessary to introduce gradually more saving prices; but of this and the mode in which it is to be brought about you on the spot must be the best judge; we leave it therefore entirely to your discretion....

If you find that a good market can be obtained for any considerable quantity of Salmon, we shall provide the necessary means in Coopers Fishermen Nets &c to prosecute that branch of business, but I could not learn in England that it was an article in much demand on the shores of the Pacific. You can however obtain certain information on this subject from the Sandwich Islands, and we shall be regulated by such as you may furnish us.

In regard to the Timber Trade also I could not learn that a market to any great extent could be obtained at Lima, Valporaizo, or the Other Spanish Towns or Settlements on that Coast, nor even at the Sandwich Islands, but we know that the last named place does afford an Outlet for a considerable quantity, and I have no doubt that the information which reached us from the Sandwich Islands as to the demand for that article at the Spanish Settlements is correct. The best way of ascertaining the fact, however, is to send a shipment at your convenience.

We are anxious that an Establishment should be formed at Nass as early as circumstances admit, to act in concert with our shipping on the coast; and if we could once get them in full operation, I have not the smallest doubt that the Trade will fall entirely into our hands, and more especially so as it appears that the Russians do not mean to afford any further encouragement to the American adventurers.

JOHN McLOUGHLIN TO JOHN ROWAND[166]

Ft. Vancouver 3 Aug. 1830

The 29th Ult. the Boston opposition after giving us an immensity of trouble took their departure, but I am given to understand another vessel is to come here.

[166] H. B. Co. Journ. No. 1038. John Rowand was the chief factor in charge of the Saskatchewan district.

GOVERNOR SIMPSON TO WILLIAM SMITH[167]

York Factory 20 Aug. 1830

I have the honor to acknowledge receipt of your valued favor of 6th March, which did not get to hand at Liverpool until just as I was on the eve of sailing, and this I trust will satisfactorily account for its not being replied to in course.

I regret exceedingly that Sir George Murray's intimation of a desire to see me at the Colonial Office did not reach me in time to be complied with; as I think I should have been able to answer any questions he might put to me touching the claims of Great Britain to the country on the west side the mountains. There are a great many Documents in my writing deposited at the Hudson's Bay House on this subject, particularly a correspondence in the year 1825 between Mr Addington (the American Secy of Legation) and myself, which contains a good deal of information thereon and to which I beg the liberty of drawing your attention when you may find it convenient to direct it to that subject.

The Hon'ble Company's affairs in this quarter, I am happy to say, look well; the Trade is in a prosperous state, (but will not be quite so profitable as last year), and the Natives are more orderly and appear better disposed than they have been for some time past.

WM. A. AITKIN TO JOHN D. CAMERON[168]

Fond du Lac 4 Sept. 1830

I have the pleasure to enclose you a copy of a letter from the Secy of the Hon. Hudsons Bay Compy in reply to one from the President of the American Fur Compy on the subject of withholding ardent Spirits from the Indians near the line of demarcation between Great Britain and the United States. It gives me

[167] H. B. Co. Journ. No. 954. William Smith, addressed in this letter, is not the Secretary, earlier mentioned, of the Hudson's Bay Company, but one of the Honorable Committee, and a member of Parliament from Norwich.

[168] H. B. Co. Journ. No. 1038. John D. Cameron was the chief factor in charge of the Rainy Lake district.

much pleasure to find that the benevolent views of your Company have induced them to come into the measure, and I hereby assure you that altho' our people take in Liquor to the Frontier Posts, they are not to make use of a drop on their way, nor on their arrival at their Posts, until they have seen you on the subject, and then Sir if your views are the same with those which the Gentlemen of your Company in England hold on the subject, you can either make arrangements with our People to destroy the Liquor on both sides, or bury it untill it can be taken out of the Country again.

Captain Simpson to John McLoughlin[169]

"Cadboro" 23 Sept. 1830

[He submits a report of his surveying and trading expedition to Nass. He has been informed that the American brigs Owhyhee and Convoy[170] are at Port Discovery and in the Straits of Fuca.]

With respect to its [Nass] proving a favorable trading post it certainly appears a Country abounding in Beavers (& those of a good quality), tho' the trade owing to the frequent visits of the American Coasters will be at a high Rate, could parties be sent up the River to trade I imagine they could be procured at a much cheaper rate. On the morning of the 3rd we sail'd from Nass, in the following afternoon Cape Northumberland N. W. & Cape Manning West, we fell in with the American ship Louisa of Boston, Lambert,[171] employed in the Fur trade; she has been on the coast for several months and had for a Consort the Griffon Brig, Taylor. This vessel I learnt had been sold on her going from the coast to the Sandwich Islands, by her proprietors, Americans,[172] to a company in China who have a gentleman of the name of Cole acting for them as agent at the Sandwich Islands or in his absence Mr Charlton. A N. W. cargo was purchased at the Islands by these gentlemen & the Brig sent back with it to the

[169] H. B. Co. Journ. No. 1062.

[170] Both these brigs were in the service of Josiah Marshall of Boston.

[171] Captain Lambert was in the service of the Boston firm of William Baker and Company. He was associated later in the Columbia with Nathaniel Wyeth.

[172] Bryant and Sturgis of Boston were the owners of this vessel in 1828.

coast. Capt. Lambert believed she sail'd under the English Flag. He inform'd me also that the American brig Convoy had left that part of the Coast some time ago having first sold his N. W. Cargo to him & Captain Taylor. By his accounts Sea Otters were very scarce this Season but land Furs on the increase; after a short visit we parted company, the Louisa proceeded up the straits of Clarence & we towards Dixons Strs. Contrary winds & close fogs, prevailing during our passage down the straits we did not clear them untill the 7th in the evening. The Eagle continued in company till the 13th when she parted in a gale of wind from the E. & we saw nothing more of her untill our return into the Columbia which in consequence of contrary winds did not take place untill the afternoon of 23rd. The Eagle had arrived on the evening of the 20th. On the 22nd we saw a strange Brig which from her appearance & the course she was steering S. W. I took for the American Brig Convoy on her way to the Sandwich Islands after having left the Straits of Fucca.

The unexpected length of our Voyage in consequence of a succession of contrary winds prevented our visiting ports for the purpose of trading which I regret as a favourable impression might have been made by visiting a few places tho' I must state the Americans appear to have goods more in demand on this part of the coast than us. Arms & ammunition they sell without limits & ardent spirits in great abundance & these articles with the exception of Blankets I found in greatest demand at Nass. Of the first of these articles I sold none, as for the last, half stock'd Green I had on board, they offered only one Beaver Skin. I regretted being under the necessity of selling a quantity of the latter as I found it impossible to trade without it nor do I see how it can well be avoided till opposition is done off the Coast....

JOHN McLOUGHLIN TO GOVERNOR & COMMITTEE[173]

Ft. Vancouver 11 Oct. 1830

[Account of the wreck of the "Isabella."]

[Coastal trade] We can never bring the Indians to the old prices, of five Beaver for one Blanket, and I do not know if ever

[173] H. B. Co. Journ. No. 1039.

we will be able to increase the present price of one Large Beaver for a Blanket.

[Captain Simpson on his way to Nass reported an American coaster in the Straits of De Fuca. He left the "Vancouver" to oppose her.]

The Intermitting Fever (for the first time since the trade of this Department was established) has appeared at this place and carried off three fourths of the Indian population in our vicinity—at present there are fifty-two of our people on the sick list, in which number is Mr. Ogden, but thanks be to God for his great goodness all our people are on the convalescent list.

The Boston Brig, Owhyhee, Capt. Dominis which arrived here in Feby 1829 sailed from this in July last. Since her departure we have had no opposition but we have been obliged to keep our parties running to Indians as much as ever to prevent their having any number of skins in the event of any coaster coming here.

Our crop, except 36 bu. barley sown on the 11 July after the water was fallen and which is now almost ready to cut, is all threshed. It yielded

927 bu. Wheat
120 " Early peas
192 " Grey "
297 " White "
600 " Indian Corn
150 " Oats
86 " Barley

And we have remaining of former years

1100 bu. Wheat
300 " Barley
80 cwt. Flour.

In short we have wheat and flour for two years, and more than a years stock of peas and corn. Hereafter we will not endeavour to do more than keep up the quantity of wheat, but to increase our peas and corn till we have a two years stock.

JOHN McLOUGHLIN TO CAPTAIN SIMPSON[174]

Ft. Vancouver 24 Nov. 1830

We are informed a considerable quantity of Beaver is collected at Montery and its vicinity. You can pay it 17/6 in Goods at 100 p. cent advance on prime cost, or in Bills on England at 10/ p. lb. but you ought not to draw for a less sum than £25. Sea otters you will pay in Goods at the above advance from twenty-five to thirty dollars, and in Bills on England or in cash from 18 to 24 Dollars.

You will endeavour to ascertain if there are any settlers on the Bonaventura,[175] and if there would be any objections to our sending a party of Trappers to that part of the country or to the Bay of St. Francisco. This information you could only get from private sources, and it is very uncertain whether even if we had leave that we would send. However as Beaver are numerous about that place it is well to ascertain the point and you will also endeavour to learn if we could be allowed to take Cattle, Horses and Mules out of California.

You will demand if you think it safe the debt due to the late N. W. Company by the Government of California.

If you become acquainted with any of the Missions you may tell them we will undertake to import any article they may wish from England.

JOHN McLOUGHLIN TO GOVERNOR & COMMITTEE[176]

Ft. Vancouver 24 Nov. 1830

[Paraphrased]

Fever broke out with increased violence since last letter, and at one time 75 were on sick list; now however it is reduced to 45. The Indians who were frightened at the mortality amongst them came in numbers to camp alongside of us, giving as a reason that

[174] *Ibid.*

[175] The Bonaventura River is the present Sacramento. For years the name was applied in maps of North America to a mythical river of the West which was supposed to flow directly from the interior to the Pacific.

[176] *Ibid.*

satisfaction to say, has, ever since that period, been in a state of the most perfect tranquillity, beneficial as well to the Indian population as to the parties interested and engaged in the trade.

Previous to that period, an unrestricted supply of spirituous liquor, then an important article of trade, led to the commission of crimes, to the injury of health, and to a state of demoralization among the native population truly lamentable. The measures since taken by the Council in the country, under the instructions of the Board of Direction in England, to remedy those evils have been attended with the happiest results: drunkenness is now of very rare occurrence in any part of the country, and quite unknown throughout the extended district situated to the northward of the Saskatchewaine and Churchill rivers occupied by the Chipewyan, Beaver Indian, Cree, Yellow Knife, Hare, Dog Rib and other tribes throughout the numerously inhabited and widely extended plain country to the southward of Saskatchewaine; in the country situated between the Rocky Mountains and the shores of the Pacific, watered by the Columbia river and its tributaries, in the country known by the name of New Caledonia, situated inland, to the northward of the Columbia river, and among the Chippewa tribes on the shores and interior country of Lakes Superior and Huron the introduction and use of spirituous and other intoxicating liquors have been strictly prohibited, except in very rare cases for medicinal purposes.

The first introduction of this measure was so unpopular among the natives as to endanger the safety of the trading establishments, rendering it necessary to maintain a large force for their protection, at a heavy expense; and it was only by compensating them for the loss of this baneful indulgence by large gratuities, consisting of presents of British manufacture, that they became reconciled to the privation. In other parts of the country, where it could not, in safety to the white population, be entirely prohibited, the use of it is now gradually diminishing, so as at this time to be no longer an evil; and in no part of the countries through which the Hudson's Bay Company's operations extend are spirituous or intoxicating liquors of any description sold to Indians, or used as a medium of barter or trade. But so inseparable is drunkenness or the abuse of spirituous liquors from opposition in the Indian trade, that on the north-west coast, where we have to contend with the Americans and Russians, and even on the banks of the St. Lawrence and Ottawa rivers, which are exposed to competition in trade, and where the Indians are partially civilized, I am sorry to say our utmost efforts to check it have been unavailing.

A confirmation of these statements is to be seen by reference to the exportations of spirituous liquors to Hudson 's Bay, which, since the year 1821, do not exceed on the average 43 puncheons of rum annually for the supply of the whole country situated to the eastward of the Rocky Mountains, comprised in the License of trade granted to the Company, as well as the Company's territories, the population of which, including servants, may be estimated at 120,000 souls, no spirituous liquors having up to this period been distilled in the country.

During the competition in trade previous to the year 1821 (when the exclusive management fell into the hands of the Hudson 's Bay Company) it was found impossible to take any effectual measure towards the civilization or moral and religious improvement of the native population. Since that period the Company have established two Protestant missions, under the management of their chaplains at Red River Settlement, where there are likewise two Catholic missions and 13 [?] schools.

In this Settlement there are resident several thousand Indians and half-breeds, drawn together from all parts of the country, with a view to their civilization and moral and religious improvement. These people have abandoned the chase, and now devote themselves to agricultural pursuits, and it is gratifying to be enabled to say that the zealous endeavours of our missionaries have been most successful.

The Hudson 's Bay Company have likewise established missions and schools at several of their principal depôts or posts on the Columbia river, west side of the Rocky Mountains, under the management of another of their chaplains, and at the Red River and Columbia schools, Indian children are educated belonging to many of the distant tribes, who, after attaining the age of manhood, are allowed the option of returning to their homes, becoming agriculturists at Red River Settlement, or entering into the Company's service. We are using our utmost endeavours in every other part of the country, where the climate and soil admit of it, to collect the Indians into villages, and direct their attention to agriculture, as the first step towards civilization. This operation is, however, attended with much difficulty, from their erratic habits, and the scanty and precarious subsistence afforded by the chase, which prevents their keeping together in considerable numbers, and applying themselves to husbandry and the pursuits of civilized life, and compels them to separate into small parties of single families, and to wander about in search of food, under circumstances where it is impossible for the missionary to follow them.

I can say, without fear of contradiction, from my intimate knowledge of the country and natives, and of the mode in which the business was conducted, both previous and subsequent to the period since which the exclusive trade has been in the hands of the Company, having held the situation I now have the honour of filling for many years, during which I have been in constant communication with the different tribes inhabiting these extensive countries, and I say it with peculiar satisfaction, that their condition is much ameliorated.

When competition in trade existed, the encouragement afforded to the Indians to make large collections of skins led to the destruction of the fur-bearing animals of all ages and sexes, and at all seasons. If this system had been continued much longer, those animals, which were rapidly decreasing in numbers, would have been almost entirely extirpated. Instead of exhausting the country, we now use every means in our power to preserve it, by withdrawing our trading posts, and the Indians attached to them, for a time from such parts as have been impoverished, so as to enable them to recruit; and by discouraging hunting during the seasons when the females are bearing and rearing their young, the animals are now becoming numerous. The employment we afford at those seasons to many of the Indians, whereby they are brought into frequent communication and intercourse with our officers and servants, tends towards their gradual civilization and improvement; and we find our own interests promoted by an equitable and liberal system of trade and management.

Our different trading establishments are the resort or refuge of many of the natives, who, from age, infirmity or other causes, are unable to follow the chase; they have the benefit of the care and attention, free of expense, of our medical men, of whom about 12 are usually employed in the service, every trading establishment being, in fact, an Indian hospital; advantages which were not and could not have been afforded to them during the competition in trade. In short, I have no hesitation in saying that the native population of the countries through which the Hudson's Bay Company's business extends never derived any real benefit from their intercourse with the whites until the fur trade became exercised under the existing License. In proof of this, the population of some of the tribes, previous to that time sensibly diminishing, is now increasing; and from my experience of the times of opposition, I can further say, that if the trade were again thrown open to competition, all the horrors of the late contest would break out afresh; drunkenness and demoralization would have their former sway, not only among the natives but among the whites, whom we are now enabled to keep under proper subordination, which was never the case during the excitement occasioned by the rivalship in trade; the fur-bearing animals would in the course of a very few years become nearly extinct; and the inevitable consequences would be, the desertion of the natives by the traders, the latter having no longer any inducement to remain among them; that unfortunate population, thus left to their own resources, must inevitably perish from cold and hunger, the use of the bow and arrow, and other rude implements, formerly affording them the means of feeding and clothing themselves, being now unknown, and our guns, ammunition, fishing-tackle, iron works, cloth, blankets and other manufactures having become absolutely necessary to their very existence. The country in which the Hudson's Bay Company now trade is divided into four great districts, known by the names of the Northern, Southern, Columbia and Montreal Departments, in which there are 136 establishments, besides hunting expeditions and shipping, affording employment to 25 chief factors, 27 chief traders, 152 clerks, and about 1200 regular servants, besides the occasional labour in boating and other services of a great number of the natives.

Previous to 1821 the business of the Columbia department was very limited; but it has since been very greatly extended at much expense, and, I am sorry to add, at a considerable sacrifice of life among the Company's officers and servants, owing to the fierce, treacherous and blood-thirsty character of its population, and the dangers of the navigation; it now comprehends 22 trading establishments, besides several migratory, hunting and trading expeditions, and six armed vessels on the north-west coast.

The fur trade is the principal branch of business at present in the country situated between the Rocky Mountains and the Pacific Ocean. On the banks of the Columbia river, however, where the soil and climate are favourable to cultivation, we are directing our attention to agriculture on a large scale, and there is every prospect that we shall soon be able to establish important branches of export trade from thence in the articles of wool, tallow, hides, tobacco, and grain of various kinds.

I have also the satisfaction to say, that the native population are beginning to profit by our example, as many, formerly dependent on hunting and fishing, now maintain themselves by the produce of the soil.

The country situated between the northern bank of the Columbia river, which empties itself into the Pacific, in lat. 46° 20″, and the southern bank of Frazer's river, which empties itself into the Gulf of Georgia, in lat. 49°, is remarkable for the salubrity of its climate and excellence of its soil, and possesses, within the Straits of De Fuca, some of the finest harbours in the world, being protected from the weight of the Pacific by Vancouver's and other islands. To the southward of the Straits of De Fuca, situated in lat. 48° 37″, there is no good harbour nearer than the bay of St. Francisco, in lat. 37° 48″, as the broad shifting bar off the mouth of the Columbia, and the tortuous channel through it, renders the entrance of that river a very

granted them certain territories in North America described in that Charter, together with exclusive privileges of trade, etc., etc. Between the years 1670 and 1690, a period of 20 years, the profits appear to have been very large, as, notwithstanding losses sustained by the capture of the Company's establishments by the French in the years 1682 to 1688, amounting to £118,014, they were enabled to make a payment to the proprietors in 1684 of 50 per cent; another payment in 1688 of 50 per cent; and of a further payment in 1689 of 25 per cent.

In 1690 the stock was trebled without any call being made, besides affording a payment to the proprietors of 25 per cent on the increased or newly-created stock; in the years 1692, 1694, 1696 and 1697, the Company incurred loss and damage, to the amount of £97,500, by other captures of their establishments by the French.

These losses appear to have rendered it necessary for the Company to borrow money, on which they paid six per cent interest; they were enabled, nevertheless, in 1720, again to treble their capital stock, with only a call of 10 per cent on the proprietors, and, notwithstanding another heavy loss sustained, by the capture of their establishments by the French under La Perouse, in 1782, they appear to have been enabled to pay dividends of from 5 to 12 per cent, averaging nine per cent, and showing, as nearly as I am able to judge from the defective state of the books during the past century, profits on the originally subscribed capital stock actually paid up of between 60 and 70 per cent per annum from the year 1690 to 1800.

Up to this period the Hudson's Bay Company had no great cause for complaint of interference with their inland trade, and if they had been left unmolested, or been protected in the undisturbed possession of it, and of the rights and privileges vested in them by their Charter, they would in all probability have continued in the enjoyment of the advantages they were then deriving from their labours and exertions in those remote and little frequented wilds.

But about that period their rights of territory and trade were invaded by rival traders, which led to animosities, feuds and dangerous navigation even to vessels of small draught of water.

The possession of that country to Great Britain may become an object of very great importance, and we are strengthening that claim to it (independent of the claims of prior discovery and occupation for the purpose of Indian trade) by forming the nucleus of a colony through the establishment of farms, and the settlement of some of our retiring officers and servants as agriculturists.

Our population in Red River Settlement amounts to about 5000 souls, say about 2000 whites, and about 3000 half breeds and Indians. The population, at the close of the late contest in trade, did not amount to as many hundreds; but so pernicious was the excitement occasioned by the contest, even among that small population, that it was then frequently the scene of bloodshed, robbery and riot; and in one of these riots, in the year 1816, 22 persons were killed, and several wounded; among the former was Mr. Semple, Governor of the Company's territories, a man of judgment and discretion, and of the most amiable and benevolent character.

The blessings of tranquillity, however, immediately followed the cessation of that contest, peaceful industry having reigned in the Settlement ever since, and offences so few as rarely to call for magisterial interference. Our population, however, is now so large, and increasing so rapidly, both as regards Indians and half-breeds, and whites, that the time has arrived when it is no longer safe to trust the peace of the Settlement solely to the good-will of its inhabitants. I, therefore, consider it highly necessary to the security of lives and property, that a court of justice, for the trial of civil and criminal cases, with an efficient police to support the civil power, should be established there without delay.

J. H. PELLY TO THE LORDS OF THE COMMITTEE OF THE PRIVY COUNCIL FOR TRADE[179]

London 7 Feb. 1838

....The Hudson's Bay Company was incorporated in the year 1670, under a Royal Charter of Charles the Second, which

[179] *Ibid.*, 543.

breaches of the peace, extending to the loss of lives, and considerable destruction of property, injurious to the native Indians, by reason of the unrestricted use of spirituous liquors and other demoralizing influence, consequent on opposition, and so prejudicial to the interests of the Hudson's Bay Company, that between 1800 and 1821, a period of 22 years, their dividends were, for the first eight years, reduced to four per cent; during the next six years they could pay no dividend at all; and for the remaining eight years they could only pay four per cent.

During a long succession of years, while this destructive contest existed, very frequent applications for protection and redress were made by the Hudson's Bay Company to His Majesty's Government, as may be seen by reference to the records of the Colonial Office, but without avail, and scenes of bloodshed, robbery and demoralization, revolting to humanity, were allowed to pass without any effectual measures being taken to punish or prevent them, although the Hudson's Bay Company had every claim on Government to support them in their just rights of territory and trade.

At length, in the year 1821, when the violence of the contest had nearly exhausted the means of both parties, an arrangement was entered into between them, by which their interests became united, under the management of the Hudson's Bay Company.

The proprietary were then called upon to pay £100 per cent upon their capital, which, with the stock in trade of both parties in the country, formed a capital stock of £400,000, on which four per cent dividend was paid in the years 1821 to 1824, and from that time to the present, half-year dividends of five per cent, with a bonus of 10 per cent from the year 1828 to 1832, and since that an average bonus of six per cent until last year, when none was paid.

When your Lordships come to consider the very hazardous nature of the trade, requiring a degree of enterprise unknown to almost any other business, together with the heavy losses to which the parties interested therein were subjected for a long series of years, from want of protection and support, which they had a right to expect from His Majesty's Government, I feel assured your Lordships will join me in opinion that the profits now arising from the business are no more than a fair return for the capital employed, and the services the Hudson's Bay Company are rendering the mother country in securing to it a branch of commerce which they are at present wresting out of the hands of foreigners, subjects of Russia and the United States of America, but which the Company would have been unable to prosecute, had they not been protected by the License of exclusive trade they now hold.

In looking at these profits, however, it should be borne in mind that Hudson's Bay stock, in like manner as in all other stocks, changes hands very frequently, and that the price of the stock is entirely regulated by the return it produces, thereby affording to the bulk of the present proprietors little more than six per cent for their money....

That the peace and tranquillity of the country has been restored; that the abuse of spirituous liquors has been discontinued; that the condition of the native population is greatly ameliorated; and that the commercial interests of Great Britain are improving under the management of the Hudson's Bay Company through the provisions of that Act, will appear manifest by the report of Mr. Simpson....

The principal benefit the Company derive from the exclusive License of trade is the peaceable occupation of their own proper territory, from which they draw nearly the whole of the profits of their trade, and for the protection of which they have a right to look to the Government in common with the rest of Her Majesty's subjects, as the trade of the country embraced in the Royal License is as yet of very little benefit to them, and affords greater advantages to the mother country in the employment of shipping, and in the revenue arising from imports and exports, than the Company derive from it.

The country denominated "Indian Territories," comprehended in the Royal License, is principally situated on the west side of the Rocky Mountains, the most valuable part thereof being the north-west coast, bordering on the shores of the Pacific.

For many years previous to the grant of exclusive trade to the

Hudson's Bay Company, the trade of that coast was engrossed by the subjects of the United States of America and Russia, the only establishment occupied by British traders being "Astoria" afterwards named "Fort George" at the mouth of the Columbia River, while no attempt was made, through the means of shipping, to obtain any part of the trade of the coast; and so unprofitable was it in the years 1818, 1819, 1820, 1821 and 1822, and so difficult of management, that several of the leading and most intelligent persons in the country strongly recommended that the Company should abandon it altogether. The Company, however, felt that the honour of the concern would, in a certain degree, be compromised were they to adopt that recommendation, holding as they did under Government the License in question, and with a degree of energy and enterprise, which, I feel assured your Lordships will admit, reflects much credit on themselves and on their officers and servants in the country, they directed their efforts so vigorously to that branch of the business, that they compelled the American adventurers, one by one, to withdraw from the contest, and are now pressing the Russian Fur Company so closely, that although that association is supported by its government to the extent of affording them the assistance of a strong military guard at each of their establishments, which, with their shipping, are officered by naval and military officers of the Imperial army and navy, we are gaining ground upon them, and hope at no very distant period to confine them to the trade of their own proper territory.

The outlay and expense attending this competition in trade are so heavy, that the profits are yet but in perspective, none worthy of notice having been realized, the result showing some years a trifling loss, and in others a small gain, fluctuating according to the degree of activity with which the contest is maintained; but by energy and perseverance, we hope, in due time, to bring it to a more favourable issue, if the facilities of protection now required of Her Majesty's Government be afforded.

This trade, nevertheless, affords employment to about 1000 men, occupying 21 permanent trading establishments, two migratory, trading and trapping expeditions, a steam vessel, and five sailing vessels from 100 to 300 tons burthen, all armed, and so dangerous is the trade, that I lament to say that it has not been unattended with loss of life....

That the Hudson's Bay Company have the strongest possible claims upon Her Majesty's Government for a renewal of the exclusive License of trade, without any rent or pecuniary consideration whatsoever, cannot, I should hope, admit of a question after the explanation I have given; but when it is considered that the greater part of the country to which the License applies is Indian country, opened by treaty to citizens of the United States of America, as well as to British subjects, and, consequently, the License of exclusive trade does not protect the Company from the competition of citizens of the United States, it must appear evident that no substantial benefit is likely to arise from the boon we are soliciting, beyond the probable means of affording peace to our own territories, in the tranquillity of which Her Majesty's Government ought to feel as deep an interest as the stockholders of the Hudson's Bay Company....

APPENDIX B

I

Note 4, *ante*, 3.

North or light canoes were the express canoes of the fur trade. They were designed for rapid transport on streams much broken by falls, or where portages were long and numerous as in the northern territories of the Hudson's Bay Company. They measured about twenty-five feet in length and four or five feet in width, and they took a crew of eight or nine men, together with two or three passengers and supplies. They were made extraordinarily light so that when empty they could be carried over short portages by two men. They were made of sheets of birch bark a quarter of an inch in thickness, which were sewed together with wattap, the root of the spruce split into threads, and the seams were made water tight with pine-tree gum. The inner surface was reinforced by a light coat of lathing, which was held in place by cedar ribs bent bow shape and inserted into the edge of the gunwales, giving the vessel firmness and strength. Bow and stern of a North canoe rose in graceful curves a foot above the level of the gunwales and were gaudily painted with mystical figures which were believed by the superstitious voyageurs to make for increased speed. Craft so frail was frequently in need of repairs. For that purpose every North canoe carried spare supplies of birch bark, wattap and gum. Mending was simple and was done with despatch, an ordinary rip requiring but an hour to close up. North canoes were express carriers rather than freighters. But the North West Company for years used them as general carriers. One of the important reforms which Governor Simpson made early in his administration was to relegate them to express uses and to substitute the prosaic but efficient York boats for freighting purposes wherever water conditions permitted. Beside North canoes, there were in use in the fur trade half canoes and single canoes; also Montreal canoes or *canôts du maitre* with a capacity twice that of North canoes, designed for rapid transport on comparatively open waters like those of the Ottawa. For a good contemporary drawing of a North canoe and its load see Sir William Schooling, *The Hudson's Bay Company* (London, 1920), 32.

II

Note 12, *ante*, 8.

Pemmican is a concentrated meat preparation that was used by the Hudson's Bay Company and other British fur-trading companies as regular voyaging provision. It was made ordinarily from buffalo meat, though venison and the flesh of other game could also be treated in the same way. The lean of the flesh was cut into thin broad slices which were hung up to dry in the sun or before a fire. Drying took about two days. The strips were then reduced to a pulp by pounding with a wooden flail on a sheet of rawhide spread out on the prairie. Bags made from buffalo hide were packed about half full with the pulp, after which an almost equal weight of melted buffalo fat was stirred in to a total of ninety pounds. Meat and fat hardened together after which the bag was securely sewed up.

Pemmican was almost ideal voyaging provision. It occupied little space in a canoe, for it is one of the most concentrated of foods, a fact which commends it still to arctic explorers. It was convenient to pack into canoes or to carry over portages by reason of its bag form. When properly protected from wet and mold it could be kept indefinitely. It could be eaten cooked or uncooked, which recommended it particularly for long canoe voyages where haste was necessary. For all these reasons it was an item of major importance in fur trade economy. Pemmican made possible the development of the interior communication system of the North West Company, and it was on this foundation, also, that Simpson built the remarkable transportation system of the Hudson's Bay Company.

Pemmican was manufactured for the Hudson's Bay Company

in the buffalo country about Pembina and around the provision posts of the Saskatchewan River on a large scale. The famous summer buffalo hunts of the Red River half-breeds and much of the takings of the early fall hunts were devoted to it, as well as a portion of the later autumn hunts. Lean meat only and tallow were used for this purpose, the remainder of the flesh being preserved by drying or smoking or by cold when taken in the late autumn. One buffalo, using the lean meat only, produced one bag of pemmican. South of the international border pemmican was not much made, the Indians and whites there preserving their meat by drying or jerking.

Pemmican was eaten on the voyage uncooked for the noon meal since the crew were not then permitted to make a stop. At other times it was eaten fried with a little flour, when that was obtainable, in the form of *richot*, or boiled with potatoes into a thick soup called *rubeiboo*. The best variety of pemmican, mixed with dried service berries or other fruit, was a fairly palatable food. But there was nothing delectable about common pemmican. "Take the scrapings from the driest outside corner of a very stale piece of cold roast-beef, add to it lumps of tallowy, rancid fat, then garnish all with long human hairs, on which string pieces, like beads upon a necklace, and short hairs of dogs or oxen, or both, and you have a fair imitation of common pemmican. Indeed, the presence of hairs in the food has suggested the inquiry whether the hair on the buffaloes from which the pemmican is made does not grow on the inside of the skin. The abundance of small stones or pebbles in pemmican also indicates the discovery of a new buffalo diet heretofore unknown to naturalists. Carefully made pemmican, flavored with berries and sugar, is nearly good; but of most persons new to the diet it may be said that, in two senses, a little of it goes a long way." H. M. Robinson, *The Great Fur Land* (London, 1879), 117. See also R. O. Merriman, "The Bison and the Fur Trade," in *Bulletin* of the Departments of History and Political and Economic Science in Queen's University, no. 53.

III

Note 14, *ante*, 8.

Such hours of labor were customary on the voyage. Between voyages, however, as a compensation, there were long intervals of idleness. Simpson has elsewhere described the typical voyaging day of the canoemen. "Weather permitting, our slumbers would be broken about one in the morning by the cry of 'Lève, lève, lève!' In five minutes, woe to the inmates that were slow in dressing; the tents were tumbling about our ears; and, within half an hour, the camp would be raised, the canoes laden, and the paddles keeping time to some merry old song. About eight o'clock, a convenient place would be selected for breakfast, about three quarters of an hour being allotted for the multifarious operations of unpacking and repacking the equipage, laying and removing the cloth, boiling and frying, eating and drinking; and, while the preliminaries were arranging, the hardier among us would wash and shave, each person carrying soap and towel in his pocket, and finding a mirror in the same sandy or rocky basin that held the water. About two in the afternoon we usually put ashore for dinner; and, as this meal needed no fire, or at least got none, it was not allowed to occupy more than twenty minutes or half an hour.

"Such was the routine of our journey, the day, generally speaking, being divided into six hours of rest and eighteen of labour. This almost incredible toil the voyageurs bore without a murmur, and generally with such a hilarity of spirit as few other men could sustain for a single forenoon.

"But the quality of the work, even more decidedly than the quantity, requires operatives of iron mould. In smooth water, the paddle is plied with twice the rapidity of the oar, taxing both arms and lungs to the utmost extent; amid shallows, the canoe is literally dragged by the men, wading to their knees or their loins, while each poor fellow, after replacing his drier half in his seat, laughingly shakes the heaviest of the wet from his legs over the gunwale, before he again gives them an inside berth; in rapids, the towing-line has to be hauled along over rocks and stumps, through swamps and thickets, excepting that, when the ground is utterly impracticable, poles are substituted, and occasionally also the bushes on the shore. Again, on the portages, where the tracks are of all imaginable kinds and degrees of badness, the canoes and their cargoes are never carried across in fewer than two or three trips—the little vessels alone monopolizing, on the first turn, the more expert half of their respective crews. Of the baggage, each man has to carry at least two pieces, estimated at a hundred and eighty pounds avoirdupois, which he suspends in slings of leather placed across the forehead, so that he has his hands free to clear the way among the branches of the standing trees and over the prostrate trunks.

"But, in addition to the separate labours of the land and the water, the poor fellows have to endure a combination of both sorts of hardship at least three or four times every day. The canoes can seldom approach near enough to the bank to enable the passengers to step ashore from the gunwale; and no sooner is a halt made, than the men are in the water to ferry us on their backs to dry ground. In this unique department of their duties they seem to take a pride; and a little fellow often ambitiously tries to get possession of the heaviest customer in the party, considerably exceeding, as has often been the case in my experience, the standard aforesaid, of two pieces of baggage." Sir George Simpson, *Narrative of a Journey Round The World* (London, 1847), I, 21-23.

IV

Note 82, *ante*, 37.

New Caledonia was a difficult transport problem for the fur companies on account of the wall of mountains that shut it in—the Rockies, the Cariboo and the Selkirk on the north and east, and the Monashee and Coastal ranges on the south and west. **The Fraser River gives no outlet because below Soda Creek it is unnavigable. The fur companies had but two means of** approach, both very difficult, one via the Pacific, the other via the East. The first was the river Columbia as far as the Okanagan with an overland trail thence via the North Thompson to a point where the Fraser becomes navigable. This route was early developed by the North West Company, and was used afterwards by the Hudson's Bay Company until 1822. The second, the eastward route, developed also by the North West Company and adopted by the Hudson's Bay Company in 1823, began at York Factory (Fort William in North West Company days), proceeded via Lake Winnipeg, Cumberland House, Frog Portage, Methye Portage and Fort Chipewyan to the Peace River, up that stream to the Rocky Mountain Portage, thence via the Parsnip River to Fort McLeod, and finally overland to Stuart Lake. A route so difficult was of course not open to York boats; nothing but North canoes could use it, and as many as six were required for the transport of the 130 "pieces" constituting the New Caledonia outfit of 1824. Nowhere else in the territories of the Hudson's Bay Company was canoe freighting on such a scale to be found, and Simpson was right when he said that this was the most tedious, harassing and expensive transport in the Indian country. The route which he proposed as an alternative ran from York Factory to Cumberland House, thence along the Saskatchewan to Edmonton, thence by an overland track to the Athabasca, thence up the Athabasca to Henry's House in Athabasca Pass, thence via Yellowhead Pass across the continental divide, and on to the headwaters of the Fraser. Such a route might have been an improvement over the old, but it never came into use. Before it could be adopted Simpson had determined to outfit New Caledonia by way again of the Columbia. See *ante*, 76 n. But that part of the proposed route which ran via Yellowhead Pass across the Rocky Mountains was long employed to bring leather from Jasper House to New Caledonia, particularly moose skins, a circumstance from which Yellowhead Pass came to be known as Leather Pass. Today this is the route of the Canadian National Railroad into British Columbia. For a good description of the Yellowhead Pass see Milton and Cheadle, *The North-West Passage by Land*, 246-258; also Malcolm McLeod, *Journal of Archibald McDonald, 1828* (Ottawa, 1872), 31, 113.

V

Note 101, *ante*, 46.

The man upon whom Simpson passes this judgment is none other than Alexander Ross, the well-known chronicler of the fur trade of the Columbia Valley. His rank at this time was that of clerk, the same he had held in the Pacific Fur Company and in the North West Company. He had been entrusted with the command of the Snake Country Expedition the preceding year, and now with the termination of his expedition he retires from the fur trade. We shall find him accepting from Governor Simpson charge of the Missionary Society School at Red River at a salary of £100, and accompanying Simpson eastward over the mountains in the spring of 1825. He spent the remainder of his life in the Red River Colony, where he published, some years before his death, the best account in existence of the earlier Snake Country Expeditions, particularly those of McKenzie, McDonald and his own. See his *Fur Hunters*. This should be read as a check on Simpson's somewhat harsh judgment. Ross published two other works connected with his early experiences which have been extensively used by historians: *The Adventures of the First Settlers on the Columbia River* (London, 1849) and *The Red River Settlement* (London, 1856). As to his Snake Country Expedition he seems to have had no intimation from Simpson that his management of it had been otherwise than satisfactory. He writes (*Fur Hunters*, II, 140, 141), "As the reader may wish to know the extent of our success in the object of our pursuit, after all our toils, I may say that, all things considered, our returns were the most profitable ever brought from the Snake Country in one year; amounting to 5000 beaver, exclusive of other peltries. I had the satisfaction of receiving, from Governor Simpson, a letter of thanks on the success of the expedition." He assures us further (232, 233) that after the meeting of the Council at Norway House Governor Simpson sent for him and urged him, though without success, to return to the Indian country, promising that "If you remain in the service you shall have the entire management of the Company's affairs in the

Snake Country guaranteed to you for a number of years, with a liberal salary." Ross dedicated his *Fur Hunters* to Simpson, and described him (II, 231) as "courteous in his manners, and active in his habits; gifted in a high degree with the power of self-command, and above all with a keen discernment of character, he appears eminently fitted by the union of these qualities for the commanding station which he so ably fills." There is a brief sketch of Ross by R. G. Thwaites in the "Introduction" to volume seven of *Early Western Travels*.

VI

Note 158, *ante*, 101.

Slavery persisted among the Indians of the Northwest Coast and of the Columbia River throughout the fur-trade period. Even at Fort Vancouver it could not be eradicated by the Hudson's Bay Company among the Indian and half-breed families of its servants. The Company was sometimes charged with deliberately perpetuating the institution as a matter of fur-trade economy. Such a charge was made in a report to Congress by W. A. Slacum, an executive agent of the United States government sent to the Columbia River in 1836-37. The charge was baseless. The Company found the difficulties of emancipation insurmountable, but so far as it could it sought to check and to minimize the evil. The policy of the Company is set forth in a despatch of the Governor and Committee to Chief Factor Douglas, written in November, 1837, probably as the result of the representations of a missionary, Rev. Herbert Beaver, who was stationed at Fort Vancouver.

"We were in hopes you would ere now have been successful in your endeavors to put an end to the inhuman and disgraceful traffic in slaves among the Indians frequenting the Establishments. We are exceedingly anxious for the accomplishment of this object, and that the condition of that much oppressed and injured race, whose sufferings at times are shocking to humanity, should be ameliorated. We are aware that many of the native Indian women, the wives of our servants, still retain the slaves they brought with them from their respective tribes. We have to desire that your best endeavors be used to obtain the emancipation of those slaves. In cases where the Company or the Gentlemen in the service have obtained the liberation of slaves by purchase, and that, after their emancipation they remain in their employ, it is necessary and proper they should enter into a written contract of servitude at fixed wages, (the amount of wages to be of course regulated by the value of their services) and all such persons must not only be virtually released from slavery, but even the term 'Slave' must on no consideration or account be applied to any inmate or resident at any of the Company's Establishments." Gov. & Com. to James Douglas, Nov. 15, 1837, H. B. Co. Gen. Letter Book No. 624.

To this despatch Douglas replied as follows: "I am most anxious to second your views for suppressing the traffic of slaves, and have taken some steps towards the attainment of that object. I regret however that the state of feeling among the natives of this river precludes every prospect of the immediate extinction of slavery, unless we resort to the very objectionable plan of a forcible emancipation. With the natives I have hitherto endeavoured to discourage the practice by the exertion of moral influence alone, carefully avoiding direct collision either with their selfish feelings or inveterate prejudices, as I do not feel justified in exposing our interests to the shock of excitement and desperate animosity which more active measures on our part might provoke. Against our own people I took a more active part, and denounced slavery as a state contrary to law, tendering to all unfortunate persons held as slaves by British subjects the fullest protection in the enjoyment of their natural rights. I soon after seized a favourable opportunity of putting the law in force by rescuing a runaway slave boy, who had been overtaken by his pursuers and brought here for punishment. He has since enjoyed his liberty and served the Company as a free labourer.

"These proceedings, so clearly destructive of the principle of slavery, would have roused a spirit of resistance in any people who know the value of liberty; but I am sorry that the effect has been scarcely felt here, and I fear that all my efforts have virtually failed in rooting out the practical evil, even within the precincts of this settlement. Of the persons ranking as slaves, some are children of tender age, others have grown up in ignorance of every useful art, whether of civilized or savage life, by which they might have earned an independent livelihood, and all classes are so destitute and friendless, that they have without exception chosen the part of continuing with their present protectors. To have urged a forcible separation in such circumstances, I must have provided them gratuitously with food and clothing, as their spiritless labour is of no value to the Company, and I feel reluctant to turn them loose into the forest, without any means of support.

"The plan I now follow, of considering every person without distinction, residing on our premises as free British subjects, who may at any time under the Company's protection, assert the exercise of their absolute and legal rights, will greatly mitigate the evils of slavery, by operating as a security against abuse, and making affection the only bond that supports the immoral system." Douglas to Gov. & Com., 18 Oct., 1838, H. B. Co. Journ. No. 1434.

When the Slacum Report of 1837 was reprinted in 1839 as part of the Cushing Report a copy of it came into the hands of Chief Factor John McLoughlin. He replied to it in a memorandum, written for the Governor and Committee, as follows: "It is incorrect that we encourage slavery, and on the reverse we avail ourselves of every opportunity to discourage it. Tho' we cannot prevent Indians having slaves, we tell the masters it is very improper to keep their fellow beings in slavery. Moreover we have redeemed several, and sent them back to their own country this very season. Some Indians of this vicinity had captured two families in the Willamette, or as they express themselves, made slaves of them. By our influence they were liberated. But strange as it may appear, there are instances in which the slave will not return to their lands; and without laying claim to doing more than our duty we can say that our influence has vastly ameliorated the situation of the slaves in every part of this country in which we have been. If the plan we adopt is followed, they will before long emancipate themselves.. . .

"You know Your Honors have sent us Instructions positively to prohibit any of the Company's servants having slaves, and prior to the receipt of your instructions my predecessors had opposed it, and one of them, J. Dugald Cameron, Esq. had emancipated the slaves of the wives of the servants and sent them from the place. But though he did this with a view to ameliorate their situation it proved the reverse, as the servants wives made a present of them to their Indian relations, who forced them to become their slaves, by whom they were treated worse than they could have been if they had been with their former mistresses at the Fort. As for me, seeing what had occurred, I did not make the servants wives send their slaves away, but availed myself of every opportunity to make them work and pay them as other Indians. The consequence is that our ploughing and harrowing is principally done by Indians and several of these Indians have claimed their liberty, in which I support them, by doing which I commit no wrong as they have been all told. We disapprove of any one having slaves, and consider every one about the Establishment as free." Remarks upon Mr. Cushing's Report, H. B. Co. Journ. No. 1742.

The Slacum account may be here added for purposes of comparison.

"The price of a slave varies from eight to fifteen blankets. Women are valued higher than men. If a slave dies within six months of the time of purchase, the seller returns one-half the purchase money. As long as the Hudson Bay Company permit their servants to hold slaves, the institution of slavery will be perpetuated. . . . The chief factor at Vancouver says the slaves are the property of the women with whom their workmen live, and do not belong to men in their employ, although I have known cases to the contrary. We shall see how this reasoning applies. These women, who are said to be the owners of the slaves, are frequently bought themselves by the men with whom they live when they are mere children; of course they have no means to purchase, until their husbands or their men make the purchase from the proceeds of their labor; and then these women are considered the ostensible owners, which neither lessens the traffic, nor ameliorates the condition of the slave. . . . The slaves are generally employed to cut wood, hunt, and fish for the families of the men employed by the Hudson Bay Company, and are ready for any extra work. Each man of the trapping parties has from two to three slaves, who assist to hunt and take care of the horses and camp; they thereby save the company the expense of employing at least double the number of men that would otherwise be required on these excursions."

VII

Note 207, *ante*, 157.

Simpson elsewhere describes the adventures of these two lost men. "On my return from the Columbia in 1825, while the grass was still so short as hardly to retain any trace of the footsteps of my party, my faithful servant Tom Taylor, and another man of the name of George Bird, dismounted to follow a red deer; and, after an unsuccessful chase, they resolved to return to our party. After halting for twenty-four hours in order to be joined by them, I gave them up for lost. At the close of six weeks, I reached Norway House on Lake Winnipeg, with a gloom on my spirits, which even the completion of a long and arduous journey could not remove. I stepped ashore, with my mind full of the sad occurrence, when who should advance to welcome me but the invaluable Tom Taylor and his companion in misfortune. Of the story of their wanderings, which might fill a volume, the outline was as follows:

"After abandoning all hope of falling upon the track of our party, they set themselves seriously to work in order to find their way to some encampment of the savages, or to one of the Company's posts. After a day or two, their ammunition was expended, and their flints became useless, while their feet were lacerated by the thorns, timber, stones, and prickly grass. They had no other clothing than their trousers and shirts, having parted from us in the heat of the day; so that they were now exposed to the chills of the night, without even the comfort of a fire—a privation which placed them, as it were, at the mercy of the wolves. From day to day, they lived on whatever the chances of the wilderness afforded them, such as roots and bark, and eggs in every stage of progress.

"At length, after fourteen days of intense suffering, despair began to take possession of their minds, and they were strongly tempted to lie down and die. Next morning, however, the instinctive love of life prevailed, and they slowly and painfully crept forward, when suddenly the sight of our track revived their energies and their hopes. Almost intoxicated with joy, they followed the clue of safety; till at length, after growing more and more indistinct for a time, it entirely disappeared from their eyes. At this awful moment of disappointment and despondency, Tom Taylor, as if led by a merciful Providence to the spot, slowly recognized the scenes of his infant rambles, though he had never seen them since his childhood.

"Life was now in the one scale almost as certainly as death was in the other; and under the influence of this definite motive of exertion, the two famished and lacerated wanderers reached before night the Company's establishment on Swan River. Being well acquainted with Mr. McDonell, the gentleman in charge, they crawled rather than walked to his private room, standing before him with their torn and emaciated limbs, while their haggard cheeks and glaring eyes gave them the appearance of maniacs. After a minute inspection of his visitors, Mr. McDonell, with the aid of sundry expletives, ascertained by degrees that one of his friends was 'The Governor's Tom'; and, having thus penetrated to the bottom of the mystery, he nursed them into condition, with the kindness of a father and the skill of a doctor, and then carried them to Norway House." Simpson, *Journey Round the World*, I, 76-78.

VIII

Note 220, *ante*, 164.

Chief Factor Donald McKenzie, one of a distinguished family of explorers and fur traders, of which other members were Sir Alexander McKenzie, the first white man to cross the North American continent to the Pacific, and Roderick McKenzie, the notable North West Company partner, was a Scot who began his service in the fur trade soon after his arrival in Canada in 1800, as a clerk in the employ of the North West Company. By 1809 he had become outstanding enough in the industry to be taken by John Jacob Astor into partnership in the Pacific Fur Company. In that service he was one of the party that in 1811-12 made the famous overland march from St. Louis to the mouth of the Columbia River to establish Astoria, with harrowing experiences which Washington Irving has so vividly described. He shared the fortunes of Astoria until 1813 when it was sold to the North West Company to avoid its capture by a British war vessel. He was then taken as a partner into the North West Company and served it in the Columbia until the coalition, distinguishing himself by resourcefulness and cool judgment, and by a series of remarkable wilderness exploits and escapes, which Alexander Ross later made the basis for part of the first volume of his *Fur Hunters*. At the coalition he became a chief factor of the Hudson's Bay Company, in which capacity he soon won the confidence of Governor Simpson, who named him in 1823 to the important post of Fort Garry to serve as unofficial adviser to an interim governor of Assiniboia. He continued in this capacity with Governor Pelly, and on the latter's withdrawal, as we have seen in the journal, was named his successor. He was Governor of Assiniboia until his own retirement from the service, guiding the destinies of the restless Red River community with notable success. Simpson gives an interesting glimpse of him at this work in 1829 in a letter to Roderick McKenzie, printed in Masson, *Les Bourgeois de la Compagnie du Nord-Ouest*, I, 59. "Your brother Donald, his lady and young folks were in high health and spirits in the month of May last when I passed ten days most agreeably with them at Red River. His government is the most easy under the sun; he settles the most knotty points with a joke and a laugh, seated on a mortar opposite the gate of his fort, and is more beloved and respected by his subjects than words can tell; he is not so stout as he was, but much more healthy and looks as if he would live forever." He spent his declining years in Mayville, New York, to which he retired in 1833 and where he died in 1851.

IX

Note 134, *ante*, 303.

Dr. McLoughlin in his "Autobiography" gives an account of this episode which differs materially from that of Simpson.

"One night in August 1828, I was surprised by the Indians making a great noise at the gate of the fort, saying that they had brought an American. The gate was opened, the man came in, but was so affected he could not speak. After sitting down some minutes to recover himself, he told us he was, he thought, the only survivor of eighteen men, conducted by the late Jedidiah Smith. All the rest, he thought, were murdered. The party left San Francisco bound to their rendezvous at the Salt Lake. They ascended the Sacramento valley, but finding no opening to cross the mountains to go east, they bent their course to the coast, which they reached at the mouth of the Rogue River, then came along the beach to the Umpqua, where the Indians stole their axe, and as it was the only axe they had, and which they absolutely required to make rafts to cross rivers, they took the chief prisoner and their axe was returned. Early the following morning Smith started in a canoe with two men and an Indian, and left orders, as usual, to allow no Indians to come into camp. But to gratify their passion for women, the men neglected to follow the order, allowed the Indians to come into camp, and at an Indian yell five or six Indians fell upon each white man. At the time, the narrator, Black, was out of the crowd, and had just finished cleaning and loading his rifle; three Indians jumped on him, but he shook them off, and seeing all his comrades struggling on the ground and the Indians stabbing them, he fired on the crowd and rushed to the woods, pursued by the Indians, but fortunately escaped; swam across the Umpqua, and came north in the hopes of reaching the Columbia, where he knew we were . . . . But . . . to our great joy Smith and his two men arrived.

"I then arranged as strong a party as I could make to recover all we could of Smith's property. I divulged my plan to none, but gave written instructions to the officer, to be opened only when he got to the Umpqua, because if known before they got there the officers would talk of it among themselves, the men would hear it and from them it would go to their Indian wives, who were spies on us, and my plan would be defeated. The plan was that the officer was, as usual, to invite the Indians to bring their furs to trade, just as if nothing had happened. Count the furs, but as the American trappers mark all their skins, keep these all separate, give them to Mr. Smith and not pay the Indians for them, telling them that they belonged to him; that they got them by murdering Smith's people.

"They denied having murdered Smith's people, but admitted they bought them of the murderers. The officers told them they must look to the murderers for the payment, which they did; and as the murderers would not restore the property they had received, a war was kindled among them, and the murderers were punished more severely than we could have done, and which Mr. Smith himself admitted . . ." S. A. Clarke, *Pioneer Days of Oregon History* (Portland, 1905), I, 216, 217.

INDEX

INDEX